T0214836

More information about this series at http://www.springer.com/series/7410

Frank Piessens · Luca Viganò (Eds.)

Principles of Security and Trust

5th International Conference, POST 2016
Held as Part of the European Joint Conferences
on Theory and Practice of Software, ETAPS 2016
Eindhoven, The Netherlands, April 2–8, 2016
Proceedings

 Springer

Editors
Frank Piessens
KU Leuven
Leuven
Belgium

Luca Viganò
King's College London
London
UK

ISSN 0302-9743 ISSN 1611-3349 (electronic)
Lecture Notes in Computer Science
ISBN 978-3-662-49634-3 ISBN 978-3-662-49635-0 (eBook)
DOI 10.1007/978-3-662-49635-0

Library of Congress Control Number: 2016932521

LNCS Sublibrary: SL4 – Security and Cryptology

Printed on acid-free paper

This Springer imprint is published by Springer Nature
The registered company is Springer-Verlag GmbH Berlin Heidelberg

ETAPS Foreword

Welcome to the proceedings of ETAPS 2016, which was held in Eindhoven, located in "the world's smartest region," also known as the Dutch Silicon Valley. Since ETAPS' second edition held in Amsterdam (1999), ETAPS returned to The Netherlands this year.

ETAPS 2016 was the 19th instance of the European Joint Conferences on Theory and Practice of Software. ETAPS is an annual federated conference established in 1998, consisting of five constituting conferences (ESOP, FASE, FoSSaCS, TACAS, and POST) this year. Each conference has its own Programme Committee and its own Steering Committee. The conferences cover various aspects of software systems, ranging from theoretical computer science to foundations to programming language developments, analysis tools, formal approaches to software engineering, and security. Organizing these conferences in a coherent, highly synchronized conference program, enables attendees to participate in an exciting event, having the possibility to meet many researchers working in different directions in the field, and to easily attend the talks of various conferences. Before and after the main conference, numerous satellite workshops took place and attracted many researchers from all over the globe.

The ETAPS conferences received 474 submissions in total, 143 of which were accepted, yielding an overall acceptance rate of 30.2 %. I thank all authors for their interest in ETAPS, all reviewers for their peer-reviewing efforts, the Program Committee members for their contributions, and in particular the program co-chairs for their hard work in running this intensive process. Last but not least, my congratulations to all the authors of the accepted papers!

ETAPS 2016 was greatly enriched by the unifying invited speakers Andrew Gordon (MSR Cambridge and University of Edinburgh, UK), and Rupak Majumdar (MPI Kaiserslautern, Germany), as well as the conference-specific invited speakers (ESOP) Cristina Lopes (University of California at Irvine, USA), (FASE) Oscar Nierstrasz (University of Bern, Switzerland), and (POST) Vitaly Shmatikov (University of Texas at Austin, USA). Invited tutorials were organized by Lenore Zuck (Chicago) and were provided by Grigore Rosu (University of Illinois at Urbana-Champaign, USA) on software verification and Peter Ryan (University of Luxembourg, Luxembourg) on security. My sincere thanks to all these speakers for their inspiring and interesting talks!

ETAPS 2016 took place in Eindhoven, The Netherlands. It was organized by the Department of Computer Science of the Eindhoven University of Technology. It was further supported by the following associations and societies: ETAPS e.V., EATCS (European Association for Theoretical Computer Science), EAPLS (European Association for Programming Languages and Systems), and EASST (European Association of Software Science and Technology). The local organization team consisted of Mark van den Brand, Jan Friso Groote (general chair), Margje Mommers, Erik Scheffers, Julien Schmaltz, Erik de Vink, Anton Wijs, Tim Willemse, and Hans Zantema.

The overall planning for ETAPS is the main responsibility of the Steering Committee, and in particular of its Executive Board. The ETAPS Steering Committee consists of an Executive Board and representatives of the individual ETAPS conferences, as well as representatives of EATCS, EAPLS, and EASST. The Executive Board consists of Gilles Barthe (Madrid), Holger Hermanns (Saarbrücken), Joost-Pieter Katoen (chair, Aachen and Twente), Gerald Lüttgen (Bamberg), Vladimiro Sassone (Southampton), and Tarmo Uustalu (Tallinn). Other members of the Steering Committee are: Parosh Abdulla (Uppsala), David Basin (Zurich), Giuseppe Castagna (Paris), Marsha Chechik (Toronto), Javier Esparza (Munich), Jan Friso Groote (Eindhoven), Reiko Heckel (Leicester), Marieke Huisman (Twente), Bart Jacobs (Nijmegen), Paul Klint (Amsterdam), Jens Knoop (Vienna), Kim G. Larsen (Aalborg), Axel Legay (Rennes), Christof Löding (Aachen), Matteo Maffei (Saarbrücken), Pasquale Malacaria (London), Tiziana Margaria (Limerick), Andrzej Murawski (Warwick), Catuscia Palamidessi (Palaiseau), Frank Piessens (Leuven), Jean-Francois Raskin (Brussels), Mark Ryan (Birmingham), Julia Rubin (Massachussetts), Don Sannella (Edinburgh), Perdita Stevens (Edinburgh), Gabriele Taentzer (Marburg), Peter Thiemann (Freiburg), Luca Vigano (London), Igor Walukiewicz (Bordeaux), Andrzej Wąsowski (Copenhagen), and Hongseok Yang (Oxford).

I sincerely thank all ETAPS Steering Committee members for all their work in making the 19th edition of ETAPS a success. Moreover, thanks to all speakers, attendees, organizers of the satellite workshops, and Springer for their support. Finally, a big thanks to Jan Friso and his local organization team for all their enormous efforts enabling ETAPS to take place in Eindhoven!

January 2016

Joost-Pieter Katoen
ETAPS SC Chair
ETAPS e.V. President

Preface

This volume contains the papers presented at POST 2016, the 5th Conference on Principles of Security and Trust, held April 4–5, 2016, in Eindhoven, The Netherlands, as part of ETAPS. Principles of Security and Trust is a broad forum related to the theoretical and foundational aspects of security and, and thus welcomes papers of many kinds: new theoretical results, practical applications of existing foundational ideas, and innovative theoretical approaches stimulated by pressing practical problems.

POST was created in 2012 to combine and replace a number of successful and long-standing workshops in this area: Automated Reasoning and Security Protocol Analysis (ARSPA), Formal Aspects of Security and Trust (FAST), Security in Concurrency (SecCo), and the Workshop on Issues in the Theory of Security (WITS). A subset of these events met jointly as an event affiliated with ETAPS 2011 under the name Theory of Security and Applications (TOSCA).

There were 35 submissions to POST 2016, 34 research papers and one tool demonstration paper. Each submission was reviewed by at least three Program Committee members, who in some cases solicited the help of outside experts to review the papers. Electronic discussion was used to decide which papers to select for the program.

The committee decided to accept 12 papers and the tool demonstration paper. In addition to the presentations of these papers, the conference program also included an invited talk by Vitaly Shmatikov, who was also one of the ETAPS unifying speakers.

We would like to thank the members of the Program Committee, the additional reviewers, the POST Steering Committee, the ETAPS Steering Committee, and the local Organizing Committee, who all contributed to the success of POST 2016. We also thank all authors of submitted papers for their interest in POST and congratulate the authors of accepted papers. Finally, we gratefully acknowledge the use of Easy-Chair for organizing the submission process, the Program Committee's work, and the preparation of this volume.

January 2016

Frank Piessens
Luca Viganò

Organization

Program Committee

Alessandro Armando	DIBRIS - University of Genoa, Italy
Lujo Bauer	Carnegie Mellon University, USA
Tom Chothia	University of Birmingham, UK
Sherman S.M. Chow	Chinese University of Hong Kong, SAR China
Michael Clarkson	George Washington University, USA
Jason Crampton	Royal Holloway, University of London, UK
Riccardo Focardi	Università Ca' Foscari, Venice, Italy
Deepak Garg	Max Planck Institute for Software Systems, Germany
Peeter Laud	Cybernetica AS, Estonia
Jay Ligatti	University of South Florida, USA
Gavin Lowe	University of Oxford, UK
Matteo Maffei	CISPA, Saarland University, Germany
Catherine Meadows	NRL, USA
Sebastian A. Mödersheim	DTU, Denmark
Frank Piessens	Katholieke Universiteit Leuven, Belgium
Alexander Pretschner	Technische Universität München, Germany
Willard Rafnsson	Chalmers University of Technology, Sweden
Tamara Rezk	Inria, France
Michael Rusinowitch	LORIA - Inria Nancy, France
P.Y.A. Ryan	University of Luxembourg, Luxembourg
Pierangela Samarati	Università degli Studi di Milano, Italy
Deian Stefan	Stanford University, USA
Nikhil Swamy	Microsoft Research, USA
Vanessa Teague	University of Melbourne, Australia
Luca Viganò	King's College London, UK

Additional Reviewers

Bao, Long	Kordy, Barbara
Benitez, Sergio	Lai, Russell W.F.
Bielova, Nataliia	Lovat, Enrico
Chen, Yu	Merlo, Alessio
Chevalier, Yannick	Muehlberg, Jan Tobias
Costa, Gabriele	Ranise, Silvio
Heiberg, Sven	Roenne, Peter
Hess, Andreas	Zhang, Tao
Kelbert, Florian	Zhao, Yongjun

Contents

Information Flow

Faceted Dynamic Information Flow via Control and Data Monads

Thomas Schmitz[1]([✉]), Dustin Rhodes[1], Thomas H. Austin[2],
Kenneth Knowles[1], and Cormac Flanagan[1]

[1] University of California Santa Cruz, Santa Cruz, USA
tschmitz@ucsc.edu
[2] San José State University, San Jose, USA

Abstract. An application that fails to ensure information flow security may leak sensitive data such as passwords, credit card numbers, or medical records. News stories of such failures abound. Austin and Flanagan [2] introduce faceted values – values that present different behavior according to the privilege of the observer – as a dynamic approach to enforce information flow policies for an untyped, imperative λ-calculus.

We implement faceted values as a Haskell library, elucidating their relationship to types and monadic imperative programming. In contrast to previous work, our approach does not require modification to the language runtime. In addition to pure faceted values, our library supports faceted mutable reference cells and secure facet-aware socket-like communication. This library guarantees information flow security, independent of any vulnerabilities or bugs in application code. The library uses a *control* monad in the traditional way for encapsulating effects, but it also uniquely uses a second *data* monad to structure faceted values. To illustrate a non-trivial use of the library, we present a bi-monadic interpreter for a small language that illustrates the interplay of the control and data monads.

1 Introduction

When writing a program that manipulates sensitive data, the programmer must prevent misuse of that data, intentional or accidental. For example, when one enters a password on a web form, the password should be communicated to the site, but not written to disk. Unfortunately, enforcing these kinds of *information flow* policies is problematic. Developers primarily focus on correct functionality; security properties are prioritized only after an attempted exploit.

Just as memory-safe languages relieve developers from reasoning about memory management (and the host of bugs resulting from its *mis*management), information flow analysis enforces security properties in a systemic fashion. Information flow controls require a developer to mark sensitive information, but otherwise automatically prevent any "leaks" of this data. Formally, we call this

© Springer-Verlag Berlin Heidelberg 2016
F. Piessens and L. Viganò (Eds.): POST 2016, LNCS 9635, pp. 3–23, 2016.
DOI: 10.1007/978-3-662-49635-0_1

property *noninterference*; that is, public outputs do not depend on private inputs[1].

Secure multi-execution [9,16,23] is a relatively recent and popular information flow enforcement technique. A program execution is split into two versions: the "high" execution has access to sensitive information, but may only write to private channels; the "low" execution may write to public channels, but cannot access any sensitive information. This elegant approach ensures noninterference.

Faceted evaluation is a technique for simulating secure multi-execution with a single process, using special *faceted values* that contain both a public view and a private view of the data. With this approach, a single execution can provide many of the same guarantees that secure multi-execution provides, while achieving better performance.

This paper extends the ideas of faceted values from an untyped variant of the λ-calculus [2] to Haskell and describes the implementation of faceted values as a Haskell library. This approach provides a number of benefits and insights.

First, whereas prior work on faceted values required the development of a new language semantics, we show how to incorporate faceted values within an existing language via library support.

Second, faceted values fit surprisingly well (but with some subtleties) into Haskell's monadic structure. As might be expected, we use an IO-like monad called FIO to support imperative updates and I/O operations. We also use a second type constructor Faceted to describe faceted values; for example, the faceted value ⟨k ? 3 : 4⟩ has type Faceted Int. Somewhat surprisingly, Faceted turns out to also be a monad, with natural definitions of the corresponding operations that satisfy the monad axioms [34]. These two monads, FIO and Faceted, naturally interoperate via an associated product function [17] that supports switching from the FIO monad to the Faceted monad when necessary (as described in more detail below).

This library guarantees the traditional information flow security property of termination-insensitive noninterference, independent of any bugs, vulnerabilities, or malicious code in the client application.

Finally we present an application of this library in the form of an interpreter for the imperative λ-calculus with I/O. This interpreter validates the expressiveness of the Faceted library; it also illustrates how the FIO and Faceted monads flow along control paths and data paths respectively.

In summary, this paper contributes the following:

- We present the first formulation of faceted values and computations in a typed context.
- We show how to integrate faceted values into a language as a library, rather than by modifying the runtime environment.

---

[1] We refer to sensitive values as "private" and non-sensitive values as "public", as confidentiality is generally given more attention in the literature on information flow analysis. However, the same mechanism can also enforce integrity properties, such as that trusted outputs are not influenced by untrusted inputs.

-- We clarify the relationship between explicit flows in pure calculations (via the Faceted monad) and implicit flows in impure computations (via the FIO monad).
- Finally, we present an interpreter for an imperative λ-calculus with dynamic information flow. The security of the implementation is guaranteed by our library. Notably, this interpreter uses the impure monad (FIO) in the traditional way to structure computational effects, and uses the pure faceted monad (Faceted) to structure values.

2 Review of Information Flow and Faceted Values

In traditional information flow systems, information is tagged with a label to mark it as confidential to particular parties. For instance, if we need to restrict pin to *bank*, we might write:

pin = 4321^{bank}

To protect this value, we must prevent unauthorized viewers from observing it, directly or indirectly. In particular, we must defend against *explicit flows* where a confidential value is directly assigned to a public variable, and *implicit flows* where an observer may deduce a confidential value by reasoning about the program's control flow. The following code shows an explicit flow from pin to the variable x.

pin = 4321^{bank}
x = pin + 1

Taint tracking – in languages such as Perl and Ruby – suffices to track straightforward explicit flows; in contrast, implicit flows are more subtle. Continuing our example, consider the following code, which uses a mutable IORef.

```
do above2K ← newIORef False
   if (pin > 2000)
      then writeIORef above2K True
      else return ()
```

This code illustrates a simple implicit flow. After it runs, the value of above2K will reflect information about pin, even though the code never directly assigns the value of pin to above2K. There are several proposed strategies for handling these types of flows:

1. Allow the update, but mark above2K as sensitive because it was changed in a sensitive context. This strategy can help for auditing information flows "in the wild" [15], but it fails to guarantee noninterference, as shown in the *Naive* column of Fig. 1 (note that the naive computation results in True when x is True).
2. Disallow the update to above2K within the context of the sensitive conditional pin. When enforced at runtime, this technique becomes the *no-sensitive-upgrade* strategy [1, 36] illustrated in the *NSU* column of Fig. 1. Note that while this technique maintains noninterference, it also terminates the program prematurely.

3. Ignore the update to `above2K` in a sensitive context, an approach first used by Fenton [11]. This strategy guarantees noninterference by sacrificing correctness (the program's result may not be internally consistent). We show this strategy in the *Fenton* column of Fig. 1.

do	Naive	NSU	Fenton	Faceted Evaluation
		$x = \langle k$? True $: \bot \rangle$		
`y <- newIORef True`	y = True	y = True	y = True	y = True
`z <- newIORef True`	z = True	z = True	z = True	z = True
`vx <- readIORef x`	–	–	–	–
`when vx`	$pc = \{k\}$	$pc = \{k\}$	$pc = \{k\}$	$pc = \{k\}$
`  (writeIORef y False)`	y = $\langle k$? False $: \bot \rangle$	stuck	ignored	y = $\langle k$? False : True$\rangle$
`vy <- readIORef y`	–		–	–
`when vy`	–		–	$pc = \{\overline{k}\}$
`  (writeIORef z False)`	–		–	z = $\langle k$? True : False$\rangle$
`readIORef z`	–		–	–
Result:	True	stuck	False	$\langle k$? True : False$\rangle$

Fig. 1. A computation with implicit flows.

Faceted values introduce a third aspect to sensitive data. In addition to the sensitive value and its label, the following faceted value includes a default public view of '0000'.

pin = $\langle bank$? 4321 : 0000$\rangle$

Then, when we run the previous program with this faceted `pin`, the value of `above2K` is $\langle bank$? True : False$\rangle$. The bank sees the sensitive value True, but an unauthorized viewer instead sees the default value False, giving a consistent picture to the unauthorized viewer while still protecting sensitive data.

Label-based information flow systems reason about multiple principals by joining labels together (e.g. $3^A + 4^B = 7^{AB}$). In a similar manner, faceted evaluation nests faceted values to represent multiple principals, essentially constructing a tree[2] mapping permissions to values:

$$\langle k_1 ? 3 : 0 \rangle + \langle k_2 ? 4 : 0 \rangle = \langle k_1 ? \langle k_2 ? 7 : 3 \rangle : \langle k_2 ? 4 : 0 \rangle \rangle$$

Figure 1, adapted from Austin and Flanagan [2], demonstrates a classic code snippet first introduced by Fenton [11]. The example uses two conditional statements to evade some information flow controls. When this code runs, the private value x leaks into the public variable z. We represent the input x, a confidential boolean value, in faceted notation as $\langle k$? False $: \bot \rangle$ for false and $\langle k$? True $: \bot \rangle$ for true, where $\bot$ means roughly 'undefined'. Boolean reference cells y and z are

---

[2] Alternatively, a faceted value can be interpreted as a function mapping sets of labels to values, and the syntax above as merely a compact representation.

initialized to `True`; by default, they are public to maximize the permissiveness of these values.

When the input x is $\langle k\ ?\ \texttt{False} : \bot \rangle$, the value for y remains unchanged because the first **when** statement is not run. Then in the second **when** statement, y is still public, and thus z also remains public because it depends only on y. Since no private information is involved in the update to z, all information flow strategies return the public value `False` as their final result.

The case where the input x is $\langle k\ ?\ \texttt{True} : \bot \rangle$ is more interesting, as illustrated in Fig. 1. Note that if the final value appears as `True` to public observers, then the private value x has leaked. The strategies differ in the way they handle the update to y in the first conditional statement. Since this update depends upon the value of x, we must be careful to avoid the potential implicit flow from x to y. We now compare how each approach handles this update.

In the *Naive* column of Fig. 1, the strategy tracks the influence of x by applying the label k to y. Regardless, y is false during the second conditional, so z retains its public `True` value. Thus, under Naive information flow control, the result of this code sample is a public copy of x, violating noninterference.

The *No-Sensitive-Upgrade* approach instead terminates execution on this update, guaranteeing termination-insensitive noninterference, but at the cost of potentially rejecting valid programs. Stefan et al. implement this strategy in the elegant LIO library for Haskell [32]. Our work shares the motivations of LIO, but extends beyond the No-Sensitive-Upgrade strategy to support faceted values, thus enabling correct execution of more programs.

The *Fenton* strategy forbids the update to y, but allows execution to continue. This approach avoids abnormal termination, but it may return inaccurate results, as shown in Fig. 1.

Faceted evaluation solves this dilemma by simulating different executions of this program, allowing it to provide accurate results and avoid rejecting valid programs. In the *Faceted Evaluation* column, we see that the update to y results in the creation of a new faceted value $\langle k\ ?\ \texttt{False} : \texttt{True} \rangle$. Any viewer authorized to see k-sensitive data[3] can see the real value of y; unauthorized viewers instead see `True`, thus hiding the value of x. In the second conditional assignment, the runtime updates z in a similar manner and produces the final result $\langle k\ ?\ \texttt{True} : \texttt{False} \rangle$. In contexts with the k security label, this value will behave as `True`; in other contexts, it will behave as `False`. This code therefore provides noninterference, avoids abnormal termination, and provides accurate results to authorized users.

3 Library Overview

We implement faceted computation in Haskell as a library that enforces information flow security dynamically, using abstract data types to prevent buggy or malicious programs from circumventing dynamic protections. In contrast, the

---

[3] That is, authorized to see data marked as sensitive to principal k.

original formulation [2] added faceted values pervasively to the semantics of a dynamically-typed, imperative λ-calculus. Because of the encapsulation offered by Haskell's type system, we do not need to modify the language semantics. Our library is available at https://github.com/haskell-facets/haskell-faceted.

Our library is conceptually divided into the following components:

– Pure faceted values of type *a* (represented by the type `Faceted` *a*).
– Imperative faceted computations (represented by the type `FIO` *a*), which can operate on:
  • faceted reference cells (represented by the type `FioRef` *a*), and
  • facet-enabled file handles / sockets (represented by the type `FHandle`).

3.1 Pure Faceted Values: `Faceted a`

Figure 2 shows the public interface for the pure fragment of our library. This fragment tracks explicit data flow information in pure computations.

```
type Label = String

data Faceted a

public  :: a → Faceted a
faceted :: Label → Faceted a → Faceted a → Faceted a
bottom  :: Faceted a

instance Monad Faceted
```

Fig. 2. Interface for the pure fragment of the `Faceted` library.

Our implementation presumes that security labels are strings, though leaving the type of labels abstract is straightforward.

A value of type `Faceted` *a* represents multiple values, or *facets*, of type *a*. To maintain security, the facets should not be directly observable; therefore, the data type is abstract.

The function `public` injects any type *a* into the type `Faceted` *a*. It accepts a value *v* of type *a* and returns a faceted value that behaves just like *v* for any observer.

The function `faceted` constructs a value of type `Faceted` *a* from a label *k* and two other faceted values *priv* and *pub*, each of type `Faceted` *a*. To any viewer authorized to see *k*, the result behaves as *priv*; to all other observers, the result behaves as *pub* (and so on, recursively).

The value `bottom` (abbreviated ⊥) is a member of `Faceted` *a* for any *a*, and represents a lack of a value. `bottom` is used when a default value is necessary, such as in a public facet. Any computation based on `bottom` results in `bottom`.

From `faceted`, we can define various derived constructors for creating faceted values with minimal effort. For example:

```
makePrivate :: Label → a → Faceted a
makePrivate k v = faceted k (public v) bottom

makeFacets :: Label → a → a → Faceted a
makeFacets k priv pub = faceted k (public priv) (public pub)
```

The Monad instance for Faceted conveniently propagates security labels as appropriate. For example, the following code uses Haskell's do syntax to multiply two values of type Faceted Int.

```
do x ← makeFacets "k" 7 1   -- <"k" ? 7 : 1>
   y ← makeFacets "l" 6 1   -- <"l" ? 6 : 1>
   return (x * y)           -- <"k" ? <"l" ? 42 : 7> : <"l" ? 6 : 1>>
```

Here, x is an Int that is extracted from (faceted "k" 7 1), either 7 or 1. The Faceted monad instance automatically executes the remainder of the do block twice (once for each possible value of x) before collecting the various results into a faceted value. The situation is similar for y, so the final faceted value is a tree with four leaves.

3.2 Faceted Reference Cells: FIO a and FioRef a

For the pure language of Sect. 3.1, information flow analysis is straightforward because all dependencies between values are explicit; there are no *implicit flows*. An implicit flow occurs when a value is computed based on side effects that depend on private data, as in the following example, where x is an IORef with initial value 0.

```
do if secret == 42                      -- working in IO monad
     then writeIORef x 1
     else writeIORef x 2
   readIORef x
```

The return value will be 1 if and only if secret == 42.

Suppose we opt to protect the confidentiality of secret by setting secret = makePrivate k 42. The type of secret is now Faceted Int. Then our example can be reformulated:

```
do n ← secret                           -- working in Faceted monad
   return $ do if n == 42                -- working in IO monad
                 then writeIORef x 1
                 else writeIORef x 2
               readIORef x
```

The outer do begins a computation in the Faceted monad, with the value 42 bound to n. This expression has type Faceted (IO Int), so it cannot be "run" as part of a Haskell program. Thus, the pure fragment of our library described so far prevents *all* implicit flows, even those that are safe.

Guided by the types, we seek a way to convert a value of type Faceted (IO a) to a value of type IO (Faceted a). The latter could then be run to yield a value of type Faceted a, where the facets account for any implicit flows.

```
data Branch = Private Label | Public Label
type PC     = [Branch]

data FIO a

instance Monad FIO

runFIO :: FIO a → PC → IO a
prod :: Faceted (FIO (Faceted a)) → FIO (Faceted a)

data FioRef a
newFioRef   :: Faceted a → FIO (FioRef (Faceted a))
readFioRef  :: FioRef (Faceted a) → FIO (Faceted a)
writeFioRef :: FioRef (Faceted a) → Faceted a → FIO (Faceted ())
```

Fig. 3. Interface for FIO and FioRef.

Faceted IO computations take place in the FIO monad (the name is short for "Faceted I/O"). Figure 3 shows the public interface for this fragment of the library. When faceted data influences control flow, the result of a computation implicitly depends on the observed facets; the implementation of FIO transparently tracks this information flow.

The Monad instance for FIO allows sequencing computations in the usual way, so FIO acts as a (limited) drop-in replacement for IO. If fio1 and fio2 each have type FIO Int, then the following expression also has type FIO Int:

```
do x ← fio1
   y ← fio2
   return (x * y)
```

The function runFIO converts a value of type FIO a to a value of type IO a. The side effects in this IO computation will respect the information flow policy.

runFIO takes one additional argument: an initial value for a data structure called pc (for "program counter label"), which is used for tracking the branching of the computation. To guarantee security, it may be necessary to execute parts of the program multiple times – once for observers who may view k-sensitive data, and again for observers who may not. During the former branch of computation, the pc will contain the value Private k; during the latter branch, it will contain Public k.

The pc argument to runFIO allows controlling the set of observers whose viewpoints are considered during faceted computation. The empty pc, denoted [], will force simulation of all possible viewpoints.

A value of type FioRef a (short for "facet-aware IORef") is a mutable reference cell where initialization, reading, and writing are all FIO computations that operate on Faceted values and that account for implicit flows accordingly.

Figure 3 presents the public interface to FioRef a, which parallels that of conventional reference cells of type IORef a.

To write side-effecting code that depends on a faceted value, the `Faceted` and `FIO` monads must be used together. The library function `prod` enables this interaction.

Using these library functions, our running example finally looks as follows.

```
do x ← newFioRef (public 0)                    -- working in FIO monad
   prod $ do v ← secret                        -- working in Faceted monad
             return $ if v == 42
                      then writeFioRef x (public 1)
                      else writeFioRef x (public 2)
   readFioRef x
```

As hinted earlier, the inner do block has type `Faceted (FIO (Faceted ()))` and so cannot compose with the other actions in the outer do block. To rectify this, the function `prod` is enclosing the inner do block, converting it to type `FIO (Faceted ())`.

In this example, the value read from `x` will be `faceted` k `1` `0`, which correctly accounts for the influence from `secret`. In Sect. 4, we will explain the machinery that implements this secure behavior.

3.3 Faceted I/O: `FHandle`

Faceted I/O differs from reference cells in that the network and file system, which we collectively refer to as the *environment*, lie outside the purview of our programming language. The environment has no knowledge of facets and cannot be retrofitted. Additionally, there are other programs able to read from and write to the file system. We assume that the environment appropriately restricts other users of the file handles, and we provide facilities within Haskell to express and enforce the relevant information flow policy.

Figure 4 shows the core of the public interface for facet-aware file handles, type `FHandle`.

```
        data FHandle

        type View = [Label]

        openFileFio :: View → FilePath → IOMode → FIO FHandle
        closeFio :: FHandle → FIO ()

        getCharFio :: FHandle → FIO (Faceted Char)
        putCharFio :: FHandle → Faceted Char → FIO ()
```

Fig. 4. Interface for `FHandle`.

We support policies that associate with each file handle h a set of labels $view_h$ of type `View`. This view indicates the confidentiality for data read from and written to h. Intuitively, if a view contains a label k, then that view is allowed to see data that is confidential to k.

The function `openFileFio` accepts a view $view_h$ along with a file path and mode and returns a (computation that returns a) facet-aware handle h protected by the policy $view_h$.

When writing to h via `putCharFio`, the view $view_h$ describes the confidentiality assured by the external environment for data written to h. In other words, we trust that the external world will protect the data with those labels in $view_h$.

When reading from a handle h via `getCharFio`, we treat $view_h$ as the confidentiality expected by the external world for data read from h. In other words, we certify that we protect the data received from h. For example, in the following computation, the character read from h is observable only to views that include labels "k" and "l".

```
do h ← openFileFio ["k", "l"] "/tmp/socket.0" ReadMode
   getCharFio h
```

4   Formal Semantics

In this section, we formalize the behavior of the Haskell library as an operational semantics and prove that it guarantees termination-insensitive noninterference.

Figures 5 and 6 show the formal syntax. The syntactic class t represents Haskell programs, k is a label, and σ is a "store" mapping addresses a to values, and mapping file handles h to strings of characters ch.

For ease of understanding, we separate the set of values into three syntactic classes. *FacetedValue* contains values in the `Faceted` monad; *FioAction* contains

$$
\begin{array}{lll}
ch \in Character & & \\
k \ \in Label & & \\
t \ \in Term & ::= x & \\
& \mid \lambda x.t & \\
& \mid t\ t & \\
& \mid ch & \text{Character} \\
& \mid k & \text{Label} \\
& \mid F & \text{Faceted values} \\
& \mid \texttt{return}^{\textsf{Fac}}\ t & \\
& \mid \texttt{bind}^{\textsf{Fac}}\ t\ t & \\
& \mid A & \text{FIO actions} \\
F \in FacetedValue & ::= \texttt{public}\ t \mid \texttt{faceted}\ t\ t\ t \mid \texttt{bottom} & \\
A \in FioAction & ::= \texttt{return}^{\textsf{FIO}}\ t \mid \texttt{bind}^{\textsf{FIO}}\ t\ t \mid \texttt{prod}\ t & \\
& \mid \texttt{newFioRef}\ t \mid \texttt{readFioRef}\ t \mid \texttt{writeFioRef}\ t\ t & \\
& \mid \texttt{getCharFio}\ t \mid \texttt{putCharFio}\ t\ t &
\end{array}
$$

Fig. 5. Source syntax.

$$
\begin{aligned}
a &\in Address \\
h &\in Handle \\
t &\in Term && ::= \ldots \mid v \\
v &\in Value && ::= F \mid A \mid \lambda x.t \mid ch \mid k \mid a \mid h \\
E &\in EvalContext && ::= \bullet\, t \mid \mathbf{bind}^{\mathsf{Fac}}\, \bullet\, t \\
\sigma &\in Store && = (Address \rightarrow Value) \cup (Handle \rightarrow String)
\end{aligned}
$$

Fig. 6. Runtime syntax.

computations in the impure FIO monad; and *Value* contains both of these, as well as ordinary values: closures, characters, labels, addresses, and handles.

We define the operational semantics with two big-step evaluation judgments.

- $t \Downarrow v$ means that the pure Haskell expression t evaluates to the value v.
- $\sigma, A \Downarrow_{pc}^{\mathsf{FIO}} \sigma', v$ means that the Haskell program "main = runFIO A pc" changes the store from σ to σ' and yields the result v.

$\boxed{t \Downarrow v}$ **Pure evaluation.**

$$
\frac{}{v \Downarrow v} \;\; [\text{E-VAL}]
\qquad\qquad
\frac{}{\mathbf{return}^{\mathsf{Fac}}\, t \Downarrow \mathbf{public}\, t} \;\; [\text{E-RET}]
$$

$$
\frac{t[x := t_1] \Downarrow v}{(\lambda x.t)\, t_1 \Downarrow v} \;\; [\text{E-APP}]
\qquad\qquad
\frac{t_2\, t_1 \Downarrow v}{\mathbf{bind}^{\mathsf{Fac}}\, (\mathbf{public}\, t_1)\, t_2 \Downarrow v} \;\; [\text{E-BIND-P}]
$$

$$
\begin{array}{c}
t \text{ not a value} \\
t \Downarrow v_1 \\
E[v_1] \Downarrow v_2 \\
\hline
E[t] \Downarrow v_2
\end{array} \;\; [\text{E-CTXT}]
\qquad
\frac{v = \mathbf{faceted}\, t_1\, (\mathbf{bind}^{\mathsf{Fac}}\, t_2\, t_4)\, (\mathbf{bind}^{\mathsf{Fac}}\, t_3\, t_4)}{\mathbf{bind}^{\mathsf{Fac}}\, (\mathbf{faceted}\, t_1\, t_2\, t_3)\, t_4 \Downarrow v} \;\; [\text{E-BIND-F}]
$$

$$
\frac{}{\mathbf{bind}^{\mathsf{Fac}}\, \mathbf{bottom}\, t \Downarrow \mathbf{bottom}} \;\; [\text{E-BIND-B}]
$$

Fig. 7. Semantics (part 1).

Figure 7 depicts the pure derivation rules. These rules describe a call-by-name λ-calculus with opaque constants and two library functions: $\mathbf{return}^{\mathsf{Fac}}$ and $\mathbf{bind}^{\mathsf{Fac}}$. These monad operators for Faceted are particularly simple because it is a free monad: $\mathbf{bind}^{\mathsf{Fac}}\, F\, v$ replaces the public "leaves" of the faceted value F with new faceted values obtained by calling v.

Figure 8 shows the impure derivation rules. The FIO monad operations (defined by [F-RET] and [F-BIND]) are typical of a state monad. The pc annotation propagates unchanged through these trivial rules.

The next five rules define prod, whose type is:

```
Faceted (FIO (Faceted a)) -> FIO (Faceted a)
```

$$\frac{t \Downarrow v}{\sigma, \mathtt{return}^{\mathsf{FIO}}\ t \Downarrow^{\mathsf{FIO}}_{pc} \sigma, v} \quad \text{[F-RET]}$$

$$\frac{\begin{array}{c} t_1 \Downarrow A_1 \\ \sigma_0, A_1 \Downarrow^{\mathsf{FIO}}_{pc} \sigma_1, v_1 \\ t_2\ v_1 \Downarrow A_2 \\ \sigma_1, A_2 \Downarrow^{\mathsf{FIO}}_{pc} \sigma_2, v_2 \end{array}}{\sigma_0, \mathtt{bind}^{\mathsf{FIO}}\ t_1\ t_2 \Downarrow^{\mathsf{FIO}}_{pc} \sigma_2, v_2} \quad \text{[F-BIND]}$$

$$\frac{\begin{array}{c} t \Downarrow \mathtt{public}\ t' \\ t' \Downarrow A \\ \sigma, A \Downarrow^{\mathsf{FIO}}_{pc} \sigma', v \end{array}}{\sigma, \mathtt{prod}\ t \Downarrow^{\mathsf{FIO}}_{pc} \sigma', v} \quad \text{[F-PROD-P]}$$

$$\frac{t \Downarrow \mathtt{bottom}}{\sigma, \mathtt{prod}\ t \Downarrow^{\mathsf{FIO}}_{pc} \sigma, \mathtt{bottom}} \quad \text{[F-PROD-B]}$$

$$\frac{\begin{array}{c} t \Downarrow \mathtt{faceted}\ t_k\ t_1\ t_2 \\ t_k \Downarrow k \qquad k \in pc \\ \sigma, \mathtt{prod}\ t_1 \Downarrow^{\mathsf{FIO}}_{pc} \sigma', v_1 \end{array}}{\sigma, \mathtt{prod}\ t \Downarrow^{\mathsf{FIO}}_{pc} \sigma', v_1} \quad \text{[F-PROD-F1]}$$

$$\frac{\begin{array}{c} t \Downarrow \mathtt{faceted}\ t_k\ t_1\ t_2 \\ t_k \Downarrow k \qquad \overline{k} \in pc \\ \sigma, \mathtt{prod}\ t_2 \Downarrow^{\mathsf{FIO}}_{pc} \sigma', v_2 \end{array}}{\sigma, \mathtt{prod}\ t \Downarrow^{\mathsf{FIO}}_{pc} \sigma', v_2} \quad \text{[F-PROD-F2]}$$

$$\frac{\begin{array}{c} t \Downarrow \mathtt{faceted}\ t_k\ t_1\ t_2 \\ t_k \Downarrow k \qquad k \notin pc \qquad \overline{k} \notin pc \\ \sigma_0, \mathtt{prod}\ t_1 \Downarrow^{\mathsf{FIO}}_{pc \cup \{k\}} \sigma_1, v_1 \\ \sigma_1, \mathtt{prod}\ t_2 \Downarrow^{\mathsf{FIO}}_{pc \cup \{\overline{k}\}} \sigma_2, v_2 \end{array}}{\sigma_0, \mathtt{prod}\ t \Downarrow^{\mathsf{FIO}}_{pc} \sigma_2, \mathtt{faceted}\ k\ v_1\ v_2} \quad \text{[F-PROD-F3]}$$

$$\frac{\begin{array}{c} t \Downarrow F \\ a \notin dom(\sigma) \\ v' = \langle\langle pc\ ?\ F : \mathtt{bottom}\rangle\rangle \end{array}}{\sigma, \mathtt{newFioRef}\ t \Downarrow^{\mathsf{FIO}}_{pc} \sigma[a := v'], a} \quad \text{[F-NEW]}$$

$$\frac{t \Downarrow a}{\sigma, \mathtt{readFioRef}\ t \Downarrow^{\mathsf{FIO}}_{pc} \sigma, \sigma(a)} \quad \text{[F-READ]}$$

$$\frac{\begin{array}{c} t_1 \Downarrow a \\ t_2 \Downarrow F \\ \sigma' = \sigma[a := \langle\langle pc\ ?\ F : \sigma(a)\rangle\rangle] \end{array}}{\sigma, \mathtt{writeFioRef}\ t_1\ t_2 \Downarrow^{\mathsf{FIO}}_{pc} \sigma', v} \quad \text{[F-WRITE]}$$

$$\frac{\begin{array}{c} t \Downarrow h \\ pc \text{ is not visible to } view_h \end{array}}{\sigma, \mathtt{getCharFio}\ t \Downarrow^{\mathsf{FIO}}_{pc} \sigma, \mathtt{bottom}} \quad \text{[F-GET-2]}$$

$$\frac{\begin{array}{c} t \Downarrow h \\ L = view_h \\ pc \text{ is visible to } L \\ ch_1 \ldots ch_n = \sigma(h) \\ \sigma' = \sigma[h := ch_2 \ldots ch_n] \\ pc' = L \cup \{\overline{k} \mid k \notin L\} \\ v = \langle\langle pc'\ ?\ \mathtt{public}\ ch_1 : \mathtt{bottom}\rangle\rangle \end{array}}{\sigma, \mathtt{getCharFio}\ t \Downarrow^{\mathsf{FIO}}_{pc} \sigma', v} \quad \text{[F-GET]}$$

$$\frac{\begin{array}{c} t_1 \Downarrow h \\ L = view_h \\ pc \text{ is visible to } L \\ t_2 \Downarrow F \\ ch = L(F) \\ \sigma' = \sigma[h := \sigma(h)ch] \end{array}}{\sigma, \mathtt{putCharFio}\ t_1\ t_2 \Downarrow^{\mathsf{FIO}}_{pc} \sigma', F} \quad \text{[F-PUT]}$$

$$\frac{\begin{array}{c} t_1 \Downarrow h \\ L = view_h \\ pc \text{ is not visible to } L \\ t_2 \Downarrow F \end{array}}{\sigma, \mathtt{putCharFio}\ t_1\ t_2 \Downarrow^{\mathsf{FIO}}_{pc} \sigma, F} \quad \text{[F-PUT-2]}$$

Fig. 8. Semantics (part 2).

The input, a faceted action, is transformed into an action that returns a faceted value. This process is straightforward for public and bottom; the public constructor is simply stripped away to reveal the action underneath, while bottom is simply transformed into a no-op. For faceted, the corresponding rule is [F-PROD-F3], where the process *bifurcates* into two subcomputations whose results are combined into a `faceted` result value. However, there is no need to bifurcate repeatedly for the same label k, so the bifurcation is remembered by adding k (or $\bar{k}$) to the pc annotation on each subcomputation. Subsequently, the optimized rules [F-PROD-F1] and [F-PROD-F2] will apply. Rather than bifurcating the computation, these rules will execute only the one path of computation that is relevant to the current pc.

The remainder of Fig. 8 shows the rules for creation and manipulation of reference cells, and for input and output.

[F-NEW] describes the creation of a new faceted reference cell. To preserve the noninterference property, the cell is initialized with a faceted value that hides the true value from observers that should not know about the cell. The notation $\langle\langle \bullet \; ? \; \bullet : \bullet \rangle\rangle$ means:

$$\langle\langle \emptyset \; ? \; v_1 : v_2 \rangle\rangle = v_1$$
$$\langle\langle \{k\} \cup pc \; ? \; v_1 : v_2 \rangle\rangle = \texttt{faceted } k \; \langle\langle pc \; ? \; v_1 : v_2 \rangle\rangle \; v_2$$
$$\langle\langle \{\bar{k}\} \cup pc \; ? \; v_1 : v_2 \rangle\rangle = \texttt{faceted } k \; v_2 \; \langle\langle pc \; ? \; v_1 : v_2 \rangle\rangle$$

[F-READ] and [F-WRITE] read and write these reference cells. [F-READ] is simple because the values in the store σ will already be appropriately faceted. To prevent implicit flows, [F-WRITE] must incorporate the pc into the label of the stored value stored.

The final rules handle input and output. Each must first confirm that the file handle h is compatible with the current pc. The notation "pc is visible to L" means

$$\forall k \in pc, k \in L \qquad \text{and} \qquad \forall \bar{k} \in pc, k \notin L,$$

i.e. L is one of the views being simulated on the current branch of computation.

In [F-GET], if pc is visible to L, then the first character ch_1 is extracted from the file. The result is a faceted value that behaves as ch_1 for view L, but as `bottom` for all other views. If pc is not visible to L, then [F-GET-2] applies and the operation is ignored; the result is simply `bottom`.

In [F-PUT], if pc is visible to L, then a character is appended to the end of the file; otherwise, [F-PUT-2] applies and the operation is ignored. The appropriate character ch must be extracted from the faceted value F using the projection $L(F)$ defined below.

4.1   Termination-Insensitive Noninterference

We first define the projection $L(v)$ of a faceted value v according to a view $L \in 2^{Label}$:

$$
\begin{aligned}
L(\texttt{faceted } k \; v_1 \; v_2) &= L(v_1) && \text{if } k \in L \\
L(\texttt{faceted } k \; v_1 \; v_2) &= L(v_2) && \text{if } k \notin L \\
L(v) &= v && \text{otherwise.}
\end{aligned}
$$

Similarly, we define the projection $L(\sigma)$ of a store σ according to a view L:

$$L(\sigma)(a) = L(\sigma(a))$$

$$L(\sigma)(h) = \begin{cases} \sigma(h) & \text{if } L = view_h \\ \epsilon & \text{otherwise} \end{cases}$$

where ϵ denotes the empty string. In words, the projected store maps each address to the projection of the stored value, and the projected store maps each handle either to the real file contents (if the viewer is $view_h$) or to ϵ.

With these definitions of projection, we can now define noninterference.

Theorem 1 (Termination-Insensitive Noninterference).
Assume:

$$L(\sigma_1) = L(\sigma_2) \qquad \sigma_1, A \Downarrow_\emptyset^{\text{FIO}} \sigma_1', v_1 \qquad \sigma_2, A \Downarrow_\emptyset^{\text{FIO}} \sigma_2', v_2$$

Then:

$$L(\sigma_1') = L(\sigma_2') \qquad\qquad L(v_1) = L(v_2).$$

In other words, if we run a program with two starting stores that are identical under the L projection, then the resulting stores and values will be identical under the L projection.

The proof is available in the extended version of this paper [29].

5   Application: A Bi-Monadic Interpreter

To demonstrate the expressiveness of the `Faceted` library, we present a monadic interpreter for an imperative λ-calculus, whose dynamic information flow security is guaranteed by the previous noninterference theorem.

The interesting aspect about this interpreter is that it uses two distinct monads.

- The `FIO` monad captures computations (called `Actions` in the code), and is propagated along control flow paths in the traditional style of monadic interpreters.
- The `Faceted` monad serves a somewhat different purpose, which is to encapsulate the many views of the underlying `RawValue`. Unlike `FIO`, this monad is propagated along data flow paths rather than along control flow paths.

Even though the interpreter's use of the `Faceted` monad is non-traditional, faceted values need exactly this monad interface – particularly considering the necessity of the monad-specific operation

$$\text{join} :: \text{Faceted (Faceted } a) \rightarrow \text{Faceted } a$$

which, for the `Faceted` monad, naturally combines two layers of security labels into a single layer.

5.1   The Interpreted Language

The source language is an imperative call-by-value λ-calculus whose abstract syntax is defined in Fig. 9. The language has variables, lambda abstractions, applications, and primitive constants for manipulating reference cells, performing I/O, and creating private values.

```
data Term =
      Var String              -- Lambdas
    | Lam String Term
    | App Term Term
    | Const Value             -- Constants
```

Fig. 9. Syntax for the bi-monadic interpreter.

To ensure that private characters are not printed to the output stream, our implementation opens the stream using the empty view.

5.2   Implementation

Figure 10 shows the core of the interpreter, the function `eval`. As usual, it takes an environment and a term and returns an action, which has type `Action = FIO (Faceted RawValue)`. The `RawValue` type includes characters, mutable references, and closures.

The most interesting code is the case for an application `App t1 t2` (lines 15–19 in Fig. 10). As usual, we use a `do` block (in the `FIO` monad) to compose the sub-evaluations of `t1` and `t2` into faceted values `v1` and `v2`. To extract each underlying function (`FnVal f`) from the faceted value `v1`, we enter a second `do` block (this time in the `Faceted` monad), and then apply `f` to `v2` to yield a result of type `Action = FIO (Faceted RawValue)`, which the `return` (on line 19) then injects into type `Faceted (FIO (Faceted RawValue))`, completing the `Faceted` do block (lines 17–19). Finally, the `prod` function on line 17 coordinates the two monads and simplifies the type to `FIO (Faceted RawValue)`, which sequentially composes with the previous sub-evaluations of `t1` and `t2`.

The remaining language features are provided by the constants below the interpreter itself: `private`, `ref`, `deref`, `assign`, and `printChar`. As for `App`, these constants must use `prod` to perform their services securely.

Figure 11 expresses our running example from Fig. 1 as a program p in the interpreted language (with some additional syntactic sugar); running the program `runFIO (eval env p) []` yields the expected result:

```
faceted "H" (public true) (public false)
```

```
 1   -- Runtime data structures.
 2   data RawValue =
 3       CharVal Char              -- Characters
 4     | RefVal (FioRef Value)     -- Mutable references
 5     | FnVal (Value → Action)    -- Functions
 6   type Value  = Faceted RawValue
 7   type Action = FIO Value
 8   type Env    = String → Value
 9
10   -- Interpreter.
11   eval :: Env → Term → Action
12   eval e (Var x)    = return $ e x
13   eval e (Lam x t)  = return $ return $ FnVal $ λv →
14                          eval (extend e x v) t
15   eval e (App t1 t2) = do v1 ← eval e t1        -- working in FIO monad
16                           v2 ← eval e t2
17                           prod $ do
18                             FnVal f ← v1        -- working in Faceted monad
19                             return $ f v2
20   eval e (Const v)  = return v
21
22   -- Constants.
23   private :: RawValue
24   private = FnVal $ λv →
25     return $ faceted "H" v bottom
26   ref :: RawValue
27   ref = FnVal $ λv → do                         -- working in FIO monad
28     ref ← newFioRef v
29     return $ return $ RefVal ref
30   deref :: RawValue
31   deref = FnVal $ λv → prod $ do                -- working in Faceted monad
32     RefVal ref ← v
33     return $ readFioRef ref
34   assign :: RawValue
35   assign = FnVal $ λv1 →
36     return $ return $ FnVal $ λv2 → prod $ do   -- working in Faceted monad
37       RefVal ref ← v1
38       rv2 ← v2
39       return $ do                               -- working in FIO monad
40         writeFioRef ref v2
41         return v2
42   printChar :: RawValue
43   printChar = FnVal $ λv → prod $ do            -- working in Faceted monad
44     CharVal c ← v
45     return $ do                                 -- working in FIO monad
46       h ← openFileFio [] "output.txt" AppendMode
47       putCharFio h (return c)
48       closeFio h
49       return v
```

Fig. 10. The bi-monadic interpreter eval function.

```
let x = ref (private true)  in
let y = ref true  in
let z = ref true  in
let vx = deref x  in
if (vx) {
    assign y false
}
let vy = deref y  in
if (vy) {
    assign z false
}
deref z
```

Fig. 11. A sample program for the interpreter. For ease of reading, we assume the availability of standard encodings for let and boolean operations.

6 Related Work

Most information flow mechanisms fall into one of three categories: run-time monitors that prevent a program execution from misbehaving; static analysis techniques that analyze the whole program and reject programs that might leak sensitive information; and finally secure multi-execution, which protects sensitive information by evaluating the same program multiple times.

Dynamic techniques dominated much of the early literature, such as Fenton's memoryless subsystems [11]. However, these approaches tend to deal poorly with *implicit flows*, where confidential information might leak via the control flow of the program; purely dynamic controls either ignore updates to reference cells that might result in implicit leaks of information [11] or terminate the program on these updates [1,36]; both approaches have obvious problems, but these techniques have seen a resurgence of interest as a possible means of securing JavaScript code, where static analysis seems to be an awkward fit [10,13,15,18].

Denning's work [6,7] instead uses a static analysis; her work was also instrumental in bringing information flow analysis into the scope of programming language research. Her approach has since been codified into different type systems, such as that of Volpano et al. [33] and the SLam Calculus [14]. Jif [21] uses this strategy for a Java-like language, and has become one of the more widespread languages providing information flow guarantees. Sabelfeld and Myers [26] provide an excellent history of information flow analysis research prior to 2003. Refer to Russo [25] for a detailed comparison of static and dynamic techniques.

Secure multi-execution [9] executes the same program multiple times representing different "views" of the data. For a simple two-element lattice of high and low, a program is executed twice: one execution can access confidential (high) data but can only write to authorized channels, while the other replaces all high data with default values and can write to public channels. This approach has since been implemented in the Firefox web browser [5] and as a Haskell library [16].

Rafnsson and Sablefeld [23] show an approach to handle declassification and to guarantee transparency with secure multi-execution.

Zanarini et al. [35] notes some challenges with secure multi-execution; specifically, it alters the behavior of programs violating noninterference (potentially introducing difficult to analyze bugs), and the multiple processes might produce outputs to different channels in a different order than expected. They further address these challenges through a *multi-execution monitor*. In essence, their approach executes the original program without modification and compares its results to the results of the SME processes; if output of secure multi-execution differs from the original at any point, a warning can be raised to note that the semantics have been altered.

Faceted evaluation [2] simulates secure multi-execution by the use of special faceted values, which track different views for data based on the security principals involved[4]. While faceted evaluation cannot be parallelized as easily, it avoids many redundant calculations, thereby improving efficiency [2]. It also allows declassification, where private data is released to public channels. Austin et al. [3] exploit this benefit to incorporate policy-agnostic programming techniques, allowing for the specification of more flexible policies than traditionally permitted in information flow systems.

Li and Zdancewic [19] implement an information flow system in Haskell, embedding a language for creating secure modules. Their enforcement mechanism is dynamic but relies on static enforcement techniques, effectively guaranteeing the security of the system by type checking the embedded code at runtime. Their system supports declassification, a critical requirement for specifying many real world security policies.

Russo et al. [24] provide a monadic library guaranteeing information flow properties. Their approach includes special declassification combinators, which can be used to restrict the release of data based on the what/when/who dimensions proposed by Sabelfeld [28].

Deviese and Piessens [8] illustrate how to enforce information flow in monadic libraries. A sequence operation $e_1 \gg e_2$ is distinguished from a bind operation $e_1 \ggg e_2$ in that there are no implicit flows with the $\gg$ operator. They demonstrate the generality of their approach by applying it to classic static [33], dynamic [27], and hybrid [12] information flow systems.

Stefan et al. [31] use a *labeled IO* (LIO) monad to guarantee information flow analysis. LIO tracks the current label of the execution, which serves as an upper bound on the labels of all data in lexical scope. IO is permitted only if it would not result in an implicit flow. It combines this notion with the concept of a *current clearance* that limits the maximum privileges allowed for an execution, thereby eliminating the termination channel. Buiras and Russo [4] show how lazy evaluation may leak secrets with LIO through the use of the *internal timing*

---

[4] Faceted values are closely related to the value pairs used by [22]; while intended as a proof technique rather than a dynamic enforcement mechanism, the construct is essentially identical.

covert channel. They propose a defense against this attack by duplicating shared thunks.

Wadler [34] describes the use of monads to structure interpreters for effectful languages. There has been great effort to improve the modularity of this technique, including the application of pseudomonads [30] and of monad transformers [20]. Both of these approaches make it possible to design an interpreter's computation monad by composing building blocks that each encapsulate one kind of effect. Our bi-monadic interpreter achieves a different kind of modularity by using separate monads for effects and values. The use of a *prod* function, which links the two monads together, is originally described by Jones and Duponcheel [17].

7   Conclusion

We show how the *faceted values* technique can be implemented as a library rather than as a language extension. Our implementation draws on the previous work to provide a library consisting primarily of two monads, which track both explicit and implicit information flows. This implementation demonstrates how faceted values look in a typed context, as well as how they might be implemented as a library rather than a language feature. It also illustrates some of the subtle interactions between two monads. Our interpreter shows that this library can serve as a basis for other faceted value languages or as a template for further Haskell work.

Acknowledgements. This research was supported by the National Science Foundation under grants CCF-1337278 and CCF-1421016.

References

1. Austin, T.H., Flanagan, C.: Efficient purely-dynamic information flow analysis. In: PLAS 2009. ACM Press, New York (2009)
2. Austin, T.H., Flanagan, C.: Multiple Facets for Dynamic Information Flow. In: POPL 2012, pp. 165–178. ACM Press, New York (2012)
3. Austin, T.H., et al.: Faceted execution of policy-agnostic programs. In: PLAS 2013, 15–26. ACM Press, New York (2013)
4. Buiras, P., Russo, A.: Lazy programs leak secrets. In: Riis Nielson, H., Gollmann, D. (eds.) NordSec 2013. LNCS, vol. 8208, pp. 116–122. Springer, Heidelberg (2013)
5. De Groef, W., et al.: FlowFox: a web browser with flexible and precise information flow control. In: CCS 2012, pp. 748–759. ACM Press, New York (2012)
6. Denning, D.E.: A lattice model of secure information flow. Commun. ACM **19**(5), 236–243 (1976)
7. Denning, D.E., Denning, P.J.: Certification of programs for secure information flow. Commun. ACM **20**(7), 504–513 (1977)
8. Devriese, D., Piessens, F.: Information Flow Enforcement in Monadic Libraries. In: TLDI 2011, pp. 59–72. ACM Press, New York (2011)
9. Devriese, D., Piessens, F.: Noninterference through secure multi-execution. In: Symposium on Security and Privacy, pp. 109–124. IEEE, Los Alamitos (2010)

10. Dhawan, M., Ganapathy, V.: Analyzing information flow in javascript-based browser extensions. In: ACSAC. IEEE (2009)
11. Fenton, J.S.: Memoryless subsystems. Comput. J. **17**(2), 143–147 (1974)
12. Le Guernic, G., Banerjee, A., Jensen, T., Schmidt, D.A.: Automata-based confidentiality monitoring. In: Okada, M., Satoh, I. (eds.) ASIAN 2006. LNCS, vol. 4435, pp. 75–89. Springer, Heidelberg (2008)
13. Hedin, D., Sabelfeld, A.: Information-flow security for a core of JavaScript. In: CSF, pp. 3–18. IEEE (2012)
14. Heintze, N., Riecke, J.G.: The SLam calculus: programming with secrecy and integrity. In: POPL, pp. 365–377. ACM (1998)
15. Jang, D., et al.: An empirical study of privacy-violating information flows in JavaScript web applications. In: ACM Conference on Computer and Communications Security, pp. 270–283 (2010)
16. Jaskelioff, M., Russo, A.: Secure multi-execution in haskell. In: Clarke, E., Virbitskaite, I., Voronkov, A. (eds.) PSI 2011. LNCS, vol. 7162, pp. 170–178. Springer, Heidelberg (2012)
17. Jones, M.P., Duponcheel, L.: Composing Monads. Technical report. Research Report YALEU/DCS/RR-1004. Yale University (1993)
18. Kerschbaumer, C., Hennigan, E., Larsen, P., Brunthaler, S., Franz, M.: Towards precise and efficient information flow control in web browsers. In: Huth, M., Asokan, N., Čapkun, S., Flechais, I., Coles-Kemp, L. (eds.) TRUST 2013. LNCS, vol. 7904, pp. 187–195. Springer, Heidelberg (2013)
19. Li, P., Zdancewic, S.: Encoding information flow in haskell. In: CSFW 2006, p.12. IEEE Computer Society, Washington, DC, USA (2006)
20. Liang, S., Hudak, P., Jones, M.: Monad transformers and modular interpreters. In: Proceedings of 22nd ACM Symposium on Principles of Programming Languages. ACM Press, New York (1995)
21. Myers, A.C.: JFlow: practical mostly-static information flow control. In: Symposium on Principles of Programming Languages (POPL), pp. 228–241. ACM (1999)
22. Pottier, F., Simonet, V.: Information flow inference for ML. ACM Trans. Program. Lang. Syst. **25**(1), 117–158 (2003)
23. Rafnsson, W., Sabelfeld, A.: Secure multi-execution: fine-grained, declassification-aware, and transparent. In: IEEE 26th Computer Security Foundations Symposium (CSF), pp. 33–48 (2013)
24. Russo, A., Claessen, K., Hughes, J.: A library for lightweight information-flow security in haskell. In: Haskell 2008, pp. 13–24. ACM, New York, NY, USA (2008)
25. Russo, A., Sabelfeld, A.: Dynamic vs. static flow-sensitive security analysis. In: CSF 2010, pp. 186–199. IEEE Computer Society, Washington, DC, USA (2010)
26. Sabelfeld, A., Myers, A.C.: Language-based information-flow security. IEEE J. Sel. Areas in Commun. **21**(1), 5–19 (2003)
27. Sabelfeld, A., Russo, A.: From dynamic to static and back: riding the roller coaster of information-flow control research. In: Pnueli, A., Virbitskaite, I., Voronkov, A. (eds.) PSI 2009. LNCS, vol. 5947, pp. 352–365. Springer, Heidelberg (2010)
28. Sabelfeld, A., Sands, D.: Declassification: dimensions and principles. J. Comput. Secur. **17**(5), 517–548 (2009)
29. Schmitz, T., et al.: Faceted dynamic information flow via control and data monads. In: University of California, Santa Cruz, Technical report UCSC-SOE-16-01 (2016)
30. Steele, G.L., Jr.: Building interpreters by composing monads. In: POPL 1994. ACM, Portland (1994)
31. Stefan, D., et al.: Flexible dynamic information flow control in haskell. In: Haskell 2011, 95–106. ACM, New York (2011)

32. Stefan, D., et al.: Flexible dynamic information flow control in Haskell, vol. 46(12). ACM (2011)
33. Volpano, D., Irvine, C., Smith, G.: A sound type system for secure flow analysis. J. Comput. Secur. 4(2–3), 167–187 (1996)
34. Wadler, P.: The essence of functional programming. In: POPL 1992. ACM, Albuquerque, New Mexico, USA (1992)
35. Zanarini, D., Jaskelioff, M., Russo, A.: Precise enforcement of confidentiality for reactive systems. In: CSF, pp. 18–32 (2013)
36. Zdancewic, S.A.: Programming languages for information security. PhD thesis. Cornell University (2002)

Asymmetric Secure Multi-execution with Declassification

Iulia Boloşteanu and Deepak Garg[✉]

Max Planck Institute for Software Systems,
Kaiserslautern and Saarbruecken, Germany
{iulia_mb,dg}@mpi-sws.org

Abstract. Secure multi-execution (SME) is a promising black-box technique for enforcing information flow properties. Unlike traditional static or dynamic language-based techniques, SME satisfies noninterference (soundness) by construction and is also precise. SME executes a given program twice. In one execution, called the high run, the program receives all inputs, but the program's public outputs are suppressed. In the other execution, called the low run, the program receives only public inputs and declassified or, in some cases, default inputs as a replacement for the secret inputs, but its private outputs are suppressed. This approach works well in theory, but in practice the program might not be prepared to handle the declassified or default inputs as they may differ a lot from the regular secret inputs. As a consequence, the program may produce incorrect outputs or it may crash. To avoid this problem, existing work makes strong assumptions on the ability of the given program to robustly adapt to the declassified inputs, limiting the class of programs to which SME applies.

To lift this limitation, we present a modification of SME, called asymmetric SME or A-SME. A-SME gives up on the pretense that real programs are inherently robust to modified inputs. Instead, A-SME requires a variant of the original program that has been adapted (by the programmer or automatically) to react properly to declassified or default inputs. This variant, called the low slice, is used in A-SME as a replacement for the original program in the low run. The original program and its low slice must be related by a semantic correctness criteria, but beyond adhering to this criteria, A-SME offers complete flexibility in the construction of the low slice. A-SME is provably sound even when the low slice is incorrect and when the low slice is correct, A-SME is also precise. Finally, we show that if the program is policy compliant, then its low slice always exists, at least in theory. On the side, we also improve the state-of-the-art in declassification policies by supporting policies that offer controlled choices to untrustworthy programs.

1 Introduction

Secure systems often rely on information flow control (IFC) to ensure that an unreliable application cannot leak sensitive data to public outputs. The standard IFC security policy is noninterference, which says that confidential or high

F. Piessens and L. Viganò (Eds.): POST 2016, LNCS 9635, pp. 24–45, 2016.
DOI: 10.1007/978-3-662-49635-0_2

inputs must not affect public or low outputs. Traditionally, noninterference and related policies have been enforced using static, dynamic, or hybrid analyses of programs [3,7,9–11,16,17,23], but it is known that such analyses cannot be sound (reject all leaky programs) and precise (accept all non-leaky programs) simultaneously. Secure multi-execution or SME is a promising recent technique that attains both soundness and precision, at the expense of more computational power [13]. Additionally, SME is a *black-box* monitoring technique that does not require access to the program's source code or binary.

Briefly, SME runs two copies of the same program, called high and low, simultaneously. The low run is given only low (public) inputs and its high (secret) outputs are blocked. The high run is given both low and high inputs, but its low outputs are blocked. Neither of the two runs can both see high inputs and produce low outputs, so SME trivially enforces noninterference. Less trivially, it can be shown that if a program is noninterfering semantically, then SME does not change its output behavior, so SME is also precise. SME has been implemented and tested in at least one large application, namely the web browser Firefox [6]. As CPU cores become cheaper, we expect SME to scale better and to be applied to other applications as well.

Whereas SME may sound like the panacea for enforcing noninterference, its deployment in practice faces a fundamental issue: Since the low run cannot be provided high inputs, what must it be provided instead? The original work on SME [13] proposes providing *default values* like 0 or null in place of high inputs. In their seminal work on enforcing declassification policies with SME [26], Vanhoef *et al.* advocate providing *policy-declassified values* in place of high inputs. In either case, the high inputs received by the low run of the program are different from the actual high inputs and may also have different semantics. Consequently, the program must be aware of, and robust to, changes in its high inputs' semantics, otherwise the low run may crash or produce incorrect outputs. This is somewhat contrary to the spirit of SME, which aims to be sound and precise on all (unmodified) programs.

Asymmetric SME (A-SME). The robustness requirement limits the programs to which SME can be applied in practice. To circumvent the limitation, a better solution or method is needed. Such a solution is the primary goal of this paper: We posit a modification of SME, called asymmetric SME or A-SME, that gives up on the SME design of executing the *same* program in the high and low runs. Instead, in A-SME, a second program that has been adapted to use declassified inputs (or default inputs in the degenerate scenario where no declassification is allowed) in place of regular high inputs is used for the low run. This second program, which we call the *low slice*, may be constructed by the programmer or by slicing the original program automatically.

In A-SME, the robustness assumption of SME changes to a semantic correctness criteria on the low slice. This correctness criteria takes the declassification policy into account. We prove three results: (a) Irrespective of the correctness of the low slice, the declassification policy is always enforced by A-SME, (b) If the low slice is correct, then A-SME is precise, and (c) If the original program complies with the declassification policy semantically, then its low slice exists, at least in theory.

Our focus here is on *reactive programs* and declassification policies that are specified separately from the monitored program. The rationale for this focus is straightforward: Both web and mobile applications are inherently reactive and, due to the open nature of the two platforms, applications cannot be trusted to declassify sensitive information correctly in their own code.

Improving Expressiveness of Policies Enforced with SME. As a secondary contribution, we improve the expressiveness of declassification policies in existing work on SME with declassification. Specifically, we improve upon the work of Vanhoef *et al.* [26] (VGDPR in the sequel). First, we allow declassification to depend on *feedback* from the program and, second, we allow the sensitivity of an input's presence to depend on policy state. We explain these two points below.

Output Feedback. We allow policy state to depend on program outputs. This feedback from the program to the policy permits the policy to offer the program controlled choices in what is declassified, without having to introspect into the state of the program. The following examples illustrate this.

Example 1. Consider a data server, which spawns a separate handler process for every client session. A requirement may be that each handler process declassifies (across the network) the data of at most one client, but the process may choose which client that is. With output feedback, the handler process can produce a special high output, seen only by the SME monitor, to name the client whose data the process wants to access. Subsequently, the policy will deny the low run any data not belonging to that client.

Example 2. Consider an outsourced audit process for income tax returns. A significant concern may be subject privacy. Suppose that the process initially reads non-identifying data about all forms (e.g., only gross incomes and pseudonyms of subjects), and then decides which 1 % of the forms it wants to audit in detail. With output feedback, we may enforce a very strong policy without interfering with the audit's functionality: The low run of the audit process can see (and, hence, leak) the detailed data of *only* 1 % of all audit forms, but it can choose *which* forms constitute the 1 %.

State-Dependent Input Presence. Like some prior work on SME [6], we consider a reactive setting, where the program being monitored reacts to inputs provided externally. In this setting, the mere *presence* of an input (not just its content) may be sensitive. SME typically handles sensitive input presence by not invoking the low run for an input whose presence is high [6,26]. Generalizing this, our policies allow the decision of whether an input's presence is high to depend on the policy state (i.e., on past inputs and outputs). This is useful in some cases, as the following example demonstrates.

Example 3. Consider a news website whose landing page allows the visitor to choose news feeds from topics like politics, sports, and social, and allows the user to interact with the feed by liking news items. When the user clicks one of these topics, its feed is displayed using AJAX, without navigating the user to another page. On the side, untrusted third-party scripts track mouse clicks for page analytics. A privacy-conscious user may want to hide her interaction with certain feeds from the tracking scripts. For example, the occurrence of a mouse click on the politics feed may be sensitive, but a similar click on the sports feed may not. Thus, the sensitivity of mouse click presence on the page depends on the topic being browsed, making the sensitivity state-dependent.

Contributions. To summarize, we make the following contributions:

- We introduce asymmetric SME (A-SME) that uses a program (the low slice) *adapted* to process declassified values in the low run (Sect. 4). This expands the set of programs on which declassification policies can be enforced precisely using SME.
- We increase the expressiveness of declassification policies in SME, by supporting program feedback and state-dependent input presence (Sect. 3).
- We prove formally that A-SME enforcement is always secure and, given a correct low slice, also precise (Sect. 4).
- We show that if the program conforms to the policy then its low slice exists, at least in theory (Sect. 5).

Proofs and other technical details omitted from this paper are provided in an appendix, available online from the authors' homepages.

Limitations. The focus of this paper is on the *foundations* of A-SME; methods for constructing the low slice are left for future work. Also, the *where* dimension of declassification, which allows a program to internally declassify information through special declassify actions, is out of the scope of this work. In the context of SME, the *where* dimension has been studied by VGDPR and independently by Rafnsson and Sabelfeld [21,22] (see Sect. 6).

2   Programming Model

We model *reactive* programs, i.e. programs invoked by the runtime when an *input* is available from the program's environment. In response, the program produces a list of *outputs* and this input-output pattern repeats indefinitely. In processing every input, the program may update its internal *memory* and during the next invocation, the runtime passes the updated memory to the program. This allows past inputs to affect the response to future inputs. Reactive programs are a ubiquitous model of computing and web browsers, servers and OS shells are all examples of reactive programs.

Let Input, Output and Memory denote the domains of inputs, outputs and memories for programs, and let $[\tau]$ denote a finite, possibly empty list of elements of type τ.

Definition 1 (Reactive program). *A reactive program p is a function of type* *Input* $\times$ *Memory* $\mapsto$ *[Output]* $\times$ *Memory.*

The program p accepts an input and its last memory and produces a list of outputs and an updated memory. We deliberately avoid introducing a syntax for reactive programs to emphasize the fact that A-SME is a black-box enforcement technique that does not care about the syntax of the program it monitors. Concretely, the program p may be written in any programming language with a distinguished syntax for inputs and outputs.

Semantics. We use the letters i, I, O and μ to denote elements of Input, [Input], [Output] and Memory. $p(i, \mu) = (O, \mu')$ means that the program p when given input i in memory μ produces the list of outputs O and the new memory μ'. A *run* of the program p, written E, is a finite sequence of the form $(i_1, O_1), \ldots, (i_n, O_n)$. The run means that starting from some initial memory, when the program is invoked sequentially on the inputs $i_1, \ldots, i_n$, it produces the output lists $O_1, \ldots, O_n$, respectively. For $E = (i_1, O_1), \ldots, (i_n, O_n)$, we define its projection to inputs $E|_i = i_1, \ldots, i_n$ and its projection to outputs $E|_o = O_1 +\!\!+ \ldots +\!\!+ O_n$, where $+\!\!+$ denotes list concatenation.

Formally, the semantics of a reactive program p are defined by the judgment $I, \mu \longrightarrow_p E$ (Fig. 1), which means that program p, when started in initial memory μ and given the sequence of inputs I, produces the run E. Here, $i :: I$ denotes the list obtained by adding element i to the beginning of the list I. Note that if $I, \mu \longrightarrow_p E$, then $E|_i = I$ and $|E| = |I|$.

$$\frac{}{[], \mu \longrightarrow_p []} R1 \qquad \frac{p(i, \mu) = (O, \mu') \qquad I, \mu' \longrightarrow_p E}{i :: I, \mu \longrightarrow_p (i, O) :: E} R2$$

Fig. 1. Reactive semantics.

3   Declassification Policies

Our A-SME monitor enforces an *application-specific* declassification policy. This policy may represent the requirements of the programmer, the site administrator, and the hosting environment, but it must be trusted. We model the policy as abstract stateful program whose state may be updated on every input and every output. The policy's state is completely disjoint from the monitored program's memory, and is inaccessible to the program directly. In each state the policy optionally produces a *declassified value*, which is made available to the low run of A-SME (the low run does not receive inputs directly). By allowing the policy state (and, hence, the declassified value) to depend on inputs, we allow for policies that, for instance, declassify the aggregate of 10 consecutive inputs, but not the individual inputs, as in the prior work of VGDPR. By additionally allowing the policy state to depend on program outputs, the policy may offer the program choices as explained and illustrated in Sect. 1, Examples 1 and 2. Finally, as illustrated in Example 3, the policy provides a function to decide whether an input's presence is high or low in a given state.

Definition 2 (Policy $\mathcal{D}$**).** *A declassification policy* $\mathcal{D}$ *is a tuple* $(S, \mathsf{upd}^i, \mathsf{upd}^o, \sigma, \pi)$, *where:*

- *S is a possibly infinite set of states. Our examples and metatheorems often specify the initial state separately.*
- $\mathsf{upd}^i : S \times Input \to S$ *and* $\mathsf{upd}^o : S \times [Output] \to S$ *are functions used to update the state on program input and output, respectively.*
- $\sigma : S \to Bool$ *specifies whether the* presence *of the last input is low or high. When* $\sigma(s) = \mathsf{true}$, *the input that caused the state to transition to s has low presence, else it has high presence.*
- $\pi : S \to Declassified$ *is the* projection *or* declassification *function that returns the declassified value for a given state. This value is provided as input to the low run when* $\sigma(s) = \mathsf{true}$. *Declassified is the domain of declassified values.*

The model of our declassification policies is inspired by the one of VGDPR, but our policies are more general because we allow the policy state to depend on program outputs and to set the input presence sensitivity. While VGDPR consider two declassification functions, one idempotent function for projecting every input to an approximate value, and another one for releasing aggregate information from past inputs, we fold the two into a single function π. See Sect. 6 for a detailed comparison of our model to VGDPR's model.

Example 4 (Declassification of aggregate inputs). Our first example is taken from VGDPR. A browsing analytics script running on an interactive webpage records user mouse clicks to help the webpage developer optimize content placement in the future. A desired policy might be to prevent the script from recording every individual click and, instead, release the average coordinates of blocks of 10 mouse clicks. Listing 1 shows an encoding of this policy. The policy's internal state records the number of clicks and the sum of click coordinates in the variables cnt and sum, respectively. The policy's input update function upd^i takes the new coordinate x of a mouse click, and updates both cnt and sum, except on every 10th click, when the avg (average) is updated and cnt and sum are reset. The projection function π simply returns the stored avg. Finally, since the last average can always be declassified, the input presence function σ always returns true. The output update function upd^o is irrelevant for this example and is not shown. (As a writing convention, we do not explicitly pass the internal state of the policy to the functions upd^i, upd^o, σ and π, nor return it from upd^i and upd^o. This state is implicitly accessible in the policy's state variables.)

Example 5 (State-dependent input presence). This example illustrates the use of the input presence function σ. The setting is that of Example 3. The policy applies to a news website where the user can choose to browse one of three possible topics:

Listing 1. INPUT AGGREGATION

Policy state s (local variables):
```
  cnt : int
  sum : int
  avg : int
```
Initialization: cnt = 0; sum = 0; avg = 0;
Update functions:
```
  upd^i (MouseClick x) =
    case cnt of
        | 9  → {cnt = 0; avg = (sum + x)/10; sum = 0; }
        | _ → {cnt = cnt + 1; sum = sum + x; }
```
Presence decision function:
```
  σ() = true.
```
Projection function:
```
  π() = avg.
```

politics, sports, or social. The declassification policy for mouse clicks is the following: On the sports page, mouse clicks are not sensitive; on the social page, the average of 10 mouse click coordinates can be declassified (as in Example 4); on the politics page, not even the existence of a mouse click can be declassified.

Listing 2 shows an encoding of this policy. The policy records the current topic being browsed by the user in the state variable st, which may take one of four values: initial, politics, sports and social. Upon an input (function upd^i), the policy state update depends on st. For st = sports, the click's coordinate x is stored in the variable last_click. For st = social, the policy mimics the behavior of Example 4, updating a click counter cnt, a click coordinate accumulator sum and the average avg once in every 10 clicks. Importantly, when st = politics, the policy state is not updated (the input is ignored). A separate component of upd^i not shown here changes st when the user clicks on topic change buttons.

The input presence function σ says that the input is high when st ∈ {politics, initial} (output is false) and low otherwise. Hence, when the user is browsing politics, not even the presence of inputs is released.

The projection function π declassifies the last click coordinate last_click when the user is browsing sports and the average of the last block of 10 clicks stored in avg when the user is browsing social topics. The value returned by the projection function is irrelevant when the user is browsing politics or has not chosen a topic (because in those states σ returns high), so these cases are not shown.

Example 6 (Output feedback: Data server). This example illustrates policy state dependence on program output, which allows feedback from the program being monitored to the policy. The setting is that of Example 1. A data server handles the data of three clients — Alice, Bob and Charlie. The policy is that the data of at most one of these clients may be declassified by a server process and the process may choose this one client. An encoding of the policy is shown in Listing 3. The policy tracks the process' choice in the variable st, which can take one of the four values: none (choice not yet made), alice, bob or charlie. To make

Listing 2. STATE-DEPENDENT INPUT PRESENCE

Policy state s (local variables):

  st : {initial, sports, politics, social}

  cnt : int

  sum : int

  last_click : int

Initialization: st = initial; cnt = 0; sum = 0; last_click = 0;

Update functions:

  upd^i(MouseClick x) =

    case st of

      | sports → {last_click = x; }

      | social →

        case cnt of

          | 10 → {cnt = 1; sum = x; }

          | _ → {cnt = cnt + 1; sum = sum + x; }

Presence decision function:

  $\sigma()$ =

    case st of

      | initial → false

      | sports → true

      | politics → false

      | social → case cnt of | 10 → true | _ → false.

Projection function:

  $\pi()$ =

    case st of

      | sports → last_click

      | social → sum/10.

the choice, the process produces an output specifying a user whose data it wants to declassify. The function upd^o records the server's choice in st if the process has not already made the choice (upd^o checks that st = none). When user data is read (i.e., a new input from the file system appears), the input update function upd^i compares st to the user whose data is read. If the two match, the read data d is stored in the policy state variable data, else *null* is stored in data. The projection function π simply declassifies the value stored in data.

Example 7 (Output feedback: Audit). This example also illustrates feedback from the program to the policy. The setting is that of Example 2, where an untrusted audit process is initially provided with pseudonyms and non-sensitive informa-tion of several client records, and later it identifies a certain fraction of these records, which must be declassified in full for further examination. We have sim-plified the example for exposition: The audit process reads exactly 100 records and then selects 1 record to be declassified for further examination. Pseudonyms are simply indices into an array maintained by the policy. An encoding of the corresponding policy is shown in Listing 4. The policy variable count counts the number of records fed to the program so far. While count is less than 100, the input update function upd^i simply stores each input record i of five fields in the

Listing 3. OUTPUT FEEDBACK: DATA SERVER

Policy state s (local variables):
  st : {none, alice, bob, charlie}
  data : file
Initialization: st = none; data = $null$;
Update functions:
  upd^o(RestrictAccessTo user) =
    if (st = none) then
      case user of
        | Alice → {st = alice; }
        | Bob → {st = bob; }
        | Charlie → {st = charlie; }
  upd^i(PrivateData (user, d)) =
    if (st = user) then {data = d; } else {data = $null$; }
Presence decision function:
  $\sigma()$ = true.
Projection function:
  $\pi()$ = data.

array records. When count reaches 100, the output update function upd^o allows the program to provide a single index idx, which identifies the record that must be declassified in full. The full record stored at this index is transferred to the variable declassified, the array records is erased and count is set to ∞ to encode that the process has made its choice.

The projection function π reveals only the index and the gross income of the last input (at index (count − 1) in records) while count is not ∞. When count has been set to ∞, the single record chosen by the process is revealed in full through the variable declassified.

4   Asymmetric SME

We enforce the declassification policies of Sect. 3 using a new paradigm that we call asymmetric SME (A-SME). A-SME builds on classic SME, but uses different programs in the high and low runs (hence the adjective asymmetric). Classic SME – as described, for example, by VGDPR – enforces a declassification policy on a reactive program by maintaining two independent runs of the given program. The first run, called the high run, is invoked on every new input and is provided the new input as-is. The second run, called the low run, is invoked for an input only when the input's presence (as determined by the policy) is low. Additionally, the low run is not given the original input, but a projected (declassified) value obtained from the policy after the policy's state has been updated with the new input. Only high outputs are retained from the high run (these are not visible to the adversary) and only low outputs are retained from the low run (these are visible to the adversary). Since the low run sees only declassified values and the high run does not produce low outputs, it must be

Listing 4. OUTPUT FEEDBACK: AUDIT

Policy state s (local variables):
  records : array[100] $*$ array[5]
  count : int
  declassified : array[5]
Initialization: records $= null$; count $= 0$; declassified $= null$;
Update functions:
  $\text{upd}^i(i) =$
    case count of
      | 100 = return;
      | x = {records[x] $= i$; count $= x + 1$; }
  $\text{upd}^o(\text{idx}) =$
    case count of
      | 100 = {declassified = records[idx]; records $= null$; count $= \infty$; }
      | _ = return;
Presence decision function:
  $\sigma() = $ true
Projection function:
  $\pi() =$
    case count of
      | ∞ = declassified
      | _ = let (idx, name, address, phone, income) = records[count $- 1$] in (idx, income)

---

the case that the low outputs depend only on declassified values. This enforces a form of noninterference.

The problem with classic SME, which we seek to address by moving to A-SME, is that even though the low and the high runs execute the *same* program, they receive completely different inputs — the high run receives raw inputs, whereas the low runs receives inputs created by the declassification policy. This leads to two problems. First, if the programmer is not aware that her program will run with SME, the low run may crash because it may not be prepared to handle the completely different types of the declassified inputs. Fundamentally, it seems impossible for the program to automatically adapt to the different inputs of the high and the low runs, because it gets no indication of which run it is executing in! Second, if the program tries to enforce the declassification policy internally (which a non-malicious program will likely do), then in the low run, the declassification is applied twice — once by the SME monitor and then internally by the program. In contrast, in a run without SME, the function is applied only once. As a consequence, one must assume that the function that implements declassification is idempotent (e.g., in VGDPR, this declassification function is called "project" and it must be idempotent). These two limitations restrict the scenarios in which SME can be used to enforce declassification policies.

To broaden the scope of enforcement of declassification policies with SME, we propose to do away with requirement that the same program be executed in the high and low runs of SME. Instead, we assume that a variant of the program that has been carefully crafted to use declassified inputs (not the raw inputs) exists. This variant, called the low slice, is used in the low run instead of the original program. The resulting paradigm is what we call asymmetric SME or A-SME. Before delving into the details of A-SME and its semantics, we give an intuition for the low slice.

Low Slice. For a program p : Input × Memory $\mapsto$ [Output] × Memory, the low slice with respect to policy $\mathcal{D}$ is a program p_L : Declassified × Memory $\mapsto$ [Output] × Memory that produces the program's low outputs given as inputs values that have been declassified in accordance with policy $\mathcal{D}$. In other words, the low slice is the part of the program that handles only declassified data.

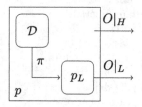

Fig. 2. Factorization of a program p into a declassification policy $\mathcal{D}$ and a low slice p_L.

A question that arises is why this low slice should even exist? Intuitively, if the program p is compliant with policy $\mathcal{D}$, then its low outputs depend only on the output of the policy $\mathcal{D}$. Hence, *semantically*, p must be equivalent to a program that composes $\mathcal{D}$ with some other function p_L to produce low outputs (see Fig. 2). It is this p_L that we call p's low slice. We formalize this intuition in Sect. 5 by proving that if the program p conforms to $\mathcal{D}$ (in a formal sense) then p_L must exist. However, note that the low slice p_L may not be syntactically extractable from the program p by any automatic transformation, in which case the programmer's help may be needed to construct p_L.

4.1 Semantics of A-SME

A-SME enforces a declassification policy $\mathcal{D}$ over a program p and its low slice p_L, together called an *A-SME-aware program*, written (p, p_L). The semantics of A-SME are defined by the judgment $I, s, \mu_H, \mu_L \Longmapsto^{\mathcal{D}}_{p, p_L} E$ (Fig. 3), which should be read: "Starting in policy state s and initial memories μ_H (for the high run) and μ_L (for the low run), the input sequence I produces the run E under A-SME and policy $\mathcal{D}$".

$$\frac{}{[], s, \mu_H, \mu_L \Longmapsto^{\mathcal{D}}_{p, p_L} []}\text{A-SME-1}$$

$$\frac{s'' = \mathsf{upd}^i(s, i) \quad \sigma(s'') = \mathsf{false} \quad p(i, \mu_H) = (O, \mu'_H) \quad s' = \mathsf{upd}^o(s'', O) \quad I, s', \mu'_H, \mu_L \Longmapsto^{\mathcal{D}}_{p, p_L} E}{i :: I, s, \mu_H, \mu_L \Longmapsto^{\mathcal{D}}_{p, p_L} (i, O|_H) :: E}\text{A-SME-2}$$

$$\frac{s'' = \mathsf{upd}^i(s, i) \quad \sigma(s'') = \mathsf{true} \quad p_L(\pi(s''), \mu_L) = (O', \mu'_L) \quad p(i, \mu_H) = (O, \mu'_H) \quad s' = \mathsf{upd}^o(s'', O) \quad I, s', \mu'_H, \mu'_L \Longmapsto^{\mathcal{D}}_{p, p_L} E}{i :: I, s, \mu_H, \mu_L \Longmapsto^{\mathcal{D}}_{p, p_L} (i, O'|_L \mathbin{+\!\!+} O|_H) :: E}\text{A-SME-3}$$

Fig. 3. Semantics of A-SME.

We define the judgment by induction on the input sequence I. Rule A-SME-1 is the base case: When the input sequence I is empty, so is the run E (when there is no input, a reactive program produces no output). Rules A-SME-2 and A-SME-3 handle the case where an input is available. In both rules, the first available input, i, is given to the policy's input update function upd^i to obtain a new policy state s''. Then, $\sigma(s'')$ is evaluated to determine whether the input's presence is high or low (rules A-SME-2 and A-SME-3, respectively).

If the input's presence is high (rule A-SME-2), then only the high run is executed by invoking p with input i. The outputs O of this high run are used to update the policy state to s' (premise $s' = upd^o(s'', O)$). After this, the rest of the input sequence is processed inductively (last premise). Importantly, any low outputs in O are discarded. The notation $O|_H$ denotes the subsequence of O containing all outputs on high (protected, non-public) channels. We assume that each output carries an internal annotation that specifies whether its channel is high or low, so $O|_H$ is defined.

If the input's presence is low (rule A-SME-3), then in addition to executing the high run and updating the policy state as described above, the low slice p_L is also invoked with the current declassified value $\pi(s'')$ to produce outputs O' and to update the low memory. Only the low outputs in O' ($O'|_L$) are retained. All high outputs in O' are discarded.

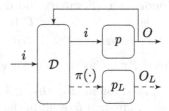

Fig. 4. Pictorial representation of A-SME semantics.

Figure 4 depicts A-SME semantics pictorially. The dashed arrows denote the case where the input's presence is low (A-SME-3). In that case, the low slice executes with the declassified value returned by the policy function π. The arrow from the output O back to the policy $\mathcal{D}$ represents the output feedback.

In the following two subsections we show that A-SME is (1) secure — it enforces policies correctly and has no false negatives, and (2) precise — if p_L is a correct low slice, then its observable behavior does not change under A-SME.

4.2 Security

We prove the security of A-SME by showing that a program running under A-SME satisfies a form of noninterference. Roughly, this noninterference says that if we take two different input sequences that result in the same declassified values, then the low outputs of the two runs of the program under A-SME are the same. In other words, the low outputs under A-SME are a function of the declassified values, so an adversary cannot learn more than the declassified values by observing the low outputs. Importantly, the security theorem makes no assumption about the relationship between p and p_L, so security holds even if a leaky program or a program that does not expect declassified values as inputs is provided as p_L.

$$\mathcal{D}^*(s, []) = []$$
$$\mathcal{D}^*(s, (i, O) :: E) = \mathcal{D}^*(\mathsf{upd}^o(s'', O), E) \qquad \text{if } s'' = \mathsf{upd}^i(s, i) \text{ and } \sigma(s'') = \mathsf{false}$$
$$\mathcal{D}^*(s, (i, O) :: E) = \pi(s'') :: \mathcal{D}^*(\mathsf{upd}^o(s'', O), E) \quad \text{if } s'' = \mathsf{upd}^i(s, i) \text{ and } \sigma(s'') = \mathsf{true}$$

Fig. 5. Function $\mathcal{D}^*$ returns values declassified by policy $\mathcal{D}$ during a run.

To formally specify our security criteria, we first define a function $\mathcal{D}^*$ (Fig. 5) that, given an initial policy state s and a program run E, returns the sequence of values declassified during that run. This function is defined by induction on E and takes into account the update of the policy state due to both inputs and outputs in E. It is similar to a homonym in VGDPR but adds policy state update due to outputs. Note that $\mathcal{D}^*$ adds the declassified value to the result only when the input presence is low (condition $\sigma(s'') = \mathsf{true}$). Equipped with the function $\mathcal{D}^*$, we state our security theorem.

Theorem 1 (Security, noninterference under $\mathcal{D}$). *Suppose* $I_1, \mu_1 \longrightarrow_p E_1$ *and* $I_2, \mu_2 \longrightarrow_p E_2$ *and* $\mathcal{D}^*(s_1, E_1) = \mathcal{D}^*(s_2, E_2)$. *If* $I_1, s_1, \mu_1, \mu_L \Longmapsto_{p, p_L}^{\mathcal{D}} E_1'$ *and* $I_2, s_2, \mu_2, \mu_L \Longmapsto_{p, p_L}^{\mathcal{D}} E_2'$, *then* $E_1'|_o|_L = E_2'|_o|_L$.

Proof. By induction on the length of $I_1 \mathbin{+\!\!+} I_2$.

The theorem says that if for two input sequences I_1, I_2, the two runs E_1, E_2 of a program p result in the same declassified values (condition $\mathcal{D}^*(s_1, E_1) = \mathcal{D}^*(s_2, E_2)$), then the A-SME execution of the program on I_1, I_2 will produce the same low outputs ($E_1'|_o|_L = E_2'|_o|_L$) for any low slice p_L. Note that the precondition of the theorem is an equivalence on E_1 and E_2 obtained by execution under standard (non-A-SME) semantics, but its postcondition is an equivalence on E_1' and E_2' obtained by execution under A-SME semantics. This may look a bit odd at first glance, but this is the intended and expected formulation of the theorem. The intuition is that the theorem relates values declassified by the standard semantics to the security of the A-SME semantics.

4.3   Precision

In the context of SME, precision means that for a non-leaky program, outputs produced under SME are equal to the outputs produced without SME. In general, SME preserves the order of outputs at a given level, but may reorder outputs across levels. For instance, the rule A-SME-3 in Fig. 3 places the low outputs $O'|_L$ before the high outputs $O|_H$. So, following prior work [26], we prove precision with respect to each level: We show that the sequence of outputs produced at any level under A-SME is equal to the sequence of outputs produced at the same level in the standard (non-A-SME) execution. Proving precision for high outputs is straightforward for A-SME.

Theorem 2 (Precision for high outputs). *For any programs p and p_L, declassification policy $\mathcal{D}$ with initial state s, and input list I, if* $I, \mu_H \longrightarrow_p E$ *and* $I, s, \mu_H, \mu_L \Longmapsto_{p, p_L}^{\mathcal{D}} E'$, *then* $E|_o|_H = E'|_o|_H$.

Proof. From the semantics in Figs. 1 and 3 it can be observed that the high run of A-SME mimics (in input, memory and outputs) the execution under $\longrightarrow_p$.

To show precision for low outputs, we must assume that the low slice p_L is *correct* with respect to the original program p and policy $\mathcal{D}$. This assumption is necessary because A-SME uses p_L to produce the low outputs, whereas standard execution uses p to produce them. Recall that the low slice p_L is intended to produce the low outputs of p, given values declassified by policy $\mathcal{D}$. We formalize this intuition in the following correctness criteria for p_L.

Definition 3 (Correct low slice/correct low pair). *A program p_L of type $Declassified \times Memory \mapsto [Output] \times Memory$ and an initial memory μ_L are called a correct low pair (and p_L is called a correct low slice) with respect to policy $\mathcal{D}$, initial state s, program p and initial memory μ if for all inputs I, if $I, \mu \longrightarrow_p E$ and $\mathcal{D}^*(s, E) = R$ and $R, \mu_L \longrightarrow_{p_L} E'$, then $E|_o|_L = E'|_o|_L$.*

Based on this definition, we can now prove precision for low outputs.

Theorem 3 (Precision for low outputs). *For any programs p and p_L, declassification policy $\mathcal{D}$ with initial state s and input list I, if $I, \mu_H \longrightarrow_p E$ and $I, s, \mu_H, \mu_L \Longmapsto_{p, p_L}^{\mathcal{D}} E'$ and (μ_L, p_L) is a correct low pair with respect to $\mathcal{D}$, s, p and μ_H, then $E|_o|_L = E'|_o|_L$.*

The proof of this theorem relies on the following easily established lemma.

Lemma 1 (Low simulation). *Let $I, s, \mu_H, \mu_L \Longmapsto_{p, p_L}^{\mathcal{D}} E$ and $\mathcal{D}^*(s, E) = R$. If $R, \mu_L \longrightarrow_{p_L} E'$, then $E|_o|_L = E'|_o|_L$.*

Proof. By induction on I. Intuitively, the low run in A-SME is identical to the given run under $\longrightarrow_{p_L}$ and the high run of A-SME does not contribute any low outputs.

Proof (of Theorem 3). Let $R = \mathcal{D}^*(s, E')$ and $R, \mu_L \longrightarrow_{p_L} E''$. By Lemma 1, $E'|_o|_L = E''|_o|_L$. From Definition 3, $E|_o|_L = E''|_o|_L$. By transitivity of equality, we get that $E|_o|_L = E'|_o|_L$.

Theorem 4 (Precision). *For any programs p and p_L, declassification policy $\mathcal{D}$ with initial state s and input list I, if $I, \mu_H \longrightarrow_p E$ and $I, s, \mu_H, \mu_L \Longmapsto_{p, p_L}^{\mathcal{D}} E'$, and (μ_L, p_L) is a correct low pair with respect to $\mathcal{D}$, s, p and μ_H, then $E|_o|_L = E'|_o|_L$ and $E|_o|_H = E'|_o|_H$.*

Proof. Immediate from Theorems 2 and 3.

Remark. Rafnsson and Sabelfeld [21, 22] show that precision across output levels can be obtained for SME using barrier synchronization. We speculate that the method would generalize to A-SME as well.

5   Existence of Correct Low Slices

In this section we show that a correct low slice (more specifically, a correct low pair) of a program exists if the program does not leak information beyond what is allowed by the declassification policy.

Definition 4 (No leaks outside declassification). *A program p starting from initial memory μ does not leak outside declassification in policy $\mathcal{D}$ and initial state s if for any two input lists I_1, I_2: $I_1, \mu \longrightarrow_p E_1$ and $I_2, \mu \longrightarrow_p E_2$ and $\mathcal{D}^*(s, E_1) = \mathcal{D}^*(s, E_2)$ imply $E_1|_o|_L = E_2|_o|_L$.*

Theorem 5 (Existence of correct low slice). *If program p, starting from initial memory μ, does not leak outside declassification in policy $\mathcal{D}$ and initial state s, then there exist p_L and μ_L such that (μ_L, p_L) is a correct low pair with respect to $\mathcal{D}$, s, p and μ.*

We describe a proof of this theorem. Fix an initial memory μ. Define f, g as follows: If $I, \mu \longrightarrow_p E$, then $f(I) = E|_o|_L$ and $g(I) = \mathcal{D}^*(s, E)$. Then, Definition 4 says that $f(I)$ is a function of $g(I)$, meaning that there exists another function h such that $f(I) = h(g(I))$. Intuitively, for a given sequence of declassification values $R = \mathcal{D}^*(s, E)$, $h(R)$ is the set of low outputs of p.

For lists L_1, L_2, let $L_1 \leq L_2$ denote that L_1 is a prefix of L_2.

Lemma 2 (Monotonicity of h). *If $I_1 \leq I_2$, then $h(g(I_1)) \leq h(g(I_2))$.*

Proof. By definition, $h(g(I_1)) = f(I_1)$ and $h(g(I_2)) = f(I_2)$. So, we need to show that $f(I_1) \leq f(I_2)$. Let $\mu, I_1 \longrightarrow_p E_1$ and $\mu, I_2 \longrightarrow_p E_2$. Since $I_1 \leq I_2$, $E_1|_o|_L \leq E_2|_o|_L$, i.e., $f(I_1) \leq f(I_2)$.

We now construct the low slice p_L using h. In the execution of p_L, the low memory μ'_L at any point is the list of declassified values R that have been seen so far. We define:

$$\mu_L = []$$
$$p_L(r, R) = (h(R :: r) \setminus h(R), R :: r)$$

If R is the set of declassified values seen in the past, to produce the low output for a new declassified value r, we simply compute $h(R :: r) \setminus h(R)$. By Lemma 2, $h(R) \leq h(R :: r)$ when R and $R :: r$ are declassified value lists from the same run of p, so $h(R :: r) \setminus h(R)$ is well-defined. We then prove the following lemma, which completes the proof.

Lemma 3 (Correctness of construction). *(μ_L, p_L) defined above is a correct low pair for $\mathcal{D}$, s, p and μ if p, starting from initial memory μ, does not leak outside declassification in $\mathcal{D}$ and initial state s.*

6 Discussion

In this section, we compare some of the fine points of A-SME and prior work on SME. We often refer to the schemas of Fig. 6, which summarizes several flavors of SME described in the literature.

Input Presence Levels. SME was initially designed by Devriese and Piessens [13] to enforce noninterference on sequential programs, not reactive programs (Fig. 6a). They implicitly assume that all inputs are low presence. Thus, there are only two kinds of inputs — low content/low presence (denoted L) and high content/low presence. Following [20], we call the latter "medium"-level or M-level inputs, reserving high (H) for inputs with high presence.

   Bielova *et al.* [6] adapted SME for enforcing noninterference in a reactive setting. Though not explicitly mentioned in their paper, their approach assumes

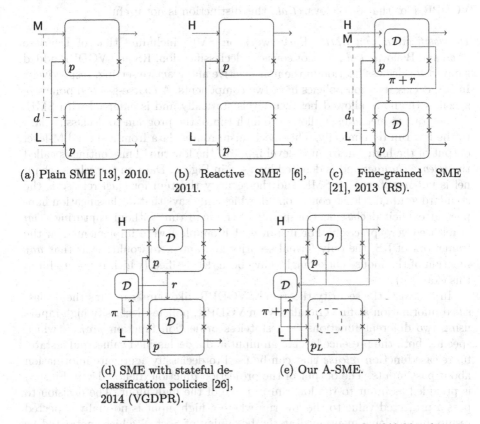

(a) Plain SME [13], 2010.

(b) Reactive SME [6], 2011.

(c) Fine-grained SME [21], 2013 (RS).

(d) SME with stateful declassification policies [26], 2014 (VGDPR).

(e) Our A-SME.

Fig. 6. Flavors of SME from literature. Red denotes information at level H, blue denotes information at level M, and black denotes information at level L. d is a default value provided to the low run when it demands an input of higher classification (Color figure online).

that an input's presence and content are classified at the same level. Consequently, in their work, inputs only have levels H and L (Fig. 6b). Bielova *et al.* also introduce the idea that for an input with high presence (level H), the low run must not be executed at all and we, as well as VGDPR [26] use this idea. In Bielova *et al.*'s work, an input's presence level is fixed by the channel on which it appears; this static assignment of input presence levels carries into all subsequent work, including that of VGDPR and of Rafnsson and Sabelfeld [21,22] (RS in the sequel). Our work relaxes this idea and permits input presence to depend on policy state.

Input Totality. RS (Fig. 6c) consider all three input levels — L, M, and H — for sequential programs with I/O. In their setup, programs demand inputs and can time how long they wait before an input is available. This allows a conceptual distinction between environments that can always provide inputs on demand and environments that cannot. In an asynchronous reactive setting like ours, VGDPR's, or that of Bielova *et al.*, this distinction is not useful.

Declassification and SME. Early work on SME, including that of Devriese *et al.* and Bielova *et al.*, did not consider declassification. RS and VGDPR added support for declassification in the non-reactive and reactive setting, respectively. In RS, declassification policies have two components. A coarse-grained policy, ρ, specifies the flows allowed between levels statically and is enforced with SME. A fine-grained mechanism allows the high run of the program to declassify data to the low run dynamically. This mechanism routes data from a special M-level output of the high run to an M-level input of the low run. This routing is called the *release channel* and is denoted by $\pi + r$ in Fig. 6c. Data on the release channel is not monitored by SME and the security theorem for such release is the standard gradual release condition [2], which only says that declassification happens at explicit declassification points of the high run, without capturing *what* is released very precisely. For instance, if Example 4 were implemented in the framework of RS, the only formal security guarantee we would get is that *any* function of the mouse clicks might have been declassified (which is not useful in this example).

   In contrast, the security theorem of VGDPR, like ours, captures the declassified information at fine granularity. In VGDPR, policies declassify high inputs using two different functions — a stateless projection function *project*, which specifies both the presence level of an input and a declassified value, and a stateful release function *release* that can be used to declassify aggregate information about past inputs. The output of the projection function (denoted π in Fig. 6d) is provided as input to the low run in place of the high input. The decision to pass a projected value to the low run where a high input is normally expected results in problems mentioned at the beginning of Sect. 4, which motivated us to design A-SME. The output of the release function (denoted r in Fig. 6d) is passed along a release channel similar to the one in RS. We find the use of two different channels redundant and thus we combine *release* and *project* into a single policy function that we call π. Going beyond VGDPR, in A-SME, the policy state may depend on program output and the input presence may depend on policy state. As illustrated in Sect. 3, this allows for a richer representation of declassification policies.

Totality of the Monitored Program. Like VGDPR, we assume that the (reactive) program being monitored is total and terminates in a finite amount of time. This rules out leaks due to the adversary having the ability to observe lack of progress, also called progress-sensitivity [1,18]. In contrast, RS do not make this termination assumption. Instead, they (meaningfully) prove progress-sensitive noninterference. This is nontrivial when the adversary has the ability to observe termination on the low run, as a scheduler must be chosen carefully. We believe that the same idea can be applied to both VGDPR's and our work if divergent behavior is permitted.

7   Related Work

(Stateful) Declassification Policies. Sabelfeld and Sands [24] survey different methods for representing and enforcing declassification policies and provide a set of four *dimensions* for declassification models. These dimensions — *what, where, when,* and *who* — have been investigated significantly in literature. Policies often encompass a single dimension, such as *what* in delimited release [23], *where* in gradual release [2], or *who* in the context of faceted values [4], but sometimes also encompass more than one dimension such as *what* and *where* in localized delimited release [3], or *what* and *who* in decentralized delimited release [17]. Our security policies encompass the *what* and *when* dimensions of declassification. We do not consider programs with explicit declassify commands (in fact, we do not consider any syntax for programs) and, hence, we do not consider the *where* dimension of declassification [21,23,26].

In the context of security policies specified separately from code, Li and Zdancewic [16] propose relaxed non-interference, a security property that applies to declassification policies written in a separate language. The policies are treated as security levels and enforced through a type system. Swamy and Hicks [25] also define policies separate from the program. They express the policies as security automata, using a new language called AIR (automata for information release). The policies maintain their own state and transition states when a release obligation is satisfied. When all obligations are fulfilled, the automaton reaches an accepting state and performs a declassification. These policies are also enforced using a type system. The language Paralocks [7] also supports stateful declassification policies enforced by a type system. There, the policies are represented as sets of Horn clauses, whose antecedents are called locks. Locks are predicates with zero or more parameters and they exhibit two states: opened (true) and closed (false). The type system statically tracks which locks are open and which locks are closed at every program point. Chong and Myers' conditional declassification policies are similar, but more abstract, and also enforced using a type system [9–11]. In the context of SME, Kashyap *et al.* [14] suggest, but do not develop, the idea of writing declassification policies as separate sub-programs. Our work ultimately draws some lineage from this idea.

Secure Multi-execution. We discussed prior work on SME in Sect. 6. Here, we mention some other work on related techniques. Khatiwala *et al.* [15] propose *data sandboxing*, a technique which partitions the program into two slices, a private slice containing the instructions handling sensitive data, and a public slice that contains the remaining instructions and uses system call interposition to control the outputs. The public slice is very similar to our low slice, but Khatiwala *et al.* trust the low slice's correctness for *security* of enforcement, while we do not. Nonetheless, we expect that the slicing method used by Khatiwala *et al.* to construct the public slice can be adapted to construct low slices for use with A-SME.

Capizzi *et al.* [8] introduce *shadow executions* for controlling information flow in an operating system. They suggest running two copies of an application with different sets of inputs: a *public copy*, with access to the network, that is supplied dummy values in place of the user's confidential data, and a *private copy*, with no access to the network, that receives all confidential data from the user.

Zanarini *et al.* [28] introduce *multi-execution monitors*, a combination of SME and monitoring, aimed at reporting any actions that violate a security policy. The multi-execution monitor runs a program in parallel with its SME-enforced version. If the execution is secure, the two programs will run in sync, otherwise, when one version performs an action different from the other, the monitor reports that the program is insecure. No support for declassification is provided.

Faceted and Sensitive Values. Faceted values [4] are a more recent, dynamic mechanism for controlling information flow. They are inspired by SME but reduce the overhead of SME by simulating the effect of multiple runs in a single run. To do this, they maintain values for different levels (called facets) separately. For a two-level lattice, a faceted value is a pair of values. Declassification corresponds to migrating information from the high facet to the low facet. We expect that in A-SME, the use of the low slice in place of the original program in the low run will result in a reduction of overhead (over SME), comparable to that attained by faceted values.

Jeeves [27] is a new programming model that uses sensitive values for encapsulating a low- and a high-confidentiality view for a given value. Like faceted values, sensitive values are pairs of values. They are parameterized with a level variable which determines the view of the value that should be released to any given sink. Jeeves' policies are represented as declarative rules that describe when a level variable may be set high or low. The policies enforce data confidentiality, but offer no support for declassification. An extension of Jeeves with faceted values [5] supports more expressive declassification policies, but output feedback is still not supported.

Generic Black-Box Enforcement. Remarkably, Ngo *et al.* [19] have recently shown that black-box techniques based on multi-execution can be used to enforce not just noninterference and declassification policies, but a large subset of what are called hyperproperties [12]. They present a generic construction for enforcing any property in this subset. Superficially, their generic construction may look similar to A-SME, but it is actually quite different. In particular, their method would enforce noninterference by choosing a second input sequence that results in the same declassified values as the given input sequence to detect if there is any discrepancy in low outputs. A-SME does not use such a construction and is closer in spirit to traditional SME.

8   Conclusion

This paper introduces asymmetric SME (A-SME) that executes a program and its low slice simultaneously to enforce a broad range of declassification policies. We prove that A-SME is secure, independent of the semantic correctness of the low slice, and also precise when the low slice is semantically correct. Moreover we show that A-SME does not result in loss of expressiveness: If the original program conforms to the declassification policy, then a correct low slice exists. Additionally, we improve the expressive power of declassification policies considered in literature by allowing feedback from the program, and by allowing input presence sensitivity to depend on the policy state.

Future Work. A-SME can be generalized to arbitrary security lattices. For each lattice level ℓ, a separate projection function π_ℓ could determine the values declassified to the ℓ-run in A-SME. For $\ell \sqsubseteq \ell'$, π_ℓ should reveal less information than $\pi_{\ell'}$, i.e., there should be some function f such that $\pi_\ell = f \circ \pi_{\ell'}$. Additionally, A-SME would require a different slice of the program for every level ℓ.

Another interesting direction for future work would be to develop an analysis either to verify the correctness of a low slice, or to automatically construct the low slice from a program and a policy. Verification will involve establishing semantic similarity of the composition of the low slice and the policy with a part of the program, which can be accomplished using static methods for relational verification. Automatic construction of the low slice should be feasible using program slicing techniques, at least in some cases.

Acknowledgments. This work was partially supported by the DFG grant "Information Flow Control for Browser Clients" under the priority program "Reliably Secure Software Systems" (RS^3).

References

1. Askarov, A., Hunt, S., Sabelfeld, A., Sands, D.: Termination-insensitive noninterference leaks more than just a bit. In: Jajodia, S., Lopez, J. (eds.) ESORICS 2008. LNCS, vol. 5283, pp. 333–348. Springer, Heidelberg (2008)
2. Askarov, A., Sabelfeld, A.: Gradual release: unifying declassification, encryption and key release policies. In: 2007 IEEE Symposium on Security and Privacy (S&P 2007), 20–23 May 2007, Oakland, pp. 207–221 (2007)

3. Askarov, A., Sabelfeld, A.: Localized delimited release: combining the what and where dimensions of information release. In: Proceedings of the 2007 Workshop on Programming Languages and Analysis for Security (PLAS 2007), pp. 53–60 (2007)
4. Austin, T.H., Flanagan, C.: Multiple facets for dynamic information flow. In: Proceedings of the 39th Annual ACM SIGPLAN-SIGACT Symposium on Principles of Programming Languages (POPL 2012), pp. 165–178 (2012)
5. Austin, T.H., Yang, J., Flanagan, C., Solar-Lezama, A.: Faceted execution of policy-agnostic programs. In: Proceedings of the Eighth ACM SIGPLAN Workshop on Programming Languages and Analysis for Security (PLAS 2013), pp. 15–26 (2013)
6. Bielova, N., Devriese, D., Massacci, F., Piessens, F.: Reactive non-interference for a browser model. In: 5th International Conference on Network and System Security (NSS 2011), pp. 97–104 (2011)
7. Broberg, N., Sands, D.: Paralocks: role-based information flow control and beyond. In: Proceedings of the 37th Annual ACM SIGPLAN-SIGACT Symposium on Principles of Programming Languages (POPL 2010), pp. 431–444 (2010)
8. Capizzi, R., Longo, A., Venkatakrishnan, V.N., Sistla, A.P.: Preventing information leaks through shadow executions (ACSAC 2008). In: Proceedings of the 2008 Annual Computer Security Applications Conference, pp. 322–331 (2008)
9. Chong, S., Myers, A.C.: Security policies for downgrading. In: Proceedings of the 11th ACM Conference on Computer and Communications Security (CCS 2004), pp. 198–209 (2004)
10. Chong, S., Myers, A.C.: Language-based information erasure. In: 18th IEEE Computer Security Foundations Workshop (CSFW-18 2005), pp. 241–254 (2005)
11. Chong, S., Myers, A.C.: End-to-end enforcement of erasure and declassification. In: Proceedings of the 21st IEEE Computer Security Foundations Symposium (CSF 2008), pp. 98–111 (2008)
12. Clarkson, M.R., Schneider, F.B.: Hyperproperties. In: Proceedings of the 21st IEEE Computer Security Foundations Symposium (CSF 2008), Pittsburgh, Pennsylvania, 23–25 June 2008, pp. 51–65 (2008)
13. Devriese, D., Piessens, F.: Noninterference through secure multi-execution. In: 31st IEEE Symposium on Security and Privacy (S&P 2010), pp. 109–124 (2010)
14. Kashyap, V., Wiedermann, B., Hardekopf, B.: Timing- and termination-sensitive secure information flow: exploring a new approach. In: 32nd IEEE Symposium on Security and Privacy (S&P 2011), 22–25 May 2011, Berkeley, pp. 413–428 (2011)
15. Khatiwala, T., Swaminathan, R., Venkatakrishnan, V.N.: Data sandboxing: a technique for enforcing confidentiality policies. In: 22nd Annual Computer Security Applications Conference (ACSAC 2006), pp. 223–234 (2006)
16. Li, P., Zdancewic, S.: Downgrading policies and relaxed noninterference. In: Proceedings of the 32nd ACM SIGPLAN-SIGACT Symposium on Principles of Programming Languages (POpPL 2005), pp. 158–170 (2005)
17. Magazinius, J., Askarov, A., Sabelfeld, A.: Decentralized delimited release. In: Yang, H. (ed.) APLAS 2011. LNCS, vol. 7078, pp. 220–237. Springer, Heidelberg (2011)
18. Moore, S., Askarov, A., Chong, S.: Precise enforcement of progress-sensitive security. In: Proceedings of the ACM Conference on Computer and Communications Security (CCS), pp. 881–893 (2012)
19. Ngo, M., Massacci, F., Milushev, D., Piessens, F.: Runtime enforcement of security policies on black box reactive programs. In: Proceedings of the 42nd Annual ACM SIGPLAN-SIGACT Symposium on Principles of Programming Languages (POpPL 2015), pp. 43–54 (2015)

20. Rafnsson, W., Hedin, D., Sabelfeld, A.: Securing interactive programs. In: 25th IEEE Computer Security Foundations Symposium (CSF 2012), pp. 293–307 (2012)
21. Rafnsson, W., Sabelfeld, A.: Secure multi-execution: fine-grained, declassification-aware, and transparent. In: 2013 IEEE 26th Computer Security Foundations Symposium, pp. 33–48 (2013)
22. Rafnsson, W., Sabelfeld, A.: Secure multi-execution: fine-grained, declassification-aware, and transparent. J. Comput. Secur. (2015). to appear
23. Sabelfeld, A., Myers, A.C.: A model for delimited information release. In: Futatsugi, K., Mizoguchi, F., Yonezaki, N. (eds.) ISSS 2003. LNCS, vol. 3233, pp. 174–191. Springer, Heidelberg (2004)
24. Sabelfeld, A., Sands, D.: Dimensions and principles of declassification. In: 18th IEEE Computer Security Foundations Workshop (CSFW-18 2005), pp. 255–269 (2005)
25. Swamy, N., Hicks, M.: Verified enforcement of stateful information release policies. In: Proceedings of the 2008 Workshop on Programming Languages and Analysis for Security (PLAS 2008), pp. 21–32 (2008)
26. Vanhoef, M., Groef, W.D., Devriese, D., Piessens, F., Rezk, T.: Stateful declassification policies for event-driven programs. In: IEEE 27th Computer Security Foundations Symposium (CSF 2014), pp. 293–307 (2014)
27. Yang, J., Yessenov, K., Solar-Lezama, A.: A language for automatically enforcing privacy policies. In: Proceedings of the 39th ACM SIGPLAN-SIGACT Symposium on Principles of Programming Languages (POpPL 2012), pp. 85–96 (2012)
28. Zanarini, D., Jaskelioff, M., Russo, A.: Precise enforcement of confidentiality for reactive systems. In: 2013 IEEE 26th Computer Security Foundations Symposium, pp. 18–32 (2013)

A Taxonomy of Information Flow Monitors

Nataliia Bielova[✉] and Tamara Rezk

Inria, Sophia Antipolis, France
{nataliia.bielova,tamara.rezk}@inria.fr

Abstract. We propose a rigorous comparison of information flow monitors with respect to two dimensions: soundness and transparency.

For soundness, we notice that the standard information flow security definition called Termination-Insensitive Noninterference (TINI) allows the presence of termination channels, however it does not describe whether the termination channel was present in the original program, or it was added by a monitor. We propose a stronger notion of noninterference, that we call Termination-Aware Noninterference (TANI), that captures this fact, and thus allows us to better evaluate the security guarantees of different monitors. We further investigate TANI, and state its formal relations to other soundness guarantees of information flow monitors. For transparency, we identify different notions from the literature that aim at comparing the behaviour of monitors. We notice that one common notion used in the literature is not adequate since it identifies as better a monitor that accepts insecure executions, and hence may augment the knowledge of the attacker. To discriminate between monitors' behaviours on secure and insecure executions, we factorized two notions that we call true and false transparency. These notions allow us to compare monitors that were deemed to be incomparable in the past.

We analyse five widely explored information flow monitors: no-sensitive-upgrade (NSU), permissive-upgrade (PU), hybrid monitor (HM), secure multi-execution (SME), and multiple facets (MF).

1   Introduction

Motivated by the dynamic nature and an extensive list of vulnerabilities found in web applications in recent years, several dynamic enforcement mechanisms in the form of information flow monitors [5–7,9,12,14,17,23,27,33], have been proposed. In the runtime monitor literature [8,13], two properties of monitors are considered specially important: soundness and transparency. In this work, we rigorously compare information flow monitors with respect to these two dimensions. We analyse five widely explored information flow monitor techniques: no-sensitive-upgrade (NSU) [33], permissive-upgrade (PU) [6], hybrid monitor (HM) [14], secure multi-execution (SME) [12], and multiple facets (MF) [7].

Soundness. An information flow monitor is sound when it ensures that observable outputs comply with a given information flow policy. In the case of noninterference, the monitor must ensure equal observable outputs if executions start

© Springer-Verlag Berlin Heidelberg 2016
F. Piessens and L. Viganò (Eds.): POST 2016, LNCS 9635, pp. 46–67, 2016.
DOI: 10.1007/978-3-662-49635-0_3

in equal observable inputs. We notice that some monitoring techniques introduce new termination channels, whereas others don't. The standard information flow security definition called *Termination-Insensitive Noninterference (TINI)* does not account for termination: only initial memories in which the program terminates should lead to equal observable outputs. Thus, TINI allows the presence of termination channels, however it does not describe whether the termination channel was present in the original program, or it was added by a monitor. *Termination-Sensitive Noninterference* (TSNI), on the other hand, is a stronger policy that disallows the presence of any termination channel. However, most information flow monitors do not satisfy TSNI. Hence, existing definitions do not allow us to discriminate between different monitors with respect to the security guarantees that they provide. We propose a notion of noninterference, stronger than TINI but weaker than TSNI, that we call *Termination-Aware Noninterference (TANI)*, that captures the fact that the monitor does not introduce a new termination channel, and thus allows to better evaluate the security guarantees of different monitors. We discovered that HM, SME, and MF do satisfy TANI, while NSU and PU do not satisfy TANI.

Example 1 (NSU introduces a termination channel). Consider the following program, where each variable can take only two possible values: 0 and 1.

```
1 if h = 0 then l = 1;                                          Program 1
2 output l
```

This program is leaking confidential information – upon observing output l=0 (l=1), it's possible to derive that h=1 (h=0). In spite of this fact, NSU allows the execution of this program starting in a memory [h=1, l=0] and blocks the execution otherwise, thus introducing a new termination channel.

Transparency. An information flow monitor is transparent when it preserves program semantics if the execution complies with the policy. In the case of noninterference, the monitor must produce the same output as an original program execution with a value that only depends on observable inputs. We identify different common notions from the literature that aim at comparing the behaviour of monitors: precision, permissiveness, and transparency. We notice that permissiveness is not adequate since it identifies as better a monitor that accepts insecure executions, and hence may augment the knowledge of the attacker, given that the attacker has knowledge based on the original executions. To discriminate between monitors' behaviours on secure and insecure executions, we factorized two notions that we call true and false transparency. *True transparency* corresponds to the standard notion of transparency in the field of runtime monitoring: the ability of a monitor to preserve semantics of secure executions. An information flow monitor is *false transparent* when it preserves semantics of the original program execution that does not comply with the security policy. False transparency might seem contradictory to soundness at first sight but this is not the case since information flow is not a property of one execution [2,24] but a property of several executions, also called a hyperproperty [11,29]. These two notions of transparency allow us to compare monitors that were deemed to be incomparable in the past. In particular, we prove that HM is *more TSNI precise* (more true transparent for the set of TSNI secure programs) than NSU and NSU is more false transparent than HM. Proofs can be found in the companion technical report [1].

Our contributions are the following:

1. We propose a new information flow policy called termination-aware noninterference (TANI) that allows us to evaluate monitors according to their soundness guarantees. We prove that TANI is stronger than TINI but weaker than TSNI that disallows any termination channels.
2. We identify two different notions of transparency that are used in the literature as the same notion and we call them true and false transparency.
3. We generalize previous results from Hedin et al. [16]: we show that dynamic and hybrid monitors become comparable when the two flavors of transparency are separated into true and false transparency.
4. We analyse and compare five major monitors previously proved sound for TINI: NSU, PU, HM, SME and MF. Table 1 in Sect. 8 summarizes our results for TANI, true and false transparency.

2   Knowledge

We assume a two-element security lattice with $L \sqsubseteq H$ and we use $\sqcup$ as the least upper bound. A security environment Γ maps program variables to security levels. By μ_L we denote a projection of low variables of the memory μ, according to an implicitly parameterized security environment Γ. The program semantics is defined as a big-step evaluation relation $(P, \mu) \Downarrow (v, \mu')$, where P is a program that produces only one output v at the end of execution. We assume that v is visible to the attacker at level L and that the program semantics is deterministic. The attacker can gain knowledge while observing output v. Following Askarov and Sabelfeld [3,4], we define knowledge as a set of low-equal memories, that lead to the program observation v.

Definition 1 (Knowledge). *Given a program P, the low part μ_L of an initial memory μ, and an observation v, the* knowledge *for semantics relation $\Downarrow$ is a set of memories that agree with μ on low variables and can lead to an observation v: $k_\Downarrow(P, \mu_L, v) = \{\mu' \mid \mu_L = \mu'_L \land \exists \mu''.(P, \mu') \Downarrow (v, \mu'')\}$.*

Notice that knowledge corresponds to *uncertainty* about the environments in the knowledge set: any environment is a possible program input. The attacker believes that the environments outside of the knowledge set are *impossible* inputs. Upon observing a program output, the uncertainty might decrease because the new output may render some inputs impossible. This means that the knowledge set may become smaller, thus increasing the knowledge of the attacker.

To specify a security condition, we define what it means for an attacker not to gain any knowledge. Given a program P, and a low part μ_L of an initial memory μ, the attacker's knowledge before the execution of the program is a set of memories that agree with μ on low variables. This set is an equivalence class of low-equal memories: $[\mu]_L = \{\mu' \mid \mu_L = \mu'_L\}$.

Definition 2 (Possible outputs). *Given a program P and the low part μ_L of an initial memory μ, a set of observable outputs for semantics relation $\Downarrow$ is:*
$$\mathcal{O}_{\Downarrow}(P, \mu_L) = \{v \mid \exists \mu', \mu''. \ \mu_L = \mu'_L \wedge (P, \mu') \Downarrow (v, \mu'')\}.$$

In the following, we don't write the semantics relation $\Downarrow$ when we mean the program semantics; the definitions in the rest of this section can be also used with the subscript parameter $\Downarrow$ when semantics has to be explicit.

We now specify the security condition as follows: by observing a program output, the attacker is not allowed to gain any knowledge.

Definition 3 (Termination-Sensitive Noninterference). *Program P is termination-sensitively noninterferent for an initial low memory μ_L, written $TSNI(P, \mu_L)$, if for all possible observations $v \in \mathcal{O}(P, \mu_L)$, we have*

$$[\mu]_L = k(P, \mu_L, v)$$

A program P is termination-sensitively noninterferent, *written $TSNI(P)$, if for all possible initial memories μ, $TSNI(P, \mu_L)$.*

The above definition is *termination-sensitive* because it does not allow an attacker to learn the secret information from program divergence. Intuitively, if the program terminates on all low-equal memories, and it produces the same output v then it satisfies TSNI. If the program doesn't terminate on some of the low-equal memories, then for all possible observations v, the knowledge $k(P, \mu_L, v)$ becomes a subset of $[\mu]_L$ and doesn't satisfy the definition.

Example 2. Consider Program 2. If the attacker observes that l=1, then he learns that h was 0, and if the attacker doesn't see any program output (divergence), the attacker learns that h was 1. TSNI captures this kind of information leakage, hence TSNI doesn't hold.

```
1 l = 1;
2 (while (h=1) do skip);
3 output l
```
Program 2

Proposition 1. *$TSNI(P)$ holds if and only if for all pairs of memories μ^1 and μ^2, we have: $\mu^1_L = \mu^2_L \wedge \exists \mu'.(P, \mu^1) \Downarrow (v_1, \mu') \Rightarrow \exists \mu''.(P, \mu^2) \Downarrow (v_2, \mu'') \wedge v_1 = v_2$.*

Termination-sensitive noninterference sometimes is too restrictive as it requires a more sophisticated program analysis or monitoring that may reject many secure executions of a program. A weaker security condition, called *termination-insensitive noninterference (TINI)*, allows information flows through program divergence, while still offering information flow security.

To capture this security condition, we follow the approach of Askarov and Sabelfeld [4], by limiting the allowed attacker's knowledge to the set of low-equal memories where the program terminates. Since termination means that some output is observable, a set that we call a *termination knowledge*, is a union of all knowledge sets that correspond to some program output: $\bigcup_{v'} k(P, \mu_L, v')$.

Definition 4 (Termination-Insensitive Noninterference). *Program P is termination-insensitively noninterferent for an initial low memory μ_L, written $TINI(P, \mu_L)$, if for all possible observations $v \in \mathcal{O}(P, \mu_L)$, we have*

$$\bigcup_{v' \in \mathcal{O}(P, \mu_L)} k(P, \mu_L, v') = k(P, \mu_L, v).$$

A program P is termination-insensitively noninterferent, written $TINI(P)$, if for all possible initial memories μ, $TINI(P, \mu_L)$.

Example 3. TINI recognises the Program 2 as secure, since the attacker's *termination knowledge* is only a set of low-equal memories where the program terminates. For example, for $\mu_L = $ [l=0], only one observation l=1 is possible when h=0, therefore *TINI* holds: $\bigcup_{v' \in \{1\}} k(P, \text{l=0}, v') = [\text{h=0}, \text{ l=0}] = k(P, \text{l=0}, 1)$.

Proposition 2. *$TINI(P)$ holds if and only if for all pairs of memories μ^1 and μ^2, we have: $\mu_L^1 = \mu_L^2 \wedge \exists \mu'.(P, \mu^1) \Downarrow (v_1, \mu') \wedge \exists \mu''.(P, \mu^2) \Downarrow (v_2, \mu'') \Rightarrow v_1 = v_2$.*

3 Monitor Soundness

In this section, we consider dynamic mechanisms for enforcing information flow security. For brevity, we call them "monitors". The monitors we consider are purely dynamic monitors, such as NSU and PU, hybrid monitors in the style of Le Guernic et al. [20,21] that we denote by HM, secure multi-execution (SME), and multiple facets monitor (MF). All the mechanisms we consider have deterministic semantics denoted by $\Downarrow_M$, where M represents a particular monitor. All the monitors enforce at least *termination-insensitive noninterference (TINI)*.[1] Since TINI accepts termination channels, it also allows the monitor to introduce new termination channels even if an original program did not have any. In the next section, we will propose a new definition for soundness of information flow monitors, capturing that a monitor should not introduce a new termination channel. But, first, we set up the similar definitions of termination-sensitive and -insensitive noninterference for a monitored semantics. Instead of using a subscript $\Downarrow_M$ for a semantics of a monitor M, we will use a subscript M.

---

[1] This is indeed a lower bound since some monitors, like SME, also enforce termination- and time-sensitive noninterference.

Definition 5 (Soundness of TSNI enforcement). *Monitor M soundly enforces* termination-sensitive noninterference, *written* $TSNI(M)$, *if for all possible programs* P, $TSNI_M(P)$.

Proposition 1 proves that this definition of TSNI soundness is equivalent to the standard two-run definition if we substitute the original program semantics with the monitor semantics. Similarly, to define a sound TINI monitor, we restate Definition 4 of TINI with the monitored semantics. The definition below is equivalent to the standard two-run definition (see Proposition 2).

Definition 6 (Soundness of TINI enforcement). *Monitor M soundly enforces* termination-insensitive noninterference, *written* $TINI(M)$, *if for all possible programs* P, $TINI_M(P)$.

This definition compares the initial knowledge and the final knowledge of the attacker under the monitor semantics. But in practice, an attacker has also the initial knowledge of the original program semantics (see Example 1).

4   Termination-Aware Noninterference

We propose a new notion of soundness for the monitored semantics, called *Termination-Aware Noninterference (TANI)* that does not allow a monitor to introduce a new termination channel.

Intuitively, all the low-equal memories, on which the original program terminates, should be treated by the monitor in the same way, meaning the monitor should either produce the same result for all these memories, or diverge on all of them. In terms of knowledge, it means that the knowledge provided by the monitor, should be smaller or equal than the knowledge known by the attacker before running the program. Additionally, in the case the original program always diverges, TANI holds if the monitor also always diverges or if the monitor always terminates in the same value.

Definition 7 (Termination-Aware Noninterference). *A monitor* $\Downarrow_M$ *is* Termination-Aware Noninterferent (TANI), *written* $TANI(M)$, *if for all programs* P, *initial memories* μ, *and possible observations* $v \in \mathcal{O}_M(P, \mu_L)$, *we have:*

- $\mathcal{O}(P, \mu_L) \neq \emptyset \implies \bigcup_{v' \in \mathcal{O}(P, \mu_L)} k(P, \mu_L, v') \subseteq k_M(P, \mu_L, v)$
- $\mathcal{O}(P, \mu_L) = \emptyset \implies (\mathcal{O}_M(P, \mu_L) = \emptyset \lor [\mu]_L = k_M(P, \mu_L, v))$

Notice that, for the case that the original program sometimes terminate $(\mathcal{O}(P, \mu_L) \neq \emptyset))$, we do not require equality of the two sets of knowledge since the knowledge set of the monitored program can indeed be bigger than the knowledge set of the attacker before running the program[2]. The knowledge set may increase when a monitor terminates on the memories where the original program did not terminate (e.g., SME from Sect. 5 provides such enforcement).

---

[2] Remember that the bigger knowledge set corresponds to the smaller knowledge or to the increased uncertainty.

Example 4 (TANI enforcement). Coming back to Program 1, TANI requires that on two low-equal memories [h=0, l=0] and [h=1, l=0] where the original program terminates, the monitor behaves in the same way: either it terminates on both memories producing the same output, or it diverges on both memories.

It is well-known that TSNI is a strong form of noninterference that implies TINI. We now formally state the relations between TINI, TANI and TSNI.

Theorem 1. $TSNI(M) \Rightarrow TANI(M)$ *and* $TANI(M) \Rightarrow TINI(M)$.

5   Which Monitors Are TANI?

We now present five widely explored information flow monitors and prove whether these monitors comply with TANI. In order to compare the monitors, we first model all of them in the same language. Thus, our technical results are based on a simple imperative language with one output (see Fig. 1). The language's expressions include constants or values (v), variables (x) and operators $(\oplus)$ to combine them. We present the standard big-step program semantics in Fig. 2.

$$P ::= S; \text{ output } x$$
$$S ::= \text{skip} \mid x := e \mid S_1; S_2 \mid \text{if } x \text{ then } S_1 \text{ else } S_2 \mid \text{while } x \text{ do } S$$
$$e ::= v \mid x \mid e_1 \oplus e_2$$

Fig. 1. Language syntax

$$\text{SKIP} \frac{}{(\text{skip}, \mu) \Downarrow \mu} \qquad \text{ASSIGN} \frac{}{(x := e, \mu) \Downarrow \mu[x \mapsto [\![e]\!]_\mu]} \qquad \text{SEQ} \frac{(S_1, \mu) \Downarrow \mu' \quad (S_2, \mu') \Downarrow \mu''}{(S_1; S_2, \mu) \Downarrow \mu''}$$

$$\text{IF} \frac{[\![x]\!]_\mu = \alpha \quad (S_\alpha, \mu) \Downarrow \mu'}{(\text{if } x \text{ then } S_{true} \text{ else } S_{false}, \mu) \Downarrow \mu'} \qquad \text{WHILE} \frac{(\text{if } x \text{ then } S; \text{while } x \text{ do } S \text{ else skip}, \mu) \Downarrow \mu'}{(\text{while } x \text{ do } S, \mu) \Downarrow \mu'}$$

$$\text{OUTPUT} \frac{[\![x]\!]_\mu = v}{(\text{output } x, \mu) \Downarrow (v, \mu)}$$

where $[\![x]\!]_\mu = \mu(x)$, $[\![v]\!]_\mu = v$ and $[\![e_1 \oplus e_2]\!]_\mu = [\![e_1]\!]_\mu \oplus [\![e_2]\!]_\mu$

Fig. 2. Language semantics

The semantics relation of a command S is denoted by $pc \vdash (\Gamma, S, \mu) \Downarrow_M (\Gamma', \mu')$ where pc is a program counter, M is the name of the monitor and Γ is a security environment mapping variables to security levels. All the considered monitors are flow-sensitive, and Γ may be updated during the monitored execution. We assume that the only output produced by the program is visible to the attacker at level L. Since our simple language supports only one output at the end of the program, the OUTPUT rule of the monitors is defined only for $pc = L$, and thus only checks the security level of an output variable x.

No-Sensitive Upgrade (NSU). The *no-sensitive upgrade approach* (NSU) first proposed by Zdancewic [33] and later applied by Austin and Flanagan [5] is based on a purely dynamic monitor that controls only one execution of the program. To avoid implicit information flows, the NSU disallows any upgrades of a low security variables in a high security context. Consider Program 1: since the purely dynamic monitor accepts its execution when h=1, it should block the execution when h=0 to enforce TINI. NSU does so by blocking the second execution since the low variable l is updated in a high context

$$\text{SKIP} \ \frac{}{pc \vdash (\Gamma, \mathsf{skip}, \mu) \Downarrow_{\text{NSU}} (\Gamma, \mu)}$$

$$\text{ASSIGN} \ \frac{[\![e]\!]_\mu = v \qquad pc \sqsubseteq \Gamma(x) \qquad \Gamma' = \Gamma[x \mapsto \Gamma(e) \sqcup pc]}{pc \vdash (\Gamma, x := e, \mu) \Downarrow_{\text{NSU}} (\Gamma', \mu[x \mapsto v])}$$

$$\text{SEQ} \ \frac{pc \vdash (\Gamma, S_1, \mu) \Downarrow_{\text{NSU}} (\Gamma', \mu') \qquad pc \vdash (\Gamma', S_2, \mu') \Downarrow_{\text{NSU}} (\Gamma'', \mu'')}{pc \vdash (\Gamma, S_1; S_2, \mu) \Downarrow_{\text{NSU}} (\Gamma'', \mu'')}$$

$$\text{IF} \ \frac{[\![x]\!]_\mu = \alpha \qquad pc \sqcup \Gamma(x) \vdash (\Gamma, S_\alpha, \mu) \Downarrow_{\text{NSU}} (\Gamma', \mu')}{pc \vdash (\Gamma, \mathsf{if}\ x\ \mathsf{then}\ S_{true}\ \mathsf{else}\ S_{false}, \mu) \Downarrow_{\text{NSU}} (\Gamma', \mu')}$$

$$\text{WHILE} \ \frac{pc \vdash (\Gamma, \mathsf{if}\ x\ \mathsf{then}\ S; \mathsf{while}\ x\ \mathsf{do}\ S\ \mathsf{else}\ \mathsf{skip}, \mu) \Downarrow_{\text{NSU}} (\Gamma', \mu')}{pc \vdash (\Gamma, \mathsf{while}\ x\ \mathsf{do}\ S, \mu) \Downarrow_{\text{NSU}} (\Gamma', \mu')}$$

$$\text{OUTPUT} \ \frac{[\![x]\!]_\mu = v \qquad \Gamma(x) = L}{L \vdash (\Gamma, \mathsf{output}\ x, \mu) \Downarrow_{\text{NSU}} (v, \Gamma, \mu)}$$

Fig. 3. NSU semantics

Our NSU formalisation for a simple imperative language is similar to that of Bichhawat *et al.* [10]. The main idea of NSU appears in the ASSIGN rule: the monitor blocks "sensitive upgrades" when a program counter level pc is not lower than the level of the assigned variable x. Figure 3 represents the semantics of NSU monitor. We use $\Gamma(e)$ as the least upper bound of all variables occurring in expression e. If e contains no variables, then $\Gamma(e) = L$. NSU was proven to enforce termination-insensitive noninterference (TINI) (see [5, Theorem 1]).

Example 5 (NSU is not TANI). Consider Program 1 and an initial memory [h=1, l=0]. NSU does not satisfy TANI, since the monitor terminates only on one memory, i.e., $k_M(P, \mu_L, v) = $ [h=1, l=0], while the original program terminates on both memories, low-equal to [l=0].

Permissive Upgrade (PU). The NSU approach suffices to enforce TINI, however it often blocks a program execution pre-emptively. Consider Program 3.

This program is TINI, however NSU blocks its execution starting in memory [h=0, l=0] because of a sensitive upgrade under a high security context.

```
1 if h = 0 then l = 1;                                    Program 3
2 l := 0;
3 output l
```

Austin and Flanagan proposed a less-restrictive strategy called *permissive upgrade* (PU) [6]. Differently from NSU, it allows the assignments of low variables under a high security context, but labels the updated variable as *partially-leaked* or '*P*'. Intuitively, P means that the content of the variable is H but it may be L in other executions. If later in the execution, there is a branch on a variable marked with P, or such variable is to be output, the monitor stops the execution.

$$\text{ASSIGN} \ \frac{[\![e]\!]_\mu = v \qquad \Gamma' = \Gamma[x \mapsto \Gamma(e) \sqcup \text{lift}(pc, \Gamma(x))]}{pc \vdash (\Gamma, x := e, \mu) \Downarrow_{\textbf{PU}} (\Gamma', \mu[x \mapsto v])}$$

$$\text{IF} \ \frac{\Gamma(x) \neq P \qquad [\![x]\!]_\mu = \alpha \qquad pc \sqcup \Gamma(x) \vdash (\Gamma, S_\alpha, \mu) \Downarrow_{\textbf{PU}} (\Gamma', \mu')}{pc \vdash (\Gamma, \text{if } x \text{ then } S_{true} \text{ else } S_{false}, \mu) \Downarrow_{\textbf{PU}} (\Gamma', \mu')}$$

where

$$\text{lift}(pc, l) = \begin{cases} L & \text{if } pc = L \\ H & \text{if } pc = H \wedge l = H \\ P & \text{if } pc = H \wedge l \neq H \end{cases}$$

Fig. 4. PU semantics

We present a permissive upgrade monitor (PU) for a two-point lattice extended with label P with $H \sqsubset P$. The semantics of PU is identical to the one of NSU (see Fig. 3) except for the ASSIGN and IF rules, that we present in Fig. 4. Rule ASSIGN behaves like the ASSIGN rule of NSU, if $pc \sqsubseteq \Gamma(x)$ and $\Gamma(x) \neq P$. Otherwise, the assigned variable is marked with P. Rule IF is similar to the rule IF in NSU, but the semantics gets stuck if the variable in the test condition is partially leaked. PU was proven to enforce TINI (see [6, Theorem 2]). However, PU is not TANI since it has the same mechanism as NSU for adding new termination channels.

Example 6 (PU is not TANI). Consider Program 1 and an initial memory [h=1, l=0]. PU does not satisfy TANI, since the monitor terminates only on one memory, i.e., $k_M(P, \mu_L, v) = $ [h=1, l=0], while the original program terminates on both memories, low-equal to [l=0].

Hybrid Monitor (HM). Le Guernic *et al.* were the first to propose a *hybrid monitor* (HM) [14] for information flow control that combines static and dynamic analysis. This mechanism statically analyses the non-executed branch of each test in the program, collecting all the possibly updated variables in that branch. The security level of such variables are then raised to the level of the test, thus preventing information leakage.

Example 7. Consider Program 1 and its execution starting in [h=1, 1=0]. This execution is modified by HM because the static analysis discovers that variable 1 could have been updated in a high security context in an alternative branch.

$$\text{ASSIGN} \quad \frac{[\![e]\!]_\mu = v \qquad \Gamma' = \Gamma[x \mapsto pc \sqcup \Gamma(e)]}{pc \vdash (\Gamma, x := e, \mu) \Downarrow_{\mathsf{HM}} (\Gamma', \mu[x \mapsto v])}$$

$$\text{IF} \quad \frac{\Gamma'' = \mathsf{Analysis}(S_{\neg\alpha}, pc \sqcup \Gamma(x), \Gamma)}{[\![x]\!]_\mu = \alpha \qquad pc \sqcup \Gamma(x) \vdash (\Gamma, S_\alpha, \mu) \Downarrow_{\mathsf{HM}} (\Gamma', \mu')}{pc \vdash (\Gamma, \text{if } x \text{ then } S_{true} \text{ else } S_{false}, \mu) \Downarrow_{\mathsf{HM}} (\Gamma' \sqcup \Gamma'', \mu')}$$

$$\text{OUTPUT} \quad \frac{\Gamma(x) = L \Rightarrow v = [\![x]\!]_\mu \qquad \Gamma(x) \neq L \Rightarrow v = \mathsf{default}}{L \vdash (\Gamma, \text{output } x, \mu) \Downarrow_{\mathsf{HM}} (v, \Gamma, \mu)}$$

Fig. 5. HM semantics

The semantics of HM is identical to NSU except for the ASSIGN, IF and OUTPUT rules that we show in Fig. 5. The ASSIGN rule does not have any specific constraints. The static analysis $\mathsf{Analysis}(S, pc, \Gamma)$ in the IF rule explores variables assigned in S and upgrades their security level according to pc. We generalize the standard notation $\Gamma[x \mapsto l]$ to sets of variables and use $\mathsf{Vars}(S)$ for the sets of variables assigned in command S.

$$\mathsf{Analysis}(S, pc, \Gamma) = \Gamma[\{y \mapsto pc \sqcup \Gamma(y) \mid y \in \mathsf{Vars}(S)\}]$$

HM was previously proven to enforce TINI [14, Thm.1] and we prove in the companion technical report [1] that HM satisfies TANI.

Theorem 2. *HM is TANI.*

Secure Multi-Execution (SME). Devriese and Piessens were the first to propose secure multi-execution (SME) [12]. The main idea of SME is to execute the program multiple times: one for each security level. Each execution receives only inputs visible to its security level and a fixed default value for each input that should not be visible to the execution. Different executions are executed with a low priority scheduler to avoid leaks due to divergence of high executions because SME enforces TSNI.

Example 8 (SME "fixes" termination channels). Consider Program 4:

```
1 if l = 0 then                                           Program 4
2    while h=0 do skip;
3 else
4    while h=1 do skip;
5 output 1
```

Assume $\mu_L = [1=0]$ and the default high value used by SME is $h=1$. Then, there exists a memory $\mu' = [h=0, 1=0]$, low-equal to μ_L, on which the original program doesn't terminate: $\mu' \notin \bigcup_{v'} k(P, \mu_L, v')$, but SME terminates: $\mu' \in k_M(P, \mu_L, 1=0)$. Notice that SME makes the attacker's knowledge smaller.

$$\text{SME} \quad \frac{(P, \mu \downarrow_\Gamma) \Downarrow (v, \mu') \qquad \mu''' = \begin{cases} \mu' \odot_\Gamma \mu'' & \text{if } \exists \mu''.(P, \mu) \Downarrow (v', \mu'') \\ \mu' \odot_\Gamma \bot & \text{otherwise} \end{cases}}{pc \vdash (\Gamma, P, \mu) \Downarrow_{\text{SME}} (v, \Gamma, \mu''')}$$

$$\text{where} \quad \mu \downarrow_\Gamma (x) = \begin{cases} \mu(x) & \Gamma(x) = L \\ \text{default} & \Gamma(x) = H \end{cases} \qquad \mu' \odot_\Gamma \mu''(x) = \begin{cases} \mu'(x) & \Gamma(x) = L \\ \mu''(x) & \Gamma(x) = H \end{cases}$$

Fig. 6. SME semantics

The SME adaptation for our while language is given in Fig. 6, with executions for levels L and H. The special value $\bot$ represents the idea that no value can be observed and we overload the symbol to also denote a memory that maps every variable to $\bot$. Using memory $\bot$ we simulate the low priority scheduler of SME in our setting: if the execution corresponding to the H security level does not terminate, the SME semantics still terminates. In this case all the variables with level H, which values should correspond to values obtained in the normal execution of the program, are given value $\bot$.

SME was previously proven TSNI [12, Theorem 1] and we prove that it also enforces TANI: this can be directly inferred from our Theorem 1.

Theorem 3. *SME is TANI.*

Multiple Facets. Austin and Flanagan proposed multiple facets (MF) in [7]. In MF, each variable is mapped to several values or facets, one for each security level: each value corresponds to the view of the variable from the point of view of observers at different security levels. The main idea in MF is that if there is a sensitive upgrade, MF semantics does not update the observable facet. Otherwise, if there is no sensitive upgrade, MF semantics updates it according to the original semantics.

Example 9. Consider the TINI Program 5. In MF, the output observable at level L (or the L facet of variable 1) is always the initial value of variable 1 since MF will not update a low variable in a high context. Therefore, all the executions of Program 5 starting with 1=1 are modified by MF, producing the output 1=1.

```
1 if h = 0 then 1 = 0 else 1=0;                    Program 5
2 output 1
```

MF RULE
$$\boxed{\dfrac{pc \vdash (\Gamma, P, \mu \uparrow_\Gamma) \downarrow_{MF} (\langle v_1 : v_2 \rangle, \Gamma', \hat{\mu})}{pc \vdash (\Gamma, P, \mu) \Downarrow_{MF} (v_2, \Gamma', \hat{\mu} \downarrow_{\Gamma'})}}$$
SKIP
$$\dfrac{}{pc \vdash (\Gamma, \text{skip}, \hat{\mu}) \downarrow_{MF} (\Gamma, \hat{\mu})}$$

ASSIGN
$$[e]\hat{\mu} = \langle v_1 : v_2 \rangle \qquad \hat{v} = \begin{cases} \langle v_1 : \hat{\mu}(x)_2 \rangle & \text{if } pc = H \wedge \Gamma(x) = L \\ \langle v_1 : v_2 \rangle & \text{if } pc = L \vee \Gamma(x) \neq L \end{cases}$$
$$\Gamma'(y) = \begin{cases} \Gamma(e) & \text{if } pc = L \wedge y = x \\ \Gamma(y) & \text{otherwise} \end{cases}$$
$$\overline{pc \vdash (\Gamma, x := e, \hat{\mu}) \downarrow_{MF} (\Gamma', \hat{\mu}[x \mapsto \hat{v}])}$$

SEQ
$$\dfrac{pc \vdash (\Gamma, S_1, \hat{\mu}) \downarrow_{MF} (\Gamma', \hat{\mu}') \qquad pc \vdash (\Gamma', S_2, \hat{\mu}') \downarrow_{MF} (\Gamma'', \hat{\mu}'')}{pc \vdash (\Gamma, S_1; S_2, \hat{\mu}) \downarrow_{MF} (\Gamma'', \hat{\mu}'')}$$

IF-HIGH
$$\dfrac{[x]\hat{\mu} = \langle \alpha_1 : \alpha_2 \rangle \qquad pc = H \vee \Gamma(x) = H \qquad H \vdash (\Gamma, S_{\alpha_1}, \hat{\mu}) \downarrow_{MF} (\Gamma', \hat{\mu}')}{pc \vdash (\Gamma, \text{if } x \text{ then } S_{true} \text{ else } S_{false}, \hat{\mu}) \downarrow_{MF} (\Gamma', \hat{\mu}')}$$

IF-LOW
$$\dfrac{[x]\hat{\mu} = \langle \alpha_1 : \alpha_2 \rangle \qquad pc = L \wedge \Gamma(x) = L}{L \vdash (\Gamma, S_{\alpha_1}, \hat{\mu}) \downarrow_{MF} (\Gamma', \hat{\mu}_1) \qquad L \vdash (\Gamma, S_{\alpha_2}, \hat{\mu}) \downarrow_{MF} (\Gamma', \hat{\mu}_2)}{pc \vdash (\Gamma, \text{if } x \text{ then } S_{true} \text{ else } S_{false}, \mu) \downarrow_{MF} (\Gamma', \hat{\mu}_1 \otimes_\Gamma \hat{\mu}_2)}$$

WHILE
$$\dfrac{pc \vdash (\Gamma, \text{if } x \text{ then } S; \text{while } x \text{ do } S \text{ else skip}, \hat{\mu}) \downarrow_{MF} (\Gamma', \hat{\mu}')}{pc \vdash (\Gamma, \text{while } x \text{ do } S, \hat{\mu}) \downarrow_{MF} (\Gamma', \hat{\mu}')}$$

OUTPUT
$$\dfrac{[x]\hat{\mu} = \hat{v}}{L \vdash (\Gamma, \text{output } x, \hat{\mu}) \downarrow_{MF} (\hat{v}, \Gamma, \hat{\mu})}$$

where
$$[\hat{v}]\hat{\mu} = \hat{v}, \quad [x]\hat{\mu} = \hat{\mu}(x)$$
$$[e_1 \oplus e_2]\hat{\mu} = \langle v_1 \oplus v_2 : v_1' \oplus v_2' \rangle, \text{ where } [e_1]\hat{\mu} = \langle v_1 : v_1' \rangle, [e_2]\hat{\mu} = \langle v_2 : v_2' \rangle$$
$$\hat{\mu}_1 \otimes_\Gamma \hat{\mu}_2(x) = \begin{cases} \hat{\mu}_1(x) & \text{if } \Gamma(x) = H \\ \langle \hat{\mu}_1(x)_1 : \hat{\mu}_2(x)_2 \rangle & \text{if } \Gamma(x) = L \end{cases}$$
$$\mu \uparrow_\Gamma (x) = \begin{cases} \langle \mu(x) : \mu(x) \rangle & \text{if } \Gamma(x) = L \\ \langle \mu(x) : \bot \rangle & \text{if } \Gamma(x) = H \end{cases} \qquad \hat{\mu} \downarrow_\Gamma (x) = \begin{cases} \hat{\mu}(x)_1 & \text{if } \Gamma(x) = H \\ \hat{\mu}(x)_2 & \text{if } \Gamma(x) = L \end{cases}$$

Fig. 7. Multiple Facets semantics

Our adaptation of MF semantics is given in Fig. 7 where we use the following notation: a faceted value, denoted $\langle v_1 : v_2 \rangle$, is a pair of values v_1 and v_2. The first value presents the view of an observer at level H and the second value the view of an observer at level L. In the syntax, we interpret a constant v as the faceted value $\langle v : v \rangle$. Faceted memories, ranged over $\hat{\mu}$, are mappings from variables to faceted values. We use the notation $\hat{\mu}(x)_i$ ($i \in \{1, 2\}$) for the first or second projection of a faceted value stored in x. As in SME, the special value $\perp$ represents the idea that no value can be observed. MF was previously proven TINI [7, Theorem 2] and we prove that it satisfies TANI.

Theorem 4. *MF is TANI.*

6   Precision, Permissiveness and Transparency

A number of works on dynamic information flow monitors try to analyse precision of monitors. Intuitively, precision describes how often a monitor blocks (or modifies) secure programs. Different approaches have been taken to compare precision of monitors, using definitions such as "precision", "permissiveness" and "transparency". We propose a rigorous comparison of these definitions.

In the field of runtime monitoring, a monitor should provide two guarantees while enforcing a security property: soundness and transparency. *Transparency* [8] means that whenever an execution satisfies a property in question, the monitor should output it without modifications[3].

Precision (versus well typed programs). Le Guernic et al. [21] were among the first to start the discussion on transparency for information flow monitors. The authors have proved that their hybrid monitor accepts all the executions of a program that is well typed under a flow-insensitive type system similar to the one of Volpano et al. [31]. Le Guernic [19] names this result as *partial transparency*. Russo and Sabelfeld [25] prove a similar result: they show that a hybrid monitor accepts all the executions of a program that is well typed under the flow-sensitive type system of Hunt and Sands [18].

Precision (versus secure programs). Devriese and Piessens [12] propose a stronger notion, called *precision*, that requires a monitor to accept all the executions of all secure programs. Notice that this definition is stronger because not only the monitor should recognise the executions of well typed programs, but also of secure programs that are not well typed. Devriese and Piessens have proven that such precision guarantee holds for SME versus TSNI programs.

Transparency (versus secure executions). As a follow-up, Zanarini et al. [32] have proven that another monitor based on SME satisfies *transparency for TSNI*. This monitor accepts all the TSNI executions of a program, even if the program itself is insecure.

---

[3] Bauer et al. [8] actually provide a more subtle definition, saying a monitor should output a semantically equivalent trace.

Permissiveness (versus executions accepted by other monitors). In his PhD thesis, Le Guernic [19] compares his hybrid monitor with another hybrid monitor that performs a more precise static analysis, and proves an *improved precision* theorem stating that whenever the first hybrid monitor accepts an execution, the second monitor accepts it as well. Following this result, Besson et al. [9] investigate other hybrid monitors and prove relative precision in the style of Le Guernic, and Austin and Flanagan [6,7] use the same definition to compare their dynamic monitors. Hedin et al. [16] name the same notion by *permissiveness* and compare the sets of accepted executions: one monitor is more permissive than another one if its set of accepted executions contains a set of accepted executions of the other monitor.

To compare precision of different information flow monitors, we propose to distinguish two notions of transparency. *True transparency* defines the secure executions accepted by a monitor, and *false transparency* defines the insecure executions accepted by a monitor.

True Transparency. We define a notion of *true transparency* for TINI. Intuitively, a monitor is true transparent if it accepts all the TINI executions of a program.

Definition 8 (True Transparency). *Monitor M is true transparent if for any program P, and any memories μ, μ' and output v, the following holds:*

$$TINI(P, \mu_L) \wedge (P, \mu) \Downarrow (v, \mu') \Rightarrow (P, \mu) \Downarrow_M (v, \mu')$$

There is a well-known result that a truncation automata cannot recognise more than computable safety properties [15,28]. Since noninterference can be reduced to a safety property that is not computable [29], and NSU and PU can be modeled by truncation automata, it follows that they are not true transparent. We show that the monitors of this paper, that cannot be modeled by truncation automata, are not true transparent for TINI neither.

Example 10 (HM is not true transparent). Consider Program 5: it always terminates with 1=0 and hence it is secure. Any execution of this program will be modified by HM because 1 will be marked as high.

Example 11 (MF is not true transparent). Consider again TINI Program 5. The MF semantics will not behave as the original program semantics upon an execution starting in [h=1, 1=1]. The sensitive upgrade of the test will assign faceted value [1=⟨0 : 1⟩] to variable 1 and the output will produce the low facet of 1 which is 1, while the original program would produce an output 0. Hence, this is a counter example for true transparency of MF.

Example 12 (SME is not true transparent for TINI). Since SME enforces TSNI, it eliminates all the termination channels, therefore even if the original program has TINI executions, SME might modify them to achieve TSNI.

Consider TINI Program 4 and an execution starting in [h=0,1=1]. SME (with default value h=1) will diverge because it's "low" execution will diverge upon h=1. Therefore, SME is not true transparent for TINI.

Even though none of the considered monitors are true transparent for TINI, this notion allows us to define a relative true transparency to better compare the behaviours of information flow monitors when they deal with secure executions.

Given a program P and a monitor M, we define a set of initial memories that lead to secure terminating executions of program P, and a monitor M does not modify these executions:

$$T(M, P) = \{\mu \mid TINI(P, \mu_{\text{L}}) \wedge \exists \mu', v.\ (P, \mu) \Downarrow (v, \mu') \Rightarrow (P, \mu) \Downarrow_M (v, \mu')\}$$

Definition 9 (Relative True Transparency). *Monitor A is* more true transparent *than monitor B, written $A \supseteq_T B$, if for any program P, the following holds: $T(A, P) \supseteq T(B, P)$.*

Austin and Flanagan [5,6] have proven that MF is more true transparent than PU and PU is more true transparent than NSU. We restate this result in our notations and provide a set of counterexamples showing that for no other couple of analysed monitors relative true transparency holds.

Theorem 5. *MF $\supseteq_T$ PU $\supseteq_T$ NSU.*

Example 13 (NSU $\not\supseteq_T$ PU, NSU $\not\supseteq_T$ HM) Consider TINI Program 3: an execution in initial memory with [h=0] is accepted by PU and HM because the security level of 1 becomes low just before the output, and it is blocked by NSU due to sensitive upgrade.

Example 14 (NSU $\not\supseteq_T$ SME, NSU $\not\supseteq_T$ MF, PU $\not\supseteq_T$ HM, PU $\not\supseteq_T$ SME and PU $\not\supseteq_T$ MF).
    Program 6 is TINI since 1' does not depend on h. With initial memory [h=0, 1=1], HM, SME (with default value chosen as 0) and MF terminate with the same output as normal execution. However, NSU will diverge due to sensitive upgrade and PU will diverge because of the branching over a partially-leaked variable 1.

```
1 if  h = 0 then 1 = 1;                                Program 6
2 if 1 = 1 then 1 = 0;
3 output 1';
```

Example 15 (HM $\not\supseteq_T$ NSU, HM $\not\supseteq_T$ PU, HM $\not\supseteq_T$ SME, HM $\not\supseteq_T$ MF). Consider Program 1 and its secure execution starting in [h=1, 1=1]. NSU, PU, SME (the default value of SME does not matter in this case) and MF terminate with the same output as original program execution, producing 1=1. However, HM modifies it because the security level of 1 is raised by the static analysis of the non-executed branch.

Example 16 (SME $\not\supseteq_T$ NSU, SME $\not\supseteq_T$ PU, SME $\not\supseteq_T$ HM, SME $\not\supseteq_T$ MF). All the terminating executions of TINI Program 4 are accepted by NSU, PU, HM and MF, while an execution starting in [h=0, 1=1] with default value for SME set to h=1 doesn't terminate in SME semantics.

Example 17 (MF $\not\supseteq_T$ HM). Program 7 is TINI for any execution. HM with [h=1,l=0,l'=0] terminates with the original output because the output variable [l'] is low. However, MF with [h=1,l=0,l'=0] doesn't terminate.

```
1 if h=0 then l=0 else l=1;
2 if l=0 then
3    while true do skip;
4 else
5    l=0
6 output l'
```

Program 7

Example 18 (MF $\not\supseteq_T$ SME). Program 5 is TINI for any execution. With [h=0, l=1] it terminates in the program semantics and SME semantics (with any default value) producing l=0. However, the MF semantics produces l=1.

Precision We have discovered that certain monitors (e.g., HM and NSU) are incomparable with respect to true transparency. To compare them, we propose a more coarse-grained definition that describes the monitors' behaviour on secure programs.

Definition 10 (Precision). *Monitor M is precise if for any program P, the following holds:*

$$TINI(P) \wedge \forall\mu.(\exists\mu', v.(P,\mu) \Downarrow (v,\mu') \Rightarrow (P,\mu) \Downarrow_M (v,\mu'))$$

This definition requires that all the executions of secure programs are accepted by the monitor. NSU, PU, HM and MF are not precise since they are not true transparent. SME is precise for TSNI, and this result was proven by Devriese and Piessens [12], however SME it not precise for TINI (see Example 12).

To compare monitors' behaviour on secure programs, we define a set of a TINI programs P, where a monitor accepts all the executions of P:

$$\mathcal{P}(M) = \{P \mid TINI(P) \wedge \forall\mu.(\exists\mu', v.(P,\mu) \Downarrow (v,\mu') \Rightarrow (P,\mu) \Downarrow_M (v,\mu'))\}$$

Definition 11 (Relative Precision). *Monitor A is more precise than monitor B, written $A \supseteq_P B$, if $\mathcal{P}(A) \supseteq \mathcal{P}(B)$.*

We have found out that no couple of the five monitors are in relative precision relation. Below we present the counterexamples that demonstrate our findings.

Example 19 (HM $\not\supseteq_P$ SME). Consider TINI Program 5. All the executions of this program are accepted by SME. However, HM modifies the program output to default because the security level of l is upgraded to H by the static analysis of the non-executed branch.

Example 20 (HM $\not\supseteq_\mathcal{P}$ NSU, HM $\not\supseteq_\mathcal{P}$ PU). Consider the following program:

```
1 l = 0;
2 if h = 0 then skip
3 else
4    while true do l = 1;
5 output l
```
Program 8

This TINI program terminates only when [h=0]. This execution is accepted by NSU and PU, but the program output is modified by HM since HM analyses the non-executed branch and upgrades the level of l to H.

Example 21 (HM $\not\supseteq_\mathcal{P}$ MF). Consider TINI Program 9. MF accepts all of its executions, while HM modifies the program output to default because the security level of l is raised to high.

```
1 l = 0;
2 if h = 0 then l = 0 else skip;
3 output l
```
Program 9

The rest of relative precision counterexamples demonstrated in Table 1 of Sect. 8 are derived from the corresponding counterexamples for relative true transparency.

Since relative precision does not hold for any couple of monitors, we propose a stronger definition of relative precision for TSNI programs. We first define a set of a TSNI programs P, where a monitor accepts all the executions of P:

$$\mathcal{P}^*(M) = \{P \mid TSNI(P) \wedge \forall \mu.(\exists \mu', v.(P, \mu) \Downarrow (v, \mu') \Rightarrow (P, \mu) \Downarrow_M (v, \mu'))\}$$

Definition 12 (Relative TSNI precision). *A monitor A is more TSNI precise than a monitor B, written $A \supseteq_\mathcal{P}^* B$, if $\mathcal{P}^*(A) \supseteq \mathcal{P}^*(B)$.*

Theorem 6. *For all programs without dead code, $HM \supseteq_\mathcal{P}^* NSU, HM \supseteq_\mathcal{P}^* PU$.*

Notice that SME was proven to be precise for TSNI programs (see [12, Theorem 2]), therefore SME is more TSNI precise than any other monitor. We demonstrate this in Table 1 of Sect. 8.

False Transparency To compare monitors with respect to the amount of insecure executions they accept, we propose the notion of *false transparency*. Notice that false transparency violates soundness.

Definition 13 (False Transparency). *Monitor M is false transparent if for any program P, for all executions starting in a memory μ and finishing in memory μ' with value v, the following holds:*

$$\neg TINI(P, \mu) \wedge (P, \mu) \Downarrow (v, \mu') \Rightarrow (P, \mu) \Downarrow_M (v, \mu').$$

Given a program P and a monitor M, we define a set of initial memories, where a program P terminates, and a monitor M is false transparent for P:

$$\mathcal{F}(M, P) = \{\mu \mid \neg TINI(P, \mu_L) \wedge \exists \mu', v.(P, \mu) \Downarrow (v, \mu') \Rightarrow (P, \mu) \Downarrow_M (v, \mu')\}$$

Definition 14 (Relative False Transparency). *Monitor A is more false transparent than monitor B, denoted $A \supseteq_{\mathcal{F}} B$, if for any program P, the following holds: $\mathcal{F}(A, P) \supseteq \mathcal{F}(B, P)$.*

Theorem 7. *The following statements hold: $NSU \supseteq_{\mathcal{F}} HM$, $PU \supseteq_{\mathcal{F}} NSU$, $PU \supseteq_{\mathcal{F}} HM$, $SME \supseteq_{\mathcal{F}} HM$, $MF \supseteq_{\mathcal{F}} NSU$, $MF \supseteq_{\mathcal{F}} PU$ and $MF \supseteq_{\mathcal{F}} HM$.*

Example 22 ($NSU \not\supseteq_{\mathcal{F}} PU$). Execution of Program 10 in the initial memory $\mu=$ [h=0, 1=0, 1'=0] is interfering since it produces an output 1=0, while an execution in the low-equal initial memory where [h=1] produces 1=1. An execution started in μ is accepted by PU but blocked by NSU.

```
1 if h = 0 then 1' = 1 else 1 = 1;            Program 10
2 output 1
```

Example 23 ($NSU \not\supseteq_{\mathcal{F}} SME$, $PU \not\supseteq_{\mathcal{F}} SME$). Execution of Program 11 starting in memory [h=0, 1=0] is not TINI and it is accepted by SME (with default value h=0). However, it is rejected by NSU because of sensitive upgrade and by PU because on the branching over a partially-leaked variable 1.

```
1 if h = 0 then 1 = 0 else 1 = 1;            Program 11
2 if 1 = 0 then 1' = 0 else 1' = 1;
3 output 1'
```

Example 24 ($NSU \not\supseteq_{\mathcal{F}} MF$). The following program always terminates in the normal semantics coping the value of h into 1. Hence all of its executions are insecure. Every execution leads to a sensitive upgrade and NSU will diverge with any initial memory. However, in the MF semantics the program will terminate with 1=0 if started with memory [h=0,1=0] since the sensitive upgrade of the true branch will assign faceted value [1=⟨0 : 0⟩] to variable 1. Hence, this is a counter example for NSU being more false transparent than MF.

```
1 if h=0 then 1=0 else 1=1;            Program 12
2 output 1
```

Example 25 ($PU \not\supseteq_{\mathcal{F}} MF$). Program 11 is not TINI for all executions. However MF with [h=1,1=1,1'=1] terminates in the same memory as normal execution, while PU will diverge because 1 is marked as a partial leak.

Example 26 ($HM \not\supseteq_{\mathcal{F}} NSU$, $HM \not\supseteq_{\mathcal{F}} PU$, $HM \not\supseteq_{\mathcal{F}} SME$, $HM \not\supseteq_{\mathcal{F}} MF$). Consider Program 1 and an execution starting in memory [h=1, 1=0]. This execution is not secure and it is rejected by HM, however NSU, PU and MF accept it. SME also accepts this execution in case the default value for h is 1.

Example 27 (SME $\not\sqsupseteq_{\mathcal{F}}$ NSU, SME $\not\sqsupseteq_{\mathcal{F}}$ PU). Execution of Program 13 starting in memory [h=0, l=0] is interfering and it is accepted by both NSU and PU, producing an output l=0. However, SME (with default value chosen as 1) modifies this execution and produces l=1.

```
1 if l = 0 then
2    if h = 1 then l = 1 else skip
3 else
4    if h = 0 then l = 0 else skip
5 output l
```
                                                                    Program 13

Example 28 (SME $\not\sqsupseteq_{\mathcal{F}}$ MF and MF $\not\sqsupseteq_{\mathcal{F}}$ SME). Program 14 is not TINI if possible values of h are 0, 1, and 2. MF with [h=1,l=1] terminates in the same memory than normal execution but SME (with default value 0) always diverges.

```
1 if h = 0 then
2    while true do skip;
3 else
4    if h=1 then l=1 else l=2;
5 output l;
```
                                                                    Program 14

On the other hand, with initial memory [h=1, l=0], SME (using default value 1) terminates in the same memory as the normal execution, producing l=1 but MF produces a different output l=0.

7   Related Work

In this section, we discuss the state of the art for taxonomies of information flow monitors with respect to soundness or transparency.

For soundness, no work explicitly tries to classify information flow monitors. However, it is folklore that TSNI, first proposed in [30], is a strong form of noninterference that implies TINI. Since most well-known information flow monitors are proven sound only for TINI [5–7,14,33], it is easy, from the soundness perspective, to distinguish SME from other monitors because SME is proven sound for TSNI [12]. However, to the best of our knowledge, no work tries to refine soundness in order to obtain a more fine grain classification of monitors as we achieve with the introduction of TANI.

For transparency, Devriese and Piessens [12] prove that SME is precise for TSNI and Zanarini et al. [32] notice that the result could be made more general by proving that SME is true transparent for TSNI, which makes of SME an effective enforcement [22] for TSNI. In this work, we first compare transparency for TINI: none of the monitors that we have studied is true transparent for TINI. Hedin et al. [16] compare hybrid (HM) and purely dynamic monitors (NSU and PU), and conclude that for these monitors permissiveness is incomparable. By factorizing the notion of permissiveness, we can compare HM and NSU: HM is more precise for TSNI than NSU and PU, and NSU and PU are more false transparent than HM. Using the same definition of permissiveness, Austin and Flanagan [6,7] prove that PU is more permissive than NSU and that MF is more permissive than PU. Looking at this result and the definition of MF, our intuition was that MF could accept exactly the same false transparent executions as NSU and PU. However, we discovered that not only MF is more true transparent than NSU and PU (this is an implication of Austin and Flanagan results) but also MF is strictly more false transparent than NSU and PU. Bichhawat et al. [10] propose two non-trivial generalizations of PU, called puP and puA, to arbitrary lattices and show that puP and puA are incomparable w.r.t. permissiveness. It remains an open question if puP and puA can be made comparable by discriminating true or false transparency, as defined in our work.

8 Conclusion

In this work we proposed a new soundness definition for information flow monitors, that we call *Termination-Aware Noninterference* (TANI). It determines whether a monitor adds a new termination channel to the program. We have proven that HM, SME and MF, do satisfy TANI, whereas NSU and PU introduce new termination channels, and therefore do not satisfy TANI.

We compare monitors with respect to their capability to recognise secure executions, i.e., true transparency [8]. Since it does not hold for none of the considered monitors, we weaken this notion and define *relative true transparency*, that determines "which monitor is closer to being transparent". We then propose even a more weaker notion, called *precision*, that compares monitor behaviours on secure programs, and allows us to conclude that HM is more TSNI precise than NSU and PU that previously were deemed incomparable [16]. We show that the common notion of permissiveness is composed of *relative true and false transparency* and compare all the monitors with respect to these notions in Table 1.

Table 1. Taxonomy of five major information flow monitors

	NSU	PU	HM	SME	MF	
NSU		$\not\supseteq_P \not\supseteq_F$	$\not\supseteq_P \not\supseteq_F$	$\not\supseteq_P \not\supseteq_F$	$\not\supseteq_P \not\supseteq_F$	$\supseteq_T$ more true TINI transparent than
PU	$\supseteq_T \supseteq_F$		$\not\supseteq_P \supseteq_F$	$\not\supseteq_P \not\supseteq_F$	$\not\supseteq_P \not\supseteq_F$	$\supseteq_P$ more TINI precise than ($\not\supseteq_P \implies \not\supseteq_T$)
HM	$\supseteq_P^* \not\supseteq_F$	$\supseteq_P^* \not\supseteq_F$		$\not\supseteq_P \not\supseteq_F$	$\not\supseteq_P \not\supseteq_F$	$\supseteq_P^*$ more TSNI precise than
SME	$\supseteq_P^* \not\supseteq_F$	$\supseteq_P^* \not\supseteq_F$	$\supseteq_P^* \supseteq_F$		$\supseteq_P^* \not\supseteq_F$	$\supseteq_F$ more false TINI transparent than
MF	$\supseteq_T \supseteq_F$	$\supseteq_T \supseteq_F$	$\not\supseteq_P \supseteq_F$	$\not\supseteq_P \not\supseteq_F$		▪ Monitor is TANI
						▪ Monitor is TSNI, hence TANI

For simplicity, we consider a security lattice of only two elements, however we expect our results to generalise to multiple security levels. In future work, we plan to compare information flow monitors with respect to other information flow properties, such as declassification [26].

Acknowledgment. We would like to thank Ana Almeida Matos for her valuable feedback and interesting discussions that has lead us to develop the main ideas of this paper, Aslan Askarov for his input to the definition of TANI, and anonymous reviewers for feedback that helped to improve this paper. This work has been partially supported by the ANR project AJACS ANR-14-CE28-0008.

References

1. A Taxonomy of Information Flow Monitors Technical report. https://team.inria.fr/indes/taxonomy
2. Abadi, M., Lamport, L.: Composing specifications. ACM Trans. Program. Lang. Syst. **15**(1), 73–132 (1993)
3. Askarov, A., Sabelfeld, A., Gradual release: unifying declassification, encryption and key release policies. In: IEEE Symposium on Security and Privacy, pp. 207–221 (2007)
4. Askarov, A., Sabelfeld, A.: Tight enforcement of information-release policies for dynamic languages. In: Proceedings of the 22nd IEEE Computer Security Foundations Symposium, CSF 2009, pp. 43–59. IEEE Computer Society (2009)
5. Austin, T.H., Flanagan, C.: Efficient purely-dynamic information flow analysis. In PLAS 2009, pp. 113–124 (2009)
6. Austin, T.H., Flanagan, C.: Permissive dynamic information flow analysis. In: PLAS 2010, pp. 3:1–3:12. ACM (2010)
7. Austin, T.H., Flanagan, C.: Multiple facets for dynamic information flow. In: Proceeding of the 39th Symposium of Principles of Programming Languages. ACM (2012)
8. Bauer, L., Ligatti, J., Walker, D.: Edit automata: enforcement mechanisms for run-time security policies. Int. J. Inf. Secur. **4**(1–2), 2–16 (2005)
9. Besson, F., Bielova, N., Jensen, T.: Hybrid information flow monitoring against web tracking. In: CSF 2013, pp. 240–254. IEEE (2013)
10. Bichhawat, A., Rajani, V., Garg, D., Hammer, C.: Generalizing permissive-upgrade in dynamic information flow analysis. In: Proceedings of the Ninth Workshop on Programming Languages, Analysis for Security, PLAS 2014, pp. 15:15–15:24. ACM (2014)
11. Clarkson, M.R., Schneider, F.B.: Hyperproperties. J. Comput. Secur. **18**(6), 1157–1210 (2010)
12. Devriese, D., Piessens, F.: Non-interference through secure multi-execution. In: Proceeding of the Symposium on Security and Privacy, pp. 109–124. IEEE (2010)
13. Erlingsson, U.: The Inlined Reference Monitor Approach to Security Policy Enforcement. PhD thesis, Cornell University (2003)
14. Le Guernic, G., Banerjee, A., Jensen, T., Schmidt, D.A.: Automata-based confidentiality monitoring. In: Okada, M., Satoh, I. (eds.) ASIAN 2006. LNCS, vol. 4435, pp. 75–89. Springer, Heidelberg (2008)
15. Hamlen, K.W., Morrisett, G., Schneider, F.B.: Computability classes for enforcement mechanisms. ACM Trans. Program. Lang. Syst. **28**(1), 175–205 (2006)
16. Hedin, D., Bello, L., Sabelfeld, A.: Value-sensitive hybrid information flow control for a javascript-like language. In: IEEE 28th Computer Security Foundations Symposium, CSF (2015)
17. Hedin, D., Sabelfeld, A.: Information-flow security for a core of JavaScript. In: Proceeding of the 25th Computer Security Foundations Symposium, pp. 3–18. IEEE (2012)

18. Hunt, S., Sands, D.: On flow-sensitive security types. In: POPL 2006, pp. 79–90. ACM, New York, January 2006
19. Le Guernic, G.: Confidentiality Enforcement Using Dynamic Information Flow Analyses. PhD thesis, Kansas State University and University of Rennes 1 (2007)
20. Le Guernic, G.: Precise dynamic verification of confidentiality. In: Proceeding of the 5th International Verification Workshop, CEUR Workshop Proceeding, vol. 372, pp. 82–96 (2008)
21. Le Guernic, G., Banerjee, A., Jensen, T., Schmidt, D.A.: Automata-based confidentiality monitoring. In: Okada, M., Satoh, I. (eds.) ASIAN 2006. LNCS, vol. 4435, pp. 75–89. Springer, Heidelberg (2008)
22. Ligatti, J., Bauer, L., Walker, D.W.: Enforcing non-safety security policies with program monitors. In: di Vimercati, S.C., Syverson, P.F., Gollmann, D. (eds.) ESORICS 2005. LNCS, vol. 3679, pp. 355–373. Springer, Heidelberg (2005)
23. Almeida-Matos, A., Fragoso Santos, J., Rezk, T.: An information flow monitor for a core of DOM. In: Maffei, M., Tuosto, E. (eds.) TGC 2014. LNCS, vol. 8902, pp. 1–16. Springer, Heidelberg (2014)
24. McLean, J.: A general theory of composition for a class of "possibilistic" properties. IEEE Trans. Softw. Eng. **22**(1), 53–67 (1996)
25. Russo, A., Sabelfeld, A.: Dynamic vs. Static flow-sensitive security analysis. In: Proceeding of the 23rd Computer Security Foundations Symposium, pp. 186–199. IEEE (2010)
26. Sabelfeld, A., Sands, D.: Declassification: dimensions and principles. J. Computer Secur. **17**(5), 517–548 (2009)
27. Santos, J.F., Rezk, T.: An information flow monitor-inlining compiler for securing a core of javascript. In: ICT Systems Security and Privacy Protection 29th IFIP TC 11 International Conference, SEC 2014 (2014)
28. Schneider, F.: Enforceable security policies. ACM Trans. Inf. Syst. Secur. **3**(1), 30–50 (2000)
29. Terauchi, T., Aiken, A.: Secure information flow as a safety problem. In: Hankin, C., Siveroni, I. (eds.) SAS 2005. LNCS, vol. 3672, pp. 352–367. Springer, Heidelberg (2005)
30. Volpano, D., Smith, G.: Eliminating covert flows with minimum typings. In: Proceeding 10th IEEE Computer Security Foundations Workshop, pp. 156–168. Society Press (1997)
31. Volpano, D., Smith, G., Irvine, C.: A sound type system for secure flow analysis. J. Comput. Secur. **4**(2–3), 167–187 (1996)
32. Zanarini, D., Jaskelioff, M., Russo, A.: Precise enforcement of confidentiality for reactive systems. In: IEEE 26th Computer Security Foundations Symposium, pp. 18–32 (2013)
33. Zdancewic, S.A.: Programming languages for information security. PhD thesis, Cornell University (2002)

On Improvements of Low-Deterministic Security

Joachim Breitner, Jürgen Graf, Martin Hecker[(✉)], Martin Mohr,
and Gregor Snelting

Karlsruhe Institute of Technology, Karlsruhe, Germany
{breitner,graf,martin.hecker,martin.mohr,gregor.snelting}@kit.edu

Abstract. Low-security observable determinism (LSOD), as introduced
by Roscoe and Zdancewic [18,24], is the simplest criterion which guarantees probabilistic noninterference for concurrent programs. But LSOD
prohibits any, even secure low-nondeterminism. Giffhorn developed an
improvement, named RLSOD, which allows some secure low-nondeterminism, and can handle full Java with high precision [5].

In this paper, we describe a new generalization of RLSOD. By
applying aggressive program analysis, in particular dominators for multi-
threaded programs, precision can be boosted and false alarms minimized.
We explain details of the new algorithm, and provide a soundness proof.
The improved RLSOD is integrated into the JOANA tool; a case study
is described. We thus demonstrate that low-deterministic security is a
highly precise and practically mature software security analysis method.

Keywords: Information flow control · Probabilistic noninterference ·
Program analysis

1 Introduction

Information flow control (IFC) analyses a program's source or byte code for leaks,
in particular violations of confidentiality and integrity. IFC algorithms usually
check some form of noninterference; sound IFC algorithms guarantee to find all
possible leaks. For multi-threaded programs, probabilistic noninterference (PN)
as introduced in [19–21] is the established security criterion. Many algorithms
and definitional variations for PN have been proposed, which vary in soundness,
precision, scalability, language restrictions, and other features.

One of the oldest and simplest criteria which enforces PN is low-security
observational determinism (LSOD), as introduced by Roscoe [18], and improved
by Zdancewic, Huisman, and others [10,24]. For LSOD, a relatively simple static
check can be devised; furthermore LSOD is scheduler independent – which is a
big advantage. However Huisman and other researchers found subtle problems
in earlier LSOD algorithms, so Huisman concluded that scheduler-independent
PN is not feasible [9]. Worse, LSOD strictly prohibits any, even secure low-
nondeterminism – which kills LSOD from a practical viewpoint.

© Springer-Verlag Berlin Heidelberg 2016
F. Piessens and L. Viganò (Eds.): POST 2016, LNCS 9635, pp. 68–88, 2016.
DOI: 10.1007/978-3-662-49635-0_4

It is the aim of this paper to demonstrate that improvements to LSOD can be devised, which invalidate these earlier objections. An important step was already provided by Giffhorn [4,5] who discovered that

1. an improved definition of low-equivalent traces solves earlier soundness problems for infinite traces and nonterminating programs.
2. flow- and context-sensitive program analysis is the key to a precise and sound LSOD algorithm.
3. the latter can naturally be implemented through the use of program dependence graphs.
4. additional support by precise points-to analysis, may-happen-in-parallel analysis, and exception analysis makes LSOD work and scale for full Java.
5. secure low-nondeterminism can be allowed by relaxing the strict LSOD criterion, while maintaining soundness.

Giffhorn's RLSOD (Relaxed LSOD) algorithm requires – like many other algorithms, e.g. [20,21] – that the scheduler is probabilistic. RLSOD is integrated into the JOANA IFC tool (joana.ipd.kit.edu), which has successfully been applied in various projects [5–7,11,12,14].

In this paper, we describe new improvements for RLSOD, which boost precision and reduce false alarms compared to original LSOD and RLSOD. We first recapitulate technical properties of PN, LSOD, and RLSOD. We then introduce the improved criterion, which is based on the notion of dominance in threaded control flow graphs. We explain the definition using examples, provide soundness arguments, and present a case study, namely a prototypical e-voting system with multiple threads. Our work builds heavily on our earlier contributions [5,7], but the current paper is aimed to be self-contained.

2   Probabilistic Noninterference

IFC aims to guarantee that no violations of confidentiality or integrity may occur. For confidentiality, usually all values in input, output, or program states

```
1  void main():
2     read(H);
3     if (H < 1234)
4        print(0);
5     L = H;
6     print(L);
```

```
1  void main():
2     fork thread_1();
3     fork thread_2();
4  void thread_1():
5     read(L);
6     print(L);
7  void thread_2():
8     read(H);
9     L = H;
```

```
1   void main():
2      fork thread_1();
3      fork thread_2();
4   void thread_1():
5      longCmd();
6      print("PO");
7   void thread_2():
8      read(H);
9      while (H != 0)
10        H--;
11     print("ST");
```

Fig. 1. Some leaks. Left: explicit and implicit, middle: possibilistic, right: probabilistic. For simplicity, we assume that read(L) reads low variable L from a low input channel; print(H) prints high variable H to a high output channel. Note that reads of high variables are classified high, and prints of low variables are classified low.

are classified as "high" (secret) or "low" (public), and it is assumed that an attacker can read all low values, but cannot see any high value.[1]

Figure 1 presents small but typical confidentiality leaks. As usual, variable H is "High" (secret), L is "Low" (public). Explicit leaks arise if (parts of) high values are copied (indirectly) to low output. Implicit leaks arise if a high value can change control flow, which can change low behaviour (see Fig. 1 left). Possibilistic leaks in concurrent programs arise if a certain interleaving produces an explicit or implicit leak; in Fig. 1 middle, interleaving order 5, 8, 9, 6 causes an explicit leak. Probabilistic leaks arise if the probability of high output is influenced by low values; in Fig. 1 right, H is never copied to L, but if the value of H is large, probability is higher that "POST" is printed instead of "STPO".

2.1   Sequential Noninterference

To formalize RLSOD, let us start with the classical definition of sequential non-interference. The classic definition assumes that a global and static classification $cl(v)$ of all program variables v as secret (H) or public (L) is given. Note that flow-sensitive IFC such as RLSOD does *not* use a static, global classification of variables; this will be explained below.

Definition 1 (Sequential noninterference). *Let $\mathcal{P}$ be a program. Let s, s' be initial program states, let $[\![\mathcal{P}]\!](s)$, $[\![\mathcal{P}]\!](s')$ be the final states after executing $\mathcal{P}$ in state s resp. s'. Noninterference holds iff*

$$s \sim_L s' \implies [\![\mathcal{P}]\!](s) \sim_L [\![\mathcal{P}]\!](s').$$

The relation $s \sim_L s'$ means that two states are low-equivalent, that is, coincide on low variables: $cl(v) = L \implies s(v) = s'(v)$. Classically, program input is assumed to be part of the initial states s, s', and program output is assumed to be part of the final states; the definition can be generalized to work with explicit input and output streams. Truly interactive programs lead to the problem of termination leaks [1], which will not be explored in this paper.

2.2   Probabilistic Noninterference

In multi-threaded programs, fine-grained interleaving effects must be accounted for, thus traces are used instead of states. A trace is a sequence of events $t = (\bar{s}_1, o_1, \underline{s}_1), (\bar{s}_2, o_2, \underline{s}_2), \ldots, (\bar{s}_\nu, o_\nu, \underline{s}_\nu), \ldots$, where the o_ν are operations (i.e. dynamically executed program statements c_ν; we write $stmt(o_\nu) = c_\nu$. $\bar{s}_\nu, \underline{s}_\nu$ are the states before resp. after executing o_ν. For the time being we assume traces to be terminating; subtleties of nontermination are discussed later.

---

[1] A more detailed discussion of IFC attacker models can be found in e.g. [5]. Note that JOANA allows arbitrary lattices of security classifications, not just the simple $\bot = L \leq H = \top$ lattice. Note also that integrity is dual to confidentiality, but will not be discussed here. JOANA can handle both.

```
1  void main():
2    L = 0;
3    fork thread_1();
4    fork thread_2();
5  void thread_1():
6    L = 42;
7    read(H);
8  void thread_2():
9    L = H;
10   print(L);
```

```
1  void main():
2    L = 0;
3    fork thread_1();
4    fork thread_2();
5  void thread_1():
6    L = 42;
7    read(H);
8  void thread_2():
9    print(L);
10   L = H;
```

```
1   void main():
2     L = 0;
3     read(H);
4     while (H2>0)
5       {H2--;}
6     fork thread_1();
7     fork thread_2();
8   void thread_1():
9     L = 42;
10    read(H);
11  void thread_2():
12    print(L);
13    L = H;
```

Fig. 2. Left: insecure program, obvious explicit leak. Middle: secure program, RLSOD + flow sensitivity avoid false alarm. Right: only iRLSOD avoids false alarm.

For PN, the notion of low-equivalent traces is essential. Classically, traces are low equivalent if for every $(\overline{s}_\nu, o_\nu, \underline{s}_\nu) \in t$, $(\overline{s'}_\nu, o_\nu, s'_\nu) \in t'$, it holds that $\overline{s}_\nu \sim_L \overline{s'}_\nu$ and $\underline{s}_\nu, \sim_L s'_\nu$. This definition enforces a rather restrictive lock-step execution of both traces. Later definitions (e.g. [20]) use stutter equivalence instead of lock-step equivalence; thus allowing one execution to run faster than the other ("stuttering" means that one trace performs additional operations which do not affect public behaviour). In our flow-sensitive setting, we achieve the same effect by demanding that not only program variables are classified, but also all program statements $(cl(c) = H$ or $cl(c) = L)$, and thus operations in traces: $cl(o) = cl(stmt(o))$. Note that it is not necessary for the engineer to provide classifications for all program statements, as most of the $cl(c)$ can be computed automatically (see below). Low equivalence then includes filtering out high operations from traces. This leads to

Definition 2 *1. The low-observable part of an event is defined as*

$$E_L((\overline{s}, o, \underline{s})) = \begin{cases} (\overline{s}\,|_{use(o)}, o, \underline{s}\,|_{def(o)}), & \text{if } cl(stmt(o)) = L \\ \epsilon, & \text{otherwise} \end{cases}$$

where $def(o)$, $use(o)$ are the variables defined (i.e. assigned) resp. used in o.
2. The low-observable subtrace of trace t is

$$E_L(t) = map(E_L)(filter(\lambda e.E_L(e) \neq \epsilon)(t)).$$

3. Traces t, t' are low-equivalent, written $t \sim_L t'$, if $E_L(t) = E_L(t')$.

Note that the flow-sensitive projections $s|_{def}(o)$, $s|_{use}(o)$ are usually much smaller than a flow-insensitive, statically defined low part of s; resulting in more traces to be low-equivalent without compromising soundness. This subtle observation is another reason why flow-sensitive IFC is more precise.

PN is called "probabilistic", because it essentially depends of the probabilities for certain traces under certain inputs: $P_i(t)$ is the probability that a specific trace t is executed under input i; and $P_i([t]_L)$ is the probability that some trace

$t' \in [t]_L$ (i.e. $t' \sim_L t$) is executed under i. Note that the $t' \in [t]_L$ cannot be distinguished by an attacker, as all $t' \in [t]_L$ have the same public behaviour.

The following PN definition is classical, and uses explicit input streams instead of initial states. For both inputs the same initial state is assumed, but it is assumed that all input values are classified low or high. Inputs i, i' are low equivalent ($i \sim_L i'$) if they coincide on low values: $cl(i_\nu) = L \wedge cl(i'_\nu) = L \implies i_\nu = i'_\nu$. The definition relies on our flow-sensitive $t \sim_L t'$.

Definition 3 (Probabilistic noninterference). *Let i, i' be input streams; let $T(i)$ be the set of all possible traces of program $\mathcal{P}$ for input i, $\Theta = T(i) \cup T(i')$. PN holds iff*

$$i \sim_L i' \implies \forall t \in \Theta \colon P_i([t]_L) = P_{i'}([t]_L).$$

That is, if we take any trace t which can be produced by i or i', the probability that a $t' \in [t]_L$ is executed is the same under i resp. i'. In other words, **probability for any public behaviour is independent from the choice of i or i'** and thus cannot be influenced by secret input.

As $[t]_L$ is discrete (in fact recursively enumerable), P_i is a discrete probability distribution, hence $P_i([t]_L) = \sum_{t' \in [t]_L} P_i(t')$. Thus the PN condition can be rewritten to

$$i \sim_L i' \implies \forall t \colon \sum_{t' \in [t]_L} P_i(t') = \sum_{t' \in [t]_L} P_{i'}(t').$$

Applying this to Fig. 1 right, we first observe that all inputs are low equivalent as there is only high input. For any $t \in \Theta$ there are only two possibilities: `...print(''PO'')...print(''ST'')...` $\in t$ or `...print(''ST'')...print(''PO'')...` $\in t$. There are no other low events or low output, hence there are only two equivalence classes $[t]_L^1 = \{t' \mid \dots \texttt{print}(\text{``PO''}) \dots \texttt{print}(\text{``ST''}) \dots \in t'\}$ and $[t]_L^2 = \{t' \mid \dots \texttt{print}(\text{``ST``}) \dots \texttt{print}(\text{``PO''}) \dots \in t'\}$. Now if i contains a small value, i' a large value, as discussed earlier $P_i([t]_L^1) \neq P_{i'}([t]_L^1)$ as well as $P_i([t]_L^2) \neq P_{i'}([t]_L^2)$, hence PN is violated.

In practice, the $P_i([t]_L)$ are difficult or impossible to determine. So far, only simple Markov chains have been used to explicitly determine the P_i, where the Markow chain models the probabilistic state transitions of a program, perhaps together with a specific scheduler [15, 20]. Worse, the sums might be infinite (but will always converge). Practical examples with explicit probabilities can be found in [4,5]. Here, as a sanity check, we demonstrate that for sequential programs PN implies sequential noninterference. Note that for sequential (deterministic) programs $|T(i)| = 1$, and for the unique $t \in_1 T(i)$ we have $P_i(t) = 1$.

Lemma 1. *For sequential programs, probabilistic noninterference implies sequential noninterference.*

Proof. Let $s \sim_L s'$. For sequential NI, input is part of the initial states, thus we may conclude $i \sim_L i'$ and apply the PN definition. Let $t'' \in \Theta$. As $\mathcal{P}$ is sequential, $t'' = t \in_1 T(i)$ or $t'' = t' \in_1 T(i')$. WloG let $t'' = t$. Due to PN,

$P_i([t]_L) = P_{i'}([t]_L)$, due to sequentiality $P_i([t]_L) = P_i(t) = P_{i'}(t') = 1$, thus $P_{i'}([t]_L) = P_{i'}(t') = 1$. That is, with probability 1 the trace t' executed under i' is low equivalent to t. Thus in particular the final states in t resp. t' must be low equivalent. Hence $s \sim_L s'$ implies $[\![\mathcal{P}]\!](s) \sim_L [\![\mathcal{P}]\!](s')$.   □

2.3 Low-Deterministic Security

LSOD is the oldest and still the simplest criterion which enforces PN. LSOD demands that low-equivalent inputs produce low-equivalent traces. LSOD is scheduler independent and implies PN (see lemma below). It is intuitively secure: changes in high input can never change low behaviour, because low behaviour is enforced to be deterministic. This is however a very restrictive requirement and eventually led to popular scepticism against LSOD.

Definition 4 (Low-security observational determinism). *Let i, i' be input streams, Θ as above. LSOD holds iff*

$$i \sim_L i' \implies \forall t, t' \in \Theta : t \sim_L t'.$$

Under LSOD, all traces t for input i are low-equivalent: $T(i) \subseteq [t]_L$, because $\forall t' \in T(i) : t' \sim_L t$. If there is more than one trace for i, then this must result from high-nondeterminism; low behaviour is strictly deterministic.

Lemma 2. *LSOD implies PN.*

Proof. Let $i \sim_L i', t \in \Theta$. WloG let $t \in T(i)$.

Due to LSOD, we have $T(i) \subseteq [t]_L$. As $P_i(t') = 0$ for $t' \notin T(i)$, we have

$$P_i([t]_L) = \sum_{t' \in [t]_L} P_i(t') = \sum_{t' \in T(i)} P_i(t') = 1$$

and likewise $P_{i'}([t]_L) = 1$, so $P_i([t]_L) = P_{i'}([t]_L)$ holds. □

Zdancewic [24] proposed the first IFC analysis which checks LSOD. His conditions require that

1. there are no explicit or implicit leaks,
2. no low observable operation is influenced by a data race,
3. no two low observable operations can happen in parallel.

The last condition imposes the infamous LSOD restriction, because it explicitely disallows that a scheduler produces various interleavings which switch the order of two low statements which may happen in parallel, and thus would generate low nondeterminism. Besides that, the conditions can be checked by a static program analysis; Zdancewic used a security type system.

As an example, consider Fig. 2. In Fig. 2 middle, statements `print(L)` and `L=42` – which are both classified low – can be executed in parallel, and the scheduler nondeterministically decides which executes first; resulting in either 42 or 0 to be printed. Thus there is visible low nondeterminism, which is prohibited by classical LSOD. The program however is definitely secure according to PN.

3   RLSOD

In this section, we recapitulate PDGs, their application for LSOD, and the original RLSOD improvement. This discussion is necessary in order to understand the new improvements for RLSOD.

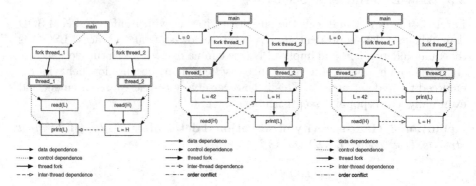

Fig. 3. Left to right: PDGs for Fig. 1 middle, and for Fig. 2 left and middle.

3.1   PDGs for IFC

Snelting et al. introduced Program Dependence Graphs (PDGs) as a device to check integrity of software [22]. Later the approach was expanded into the JOANA IFC project. It was shown that PDGs guarantee sequential noninterference [23], and that PDGs provide improved precision as they are naturally flow- and context-sensitive [7].

In this paper, we just present three PDG examples and some explanations. PDG nodes represent program statements or expressions, edges represent data dependencies, control dependencies, inter-thread data dependencies, or summary dependencies. Figure 3 presents the PDGs for Fig. 1 middle, and for Fig. 2 left and middle. The construction of precise PDGs for full languages is absolutely nontrivial and requires additional information such as points-to analysis, exception analysis, and thread invocation analysis [7]. We will not discuss PDG details; it is sufficient to know the *Slicing Theorem*:

Theorem [8]. If there is no PDG path $a \rightarrow^* b$, it is guaranteed that statement a can never influence statement b. In particular, values computed in a cannot influence values computed in b.

Thus all statements which might influence a specific program point b are those on backward paths from this point, the so-called "backward slice" $BS(b)$. In particular, information flow $a \rightarrow^* b$ is only possible if $a \in BS(b)$. There are stronger versions of the theorem, which consider only paths which can indeed be dynamically executed ("realizable" paths); these make a big difference in precision e.g. for programs with procedures, objects, or threads.

As an example, consider Fig. 3. The left PDG has a data dependency edge from L=H; to print(L);, because L is defined in line 9 (Fig. 2 left), used in line 10, there is a path in the control flow graph (CFG) from 9 to 10, and L is not reassigned ("killed") on the path. Thus there is a PDG path from read(H); to print(L);, representing an illegal flow from line 7 to line 10 (a simple explicit leak). In Fig. 3 right, there is no path from L=H; to print(L); due to flow sensitivity: no scheduler will ever execute L=H; before print(L);. Hence no path from read(H) to print(L); exists, and it is guaranteed that the printed value of L is not influenced by the secret H.

In general, the multi-threaded PDG can be used to check whether there are any explicit or implicit leaks; technically it is required that no high source is in the backward slice of a low sink. This criterion is enough to guarantee sequential noninterference [23]. For probabilistic noninterference, according to the Zdancewic LSOD criterion one must additionally show that public output is not influenced by execution order conflicts such as data races, and that there is no low nondeterminism. This can again be checked using PDGs and an additional analysis called "May happen in parallel" (MHP); the latter will uncover potential execution order conflicts or races. Several precise and sound MHP algorithms for full Java are available today.

Note that the slicing theorem does not cover physical side channels such as power consumption profiles, nor does it cover corrupt schedulers or defective hardware; it only covers "genuine" program behaviour.

In the following, we will need some definitions related to PDGs. For more details on PDGs, MHP, flow- context-, object- and time-sensitivity, see [7].

Definition 5.   *1. Let $G = (N, \rightarrow)$ be a PDG, where N consists of program statements and expressions, and $\rightarrow$ comprises data dependencies, control dependencies, summary dependencies, and inter-thread dependencies. The (context-sensitive) backward slice for $n \in N$ is defined as*

$$BS(n) = \{m \mid m \rightarrow^*_{realizeable} n\}$$

where $\rightarrow^*_{realizeable}$ includes only context- object- and (optionally) time-sensitive paths in the PDG [7].

2. All input and output statements $n \in N$ are assumed to be classified as $cl(n) = H$ or $cl(n) = L$. Other PDG nodes need not be explicitly classified, but a classification can be computed via the flow equation

$$cl(n) = \bigsqcup_{m \rightarrow n} cl(m).$$

For an operation o in a trace t, we assume $stmt(o) \in N$ and define $cl(o) = cl(stmt(o))$.

3. We write $MHP(n, m)$ if MHP analysis concludes that n and m may be executed in parallel. Thus by interleaving there may be traces t, t' where $t = \ldots (\overline{s_n}, o_n, \underline{s_n}) \ldots (\overline{s_m}, o_m, \underline{s_m}) \ldots, \; t' = \ldots (\overline{s_m}, o_m, \underline{s_m}) \ldots (\overline{s_n}, o_n, \underline{s_n}) \ldots.$

Concerning cl it is important to note that PDGs are automatically flow-sensitive and may contain a program variable v several times as a PDG node; each occurence of v in N may have a different classification! Thus there is no global classification of variables, but only the local classification $cl(n)$ together with the global flow constraints $cl(n) = \bigsqcup_{m \to n} cl(m)$. The latter can easily be computed or checked by a fixpoint iteration on the PDG [7].

3.2 Relaxed LSOD

In his 2012 thesis, Giffhorn applied PDGs to PN. He showed that PDGs can naturally be used to check the LSOD property, and provided a soundness proof as well as an implementation for JOANA [4]. Giffhorn also found the first optimization relaxing LSOD's strict low-determinism, named RLSOD.

One issue was to plug soundness leaks which had been found in some earlier approaches to LSOD. In particular, treatment of nontermination had proven to be tricky. Giffhorn provided a new definition for low-equivalent traces, where $t \sim_L t'$ iff 1. if t, t' are both finite, as usual the low events and low memory parts must coincide (see Definition 2); 2. if wloG t is finite, t' is infinite, then this coincidence must hold up to the length of the shorter trace, *and the missing operations in t must be missing due to an infinite loop* (and nothing else); 3. for two infinite traces, this coincidence must hold for all low events, or if low events are missing in one trace, they must be missing due to an infinite loop [5].

It turned out that the last condition not only avoids previous soundness leaks, but can precisely be characterized by dynamic control dependencies in traces [5]. Furthermore, the latter can soundly and precisely be statically approximated through PDGs (which include all control dependencies). Moreover, the static conditions identified by Zdancewic which guarantee LSOD can naturally be checked by PDGs, and enjoy increased precision due to flow-, context- and object-sensitivity. Formally Giffhorn's LSOD criterion reads as follows:

Theorem 1. *Let $n, n', n'' \in N$ be PDG nodes. LSOD holds if*

1. $\forall n, n': \ cl(n) = L \wedge cl(n') = H \implies n' \notin BS(n)$,
2. $\forall n, n', n'': \ \mathrm{MHP}(n, n') \wedge \exists v \in def(n) \cap (def(n') \cup use(n')) \wedge cl(n'') = L$
   $\implies n \notin BS(n'') \wedge n' \notin BS(n'')$,
3. $\forall n, n': \ \mathrm{MHP}(n, n') \implies cl(n) = H \vee cl(n') = H$.

Proof. For proof and implementation details, see [5]. □

Applying this criterion to Fig. 1 right, it discovers a leak according to condition 3, namely low nondeterminism between lines 6 and 11; which is correct. In Fig. 2 left, a leak is discovered according to condition 1, which is also correct (cmp. PDG example above). In Fig. 2 middle and right, the explicit leak has disappeared (thanks to flow-sensitivity), but another leak is discovered according to condition 3: we have $\mathrm{MHP}(\texttt{L = 42;}, \texttt{print(L);})$, which causes a false alarm.

The example motivates the RLSOD criterion: *low nondeterminism may be allowed, if it cannot be reached from high events.* That is, there must **not** be a path in the control flow graph from some n'', where $cl(n'') = H$, to n or n', where $cl(n) = cl(n') = L$ and $\mathrm{MHP}(n, n')$. If there is no path from a high event to the low nondeterminism, no high statement can ever be executed before the nondeterministic low statements. Thus the latter can never produce visible behaviour which is influenced by high values. This argument leads to the RLSOD criterion, which replaces condition 3 above by

3'. $\forall n, n'$: $\mathrm{MHP}(n, n') \land \exists n''$: $cl(n'') = H \land (n'' \to^*_{CFG} n \lor n'' \to^*_{CFG} n')$
   $\implies cl(n) = H \lor cl(n') = H.$

This condition can be rewritten by contraposition to the more practical form

3'. $\forall n, n'$: $\mathrm{MHP}(n, n') \land cl(n) = L \land cl(n') = L$
   $\implies \forall n'' \in START \to^*_{CFG} n \cup START \to^*_{CFG} n'$: $cl(n'') = L.$

In fact the same argument not only holds for execution order conflicts, but also for data races: no data race may be in the backward slice of a low sink, *unless it is unreachable by high events.* That is, condition 2 can be improved the same way as condition 3, leading to

2'. $\forall n, n', n''$: $\mathrm{MHP}(n, n') \land \exists n'''$: $cl(n''') = H \land (n''' \to^*_{CFG} n \lor n''' \to^*_{CFG} n')$
   $\land \exists v \in def(n) \cap (def(n') \cup use(n')) \land cl(n'') = L$
   $\implies n, n' \notin BS(n'').$

By contraposition, we obtain the more practical form

2'. $\forall n, n', n''$: $\mathrm{MHP}(n, n') \land \exists v \in def(n) \cap (def(n') \cup use(n'))$
   $\land cl(n'') = L \land \big(n \in BS(n'') \lor n' \in BS(n'')\big)$
   $\implies \forall n''' \in START \to^*_{CFG} n \cup START \to^*_{CFG} n'$: $cl(n''') = L.$

In fact RLSOD, as currently implemented in JOANA, uses even more precise refinements of conditions 2' and 3' (see [4], pp. 200ff), which we however omit due to lack of space. Figure 1 right is not RLSOD, because one of the low-nondeterministic statements, namely line 11, can be reached from the high statement in line 8; thus criterion 3' is violated. Indeed the example contains a probabilistic leak. Figure 2 middle is RLSOD, because the low-nondeterminism in line 6 resp. 9 can not be reached from any high statement (condition 3'). The same holds for the data race between line 6 and line 9 – condition 2 is violated (note that in this example, $n' = n''$), but 2' holds.[2] Indeed the program is PN. Figure 2 right is however not RLSOD, because the initial read(H2) will reach any other statement. But the program is PN, because H2 does not influence any later low statement! The example shows that RLSOD does indeed reduce false alarms, but it effectively removes only false alarms on low paths beginning at program start. Anything after the first high statement will usually be reachable from that statement, and does not profit from rule 3' resp. 2'.

---

[2] That is, 2' as in [4] holds; the slightly less precise, but simpler 2' condition in the current paper is violated, but 3' as defined in the current paper holds. We thank C. Hammer and his students for this subtle observation.

Still RLSOD was a big step as it allowed – for the first time – low nondeterminism, while basically maintaining the LSOD approach. We will not present a formal soundness argument for RLSOD, as RLSOD is a special case of the improvement which will be discussed in the next section.

4   Improving RLSOD

In the following, we will generalize condition 3' to obtain a much more precise "iRLSOD" criterion. The same improvement can be applied to condition 2' as well – the usage of dominators (see below) and the soundness proof are essentially "isomorphic". It is only for reasons of space and readability that in this paper we only describe the improvement of 3'. For the same reasons, we stick to definitions 2' and 3', even though JOANA uses a slightly more precise variant (see above); the iRLSOD improvement works the same with the more precise 2' and 3'.

To motivate the improvement, consider again Fig. 1 right (program $\mathcal{P}_1$) and Fig. 2 right (program $\mathcal{P}_2$). When comparing $\mathcal{P}_1$ and $\mathcal{P}_2$, a crucial difference comes to mind. In $\mathcal{P}_2$ the troublesome high statement can reach *both* low-nondeterministic statements, whereas in $\mathcal{P}_1$, the high statement can reach only one of them. In both programs some loop running time depends on a high value, but in $\mathcal{P}_2$, the subsequent low statements are influenced by this "timing leak" in exactly the same way, while in $\mathcal{P}_1$ they are not.

In terms of the PN definition, remember that $\mathcal{P}_1$ has only two low classes $[t]_L^1 = \{t' \mid \ldots t' = \texttt{print}(\text{"PO"}) \ldots \texttt{print}(\text{"ST"}) \ldots\}$ and $[t]_L^2 = \{t' \mid t' = \ldots \texttt{print}(\text{"ST"}) \ldots \texttt{print}(\text{"PO"}) \ldots\}$. Likewise, $\mathcal{P}_2$ has two low classes $[t]_L^1 = \{t' \mid t' = \ldots \texttt{L} = 42 \ldots \texttt{print}(42) \ldots\}$ and $[t]_L^2 = \{t' \mid t' = \ldots \texttt{print}(0) \ldots \texttt{L} = 42 \ldots\}$. The crucial difference is that for $\mathcal{P}_1$, the probability for the two classes under i resp. i' is not the same (see above), but for $\mathcal{P}_2$, $P_i([t]_L^{1,2}) = P_{i'}([t]_L^{1,2})$ holds!

Technically, $\mathcal{P}_2$ contains a point c which *dominates* both low-nondeterministic statements $n \equiv \texttt{L} = 42;$, $m \equiv \texttt{print(L)}$, and all relevant high events always happen before c. Domination means that any control flow from $START$ to n or m must pass through c. In $\mathcal{P}_2$, c is the point immediately before the first fork. In contrast, $\mathcal{P}_1$ has only a trivial common dominator for the low nondeterminism, namely the $START$ node, and on the path from $START$ to $n \equiv \texttt{print}(\text{"PO"})$ there is no high event, while on the path to $m \equiv \texttt{print}(\text{"ST"})$ there is.

Intuitively, the high inputs can cause strong nondeterministic high behaviour, including stuttering. But if LSOD conditions $1 + 2$ are always satisfied, and if there are no high events in any trace between c and n resp. m, the effect of the high behaviour is always the same for n and m and thus "factored out". It cannot cause a probabilistic leak – the dominator "shields" the low nondeterminism from high influence. Note that $\mathcal{P}_2$ contains an additional high statement $m' \equiv \texttt{read(H)}$ but that is behind n (no control flow is possible from m' to n) and thus cannot influence the n, m nondeterminism.

4.1   Improving Condition 3'

The above example has demonstrated that low nondeterminism may be reachable by high events without harm, as long as these high events always happen before the common dominator of the nondeterministic low statements. This observation will be even more important if dynamically created threads are allowed (as in JOANA, cmp. Sect. 5). We will now provide precise definitions for this idea.

Definition 6 (Common dominator). *Let two statements* $n, m \in \mathcal{P}$ *be given.*

1. *Statement c is a dominator for n, written c dom n, if c occurs on every CFG path from START to n.*
2. *Statement c is a common dominator for n, m, written c cdom (n, m), if c dom $n \wedge c$ dom m.*
3. *If c cdom (n, m) and $\forall c'$ cdom (n, m): c' dom c, then c is called an immediate common dominator.*

Efficient algorithms for computing dominators can be found in many compiler textbooks. Intraprocedural immediate dominators are unique and give rise to the dominator tree; for unique immediate common dominators we write $c = idom(n, m)$.[3] Note that $START$ itself is a (trivial) common dominator for every n, m. iRLSOD works with any common dominator. We thus assume a function $cdom$ which for every statement pair returns a common dominator, and write $c = cdom(n, m)$. Note that the implementation of $cdom$ may depend on the precision requirements, but once a specific $cdom$ is chosen, c depends solely on n and m. We are now ready to formally define the improved RLSOD criterion.

Definition 7 (iRLSOD). *iRLSOD holds if LSOD conditions 1 and 2 hold for all PDG nodes, and if*

$$3''. \ \forall n, n' : \ \mathrm{MHP}(n, n') \wedge cl(n) = cl(n') = L \wedge c = cdom(n, n')$$
$$\implies \forall n'' \in c \to^*_{CFG} n \cup c \to^*_{CFG} n' : cl(n'') = L.$$

iRLSOD is most precise (generates the least false alarms) if $cdom = idom$, because in this case it demands $cl(n'') = L$ for the smallest set of nodes "behind" the common dominator. Figure 4 illustrates the iRLSOD definition. Note that the original RLSOD trivially fulfils condition 3", where $cdom$ always returns $START$. Thus iRLSOD is a true generalization.

4.2   Classification Revisited

Consider the program in Fig. 5 middle/right. This example contains a probabilistic leak as follows. H influences the running time of the first while loop, hence H influences whether line 10 or line 18 is performed first. The value of tmp2 influences the running time of the second loop, hence it also influences whether L1 or

---

[3] In programs with procedures and threads, immediate dominators may not be unique due to context-sensitivity [2]. Likewise, the dominator definition must be extended if the same thread can be spawned several times. Both issues are not discussed here.

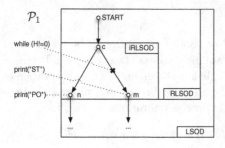 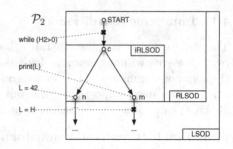

Fig. 4. Visualization of LSOD vs. RLSOD vs. iRLSOD. CFGs for Fig. 1 right resp. Fig. 2 right are sketched. n/m produces low nondeterminism, c is the common dominator. LSOD prohibits any low nondeterminism; RLSOD allows low nondeterminism which is not reachable by any high events; iRLSOD allows low nondeterminism which may be reached by high events if they are before the common dominator. The marked regions are those affected by low nondeterminism; inside these regions no high events are allowed. Thus iRLSOD is much more precise.

L2 is printed first. Thus H indirectly influences the execution order of the final print statements. Indeed the program is not RLSOD, as the print statements can be reached from the high statement in line 3 (middle). Applying iRLSOD, the common dominator for the two print statements is line 10.

The classification of line 10 is thus crucial. Assume $cl(10) = H$, then this classification automatically propagates in the PDG (due to the standard flow equation $cl(n) = \bigsqcup_{m \to n} cl(m)$) and lines 12/13 are classified high. iRLSOD is violated, and the probabilistic leak discovered.

But according to the flow equation, only line 3 is explicitly high and only lines 4, 7, 8 are PDG-reachable from 3. Thus $cl(10) = L$. Hence iRLSOD would be satisfied because 3,4,7,8 are *before* the common dominator. The leak would go undiscovered! This is not a flaw in condition 3", but an incompleteness in the standard flow equation – it must be extended for low nondeterminism.

In general, the rule is as follows. The standard flow equation $cl(n) = \bigsqcup_{m \to n} cl(m)$ expresses the fact that if a high value can reach a PDG node m upon which n is dependent, then the high value can also reach n. Likewise, if there is low nondeterminism with $\text{MHP}(n, m)$, and $idom(n, m) = c$, and the path $c \to^*_{CFG} n$ violates iRLSOD – that is, it contains high statements – then the high value can reach n. Thus $cl(n) = H$ must be enforced. This rule must be applied recursively until a fixpoint is reached.[4]

Definition 8 (Classification in PDGs). *A PDG $G = (N, \to)$ is classified correctly, if*

1. $\forall n \in N: cl(n) \geq \bigsqcup_{m \to n} cl(m)$,
2. $\forall n, m \in N: \text{MHP}(n, m) \land c = idom(n, m) \land \exists c' \in c \to^*_{CFG} n, cl(c') = H$
   $\implies cl(n) = H$.

---

[4] In case n was manually classified low, a trivial explicit leak has been discovered. Same for the standard flow equation [7].

In condition 1, $\geq$ must be used because 2 can push $cl(n)$ higher than $\bigsqcup_{m\to n} cl(m)$. In the example, the rule enforces line 10 to be classified high, as we have $MHP(10, 18) = 6$, and on the path from 6 to 10, lines 7 and 8 are high.

4.3 Soundness Arguments

Before we discuss soundness, let us point out an assumption which is standard for PN, namely that the scheduler is truly probabilistic. In particular, it maintains no state of its own, does not look at program variables, and the relative chance of two threads to be scheduled next is independent of other possibly running threads. The necessity of this assumption was stressed by various authors, e.g. [20]. Indeed a malicious scheduler can read high values to construct an explicit flow by scheduling, as in {H=0;||H=1;} {L=0;||L=1;}: the scheduler can leak H by scheduling the L assignments after reading H, such that the first visible L assignment represents H. Even if the scheduler is not malicious, but follows a deterministic strategy which is known to the attacker, leaks can result. As an example, consider Fig. 5 left. Assume deterministic round robin scheduling which executes 3 basic statements per time slice. Then for H=1 statements 2,3,4,9,5 are executed, while for H=0, statements 2,4,5,9 are executed. Thus the attacker can observe the public event sequence $9\to5$ resp. $5\to9$, leaking H. However under the assumption of truly probabilistic scheduling, Fig. 5 left is iRLSOD.

In the following, let $t_1 \cdots$ be the set of traces beginning with t_1, so that $P_i(t_1 \cdots) = \sum_{t=t_1 \cdot t_2} P_i(t)$ is the probability that execution under input i begins with t_1. We denote with $P_i(t_2 \mid t_1) = P_i(t_1 \cdot t_2)/P_i(t_1 \cdots)$ the conditional probability that after t_1, execution continues with t_2. This notion extends to sets of traces: $P_i(T' \mid T) = \sum_{t \in T' \cdot T} P_i(t)/\sum_{t \in T} P_i(t \cdots)$.

For the following soundness theorem, we assume that there is only one point of low-nondeterminism. In this case LSOD conditions 1, 2 and 3 hold for the whole program, except for the one point where low-nondeterminism is possible and only the iRLSOD condition 3" holds.

```
1  thread1(){
2    if (H) {
3      skip;};
4    fork Thread2();
5    print(17);
6  }
7
8  thread2() {
9    print(42);
10 }
```

```
1  thread1() {
2    tmp = 1;
3    if (H) {
4      tmp = 100;
5    }
6    fork thread2();
7    while (tmp > 0) {
8      tmp = tmp − 1;
9    }
10   tmp2 = 1;
11   fork thread3();
12   while (tmp2 > 0) {
13     tmp2 = tmp2 − 1;
14   }
15   print(L1);
16 }
```

```
17 thread2() {
18   tmp2 = 100;
19 }
20
21 thread3() {
22   print(L2);
23 }
```

Fig. 5. Left: deterministic round-robin scheduling may leak. Middle/Right: a leak which goes undiscovered if classification of statements is incomplete.

Theorem 2. *Let iRLSOD hold for $\mathcal{P}$, where $\mathcal{P}$ contains only one pair n, n' of low-nondeterministic statements:* $\mathrm{MHP}(n, n'), cl(n) = cl(n') = L$.

Now let $i \sim_L i'$, let $t \in \Theta$. Then

$$P_i([t]_L) = P_{i'}([t]_L).$$

Proof. (sketch). If t contains neither n nor n', LSOD holds and thus the PN condition $P_i([t]_L) = P_{i'}([t]_L)$ trivially holds.

Thus we assume, without loss of generality, that n occurs on t, and before a possible occurence of n'. Let $c = cdom(n, n')$.

The iRLSOD conditions ensures that t can be decomposed as $t_1 \cdot c \cdot t_2 \cdot n \cdot t_3$, and furthermore all low events on t_2 are on the control path from c to n or n', while any high events are from possible other threads. These other threads cannot have any low operations in t_2, as that would form another MHP-pair with n and n'. Correspondingly, $i = i_1 i_c i_2 i_n i_3$, where i_ν is consumed by t_ν.

Any trace $t' \sim_L t$ necessarily contains c and n and can be decomposed analogously and uniquely, with $t'_1 \sim_L t_1$, $t'_2 \sim_L t_2$ and $t'_3 \sim_L t_3$. Therefore, we have

$$P_i([t]_L) = P_i([t_1 \cdots]_L) \cdot P_i(c \cdot [t_2]_L \cdot n \cdots \mid [t_1]_L) \cdot P_i(t_3 \mid [t_1 \cdot c \cdot t_2]_L \cdot n).$$

by the chain rule for conditional probabilities, and the same for $i' = i'_1 i'_c i'_2 i'_n i'_3$.

We show $P_i([t]_L) = P_{i'}([t]_L)$ by equating these factors:

- We have $P_i([t_1 \cdots]_L) = P_{i'}([t_1 \cdots]_L)$: There is no low nondeterminism in the part of the CFG that produced this initial segment of the trace, and by the usual soundness argument for LSOD (cmp. Lemma 2), we find that $P_i([t_1 \cdots]_L) = 1$, and analogously for i'.
- We have $P_i(c \cdot [t_2]_L \cdot n \cdots \mid [t_1]_L) = P_{i'}(c \cdot [t_2]_L \cdot n \cdots \mid [t_1]_L)$: If there were no other, high threads, $c \cdot t_2 \cdot n$ would consist exclusively of low events. Since we assume a scheduler that does neither maintain its own state nor looks at the value of variables, the probabilities depend only on the part of i resp. i' that is consumed by the trace between c and n, namely i_2 resp. i'_2. As t_2, t'_2 contain only low operations, i_2, i'_2 is also classified low; and as we have $i \sim_L i'$, $i_2 = i'_2$ must hold. Therefore the probabilities are equal.

  If there are other threads, which necessarily only execute high events in this part of the execution, then these may slow down t_2 resp. t'_2 (similar to "stuttering"), but, as we assume a fair scheduler, do not change their relative probabilities. Therefore, these differences are factored out by considering low equivalence classes and equality holds in this case as well.
- For $P_i(t_3 \mid [t_1 \cdot c \cdot t_2]_L \cdot n) = P_i(t_3 \mid [t_1 \cdot c \cdot t_2]_L \cdot n)$ we are again in the situation of no low nondeterminism, as any possible nondeterminism is caused by the MHP-pair (n, n'), so analogously to the initial segment, both probabilities are one.   □

Note that the restriction to a single low-nondeterministic pair still covers many applications. An inductive proof for the general case (more than one low nondeterminism pair) is work in progress.

Corollary 1. *RLSOD is sound.*

Proof. RLSOD is a special case of iRLSOD: choose $cdom(n, n') = START$.   □

5 Case Study: E-Voting

In the following, we will apply RLSOD/iRLSOD to an experimental e-voting system developed in collaboration with R. Küsters et. al. This system aims at a provably secure e-voting software that uses cryptography to ensure *computational indistinguishability*. To proof computational indistinguishability, the cryptographic functions are replaced with a dummy implementation (called an "ideal variant"). It is then checked by IFC that no explicit or implicit flow exists between plain text, secret key and encrypted message; that is, probabilistic noninterference holds for the e-voting system with dummy crypto implementation. By a theorem of Küsters, noninterference of the ideal variant implies computational indistinguishability for the system with real encryption [11,12].

The example uses a multithreaded client-server architecture to send encrypted messages over the network. It consists of 550LoC with 16 classes. The interprocedural control flow is sketched in Fig. 6; Fig. 7 contains relevant parts of the code. The main thread starts in class `Setup` in line 3ff: First it initializes encryption by generating a private and public key, then it spawns a single `Server` thread before entering of the main loop. Inside the main loop it reads a secret message from the input and spawns a `Client` that takes care of the secure

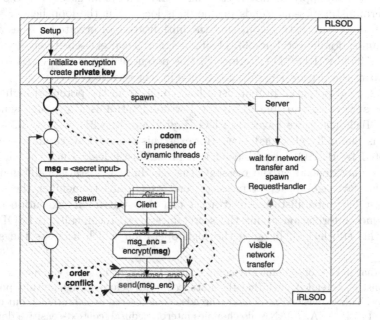

Fig. 6. CFG structure of the multithreaded server-client based message transfer.

message transfer: The client encrypts the given message and subsequently sends it via the network to the server. Note that there are multiple instances of the client thread as a new one is started in each iteration.

There are two sources of secret (HIGH) information: (1) the value of the parameter secret_bit (line 3) that decides about the content of the message; and (2) the private key of the encryption (line 33). Both are marked for JOANA with a @Source annotation. By Definition 8, (2) propagates to lines 44, 46, 5, 8 and 9 which are also classified High. Likewise, (1) propagates to lines 21 and 24, which are thus High as well.

As information sent over network is visible to the attacker, calls to the method sendMessage (line 66f) are marked as a LOW @Sink. JOANA was started in RLSOD mode, and – analysing the "ideal variant" – immediately guarantees that there are no explicit or implicit leaks. However the example contains two potential probabilistic leaks, which are both discovered by JOANA in RLSOD mode; one is later uncovered by iRLSOD to be a false alarm.

To understand the first leak in detail, remember that this e-voting code spawns new threads in a loop. This will cause low-nondeterminism, as the running times for the individual threads may vary and thus their relative execution order depends on scheduling. This low-nondeterminism is (context-sensitively) reachable from the high private-key initialization in line 44, hence RLSOD will cause an alarm (cmp. RLSOD criterion 3). Technically, we have $MHP(66, 66) \wedge cl(66) = L$; that is, line 66 is low-nondeterministic with itself (because the same thread is spawned several times). Furthermore, $START \rightarrow^*_{CFG} 44 \rightarrow^*_{CFG} 66 \wedge cl(44) = H$. Thus RLSOD criterion 3' is violated.

Now let us apply iRLSOD to this leak. The dominator for the low-nondeterministic message sends in line 66 is located at the loop header: $12 = cdom(66, 66)$.[5] Now it turns out that the initialisation of private keys lies *before* this common dominator: lines 33, 44, 46, 5, 8, and 9 context-sensitively dominate line 12. Thus by iRLSOD criterion 3", this potential leak is uncovered to be a false alarm: the private key initialisation is in fact secure!

The second potential probabilistic leak comes from the potential high influence by secret_bit in line 21 to the low-nondeterministic message sends in line 73. Technically, we have the PDG High chain $3 \rightarrow 21 \rightarrow 24 \rightarrow 62 \rightarrow 66$, but 66 is manually classified Low. However this second leak candidate is not eliminated by iRLSOD, and indeed is a probabilistic leak: since the encrypt run time may depend on the message, the scheduler will statistically generate a specific "average" order of message send executions (remember the scheduler must be probabilistic). An attacker can thus watch this execution order, and deduce information about the secret messages. Technically, iRLSOD discovers this subtle leak because the high operation which accesses the secret

---

[5] Note that in case of dynamically created threads, the definition of common dominator must be extended, such that the static *cdom* lies before *all* dynamically possible spawns. This extension for dynamic threads is not covered by definition 4, but implemented in JOANA. JOANA also handles interprocedural, context-sensitive dominators.

bit lies *behind* the common dominator, but before the low-nondeterminism: $12 = cdom(66,66) \rightarrow^*_{CFG} 21 \rightarrow^*_{CFG} 66$.

JOANA must and will report this probabilistic leak. The engineer might however decide that the leak is not dangerous. If the engineer can guarantee that the encrypt run time does *not* depend on msg, the leak may be ignored. JOANA detects both potential leaks in about 5 s on a standard PC.

6 Related Work

Zdancewic's work [24] was the starting point for us, once Giffhorn discovered that the Zdancewic LSOD criteria can naturally be checked using PDGs. Zdancewic uses an interesting definition of low-equivalent traces: low equivalence is not demanded for traces, but only for every subtrace for every low variable ("location traces"). This renders more traces low-equivalent and thus increases precision. But location traces act contrary to flow-sensitivity (relative order of variable accesses is lost), and according to our experience flow-sensitivity is essential.

While strict LSOD immediately guarantees probabilistic non-interference for any scheduler, it is much too strict for multi-threaded programs. In our current work, we considerably improved the precision of LSOD, while giving up on full scheduler independence (by restricting (i) RLSOD to truly probabilistic schedulers). Smith [20] improves on PN based on probabilistic bisimulation, where the latter forbids the execution time of any thread to depend on secret input. Just as in our work, a probabilistic scheduler is assumed; the probability of any execution step is given by a markov chain. This *weak* probabilistic bisimulation allows the execution time of threads to depend on secret input, as long as it is not made observable by writing to public variables. If the execution time up to the current point depends on secret input, their criterion allows to spawn new threads only if they do not alter public variables. In comparison, our c $cdom$ (n, m) based check *does* allow two public operations to happen in parallel in newly spawned threads, even if the execution time up to c (i.e.: a point at which at most one of the two threads involved existed) depends on secret input.

Approaches for non-interference of concurrent programs based on type systems benefit from various degrees of compositionality, a good study of which is given in [16]. Again, a probabilistic scheduler is assumed. Scheduler-independent approaches can be found in, e.g., [13,17]. The authors each identify a natural class of "robust" resp. "noninterfering" schedulers, which include uniform and round-robin schedulers. They show that programs which satisfy specific possibilistic notions of bisimilarity ("FSI-security" resp. "possibilistically noninterferent") remain probabilistically secure when run under such schedulers. Since programs like Fig. 5 left are not probabilistically secure under a round-robin scheduler, their possibilistic notion of bisimilarity require "lock-step" execution at least for threads with low-observable behaviour. Compared to iRLSOD this is more restrictive for programs, but less restrictive on scheduling.

```
 1  public class Setup {
 2
 3    public static void setup(@Source boolean secret_bit) { // HIGH input
 4      // Public−key encryption functionality for Server
 5      Decryptor serverDec = new Decryptor();
 6      Encryptor serverEnc = serverDec.getEncryptor();
 7      // Creating the server
 8      Server server = new Server(serverDec, PORT);
 9      new Thread(server).start();
10
11      // The adversary decides how many clients we create
12      while (Environment.untrustedInput() != 0) {
13        // determine the value the client encrypts:
14        // the adversary gives two values
15        byte[] msg1 = Environment.untrustedInputMessage();
16        byte[] msg2 = Environment.untrustedInputMessage();
17        if (msg1.length != msg2.length) { break; }
18
19        byte[] msg = new byte[msg1.length];
20        for(int i = 0; i < msg1.length; ++i)
21          msg[i] = (secret_bit ? msg1[i] : msg2[i]);
22
23        // spawn new client thread
24        Client client = new Client(serverEnc, msg, HOST, PORT);
25        new Thread(client).start();
26      }
27    }
28  }
29
30  public class KeyPair {
31    public byte[] publicKey;
32    @Source
33    public byte[] privateKey; // HIGH value
34  }
35
36  public final class Decryptor {
37
38    private byte[] privKey;
39    private byte[] publKey;
40    private MessagePairList log = new MessagePairList();
41
42    public Decryptor() {
43      // initialize public and secret (HIGH) keys
44      KeyPair keypair = CryptoLib.pke_generateKeyPair();
45      publKey = copyOf(keypair.publicKey);
46      privKey = copyOf(keypair.privateKey);
47    }
48
49    ...
50
51  }
52
53  public class Client implements Runnable {
54
55    private byte[] msg; private Encryptor enc;
56    private String hostname; private int port;
57    ...
58
59    @Override
60    public void run() {
61      // encrypt
62      byte[] msg_enc = enc.encrypt(msg);
63
64      // send
65      long socketID = Network.openConnection(hostname, port);
66      Network.sendMessage(socketID, msg_enc);
67      Network.closeConnection(socketID);
68    }
69  }
70
71  public class Network {
72
73    @Sink // LOW output
74    public static void sendMessage(long socketID, byte[] msg) throws NetworkError {
75      ...
76    }
77    ...
78  }
```

Fig. 7. Relevant parts of the multithreaded encrypted message passing system with security annotations for JOANA.

7 Future Work

RLSOD is already part of JOANA; we currently integrate iRLSOD into the system. We will thus be able to provide empirical precision comparisons between iRLSOD, RLSOD, and LSOD. Another issue is a generalization of Theorem 2 for multiple *MHP* pairs with corresponding multiple common dominators.

One issue which might push precision even further is lock sensitivity. The current MHP and dominator algorithms analyse thread invocations in a context-sensitive manner, but do ignore explicit locks. We started an integration of Müller-Olm's lock-sensitive Dynamic Pushdown Networks [3] into MHP, which sometimes can eliminate inter-thread dependences. The dominator computation for multi-threaded programs could profit from lock-sensitivity as well.

8 Conclusion

JOANA can handle full Java with arbitrary threads, while being sound and scaling to several 10k LOC. The decision to base PN in JOANA on low-deterministic security was made at a time when mainstream IFC research considered LSOD too restrictive. In the current paper we have shown that flow- and context-sensitive analysis, together with new techniques for allowing secure low-nondeterminism, has rehabilitated the LSOD idea.

Acknowledgements. This work was partially supported by Deutsche Forschungsgemeinschaft in the scope of SPP "Reliably Secure Software Systems", and by BMBF in the scope of the KASTEL project.

References

1. Askarov, A., Hunt, S., Sabelfeld, A., Sands, D.: Termination-insensitive noninterference leaks more than just a bit. In: Jajodia, S., Lopez, J. (eds.) ESORICS 2008. LNCS, vol. 5283, pp. 333–348. Springer, Heidelberg (2008)
2. De Sutter, B., Van Put, L., De Bosschere, K.: A practical interprocedural dominance algorithm. ACM Trans. Program. Lang. Syst. **29**(4), 19 (2007)
3. Gawlitza, T.M., Lammich, P., Müller-Olm, M., Seidl, H., Wenner, A.: Join-lock-sensitive forward reachability analysis for concurrent programs with dynamic process creation. In: Jhala, R., Schmidt, D. (eds.) VMCAI 2011. LNCS, vol. 6538, pp. 199–213. Springer, Heidelberg (2011)
4. Giffhorn, D.: Slicing of concurrent programs and its application to information flow control. Ph.D. thesis, Karlsruher Institut für Technologie, Fakultät für Informatik, May 2012
5. Giffhorn, D., Snelting, G.: A new algorithm for low-deterministic security. Int. J. Inf. Secur. **14**(3), 263–287 (2015)
6. Graf, J., Hecker, M., Mohr, M., Snelting, G.: Checking applications using security APIs with JOANA. In: 8th International Workshop on Analysis of Security APIs. http://www.dsi.unive.it/focardi/ASA8/

7. Hammer, C., Snelting, G.: Flow-sensitive, context-sensitive, and object-sensitive information flow control based on program dependence graphs. Int. J. Inf. Secur. 8(6), 399–422 (2009)

8. Horwitz, S., Prins, J., Reps, T.: On the adequacy of program dependence graphs for representing programs. In: Proceedings POPL 1988. pp. 146–157. ACM, New York, NY, USA (1988)

9. Huisman, M., Ngo, T.: Scheduler-specific confidentiality for multi-threaded programs and its logic-based verification. In: Proceedings Formal Verification of Object-Oriented Systems (2011)

10. Huisman, M., Worah, P., Sunesen, K.: A temporal logic characterisation of observational determinism. In: Proceedings of the 19th CSFW, pp. 3. IEEE (2006)

11. Küsters, R., Scapin, E., Truderung, T., Graf, J.: Extending and applying a framework for the cryptographic verification of java programs. In: Abadi, M., Kremer, S. (eds.) POST 2014 (ETAPS 2014). LNCS, vol. 8414, pp. 220–239. Springer, Heidelberg (2014)

12. Küsters, R., Truderung, T., Graf, J.: A framework for the cryptographic verification of Java-like programs. In: 2012 IEEE 25th Symposium on Computer Security Foundations (CSF). IEEE Computer Society (2012)

13. Mantel, H., Sudbrock, H.: Flexible Scheduler-independent security. In: Gritzalis, D., Preneel, B., Theoharidou, M. (eds.) ESORICS 2010. LNCS, vol. 6345, pp. 116–133. Springer, Heidelberg (2010)

14. Mohr, M., Graf, J., Hecker, M.: JoDroid: adding android support to a static information flow control tool. In: Gemeinsamer Tagungsband der Workshops der Tagung Software Engineering 2015, Dresden, Germany, 17–18 Määrz 2015, vol. 1337, pp. 140–145, CEUR Workshop Proceedings. CEUR-WS.org (2015)

15. Ngo, T.M.: Qualitative and quantitative information flow analysis for multi-threaded programs. Ph.D. thesis, University of Enschede (2014)

16. Popescu, A., Hölzl, J., Nipkow, T.: Formalizing probabilistic noninterference. In: Gonthier, G., Norrish, M. (eds.) CPP 2013. LNCS, vol. 8307, pp. 259–275. Springer, Heidelberg (2013)

17. Popescu, A., Hölzl, J., Nipkow, T.: Noninterfering schedulers. In: Heckel, R., Milius, S. (eds.) CALCO 2013. LNCS, vol. 8089, pp. 236–252. Springer, Heidelberg (2013)

18. Roscoe, A.W., Woodcock, J.C.P., Wulf, L.: Non-interference through determinism. In: Gollmann, Dieter (ed.) ESORICS 1994. LNCS, vol. 875. Springer, Heidelberg (1994)

19. Sabelfeld, A., Sands, D.: Probabilistic noninterference for multi-threaded programs. In: Proceedings of the 13th IEEE Computer Security Foundations Workshop (CSFW 2000) 3–5 July 2000, Cambridge, pp. 200–214 (2000)

20. Smith, G.: Improved typings for probabilistic noninterference in a multi-threaded language. J. Comput. Secur. 14(6), 591–623 (2006). http://iospress.metapress.com/content/4wt8erpe5eqkc0df

21. Smith, G., Volpano, D.: Secure information flow in a multi-threaded imperative language. In: Proceedings of POPL 1998, pp. 355–364. ACM, January 1998

22. Snelting, G.: Combining slicing and constraint solving for validation of measurement software. In: Cousot, Radhia, Schmidt, D.A. (eds.) SAS 1996. LNCS, vol. 1145. Springer, Heidelberg (1996)

23. Snelting, G., Robschink, T., Krinke, J.: Efficient path conditions in dependence graphs for software safety analysis. ACM Trans. Softw. Eng. Methodol. 15(4), 410–457 (2006)

24. Zdancewic, S., Myers, A.C.: Observational determinism for concurrent program security. In: Proceedings CSFW, pp. 29–43. IEEE (2003)

Tool Demonstration: JOANA

Jürgen Graf[✉], Martin Hecker, Martin Mohr, and Gregor Snelting

Karlsruhe Institute of Technology, Karlsruhe, Germany
{graf,martin.hecker,martin.mohr,gregor.snelting}@kit.edu

Abstract. JOANA is a tool for information flow control, which can handle full Java with unlimited threads and scales to ca. 100 kLOC. JOANA uses a new algorithm for checking probabilistic noninterference, named RLSOD. JOANA uses a stack of sophisticated program analysis techniques which minimise false alarms. JOANA is open source (joana.ipd.kit.edu) and offers an Eclipse GUI as well as an API.

The current tool demonstration paper concentrates on JOANA's precision. Effects of flow-sensitivity, context-sensitivity, and object-sensitivity are explained, as well as precision gains from the new RLSOD criterion.

Keywords: Information flow control · Probabilistic noninterference · Program analysis

1 Introduction

JOANA is a tool for information flow control (IFC), which discovers all confidentiality and integrity leaks in Java programs. JOANA is open source (joana.ipd.kit.edu). In this tool demonstration paper, we concentrate on the precision of JOANA. JOANA is based on sophisticated program analysis (points-to analysis, exception analysis, program dependence graphs), can handle full Java with unlimited threads, and scales to ca. 100 kLOC. JOANA minimizes false alarms through flow- context- field- object- time- and lock-sensitive analysis algorithms. JOANA guarantees to find all explicit, implicit, possibilistic, and probabilistic leaks. The theoretical foundations have been described in [2,5,10]. The GUI and specific usage aspects have been described in [3,4,6–9].

Figure 1 shows the JOANA Eclipse plugin. In the source code, input and output are annotated with security levels ("High" i.e. secret, or "Low" i.e. public; only input and output need annotations). The program contains a probabilistic leak, because the running time of the loop depends on secret input, and thus the probability that "POST" is printed instead of "STPO" due to interleaving depends on secret input. The leak is highlighted in the source code (full details on a leak are available on demand). JOANA allows arbitrary security lattices (not just "High" and "Low"). It can check confidentiality as well as integrity; in this paper we concentrate on confidentiality.

JOANA analyses Java bytecode and uses IBM's WALA analysis frontend; recently, a frontend for Android bytecode was added. JOANA offers various

© Springer-Verlag Berlin Heidelberg 2016
F. Piessens and L. Viganò (Eds.): POST 2016, LNCS 9635, pp. 89–93, 2016.
DOI: 10.1007/978-3-662-49635-0_5

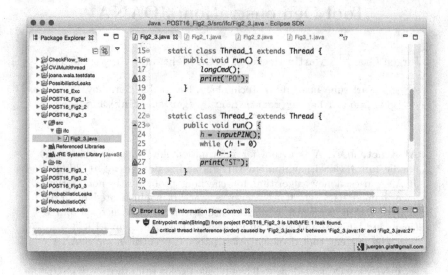

Fig. 1. JOANA GUI, discovering a probabilistic leak

options for analysis precision (e.g. object-sensitive points-to analysis, time-sensitive backward slicing). It was thus able to provide security guarantees for several examples from the literature which are considered difficult. More interesting is perhaps the successful analysis of an experimental e-voting system developed by Küsters et al. [7]. In a scalability study, the full source code of the HSQLDB database was analysed; analysis needed one day on a standard PC.

```
1  void main ():            1  void main ():            1  void main ():
2    read (H);              2    fork thread_1 ();       2    fork thread_1 ();
3    if (H < 1234)          3    fork thread_2 ();       3    fork thread_2 ();
4      print (0);           4  void thread_1 ():        4  void thread_1 ():
5    L = H;                 5    read (L);              5    longCmd;
6    print (L);             6    print (L);             6    print ("PO");
                            7  void thread_2 ():        7  void thread_2 ():
                            8    read (H);              8    read (H);
                            9    L = H;                 9    while (H != 0)
                                                        10     H--;
                                                        11   print ("ST");
```

Fig. 2. Some leaks. Left: explicit and implicit, middle: possibilistic, right: probabilistic.

Figure 2 presents small but typical confidentiality leaks (as usual, H is "High", L is "Low"). Explicit leaks arise if (parts of) secret values are copied (indirectly) to public output. Implicit leaks arise if a secret value can change control flow (which can change public behaviour). Possibilistic leaks in concurrent programs arise if a certain interleaving produces an explicit or implicit leak; in Fig. 2 middle, interleaving order 5,8,9,6 causes an explicit leak. Probabilistic leaks arise if the probability of public output is influenced be secret values; in Fig. 2 right, H is never copied to L, but if the value of H is large, probability is higher that "POST" is printed instead of "STPO".

2   Sequential Precision

JOANA was the first IFC tool which used program dependence graphs (PDGs). PDGs are naturally flow- and context-sensitive. Today PDGs for (multi-threaded) full Java are highly precise and scale up to 1 MLOC. As a prerequisite for PDGs, a precise points-to analysis and exception analysis is necessary.

```
1  void main ():              1    o1 = new O();  //O1      1  void main ():
2    read (H);                2    o2 = new O();  //O2      2    fork thread_1 ();
3    L = 2;                   3    o1.c = H;                3    fork thread_2 ();
4    H1 = f (H);              4    o2.c = L;                4  void thread_1 ():
5    L1 = f (L);              5    o3 = o2;                 5    L = 42;
6    print (L1);              6    print (o3.c);            6    read (H);
7                             7    o4 = o1;                 7  void thread_2 ():
8  int f (int x)              8    o4 = o2;                 8    print (L);
9    {return x+42;}                                         9    L = H;
```

Fig. 3. Unprecise analysis causes false alarms.

A flow-insensitive analysis will ignore statement order. In Fig. 3 right, a false alarm results if order of statements 8/9 is ignored. Flow-insensitive analysis also ignores killing definitions as in L=H; L=42; (where the second statement can be far from the first). A context-insensitive analysis will merge different calls to the same function. In Fig. 3 left, a context-insensitive analysis will merge the two calls to f and cause a false alarm. In practice, context-sensitivity is even more important for precision than flow-sensitivity. Object-sensitivity means that fields in different objects of the same class are distinguished. In Fig. 3 middle, an object-insensitive analysis will merge o1 and o2 and cause a false alarm. Object-sensitivity is difficult in case of nested or recursive object definitions, because it interferes with points-to analysis and requires additional field-sensitivity. For analysing object-oriented programs, the combination of context- and object-sensitivity is essential, as in o1.c=o1.f(H); o2.c=o1.f(L);.

Points-to analysis determines for every pointer a set of objects it may point to. In Fig. 3 middle, $pt(o1) = \{O1\}$, $pt(o3) = pt(o2) = \{O2\}, pt(o4) = \{O1, O2\}$. For precision, points-to sets should be small, but of course maintain soundness. Today, sophisticated points-to algorithms for full Java are known, however many common approaches are not efficient for PDG-based IFC. Hence, we are exploring *sweet-spots* of points-to analyses with a better precision-cost-ratio, which employ precision only where needed. The key is to taylor the points-to analysis to the concrete IFC query: First we build a PDG with an imprecise but cheap points-to analysis and compute a forward slice [5] of the high statements. From this slice, we extract the critical instances that may contain high information. In a second pass, we apply an automatically taylored points-to analysis which specifically distinguishes the critical instances.

Another issue is exception analysis, as exceptions can generate much additional control flow and spoil precision. We implemented a null pointer analysis which detects field accesses that never dereference null. We are currently implementing an analogous checker for array accesses.

3   Probabilistic Precision

Different criteria and algorithms for probabilistic noninterference (PN) have been proposed. The vast majority is not flow-sensitive (let alone context- or object-sensitive), or puts unacceptable restrictions on programs ("no low statements after high guards"); some turned out to be unsound. The simplest criterion, LSOD (low-security observational determinism) is scheduler independent and easy to implement as a program analysis. However LSOD strictly prohibits any, even secure, low-nondeterminism. For example Fig. 3 right is PN according to the original definition, but interleaving can cause low nondeterminism (in fact a race) for statements 5 and 8, hence LSOD causes a false alarm.

We found that flow-sensitivity is essential for a precise LSOD, and that LSOD can naturally be checked using PDGs for multi-threaded programs [2]. We then devised an improvement, RLSOD (relaxed LSOD), which allows low-nondeterminism if it cannot be reached from high events. The latter can be checked easily in the CFG. For example, Fig. 3 right is not LSOD but RLSOD, because the 5/8 race cannot be reached from high statements. Recently, we discovered that for low-nondeterministic statements s_1, s_2, it is enough to check high events in the control flow regions between the immediate dominator $idom(s_1, s_2)$, and $s1$ (resp. $s2$). For example assume that in `main` the initial statement `read(H)` is added. Then the 5/8 race *can* be reached from a high event, so "simple" RLSOD causes a false alarm. But the "dominator" improvement, plus flow-sensitivity (which respects the 8/9 order) will classify the example as secure – which it is according to PN.

Another issue is precision of the may-happen-in-parallel analysis, which is part of the RLSOD algorithm [2]. The current MHP analysis is context-sensitive but ignores explicit locks; recently, experiments with a lock-sensitive MHP based on pushdown networks [1] have begun.

4   Fine Tuning

JOANA supports a wide range of configuration options that allows experts to fine-tune the analysis. JOANA also comes with an automated approach to infer a reasonable configuration and additionally categorize detected leaks. Given a program and security annotations, JOANA starts with a fast but imprecise points-to analysis and subsequently applies more precise algorithms until either the maximal precision option has been reached or no leaks are detected.

JOANA helps to categorize the severity of detected information leaks as follows: (1) Flow through exceptions is ignored. Disappearing leaks are categorized as *caused by exceptions*. (2) Implicit flow through control dependencies is ignored. Leaks still detected are categorized as *explicit*, disappeared leaks as *implicit*. The result is a noninterference guarantee or a list of information leaks with source code location and categorization.

Acknowledgements. JOANA was partially supported by Deutsche Forschungsgemeinschaft in the scope of SPP "Reliably Secure Software Systems".

References

1. Gawlitza, T.M., Lammich, P., Müller-Olm, M., Seidl, H., Wenner, A.: Join-lock-sensitive forward reachability analysis for concurrent programs with dynamic process creation. In: Jhala, R., Schmidt, D. (eds.) VMCAI 2011. LNCS, vol. 6538, pp. 199–213. Springer, Heidelberg (2011)
2. Giffhorn, D., Snelting, G.: A new algorithm for low-deterministic security. Int. J. Inf. Secur. **14**(3), 263–287 (2015)
3. Graf, J., Hecker, M., Mohr, M.: Using JOANA for information flow control in Java programs - a practical guide. In: Proceedings of 6th Working Conference on Programming Languages (ATPS 2013). Lecture Notes in Informatics (LNI), vol. 215, pp. 123–138. Springer, Heidelberg (2013)
4. Graf, J., Hecker, M., Mohr, M., Snelting, G.: Checking applications using security APIs with JOANA. In: 8th International Workshop on Analysis of Security APIs, July 2015
5. Hammer, C., Snelting, G.: Flow-sensitive, context-sensitive, and object-sensitive information flow control based on program dependence graphs. Int. J. Inf. Secur. **8**(6), 399–422 (2009)
6. Küsters, R., Scapin, E., Truderung, T., Graf, J.: Extending and applying a framework for the cryptographic verification of java programs. In: Abadi, M., Kremer, S. (eds.) POST 2014 (ETAPS 2014). LNCS, vol. 8414, pp. 220–239. Springer, Heidelberg (2014)
7. Küsters, R., Truderung, T., Graf, J.: A framework for the cryptographic verification of Java-like programs. In: 2012 IEEE 25th Computer Security Foundations Symposium (CSF). IEEE Computer Society, June 2012
8. Mohr, M., Graf, J., Hecker, M.: JoDroid: adding android support to a static information flow control tool. In: Gemeinsamer Tagungsband der Workshops der Tagung Software Engineering , Dresden, Germany, 17-18 März 2015, vol. 1337 of CEUR Workshop Proceedings, pp. 140–145. CEUR-WS.org (2015)
9. Snelting, G., Giffhorn, D., Graf, J., Hammer, C., Hecker, M., Wasserrab, D.: Checking probabilistic noninterference using JOANA. IT - Inf. Technol. **56**, 280–287 (2014)
10. Wasserrab, D., Lohner, D., Snelting, G.: On PDG-based noninterference and its modular proof. In: Proceedings of PLAS 2009. ACM, June 2009

Models and Applications

Towards Fully Automatic Logic-Based Information Flow Analysis: An Electronic-Voting Case Study

Quoc Huy Do[✉], Eduard Kamburjan, and Nathan Wasser

Department of Computer Science, TU Darmstadt, Darmstadt, Germany
do@cs.tu-darmstadt.de, eduard.kamburjan@stud.tu-darmstadt.de,
wasser@informatik.tu-darmstadt.de

Abstract. Logic-based information flow analysis approaches generally are high precision, but lack automatic ability in the sense that they demand user interactions and user-defined specifications. To overcome this obstacle, we propose an approach that combines the strength of two available logic-based tools based on the KeY theorem prover: the KEG tool that detects information flow leaks for Java programs and a specification generation tool utilizing abstract interpretation on program logic. As a case study, we take a simplified e-voting system and show that our approach can lighten the user's workload considerably, while still keeping high precision.

Keywords: Test generation · Information flow · Invariant generation

1 Introduction

Information flow analysis has played an important role in ensuring security for software systems and has attracted many researchers for several decades. Most approaches analysing programs for secure information flow are either logic-based [4,26], which is precise but not automatic and difficult to apply for large programs, or over-approximation approaches such as type-based [1,17,24,27], dependency graph [14] or abstract interpretation [2], which are fully automatic with high performance but lack precision.

In this paper we propose a logic-based approach based on self-composition [3,10] and symbolic execution [19] that makes use of abstract interpretation [7] to obtain automation while still maintaining high precision in information flow analysis. It combines the strength of two available logic-based tools based on the KeY theorem prover: the KEG tool [12] that detects information flow leaks and a specification generation tool [28,30] utilizing abstract interpretation on program logic. The basic idea is to first analyse a target program with the specification generation tool in order to generate necessary specifications for unbounded loops

---

The work has been funded by the DFG priority program 1496 '"Reliably Secure Software Systems"'.

F. Piessens and L. Viganò (Eds.): POST 2016, LNCS 9635, pp. 97–115, 2016.
DOI: 10.1007/978-3-662-49635-0_6

and recursive method calls and then use the KEG tool to detect information flow leaks w.r.t. a given information flow policy. The needed loop invariants and method contracts are automatically generated by abstraction techniques, including array abstraction with symbolic pivots [30], based on abstract interpretation of partitions in an array. Loop invariants are generated without user interaction by repeated symbolic execution of the loop body and abstraction of modified variables or, in the case of arrays, the modified array elements. The invariant generation provides loop invariants which are often precise enough to be used in information leak detection.

We apply our approach in analysing two versions of a simplified e-voting system as a case study: one implementation is correct, while the other is faulty (in the sense that an information leak can happen). We show that with the correct implementation of the simplified e-voting program our approach does not report any false alarms while with the faulty implementation our approach successfully detects the leak and generates a JUnit test as witness thereof. Along with the high precision, our approach only requires users to supply a noninterference policy and preconditions for input data, but does not require any other user interactions or specifications. Our main contributions are as follows: (i) the first logic-based approach utilizing two available tools to obtain both precision and (almost) full automation in analysing information flow security, and (ii) a case study on noninterference of a simplified e-voting system showing the feasibility of our approach.

The paper is structured as follows: Sect. 2 introduces fundamental techniques used in our approach, i.e. symbolic execution and abstract interpretation. Section 3 briefly presents our logic-based leak detection approach and the implementation thereof, while the approach generating loop and method specifications is explained in Sect. 4. The combination of both tools is illustrated in Sect. 5. Section 6 demonstrates our case study and its remarks are pointed out in Sect. 7. Related work is discussed in Sect. 8 and finally Sect. 9 gives our conclusions and outlines future work.

2   Background

2.1   Symbolic Execution

Symbolic execution [19] is a powerful technique widely used in program verification, test case generation and program analysis. The main idea of symbolic execution is to run the program with symbolic input values instead of concrete ones. The central result of symbolic execution is a symbolic execution tree. Each node of the tree is annotated by its symbolic state, mapping each program location to its symbolic representation. Each path of the tree has a unique path condition that is the conjunction of all its branch conditions and represents the set of concrete executions having input values satisfying the path condition. If the program does not contain unbounded loops or recursive method calls, the symbolic execution tree is finite and covers exactly all possible concrete executions performed by the program.

In case of unbounded loops or unbounded recursive method calls a symbolic execution tree is no longer finite. One natural solution is unfolding loops or expanding invoked method calls up to a fixed depth value, generating a symbolic execution tree which is an under-approximation of the real program. Another solution is to make use of specifications as proposed in [16] to achieve a finite representation of a symbolic execution tree. This approach uses loop invariants and method contracts to describe the effect of loops and method calls. This approach gives a comprehensive view of the program's behaviour and brings scalability while still maintaining program semantics precisely. The major drawback of this approach is that specifications must be supplied in advance. In many cases this is a complex task, depending mostly on the complexity of the specific source code. Generating loop invariants as well as method specifications automatically has been an active research topic in program analysis literature.

2.2 Abstract Interpretation

Abstract interpretation [7] is a technique used in program analysis which provides a framework to lose precision within the analysis for a greater automation. When combined with symbolic execution, e.g. in [29], it allows to consider abstract symbolic values. Abstract symbolic values do not represent an unknown yet fixed concrete value, but rather in any given model the concrete value is within a set of possible concrete values – the abstract element. The abstract elements form a lattice – the abstract domain.

Given two abstract symbolic values, a_1 and a_2, the abstract domain allows to join their abstract elements, and the resulting abstract element $a_1 \sqcup a_2$ is a set which encompases at least all the possible concrete values of the two input values. This potentially loses information, as the joined element might encompase further concrete values. Information loss also occurs when abstracting a symbolic value v, i.e. finding an abstract element a such that all possible concrete values of v in a given state are within a. While information loss is inevitable, it happens in a controlled fashion and the choice of the abstract domain allows to preserve enough information for a given task, while making the set of possible values more feasable. A common choice is that the abstract domain has finite height, while the set of concrete values is infinite. This makes analysis of programs tractable and also allows fixpoint procedures, like the one presented in Sect. 4 for loop invariant generation. Abstract domains with infinite height require a widening operator in order to ensure fixpoint generation will terminate.

3 Detection of Information Flow Leaks

In this section we introduce a logic-based approach to detect (and generate exploits for) information flow leaks based on self-composition and symbolic execution that has been proposed in previous work [12] by some of the authors.

3.1   Approach

We make use of self-composition [3,10] and symbolic execution [19] to characterize and formalize information flow policies, including *noninterference* and *delimited information release* [25] as declassification. In this paper we focus on noninterference policies, the details of delimited release are explained in [12].

Given program p and the set V of all variables of p, assume that V is partitioned into two subsets H and L. Program p satisfies noninterference policy $H \nrightarrow L$ if there is no information flow from H to L. This is conventionally represented by using two program executions: p satisfies $H \nrightarrow L$ iff it holds that any two executions of p starting in initial states that coincide on L also terminate in two states that coincide on L. Above definition can be formalized using self-composition technique proposed in [10]. A self-copied program of p, denoted p′, is created by copying p′ and replacing all variables with fresh ones, such that p and p′ do not share any memory. Let V', L', H' be fresh copies of V, L, H accordingly. Then $H \nrightarrow L$ can be formalized as follows:

$$\{L \doteq L'\} p(V); p'(V') \{L \doteq L'\} \tag{1}$$

A major drawback of the formalization is that it requires program p to be analysed twice. It can be refined by making use of symbolic execution. Let SE_p and SE_p' be symbolic execution trees of p and p′. It is obvious that SE_p and SE_p' are identical except that all variables $v \in V$ (considered as symbolic inputs) in all path conditions and symbolic states of SE_p are replaced by corresponding fresh copies $v' \in V'$ in SE_p'. Thus we only need to symbolically execute p once and represent two executions of p and p′ by two symbolic execution paths of SE_p with different symbolic inputs V and V'.

For each symbolic execution path i of SE_p, we denote pc_i as its path condition. To make explicit that the symbolic final value of each program variable $v \in V$ depends on symbolic inputs and corresponding execution path, for each path i and variable v, we define function f_i^v mapping from symbolic inputs to symbolic final value of v. Let N_p be the number of symbolic execution paths of SE_p, we construct an SMT formula having the same meaning as (1):

$$\bigwedge_{0 \le i \le j < N_p} \left(\left(\bigwedge_{v \in L} v \doteq v' \right) \wedge pc_i(V) \wedge pc_j(V') \implies \bigwedge_{l \in L} f_i^l(V) \doteq f_j^l(V') \right) \tag{2}$$

To detect leaks w.r.t noninterference policy $H \nrightarrow L$, we build *insecurity formula* by negating (2) and transforming the negation into disjunctive normal form:

$$\bigvee_{l \in L} \bigvee_{0 \le i \le j < N_p} Leak(H, L, l, i, j) \tag{3}$$

where

$$Leak(H, L, l, i, j) \equiv \left(\bigwedge_{v \in L} v \doteq v' \right) \wedge pc_i(V) \wedge pc_j(V') \wedge f_i^l(V) \ne f_j^l(V') \tag{4}$$

Information flow leaks are detected by solving each formula $Leak(H, L, l, i, j)$ in (4). If it is satisfiable, there exists a forbidden information flow from some variables of H to a variable $l \in L$ and the leak can be seen by comparing two symbolic execution paths i, j. Otherwise, p is secure w.r.t the noninterference policy $H \not\rightarrow L$ if (3) is unsatisfiable.

Formula (3) can be easily extended to support detecting leaks under user-defined preconditions. Let Pre be a precondition assumed to hold at all initial states of p. To check whether p satisfies $H \not\rightarrow L$ under the assumption that Pre holds, we only need to add two conjunctions $Pre(V)$ and $Pre(V')$ into $Leak(H, L, l, i, j)$.

If p contains unbounded loops or recursive method calls, SE_p is infinite and (3) becomes unsolvable. The approach unfolding loops and expanding methods up to a fixed depth could be employed without any user interaction. Although it is useful in the sense that it can help to detect some leaks, it cannot find all possible leaks and hence cannot be used for proving secure information flow. On the other hand, the size of symbolic execution trees might be very large, thus the analysis might be very expensive. We overcome this obstacle by making use of specifications to get the finite form of SE_p as proposed in [16]. This approach represents loops and method calls as corresponding single nodes of a symbolic execution tree while keeping their semantics by using loop invariants and method contracts to contribute to relevant path conditions and to the representation of the symbolic state. For each variable v whose values can be changed during the execution of a loop or method call, its symbolic value is assigned by a fresh symbolic variable at the exit point of the loop or method call. The output value function f_i^v as well as path conditions sp_i now are represented upon $V_S = V \cup V_{fresh}$, where V_{fresh} is the set of all fresh symbolic variables created during symbolically analysing p. The approach has been implemented as a symbolic execution engine based on the verification system KeY [5], which we use as the backend for our implementation. Details and examples can be found in [12].

The precision of the information flow analysis using specifications depends mostly on the quality of the specifications. If loop invariants and method contracts are not strong enough so that they allow behaviours that are not possible in the actual program, false alarms might be raised. In the worst case when they are wrong in the sense that they exclude existing behaviours, actual leaks might not be detected. Wrong specifications can be avoided by verifying them using a program verification tool. However, refining too weak specifications is a laborious task for even an experienced user. Combining this approach with an automatic specification generation tool is a potential direction to enhance both precision and automation.

3.2 Implementation

Our approach has been implemented in a prototype tool named *KeY Exploit Generation (KEG)*[1]. KEG can automatically detect leaks in Java programs

---

[1] www.se.tu-darmstadt.de/research/projects/albia/download/exploit-generation-tool.

w.r.t user-specified information flow policies and generate exploits in form of
JUnit tests to expose them. KEG is based on KeY [5], a state-of-the-art theorem prover for Java and makes use of its symbolic execution engine [16] which
supports method and loop specifications to deal with recursive method calls and
unbounded loops. KEG supports not only primitive types but also object types
and arrays (to some extent). Comprehension expressions, such as sum, max and
min, are also supported.

Figure 1 describes KEG's work-flow. KEG checks a Java program by
analysing all specified methods w.r.t. a given information flow specification. Noninterference is a class level policy, while declassification (delimited information
release) is a method level policy. To analyse a method m, first m is symbolically
executed (using KeY) to achieve the symbolic execution tree. Afterwards, for
each information flow policy $H \not\rightarrow L$, KEG uses the method's path conditions
and the final symbolic values of the program locations modified by m to compose insecurity formulas $Leak(H, L, l, i, j)$. Those formulas are passed to a model
finder (in our case the SMT Solver Z3 [11]) to find concrete models satisfying
them. If a model has been found, it is used to configure the initial states of two
runs which expose a forbidden information flow. The generated exploit then sets
up two runs corresponding to two initial states and inspects the reached final
values of low variables to detect a leak. KEG outputs the exploited program as
an executable JUnit test.

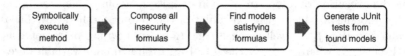

Fig. 1. Exploit generation by KEG

4   Loop Invariant Generation

4.1   KeY and Abstract Domains

The KeY tool uses symbolic execution to verify Java programs. The underlying
JavaDL calculus uses *updates* [5] to encapsulate state changes of variables and
models the heap memory as a special program variable. An elementary update
has the form $x := t$, where x is the program variable that is updated and t is a
term which is the new value for x. Parallel updates are denoted $\mathcal{U} \parallel \mathcal{U}'$, where $\mathcal{U}$
and $\mathcal{U}'$ are elementary or parallel updates. Updates can be applied to terms (or
formulas) with the $\{\cdot\}\cdot$ operator, resulting in new terms (or formulas). As the
name implies, all elementary updates contained in a parallel update are applied
simultaneously (with the rightmost update winning in case of multiple updates
to the same variable). Therefore, for example, $\{x := y \parallel y := x\}(2 * x + y)$ is
equal to $(2 * y + x)$. Updates and update applications can also be simplified: for

example, the sequential update applications $\{x := y\}\{y := x\}\phi$ can be simplified first to a parallel update application $\{x := y \parallel y := \{x := y\}x\}\phi$ and then the inner update application on x can be resolved, resulting in $\{x := y \parallel y := y\}\phi$. Further simplification gives $\{x := y\}\phi$. Updates are created during symbolic execution whenever a field or variable changes its value, e.g., this is the rule for executing variable assignments:

$$\text{assignment} \quad \frac{\Gamma \Rightarrow \{\mathcal{U}\}\{x := t\}[\ldots]\varphi, \Delta}{\Gamma \Rightarrow \{\mathcal{U}\}[x\ \texttt{=}\ t;\ \ldots]\varphi, \Delta}$$

The heap variable is updated with a special *store* function:

$$\text{assignment}_{array} \quad \frac{\Gamma \Rightarrow \{\mathcal{U}\}\{\text{heap} := store(\text{heap}, \texttt{a}, \texttt{i}, t)\}[\ldots]\varphi, \Delta}{\Gamma \Rightarrow \{\mathcal{U}\}[\texttt{a[i]}\ \texttt{=}\ t;\ \ldots]\varphi, \Delta}$$

Updates allow to postpone the application of state changes until the whole program has been executed and to analyze and manipulate pending state changes. The approach introduced in [6] uses the analysis of updates to incorporate abstract interpretation and loop invariant generation for local variables. We use abstract function symbols to denote abstract symbolic values, as described in Sect. 2.2.

With abstract functions it is possible to express *within* an update that, for example, an integer variable has a positive value. These abstract functions are denoted $\gamma_{\alpha,z}$, where α is the abstract element and $z \in \mathbb{Z}$ identifies the abstract function. A simple abstract domain for integers is pictured in Fig. 2.

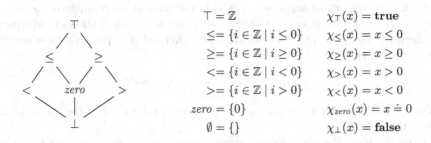

$$
\begin{aligned}
\top &= \mathbb{Z} & \chi_\top(x) &= \textbf{true} \\
\leq &= \{i \in \mathbb{Z} \mid i \leq 0\} & \chi_\leq(x) &= x \leq 0 \\
\geq &= \{i \in \mathbb{Z} \mid i \geq 0\} & \chi_\geq(x) &= x \geq 0 \\
< &= \{i \in \mathbb{Z} \mid i < 0\} & \chi_>(x) &= x > 0 \\
> &= \{i \in \mathbb{Z} \mid i > 0\} & \chi_<(x) &= x < 0 \\
zero &= \{0\} & \chi_{zero}(x) &= x \doteq 0 \\
\emptyset &= \{\} & \chi_\perp(x) &= \textbf{false}
\end{aligned}
$$

Fig. 2. Abstract domain for integers

The lattice structure allows joining updates into abstract updates that describe a set of possible value changes. E.g., the update $x := \gamma_{>,1} \parallel y := \gamma_{>,2}$ sets x to some positive value and y to another, possibly different, positive value. The additional information of the $\gamma_{\alpha,z}$ symbols can be obtained by adding the description of α to the premiss of the sequent. The description of each α is contained in the matching characteristic function χ_α.

4.2 Generation and Implementation

In [6] abstract interpretation is used to generate loop invariants for local variables. To do this, the loop is symbolically executed once and the resulting symbolic program states are joined with the initial (symbolic) program state: For each variable, the value in the update is abstracted, i.e. the smallest abstract element that contains all possible values is determined. Then all abstract elements are joined. This is repeated until a fixpoint is found, i.e. another iteration does not produce a weaker update.

Example 1. Consider the sequent

$$\Rightarrow \{\texttt{i} := 1\}[\textbf{while}(\texttt{i} > 0) \ \texttt{i} \ = \ \texttt{i-1};](\texttt{i} = 0)$$

The initial program state is expressed in the update $\texttt{i} := 0$ and symbolic execution of one iteration leads to the sequent

$$\Rightarrow \{\texttt{i} := 0\}[\textbf{while}(\texttt{i} > 0) \ \texttt{i} \ = \ \texttt{i-1};](\texttt{i} = 0)$$

Both 1 and 0 are contained in $\geq$ thus the updates are joined to $\texttt{i} := \gamma_{\geq,0}$, which is used as the pre-state in the next iteration. Another iteration produces the update $\texttt{i} := \gamma_{\geq,0} - 1$ under the premiss that $\gamma_{\geq,0} > 0$ and leads to no weaker update.

Fields of integer type can be handled analogously and simple domains for boolean and object variables/fields can be used.

In [29] this approach was extended to abstraction of arrays: Arrays are regarded as split into two parts: a (potentially) modified and an unmodified part. If the sequence of array accesses is monotonously increasing (or decreasing), then each iteration moves the splitting point further and allows to abstract all the array elements in between. With this method it is possible to generate invariants of the form

$$\forall i. \ (initial \leq i \wedge i < id) \rightarrow \chi_a(\textbf{arr}[i])$$

where *id* is the index term for the array access and *initial* is the value of *id* before the loop.

If in the loop the sequence of array access has the form $a + x * b$ in the xth iteration of the loop for some $a, b \in \mathbb{Z}$, then a more precise invariant is possible that only makes a statement about the elements actually accessed. If the sequence is not monotonous, a very weak invariant of the form

$$\forall i. \ (0 \leq i \wedge i < \textbf{arr.length}) \rightarrow (\chi_a(\textbf{arr}[i]) \vee \textbf{arr}[i] = \textbf{arr}_{old}[i])$$

can be generated, where $\textbf{arr}_{old}$ denotes the array in the state before entering the loop for the first time.

Additional forms of invariants can be extracted from the unrolled loops in the invariant generation for arrays and variables. These include simple abstraction over arbitrary terms, that can be used, e.g., to establish an order between variables. Another extension is *sum invariants* that can be generated if a variable is modified only by summing another value inside the loop. In this case after symbolic execution of the fixed point iteration all open branches contain an update of the form $x := \gamma_{\alpha,z} + t$ for the variable x in question, where $\gamma_{\alpha,z}$ is the value of x before execution of the loop body. (Also accepted are updates $x := \gamma_{\alpha,z}$ and $x := \gamma_{\alpha,z} - t$.) As an additional requirement all variables in t must have the aforementioned form $a + x * b$ in the xth iteration for some $a, b \in \mathbb{Z}$.

As it is possible that different terms are added to the variable, the execution tree is condensed into a tree that only contains the splitting nodes and the post-states. The splitting conditions in the inner nodes are used as conditions in the ternary conditional expression operator when constructing the sum formula.

Example 2. Consider the sequent

$$\Rightarrow \{i := 1 \parallel j := 2 \parallel k := 5\}[\mathbf{while}(k > 0)\{$$
$$\mathbf{if}(b) \; i \; = \; i \; + \; j;$$
$$\mathbf{else} \; i \; = \; i \; + \; k;$$
$$k\text{--};$$
$$\}](k = 0)$$

This generates the invariant update $i := \gamma_{>,z} \parallel j := 2 \parallel k := \gamma_{\geq,z}$ and the condensed tree has the following form:

As k has the form $5 - x$ in the xth iteration, it produces the invariant

$$i = 1 + \sum_{n=0}^{it} b \; ? \; \text{5-n} \; : \; 2$$

The invariant generation uses the generated invariant directly in order to potentially reach other loops or the same loop in a different program state and generate further loop invariants, but also outputs JML [22]. When the invariant is used in a proof, by application of a loop invariant rule, it is ensured that the invariant is correct, i.e. it holds before the first execution and holds after every iteration if it held before.

As the invariant consists of subformulas with fixed form, each is translated separately:

- Updates of the form $x := \gamma_{\alpha,z}$ are translated into $\chi_\alpha(x)$. The χ-functions can be rewritten to JML formulas, e.g., $\chi_>(x)$ would become $x > 0$. If several variables share the same γ-constant, the corresponding equalities are added.
- Array invariants use the same rewriting of χ-functions.
- Sum invariants are translated into JML with the \sum operator. E.g., the sum invariant in Example 2 is translated to

$$i = 1 + \text{\textbackslash sum int } n; \; n >= 0 \;\&\&\; n < \text{iter}; \; b \; ? \; \text{5-n} \; : \; 2$$

If a subformula is equal to **true**, e.g. $\chi_\top(i)$, it is omitted in the JML output.

5   Fully Automatic Approach

The logic-based information flow analysis approach proposed in Sect. 3 requires that specifications necessary for information flow analysis, i.e. loop invariants and method contracts, must be supplied by the user. This is usually a tough task and requires a considerable effort. In this section we demonstrate an approach that reduces the workload of the user towards obtaining a fully automatic analysis of information flow for Java programs. The fundamental idea is that we leave the task of generating loop invariants and method contracts to the tool proposed in Sect. 4 and use these generated specifications in the information flow analysis by KEG.

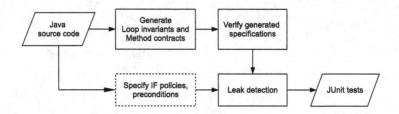

Fig. 3. Fully automatic leak detection for java programs

Figure 3 shows the combination of two tools to automatically detect information leaks in a Java program. The solid border rectangle boxes represent automatic actions performed by our tools, while the dashed border one is for manual action done by the user. If the Java program contains unbounded loops and/or recursive method calls, the specification generator is activated to generate corresponding specifications and insert them into the original source code. Generated specifications are also verified by a verification tool, here we use the theorem prover KeY. Finally, the specified program is automatically analysed w.r.t. user-defined information flow policies and other specifications (usually preconditions) using KEG to create JUnit tests helping to demonstrate discovered leaks as well as serving for regression tests.

6   E-Voting Case Study

In this section we present our case study on verifying the privacy property of an e-voting system by proving the noninterference property of a simplified, ideal Java counterpart[2].

---

[2] www.se.tu-darmstadt.de/research/projects/albia/download/e-voting-case-study/.

6.1   From Privacy to Noninterference

Our case study is a modified, extended version of the e-voting case study introduced in [20,21]. In order to prove the cryptographic privacy of the votes of honest voters, the authors constructed a cryptographic privacy game formulated in Java. In that game, the environment (the adversary) can provide two vectors $\overline{c_0}$ and $\overline{c_1}$ of choices of voters such that the two vectors yield the same result according to the counting function, otherwise the game is stopped immediately. Afterwards, the voters vote according to $\overline{c_b}$, where b is a secret bit. The adversary tries to distinguish whether the voters voted according to $\overline{c_0}$ or to $\overline{c_1}$. If they succeed, the cryptographic privacy property is broken. By defining this game, instead of proving the cryptographic privacy property of the complex e-voting system, the authors of [21] prove the noninterference property of its ideal simplified counterpart, which states that there is no information flow from secret bit b to the public result on the bulletin board. It states that if the voting machine computes the result correctly, then this result is independent of whether the voters voted according to $\overline{c_0}$ or $\overline{c_1}$.

We re-implement the simplified version of the e-voting system in [20] by a slightly more complicated version in which the system can handle an arbitrary number of candidates rather than only two. Figure 4 depicts the core of our case study program that includes two classes: Result wraps the result of the election and SimplifiedEvoting reproduces the privacy game mentioned in [21]. Class Result has one public integer array field bulletin, where bulletin[i] stores the number of votes for candidate i. Class SimplifiedEVoting has the following fields: a private logic variable secret as the secret bit, an integer variable n representing the number of candidates indexed by n consecutive integer number from 0 to $n-1$; two integer arrays votesX, votesY as two vectors of votes supplied by the adversary, where each array's element i is an integer number j (ideally $0 \leq j \leq n-1$) which mean that voter i votes for candidate j; and finally the public variable Result that can be observed by the adversary. Method privacyGame of class SimplifiedEvoting mimics the process that the result is computed using one of two vectors of votes based on the value of the secret bit. Method compute of class SimplifiedEvoting computes the result of the election using the corresponding vector of votes passed as its parameter. Line 7 is the noninterference policy claiming that there is no information flow from secret to result. To deal with this object-sensitive noninterference policy, we implement the approach introduced in [4]. We experiment using our approach on two versions of compute: one is a correct implementation, while the other is faulty.

The precondition of method privacyGame is depicted in Fig. 5, enforcing that two vectors of votes (votesX and votesY) have the same size and produce the same result before privacyGame is executed. It also makes sure that the number of candidates is greater than 1 and every single vote belongs to one of those candidates.

```
1     public class SimplifiedEVoting {
2        private boolean secret;
3        public Result result;
4        int n; //number of candidates
5        int [] votesX , votesY ;
6
7        /*! result | secret ; !*/
8
9        private Result compute(int [] votes){
10          /* implementation of compute   */
11       }
12
13       /*@requires ... @*/
14       public void privacyGame(){
15          if(secret)
16             result = compute(votesX);
17          else
18             result = compute(votesY);
19       }
20    }
21
22    public class Result {
23       public int [] bulletin;//result of votes
24       public Result(int n) {
25          if(n>0)
26             this.bulletin = new int [n];
27          else
28             this.bulletin = null;
29       }
30    }
```

Fig. 4. Simplified e-voting program

```
1  /*@requires votesX!=null && votesY != null
2     && (votesX.length == votesY.length) && (votesX.length>0) && n>=2
3     && (\forall int j; j>=0 && j<votesX.length;
4          votesX[j]>=0 && votesX[j]<n && votesY[j]>=0 && votesY[j]<n)
5     && (\forall int i; 0 <= i && i < n;
6     (\sum int j; 0 <= j && j < votesX.length; (votesX[j]==i ? 1 : 0))
7        ==
8     (\sum int j; 0 <= j && j < votesY.length; (votesY[j]==i ? 1 : 0)))
9        ;
10  @ diverges true;
11  @*/
```

Fig. 5. Precondition as JML specification of method privacyGame

6.2   Leak Detection for Correct Implementation

We first show the result of our approach for the correct implementation of method
compute as shown in Fig. 6. To check the security of the method privacyGame, it is
first symbolically executed by the KeY tool. The input file is shown in Fig. 7.

This first step symbolically executes the loop 7 times in total, opens 105 side
proofs and needs 148 s on a i5-3210M CPU with 6 GB RAM. As our system is
not optimized for speed, we suppose that it is possible to generate the invariants
in significantly less time. The output of the symbolic execution is, besides the
proof tree, a file named SimplifiedEVoting.java.mod.0, which contains the Java
file with the annotations. In Fig. 8 the result of the loop invariant generation for

```
1  private Result compute(int[] votes){
2     Result rs = new Result(n);
3     for(int i = 0; i< votes.length; i++){
4        if(votes[i]>=0 && votes[i]<n)
5           rs.bulletin[votes[i]] = rs.bulletin[votes[i]] + 1;
6     }
7     return rs;
8  }
```

Fig. 6. Correct implementation of method `compute`

```
1     \javaSource ".";
2
3     \programVariables{
4        SimplifiedEVoting2 vt;
5        int[] v;
6        Result2 r;
7     }
8
9     \problem{
10       vt != null &
11       vt.<created> = TRUE &
12       vt.<inv> &
13       vt.n >0 &
14       v != null &
15       v.<created> = TRUE &
16       wellFormed(heap) &
17       (\forall int i; (i >=0 & i <v.length -> (v[i] >= 0 & v[i] <
                 vt.n))) &
18       r = null
19       ->
20       \[{
21                    r = vt.compute(v);
22       }\](r != null)
23
24    }
```

Fig. 7. Inputfile input.key

the loop in method `compute` is depicted. The invariant is generated by calling the method `compute`, not by calling the method `privacyGame`, because the loop invariant generation is *local*, in the sense that it produces invariants valid under a given precondition. Calling `privacyGame` would produce two invariants, one for each branch, which must be combined using the splitting condition distinguishing them. This may lose precision because the splitting condition may be not fully known, thus the generating call should be to the method containing the loop.

In the next step, the file SimplifiedEVoting.java.mod.0 is renamed to SimplifiedEVoting.java and used as input for the KEG tool. KEG finished checking the program w.r.t noninterference policy in 41 s on the same system without finding any information flow leak.

6.3   Leak Detection for Faulty Implementation

Now we change the implemenation of method `compute` slightly, such that it ignores the first element in the vector of votes when calculating the result.

```
1    //@ghost int iter = 0;// AUTO_GENERATED BY KeY
2    /*@ // AUTO_GENERATED BY KeY
3          loop_invariant
4          rs.bulletin == rs.bulletin
5      && i >= 0
6      && i == (\sum int q; 0 <= q & q <iter;1 + 0)
7      && ( \forall int j_27;
8          (   0 <= j_27 & j_27 < rs.bulletin.length
9          ==>   (\sum int q_1; 0 <= q_1 & q_1 <iter; (votes[q_1] ==
                 j_27)
10                                        ? (1 + 0)
11                                        : (0))
12                == rs.bulletin[j_27]))
13     && (iter >= 0 & iter * 1 == i)
14     && i - votes.length <= 0
15     && ( \forall int j_28;
16         (j_28 < i & 0 <= j_28 ==> votes[j_28] >= 0)
17     );
18         assignable
19         rs.bulletin[*],i;
20     @*/
21
22         for(int i = 0; i< votes.length; i++){
23    //@set iter = iter + 1;// AUTO_GENERATED BY KeY
24                if(votes[i]>=0 && votes[i]<n)
25                    rs.bulletin[votes[i]] = rs.bulletin[votes[i]] +
                        1;
26         }
27         return rs;
28     }
```

Fig. 8. Annotated SimplifiedEVoting.java.mod.0

It is obviously an incorrect implementation, in that two vector of votes votesX, votesY can produce two different results even if the precondition of method privacyGame holds. The faulty implementation is given in Fig. 9.

```
1    private Result compute(int[] votes){
2       Result rs = new Result(n);
3       for(int i = 1; i< votes.length; i++){ //omit votes[0]
4          if(votes[i]>=0 && votes[i]<n)
5             rs.bulletin[votes[i]] = rs.bulletin[votes[i]] + 1;
6       }
7       return rs;
8    }
```

Fig. 9. Faulty implementation of method compute

For this method, the loop invariant generation opens 86 side proofs, executes the loop 7 times in total and needs 161 s on a i5-3210M CPU with 6 GB RAM.

The KEG tool finishes checking method privacyGame calling the faulty implementation of compute in 145 s and finds a leak. It reports that there is an implicit information flow leak caused by two different symbolic execution paths branched by the value of secret. Using precondition of method privacyGame as in Fig. 5, KEG generates input values for votesX and votesY in order to demonstrate the leak as follows:

array	element at index
	0 1 2 3 4 5 6 7 8
votesX	1 2 2 1 1 0 0 1 0
votesY	2 1 1 1 1 0 0 0 2

It is easy to see that the generated values of votesX and votesY bring the same election result by using the correct version of compute, however the results computed by the faulty method compute differ. This helps the attacker infer the value of bit secret and break the privacy property of the e-voting system.

7   Discussion

We chose the simplified e-voting system as case study for our approach for the following reasons: (i) its noninterference property has been verified using a hybrid approach [21] that is not automatic and requires the program to be modified; (ii) it is a sequential Java program having complex features of real-life object oriented programs such as reference types, arrays and object creation; and (iii) the program requires complex specifications containing comprehension sum that challenge both our specification generation tool and the KEG tool.

Comprehension expressions like sum, max and min are usually not natively supported by SMT Solver. KEG uses the SMT Solver Z3 to solve insecurity formulas. While Z3 is very powerful, it does not natively support comprehension expressions. KEG treats sum in a similar way to the approach proposed in [23], where each sum is translated into a self-contained function characterized by its axioms. The original implementation for the translation of sum (and other comprehension expressions such as max and min) binds each expression to a corresponding function that has two parameters describing the interval. For example, consider the following sum expression in JML syntax:

(\sum int i; 0 <= i && i < votes.length; votes[i])

This can be translated into a function call sum_0(0, votes.length-1), where sum_0 is characterized by the following axioms:

$$\forall x, y \in \{0, 1, .., \text{votes.length} - 1\} :$$
$$x > y \Rightarrow \text{sum\_0}(x, y) = 0 \land$$
$$x = y \Rightarrow \text{sum\_0}(x, y) = \text{votes}[x] \land$$
$$x < y \Rightarrow \text{sum\_0}(x, y) = \text{votes}[x] + \text{sum\_0}(x + 1, y)$$

This translation approach is simple but versatile and can be used for all types of comprehension expressions. The drawback of this approach is that it does not support quantification, i.e. if sum is nested in a universal expression (as shown at lines 3 - 7 in Fig. 5). To solve this problem, we tailor a new translation approach for sum if it is quantified. We extend the generated sum functions with a parameter representing the quantified variable. For example, following quantified clause in the precondition shown in Fig. 5:

```
(\forall int i; 0 <= i && i < n;
(\sum int j; 0<=j && j<votesX.length; (votesX[j]==i?1:0))
    ==
(\sum int j; 0<=j && j<votesY.length; (votesY[j]==i?1:0)))
```

can be translated into following expression:

$$\forall\, i \in \{0, 1, .., n-1\}:$$
$$\mathtt{sum\_1}(0, \mathtt{votesX.length} - 1, i) = \mathtt{sum\_2}(0, \mathtt{votesY.length} - 1, i)$$

The corresponding axioms chracterising `sum_1` and `sum_2` are also added into the insecurity formula. Although this approach allows quantifying over `sum` expressions (also other comprehensions), it is not suitable for all instances of sum and brings considerable extra workload for the SMT Solver. We do believe that there is no one-size-fits-all method translating comprehension expressions to SMT first order formulas that exists and it is necessary to optimize the translation w.r.t. each specific case.

The ability to generate invariants containing comprehension expressions (in this case sum) was crucial in this case study in order to generate a strong enough functional invariant so as to be able to prove noninterference with the KEG tool. Comprehension expressions also allow the ability to be much more precise about the value of a variable or array index term, rather than using abstraction, which is often only an over-approximation.

In general, sums and arrays interact with each other quite nicely, in that (i) programs often sum values based on the elements in an array (besides the example in this case study another simple example would be calculating the sum of all elements), but also (ii) array index terms are often sums (sometimes also expressible as an affine term, but for example a binary tree expressed in array form gets from index i to its left child node by adding $i + 1$ to the index).

Analysis of whether a comprehension expression can be used to express an invariant is quite simple in our tool, as we can see the program updates and branch conditions of all sequents resulting from symbolic execution of the loop body, thus infering sums, etc. from the actual symbolic values, rather than trying to syntactically analyse the program code.

8   Related Work

Our e-voting case study is motivated and based on the one used in [20,21]. In that paper, the authors propose a hybrid approach combining the strengths of an automatic tool (Joana [14]) and a deductive verification tool (KeY [5]) for proving noninterference property of a simple e-voting system. This approach requires programs to be extended so that the automatic tool for proving noninterference can be applied without returning any false positives. The deductive verification tool is used to prove functional properties of the e-voting program and its extended version. While enhancing the precision of the automatic tool Joana, the approach still needs a lot of user interaction in establishing and proving functional properties as program invariants.

There has been a lot of research into secure information flow. Some logic-based approaches such as [4,26] are fully precise but not fully automatic in the sense that they require from the user not only specifications for unbounded loops and recursive method calls but also non-trivial interactions with the theorem prover. On the other hand, approaches based on type systems [1,17,24,27] or those based on dependency graphs [14] are fully automatic and able to check real-life programs due to their high performance. However, these approaches share common drawbacks of over-approximation on actual information flow that lead to lack of precision and resulting false positives in many cases.

Several tools for loop invariant generation have been proposed and using abstract interpretation is among the first approaches [9]. Such tools were developed for other theorem provers, e.g. ESC/Java2 [13,18], but concentrate on checking bounds when dealing with arrays. Other approaches which are more precise concerning arrays either rely on syntactic analysis and restrictions [15] or on additional information provided together with the abstract domain [8].

9 Conclusion

We proposed a novel logic-based approach towards fully automatic information flow analysis by combining the strength of two logic-based tools. We applied it for a simplified version of an e-voting system as case study to check noninterference policy that is the counterpart of cryptographic privacy property. By the case study result, we showed that our approach is not only precise (it can detect the potential leak of an insecure program while not raising false positives for a secure program) but also automatic (it only requires user to supply expressive information flow policy and precondition describing the constraint of the initial program state). Although the case study revolves around a relatively small program, it is not a simple program and it is sufficient for exposing the strengths as well as limitations of our tools, which shows that our approach is very promising to be used for real-life programs.

For future work, we aim to extend our tools and their combination towards analysing real-life programs, which are usually large and complex. A potential solution is to use method contracts instead of simply expanding method calls, which brings compositionability, scalability and analysis re-usability. Both tools we used are adequate for this direction, in that the specification generation tool can already generate method contracts for recursive methods [28], while the KEG tool can use method contracts for leak detection. However, they need to be improved in performance as well as expanding the set of language features they support. Optimizing the specification generation towards supporting better information flow analysis is another promising direction.

Acknowledgements. We would like to thank Richard Bubel for fruitful discussions and comments.

References

1. Avvenuti, M., Bernardeschi, C., Francesco, N.D., Masci, P.: JCSI: a tool for checking secure information flow in java card applications. J. Syst. Softw. **85**(11), 2479–2493 (2012)
2. Banerjee, A., Giacobazzi, R., Mastroeni, I.: What you lose is what you leak: information leakage in declassification policies. Electron. Notes Theor. Comput. Sci. **173**, 47–66 (2007)
3. Barthe, G., D'Argenio, P.R., Rezk, T.: Secure information flow by self-composition. In: Proceedings of the 17th IEEE Workshop on Computer Security Foundations, CSFW 2004, pp. 100–114. IEEE CS(2004)
4. Beckert, B., Bruns, D., Klebanov, V., Scheben, C., Schmitt, P.H., Ulbrich, M.: Information flow in object-oriented software. In: Gupta, G., Peña, R. (eds.) LOPSTR 2013, LNCS 8901. LNCS, vol. 8901, pp. 19–37. Springer, Heidelberg (2014)
5. Beckert, B., Hähnle, R., Schmitt, P.H. (eds.): Verification of Object-Oriented Software. Lecture Notes in Computer Science, vol. 4334. Springer, Heidelberg (2007)
6. Bubel, R., Hähnle, R., Weiß, B.: Abstract interpretation of symbolic execution with explicit state updates. In: de Boer, F.S., Bonsangue, M.M., Madelaine, E. (eds.) FMCO 2008. LNCS, vol. 5751, pp. 247–277. Springer, Heidelberg (2009)
7. Cousot, P., Cousot, R.: Abstract interpretation: a unified lattice model for static analysis of programs by construction or approximation of fixpoints. In: 4th Symposium on Principles of Programming Languages (POPL), pp. 238–252. ACM (1977)
8. Cousot, P., Cousot, R., Logozzo, F.: A parametric segmentation functor for fully automatic and scalable array content analysis. SIGPLAN Not. **46**(1), 105–118 (2011)
9. Cousot, P., Halbwachs, N.: Automatic discovery of linear restraints among variables of a program. In: Proceedings of the 5th ACM SIGACT-SIGPLAN Symposium on Principles of Programming Languages, POPL 1978, pp. 84–96. ACM (1978)
10. Darvas, Á., Hähnle, R., Sands, D.: A theorem proving approach to analysis of secure information flow. In: Gorrieri, R. (ed.) Workshop on Issues in the Theory of Security. IFIP WG 1.7, SIGPLAN and GI FoMSESS. ACM (2003)
11. de Moura, L., Bjørner, N.S.: Z3: an efficient SMT solver. In: Ramakrishnan, C.R., Rehof, J. (eds.) TACAS 2008. LNCS, vol. 4963, pp. 337–340. Springer, Heidelberg (2008)
12. Do, Q., Bubel, R., Hähnle, R.: Exploit generation for information flow leaks in object oriented programs. In: Federrath, H., Gollmann, D. (eds.) ICT SystemsSecurity and Privacy Protection. IFIP Advances in Information and Communication Technology, vol. 455, pp. 401–415. Springer, Heidelberg (2015)
13. Flanagan, C., Qadeer, S.: Predicate abstraction for software verification. SIGPLAN Not. **37**(1), 191–202 (2002)
14. Graf, J., Hecker, M., Mohr, M.: Using JOANA for information flow control in java programs - a practical guide. In: Proceedings of the 6th Working Conference on Programming Languages. LNI, vol. 215, pp. 123–138. Springer, February 2013
15. Halbwachs, N., Péron, M.: Discovering properties about arrays in simple programs. SIGPLAN Not. **43**(6), 339–348 (2008)
16. Hentschel, M., Hähnle, R., Bubel, R.: Visualizing unbounded symbolic execution. In: Seidl, M., Tillmann, N. (eds.) TAP 2014. LNCS, vol. 8570, pp. 82–98. Springer, Heidelberg (2014)

17. Hunt, S., Sands, D.: On flow-sensitive security types. In: ACM SIGPLAN Notices, vol. 41, pp. 79–90. ACM (2006)
18. Janota, M.: Assertion-based loop invariant generation. In: Proceedings of the 1st International Workshop on Invariant Generation (WING 07), Wing 2004 (2007)
19. King, J.C.: Symbolic execution and program testing. Commun. ACM **19**(7), 385–394 (1976)
20. Küsters, R., Truderung, T., Beckert, B., Bruns, D., Graf, J., Scheben, C.: A hybrid approach for proving noninterference and applications to the cryptographic verification of java programs. In: Grande Region Security and Reliability Day 2013, Extended Abstract (2013)
21. Küsters, R., Truderung, T., Beckert, B., Bruns, D., Kirsten, M., Mohr, M.: A hybrid approach for proving noninterference of java programs. In: Fournet, C., Hicks, M. (eds.) 28th IEEE Computer Security Foundations Symposium (2015)
22. Leavens, G.T., Baker, A.L., Ruby, C.: JML: a java modeling language. In: Formal Underpinnings of Java Workshop (at OOPSLA 1998), pp. 404–420 (1998)
23. Leino, K.R.M., Monahan, R.: Reasoning about comprehensions with first-order SMT solvers. In: Proceedings of the 2009 ACM Symposium on Applied Computing, SAC 2009, pp. 615–622. ACM, New York (2009)
24. Myers, A.C.: JFlow: practical mostly-static information flow control. In: Proceedings of 26th ACM Symposium on Principles of Programming Languages, pp. 228–241 (1999)
25. Sabelfeld, A., Myers, A.C.: A model for delimited information release. In: Futatsugi, K., Mizoguchi, F., Yonezaki, N. (eds.) Software Security - Theories and Systems. Lecture Notes in Computer Science, vol. 3233, pp. 174–191. Springer, Heidelberg (2004)
26. Scheben, C., Schmitt, P.H.: Verification of information flow properties of JAVA programs without approximations. In: Beckert, B., Damiani, F., Gurov, D. (eds.) FoVeOOS 2011. LNCS, vol. 7421, pp. 232–249. Springer, Heidelberg (2012)
27. Volpano, D., Irvine, C., Smith, G.: A sound type system for secure flow analysis. J. Comput. Secur. **4**(2), 167–187 (1996)
28. Wasser, N.: Generating specifications for recursive methods by abstracting program states. In: Li, X., Liu, Z., Yi, W. (eds.) Dependable Software Engineering: Theories, Tools, and Applications. Lecture Notes in Computer Science, vol. 9409, pp. 243–257. Springer, Heidelberg (2015)
29. Wasser, N., Bubel, R.: A theorem prover backed approach to array abstraction. Technical. report, Department of Computer Science, Technische Universität Darmstadt, Germany , presented at the Vienna Summer of Logic 2014 5th International Workshop on Invariant Generation (2014)
30. Wasser, N., Bubel, R., Hähnle, R.: Array abstraction with symbolic pivots. Technical report, Department of Computer Science, Technische Universität Darmstadt, Germany, August 2015

Towards a Comprehensive Model of Isolation for Mitigating Illicit Channels

Kevin Falzon[1(✉)] and Eric Bodden[2]

[1] Technische Universität Darmstadt, Darmstadt, Germany
kevin.falzon@ec-spride.de
[2] Universität Paderborn and Fraunhofer IEM, Paderborn, Germany
eric.bodden@uni-paderborn.de

Abstract. The increased sharing of computational resources elevates the risk of side channels and covert channels, where an entity's security is affected by the entities with which it is co-located. This introduces a strong demand for mechanisms that can effectively isolate individual computations. Such mechanisms should be efficient, allowing resource utilisation to be maximised despite isolation.

In this work, we develop a model for uniformly describing isolation, co-location and containment relationships between entities at multiple levels of a computer's architecture and at different granularities. In particular, we examine the formulation of constraints on co-location and placement using partial specifications, as well as the cost of maintaining isolation guarantees on dynamic systems. We apply the model to a number of established attacks and mitigations.

1   Introduction

Side and *covert channels* (collectively, *illicit channels*) are fundamentally the result of imperfect isolation, where information regarding an entity's internal and potentially secret state leaks to an observer through an unregulated interface.

The position of two entities relative to each other determines the type of illicit channel that can be formed between them. For example, two processes sharing a physical core may form a channel over the memory subsystem, whereas processes on separate machines may form a network-based illicit channel. This leads to the notion of *co-location*, where entities are said to be co-located within a medium if they can leverage it to form illicit channels.

Co-location is often considered at the virtual-machine level in the context of cloud computing, yet the notion of co-location as a precursor to illicit channels extends to multiple levels of a computer's architecture. Isolation at the virtualisation level is limited in that it is *coarse-grained*, whereas one often only has to isolate parts of a virtual machine. In addition, the mechanisms used to build

---

This work was supported by the German Federal Ministry of Education and Research (BMBF) within EC SPRIDE. At the time this research was conducted, Eric Bodden was at Fraunhofer SIT and Technische Universität Darmstadt.

F. Piessens and L. Viganò (Eds.): POST 2016, LNCS 9635, pp. 116–138, 2016.
DOI: 10.1007/978-3-662-49635-0_7

illicit channels can operate at a fine granularity, and their effects may not be correctly or precisely encompassed by a coarse-grained model.

In this work, we develop a holistic model of locality that considers multiple levels of an architecture at varying granularities. This offers numerous advantages over a single-level model. Finer granularity can lead to an improvement in hardware utilisation, as fewer resources are committed to providing isolation guarantees. The ability to compare the cost of maintaining different isolation levels also allows resource allocation to be optimised dynamically, further improving utilisation. Apart from being quantifiable, the cost of maintaining isolations must be attributable, particularly in the case of cloud computing.

As scheduling and placement play a central role in co-location, the locality model must also be able to describe both temporal as well as spatial aspects of a system. Another aspect addressed by the model is the notion of *partial specification*, where entities within a system (such as tenants on a cloud) only have a partial view of their environment, and must be able to delegate their isolation requirements to external entities.

In summary, this work:

- reconciles different aspects of isolation and co-location into a unified model that can describe both temporal and spatial properties of a system at multiple architectural levels,
- examines the different levels and confinement types, and their use in defining partial specifications and isolation requirements,
- provides an operational model for migration and cost estimation, allowing different system configurations and real-world architectures to be compared and optimised, and
- demonstrates various applications of the model in analysing illicit channels.

2   Confinements

A modern computer architecture consists of a multitude of isolated environments, which are themselves contained within isolations, forming a hierarchy. The following section introduces the notions of confinement and containment.

2.1   Isolation and Containment

A computer architecture comprises a number of logical and physical *confinements*. For example, processes execute within the confines of a CPU. Confinements must themselves exist within an environment, which leads to a notion of hierarchical *containment*. Extending the previous example, multiple CPUs may be confined by a single machine, which can itself form part of a network.

Definition 1 (Confinement). *A* confinement *(equivalently,* isolation *or* locality*) denotes a boundary within which a number of sub-confinements exist. A confinement of type Γ with a name N and capability set C containing a set of sub-confinements* SB *is denoted as* $\Gamma{:}N(C)$ [SB]*.*

A confinement's name is typically dictated by its type, and serves to identify it from amongst its siblings. Capabilities are used to limit how confinements can interact and modify each other, as will be seen in Sect. 3. The capability set can be omitted when it is empty.

Illicit channels exploit the fact that certain confinements are imperfect, and do not keep their sub-confinements completely isolated from each other. Thus, confinements can be seen as introducing *locality*, where confinements that should theoretically be disjoint are connected through a channel exploiting some characteristic of their parent confinement.

Definition 2 (Containment and Co-Location). *A confinement* X *is contained within a confinement* Γ:$D(C)$ [SB] *if* $X \in SB$. *This is denoted as* $X \in D$. X *is said to be* co-located *with* Y *through* D, *written as* $X \overset{D}{\leftrightarrow} Y$, *if* $X \in D \wedge Y \in D$.

The state leaked within a confinement can potentially be observed both by its direct sub-confinements as well as their members. This gives rise to the notion of *nested containment*, where $X \in^+ D \overset{\text{def}}{=} X \in D \vee \exists D' \in D. X \in^+ D'$ and *nested co-location*, where $X \overset{D}{\Leftrightarrow} Y \overset{\text{def}}{=} X \in^+ D \wedge Y \in^+ D$.

Example 1 (Parallel Execution). Consider a CPU package with two cores (**C**) sharing an **L3** cache, each of which employs *simultaneous multithreading* (SMT) to expose two hardware threads sharing an **L1** and **L2** cache. This can be modelled as:

$$\text{CPU} \overset{\text{def}}{=} \textbf{L3}{:}0\,[\textbf{L2}{:}0\,[\textbf{L1}{:}0\,[\textbf{C}{:}0\,[]\,,\textbf{C}{:}1\,[]]]\,,\textbf{L2}{:}1\,[\textbf{L1}{:}0\,[\textbf{C}{:}2\,[]\,,\textbf{C}{:}3\,[]]]]$$

Two processes X and Y can be susceptible to an attack via **L1** cache [28] if $\exists \textbf{L1}{:}L \in^+ \text{CPU}. X \overset{L}{\Leftrightarrow} Y$, or via **L3** cache [36] if $\exists \textbf{L3}{:}L \in^+ \text{CPU}. X \overset{L}{\Leftrightarrow} Y$. The latter will hold whenever the processes execute simultaneously.   □

Note that proximity, or the depth at which two processes are co-located within the model, does not necessarily correlate with an illicit channel's bandwidth. That is, while processes that are closer to each other can generally communicate at a faster rate or perform more events per unit time than others that are further away (for example, processes sharing a cache interact with their shared resource at a higher frequency than if they were co-located through a network), not every interaction carries information relevant to the channel.

2.2 Types of Isolation

Illicit channels occur either at the software or hardware level [24], the former being a product of the algorithms used, while the latter emerge from the characteristics of a system's hardware. When considering hardware-based channels, an additional distinction between *soft* and *hard isolation* can be made [32]. Hard isolation implies that co-locations are broken by using distinct physical hardware locations, whereas soft isolation simulates distinct hardware locations by

Table 1. Types of soft and hard isolation, and their typical containments.

Hard isolation			Soft isolation		
Type	Description	Can contain	Type	Description	Can contain
Net	Network	**Net, M**	**VM**	Virtual machine	**VC, OS**
M	Machine	**L3, OS**	**VC**	Virtual CPU	**VC, P_E, Con, VM**
L3	L3 Cache	**L2**	**Con**	Container	**P**
L2	L2 Cache	**L1**	**P_E**	Control group	**Con, P**
L1	L1 Cache	**C**	**P**	Process	–
C	Physical core	**VC, P_E, Con, VM**	**OS**	Operating Sys	**P_E, Con, VM**

arbitrating access to resources, hiding their characteristics. Soft isolation is guaranteed with respect to a defined attribute. For example, a timing channel can be closed by masking the timing characteristics of caches [28], yet such a mitigation may not effectively address other potential illicit cache-level channels. Hard isolation is comprehensive, but is limited by capacity [27].

Table 1 lists the soft and hard isolation types with which this work is primarily concerned. Other granularities and isolation types can also be modelled. For example, as will be seen in Sect. 5.2, monolithic caches can be decomposed into cache sets. The confinement model places no restrictions on the types of subconfinements, which allows the description of partial specifications and incomplete system hierarchies. In practice, it follows that certain containment patterns do not occur, and that the presence of certain confinements imply the existence of a parent of a specific type. For example, a virtual CPU (**VC**) confinement would imply the existence of a **VM** to which it belongs.

Hard isolations are passive elements of a system. Conversely, certain soft isolations must be upheld through an active and ongoing process, or through a change in policy. For example, early implementations of x86 virtualisation incurred a constant overhead through dynamic binary rewriting [3], which has nowadays been significantly reduced via hardware-assisted virtualisation. Similarly, software-based approaches to securing AES added overheads [28] that were eliminated through their implementation as a special hardware-level confinement [23].

3 Managing Isolations

The core operations for modifying a containment hierarchy are confinement *creation*, *destruction* and *migration*. The latter is modelled as moving an isolation from one containment to another. The implementation of these operations varies based on the isolations involved, and may require a series of compound actions that incur multiple changes at different parts of the hierarchy. Changes to the hierarchy are effected by *agent* processes.

Definition 3 (Agent). *An agent is a confinement* $A{:}N(C^{Ag})_{\overrightarrow{T}}[Q]$, *where* **A** *denotes an agent type, N is the agent's name,* C^{Ag} *is its capability set, T is a set of confinements visible to the agent,* $\rightarrow \ \subseteq T \times T$ *is a mapping defining legal containments, and* Q *is a queue of idle confinements.*

Agents represent scheduling components that manage confinements. For example, an operating system's process scheduler can be modelled as an agent confinement that regulates movements between an idle queue and core confinements. Agents can be embedded at any part of the hierarchy. For example, a network domain controller can be modelled as an agent embedded within the network's hardware layer. Agents can move (or *migrate*) confinements using *local* and *global* scheduling operations, described in the following sections.

3.1 Local Scheduling

Local scheduling moves a confinement between an agent's idle queue and a target confinement via the *local-schedule* (L-Sc) and *local-deschedule* (L-Ds) rules, the general forms of which are defined in Fig. 1, where $\mathsf{cap}(\Gamma{:}N(C)\,[S_B]) \rightarrow C$, and $A \Cap B \overset{\text{def}}{=} A \cap B \neq \emptyset$. For a local-schedule operation, the agent process Ag issues a migration operation $(X \curvearrowright N)$ that moves X from its idle queue to the target locality N, provided that the allocation is permitted (as defined by $\rightarrow$), and that the agent holds the appropriate capabilities. Descheduling is similar, but returns the locality from a target confinement to the agent's idle queue.

An agent must share a capability with the target confinement, as well as the confinement being moved. Capability checking is modelled as an abstract operation (an intersection between capability sets), as the concrete implementation varies by confinement. For example, destroying a process requires the agent to have the process owner's user rights. Similarly, virtual machines can only be modified by agents holding the appropriate rights, which can be granted through a number of authorisation mechanisms, such as user groups, passwords, or *polkit* [2] policies.

Mutability is not modelled as an intrinsic property of a confinement, rather it is determined by the availability of its capability to agents. While hardware confinements such as caches are not typically disabled at runtime, an agent may

$$\text{L-Sc} \ \frac{\Gamma{:}N(C)\,[S_B] \qquad Ag \equiv X \curvearrowright N.Ag' \qquad C^{Ag} \Cap C \qquad C^{Ag} \Cap \mathsf{cap}(X) \qquad (X,N) \in \rightarrow}{A{:}Ag'(C^{Ag})_{\overrightarrow{T}}[Q] \qquad \Gamma{:}N(C)\,[S_B \cup \{X\}]} \ \ \scriptstyle A{:}Ag(C^{Ag})_{\overrightarrow{T}}[Q \cup \{X\}]$$

$$\text{L-Ds} \ \frac{\Gamma{:}N(C)\,[S_B \cup \{X\}] \qquad Ag \equiv X \curvearrowright Ag.Ag' \qquad C^{Ag} \Cap C \qquad C^{Ag} \Cap \mathsf{cap}(X)}{A{:}Ag'(C^{Ag})_{\overrightarrow{T}}[Q \cup \{X\}] \qquad \Gamma{:}N(C)\,[S_B]} \ \ \scriptstyle A{:}Ag(C^{Ag})_{\overrightarrow{T}}[Q]$$

Fig. 1. Local migration rules.

want to delete their representation from the model if it is certain that the threat of a channel through that confinement has been neutralised.

Example 2 (Round Robin Scheduler). Consider the CPU hierarchy defined in Example 1. An agent implementing a simple round-robin scheduler with a shared run queue can be defined as $\mathbf{A}{:}\mathrm{rr}(\mathrm{C}^{\mathrm{Ag}})_{\mathrm{T}}^{\rightarrow}[\mathrm{Q}]$, where Q contains an ordered list of processes, and $\rightarrow$ defines the allowed mapping of processes to physical cores. The default behaviour is to map all processes to all available cores, giving $\rightarrow \overset{\text{def}}{=} \{(\mathrm{X},\mathrm{Y}) \mid \mathrm{X} \in \mathrm{Q}, \mathrm{Y} = \mathbf{C}{:}\mathrm{N}(\mathrm{C})[\mathrm{SB}], \mathrm{Y} \in^{+} \mathrm{CPU}\}$. Given that $\uparrow(\mathrm{X}) \overset{\text{def}}{=} \{\mathrm{Y} \mid (\mathrm{X},\mathrm{Y}) \in \rightarrow\}$, the scheduler can be defined as a CSP-like process as follows:

$$\mathrm{RR}_{\mathrm{Q}}([\mathrm{P} \mid \mathrm{Ps}], \mathrm{C}_{\mathrm{A}}, \mathrm{C}_{\mathrm{F}}) \equiv \overset{\mathbf{C}{:}\mathrm{X} \in \uparrow(\mathrm{P}) \cap \mathrm{C}_{\mathrm{F}}}{\sqcap} \mathrm{P} \curvearrowright \mathrm{X}.\mathrm{RR}_{\mathrm{Q}}(\mathrm{Ps}, \mathrm{C}_{\mathrm{A}}, \mathrm{C}_{\mathrm{F}} \setminus \{\mathrm{X}\}) \sqcap$$
$$\overset{\mathrm{P}{:}\mathrm{P'} \in \mathbf{C}{:}\mathrm{Y} \in \mathrm{C}_{\mathrm{A}}}{\sqcap} \mathrm{P'} \curvearrowright \mathrm{rr}.\mathrm{RR}_{\mathrm{Q}}(\mathrm{Ps} \mid [\mathrm{P'}], \mathrm{C}_{\mathrm{A}}, \mathrm{C}_{\mathrm{F}} \cup \{\mathrm{Y}\})$$

where C_{A} is the set of all cores being managed by the scheduler, $[\mathrm{P} \mid \mathrm{Ps}]$ is an ordered list of processes with P as its head and Ps as its tail, and C_{F} is the set of idle cores. The process would thus be initialised as $\mathrm{RR}_{\mathrm{Q}}(\mathrm{Q}, \mathrm{Cs}, \mathrm{Cs})$, where $\mathrm{Cs} = \{\mathrm{X} \mid \mathbf{C}{:}\mathrm{X} \in^{+} \mathrm{CPU}\}$.

Next, consider the scenario where a security-sensitive process S is added to Q. If the process is susceptible to a cache-level synchronous attack [28], then one must avoid co-locating S with other processes during its execution. As formulated, the scheduler will execute processes in the order specified by the idle queue, but processes can be descheduled pre-emptively at will, meaning that every other process can potentially execute in parallel with S. Forcing processes to execute for an equal and fixed time-slice will cause S to potentially be co-scheduled with the $|\mathrm{Cs}| - 1$ processes that appear before and after it in the idle queue. Finally, changing $\rightarrow$ to ensure that S always executes by itself will prevent spatial co-location, at the cost of underutilised hardware. As a compromise, $\rightarrow$ can be varied dynamically, with the number of processes that can share cores growing proportionately to the time elapsed since the last scheduling of S. □

Configurations. Reasoning about temporal locality requires the ability to describe how a model evolves from one *configuration* to the next, where a configuration is defined as a set of confinements. The evolution of a configuration is determined by the agents it contains. The presence of multiple agent and varying scheduling policies mean that, in general, there is more than one legal next configuration. This leads to the notion of a $\mathtt{next}(\mathcal{C})$ function, which returns the set of possible configurations that can be reached from a configuration $\mathcal{C}$ through a single application of a local schedule or deschedule operation (Fig. 1). This is extended to the iterated next configuration function $\mathtt{next}^{n}(\mathcal{C})$, which returns the set of configurations reachable from $\mathcal{C}$ in n steps, defined as follows:

$$\mathtt{next}^{0}(\mathcal{C}) \overset{\text{def}}{=} \{\mathcal{C}\}$$
$$\mathtt{next}^{n}(\mathcal{C}) \overset{\text{def}}{=} \{\mathtt{next}^{n-1}(\mathcal{C'}) \mid \mathcal{C'} \in \mathtt{next}(\mathcal{C})\}$$

Finally, the configuration combination operator $\text{next}^n_{\cup}(\mathcal{C})$ is defined as:

$$\text{next}^n_{\cup}(\mathcal{C}) \overset{\text{def}}{=} \left\{ \Gamma{:}\text{N}(\text{C})\,[\text{SB}] \mid \Gamma{:}\text{N}(\text{C})\,[\text{SB}'] \in^+ \text{CFS} \right\}$$

$$\text{where } \text{SB} \overset{\text{def}}{=} \bigcup \left\{ \text{SB}'' \mid \Gamma{:}\text{N}(\text{C})\,[\text{SB}''] \in^+ \text{CFS} \right\}$$

$$\text{and } \text{CFS} \overset{\text{def}}{=} \bigcup_{0 \leq i \leq n} \bigcup \text{next}^i(\mathcal{C})$$

This effectively performs a union of every possible configuration reachable within n local scheduling operations, including intermediate configurations. The result is a graph that shows every containment combination attainable in a set sequence of steps. This can be used to represent a system's temporal behaviour as a static spatial graph. A related graph can be achieved by combining each agent's containment mapping, giving a graph of potential containments, yet this would over-approximate containments, as a scheduling policy may opt to only use a subset of mappings available to it. To simplify the operation, it is assumed that confinements can be uniquely identified by their name. Otherwise, an additional preprocessing step can be introduced.

Example 3 (Round Robin Scheduler, revisited). In Example 2, co-location with a security-sensitive process S was only considered with respect to a single moment in time, yet an access-based cache-level side channel's effects persist beyond a process' execution [28] until the security-sensitive memory blocks have been flushed. Thus, simply disabling co-scheduling during S's execution would not be sufficient to break the channel reliably.

The duration of the residual effects of caches is independent of real time, and is determined by cache evictions. For the pre-emptive round robin scheduler described earlier, the position of S in the idle queue relative to an attacker process will generally affect the illicit channel's quality, as the probability that S's sensitive cache blocks become clobbered increases with the number of processes that execute in the interim. If cache eviction patterns and process quanta are irregular, or if a fully pre-emptive scheduling policy is used, then each core in $\text{next}^\infty_{\cup}(\{\text{CPU}\})$ will contain Q.

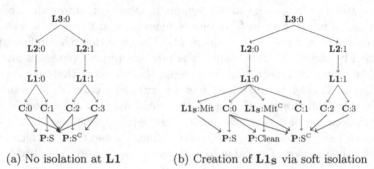

(a) No isolation at **L1**   (b) Creation of **L1$_\text{S}$** via soft isolation

Fig. 2. Cache-level co-location and mitigation via soft isolation, with arrows denoting containment.

Residual effects can be explicitly removed through a *cache-cleaning process* [37] that invalidates cache blocks, masking their timing variations. The process (henceforth referred to as CLEAN) must execute after each de-scheduling of S. Any process using the same cache that executes concurrently with S can potentially infer the timing state up to the point of CLEAN's completion. Thus, one must place an additional restriction on concurrent execution. If these two conditions can be guaranteed as invariants, then the cache has effectively been partitioned into two sub-confinements of type $\mathbf{L1_S}$ (a soft-isolated $\mathbf{L1}$), transforming the hierarchy described in Fig. 2a to that illustrated by Fig. 2b (for simplicity, S is pinned to $\mathbf{C}$:0). The partitioning serves to isolate the process S from the other processes S^C (the latter being the complement of S). Note that the processes remain co-located within $\mathbf{L1}$:0, as they are still ultimately sharing hardware locality. If the soft isolation is deemed perfect, then the $\mathbf{L1}$ confinement can be destroyed. Removing CLEAN would lead to the partitions being destroyed, and the $\mathbf{L1}$:0 confinement being recreated.   □

3.2   Global Scheduling

Local scheduling limits an agent in its procurement of isolation, as it can only make use of confinements under its direct control. An agent can be supported by additional agents external to its scope in two ways. First, an external agent can provide isolation guarantees on the parents of confinements that are being managed by an agent. For example, if an agent running within a virtual machine requires a hard isolation guarantee that a process executes alone on a core, then it must query an agent in the underlying hypervisor's scope to ensure that the $\mathbf{VC}$ confinement is placed in a dedicated $\mathbf{C}$ confinement. Secondly, an external agent serves to extend the pool of available confinements, allowing confinements to be *migrated* to a different scope. Building on the previous example, the hypervisor agent can migrate $\mathbf{VC}$ confinements amongst cores until an isolated core is provisioned. If the agent finds that all of its resources are committed, it can query additional external agents for isolations on different machines.

Migrating from one agent's scope to the next leads to the notion of *global* scheduling. Broadly, global scheduling involves two steps, namely (a) identifying a target agent which can procure the required level of isolation, and (b) migrating the confinements required to achieve isolation. The following section details how these tasks are performed.

Scopes and Renaming. In general, an agent will only have a partial view of a system. Consider the containment hierarchy illustrated in Fig. 3, which represents a minimal model $\text{next}_\circlearrowleft^\infty(\{\texttt{Machine}\})$ of a two-core compute node over which two tenant virtual machines are executing. In this model, each $\mathbf{VM}$ has an agent TA0 and TA1 running within it, whereas the infrastructure provider has an agent HYP running on the base system. The virtualisation confinement prevents a tenant's agents from enumerating the parent's confinements through standard operating-system interfaces. In addition, even if the details of the parent's confinements can somehow be inferred (for instance, through illicit channels), the tenant's agents would not have the necessary capabilities to alter them. For instance, mere knowledge of the existence of additional co-located tenants would not automatically grant a tenant's agent control over them.

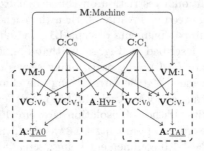

Fig. 3. Partial model showing agent scopes and boundaries.

While a tenant agent may be unaware of its parent environment's confinements, the converse does not hold. Containment relationships crossing a boundary still require that the sub-confinement be exposed to its parent. For example, while tenants in Fig. 3 might not be aware of the number of physical cores on the machine, the hypervisor must have a handle to the tenants' **VC** structures in order to manage their core pinnings[1].

The agent's position within a hierarchy also determines its view of a confinement. For example, **VC** confinements managed by HYP are seen as **C**s by processes within the tenants' **VM**s. Thus, isolation requests across scopes must be accompanied by a mechanism to rename confinements. Confinement renaming is not always straightforward, such as in the case of processes, which have a significant amount of state dispersed within their parent **OS** confinement that has to be translated on migration. For instance, a process' PID may have to be changed on migrating to a new **OS** environment [1], which would alter its internal system view. A common workaround is to employ *namespace* mechanisms, commonly in conjunction with containers [2], to encapsulate structures such as PIDs and network interfaces and separate them from the common namespace of the base **OS**. This ensures that a migrated process' structures remain internally consistent.

Isolation Constraints. A consequence of agent scoping is that changes to external confinements need to be delegated to an agent. In addition, changes cannot refer to specific external confinements, both due to scoping and security reasons.

---

[1] *Introspection* [19] can be used to characterise sub-confinements of a **VM**.

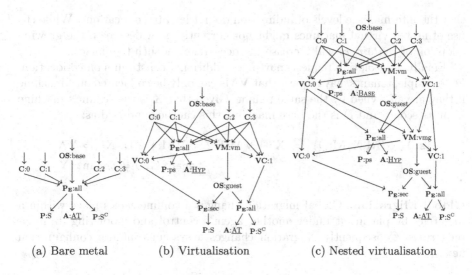

(a) Bare metal   (b) Virtualisation   (c) Nested virtualisation

Fig. 4. Environment nesting and indirection.

Consider a simple isolation condition `isolp()`, which checks whether a process exists by itself in a **C** environment, defined as follows:

$$\texttt{isolp}(\text{P:X}, \text{C:D}) \overset{\text{def}}{=} \neg \exists \text{P:Y} \in^{+} \text{D. X} \neq \text{Y}$$

The evaluation of `isolp()` varies based on the underlying system assumptions. Figure 4a illustrates a partial $\texttt{next}_{\cup}^{\infty}()$ graph of the CPU hierarchy from the perspective of an agent running within a virtualised environment (or equivalently, a non-virtualised, bare-metal environment). In this case, for D quantified over all visible confinements, $\texttt{isolp}(S, D)$ will fail (return false) due to processes sharing a process control group ALL. To comply with the isolation requirement, processes must be partitioned into two process groups contained in disjoint sets of cores.

Subsequently adding a virtualisation layer produces the containment tree shown in Fig. 4b. If multiple **VMs** execute in parallel, then the `isolp()` predicate may fail. Thus, the hypervisor agent Hyp must be queried to ensure that cores are allocated exclusively to the **VC** containing S. Given that $X \mapsto X'$ renames a confinement X into a locally-scoped confinement X', a second isolation condition $\texttt{isol}_{VC}()$ is defined and sent to HYP, where:

$$\texttt{isol}_{VC}(\text{C:X}, \text{C:D}) \overset{\text{def}}{=} X \mapsto \text{VC:X'} \wedge \neg \exists \text{VC:Y} \in \text{D. X'} \neq Y \wedge X' \overset{D}{\nleftrightarrow} Y$$

In this case, D is a free variable which must be bound by HYP. As described in the previous section, the **C** confinement must be renamed to a structure visible to HYP, namely X' . As virtualisation and containments can potentially be nested to an arbitrary depth (Fig. 4c), the $\texttt{isol}_{VC}()$ isolation request must be pushed upwards in the hierarchy, until the base confinement is reached. This ensures that the intermediate levels of indirection do not lead to co-locations. While the use of nested virtual machines might not currently be widespread, the growing adoption of *containers* will increase the occurrence of such topologies.

Finally, an isolation request may place additional constraints on co-location. For example, tenants may request that **VMs** can only be co-located on a machine if they are all owned by the same tenant. Given that X is the tenant's machine from its scope, and D is the base machine, this can be expressed as:

$$\texttt{isol}_{\mathbf{VM}}(\mathbf{M{:}X}, \mathbf{M{:}D}) \overset{\text{def}}{=} X \mapsto \mathbf{VM{:}X'} \wedge \neg \exists \mathbf{VM{:}Y} \in D.\ X' \overset{D}{\Leftrightarrow} Y \wedge$$
$$\texttt{tenant}(X') \neq \texttt{tenant}(Y)$$

Global Migration. Global migration changes a confinement's place within a hierarchy by placing it under another agent's control and modifying its mapping rules. Consequently, migration changes a system's infinite configuration $\texttt{next}_{\circlearrowleft}^{\infty}()$.

$$\text{G-Sc} \frac{\begin{array}{c} \mathbf{A{:}Src}(\mathbf{C}^{\text{Src}})_{\text{TS}}^{\rightarrow \text{Src}}\,[Q_{\text{Src}} \cup \{X\}] \qquad \mathbf{A{:}Dst}(\mathbf{C}^{\text{Dst}})_{\text{TD}}^{\rightarrow \text{Dst}}\,[Q_{\text{Dst}}] \\ \text{Dst} \in \text{TS} \qquad \text{Src} \equiv X \overset{\texttt{isol}()}{\curvearrowright} \text{Dst.Src'} \qquad D \in^{+} \{D' \mid D' \in \text{TD}\} \\ \mathbf{C}^{\text{Src}} \cap \mathbf{C}^{\text{Dst}} \qquad \mathbf{C}^{\text{Src}} \cap \texttt{cap}(X) \qquad \mathbf{C}^{\text{Dst}} \cap \texttt{cap}(D) \qquad \texttt{isol}(X, D) \end{array}}{\begin{array}{c} \mathbf{A{:}Src'}(\mathbf{C}^{\text{Src}})_{\text{TS} \setminus \{X\}}^{\rightarrow \text{Src'}}\,[Q_{\text{Src}}] \qquad \rightarrow_{\text{Src'}} \equiv \rightarrow_{\text{Src}} \setminus \{(X, Y) \mid (X, Y) \in \rightarrow_{\text{Src}}\} \\ \mathbf{A{:}Dst}(\mathbf{C}^{\text{Dst}})_{\text{TD} \cup \{X\}}^{\rightarrow \text{Dst'}}\,[Q_{\text{Dst}} \cup \{X\}] \qquad \rightarrow_{\text{Dst'}} \equiv \rightarrow_{\text{Dst}} \cup \{(X, D)\} \end{array}}$$

Fig. 5. Global migration rule.

Figure 5 defines the general rule for migrating a confinement X globally. The source agent Src initiates a migration request to a destination agent Dst with an isolation criterion $\texttt{isol}()$, which Dst attempts to match against its known and controllable confinements. Following the migration, each agent updates its containment mapping rules, with Src removing the associated mappings, and Dst adding a rule for X's allowed containments. The source and destination agents can be the same, allowing confinements to be created, destroyed, or simply remapped. The rule can be modified so that X is assigned multiple parent confinements at its destination. This allows a confinement to maintain the same number of allocated resources across migrations.

A target agent must be within the source agent's scope. Logics such as the *cloud calculus* [25] make use of a $\texttt{parent}()$ operator, which returns a handle to a confinement's parent. Agent discovery varies depending on the confinement level being considered, but it generally involves mapping an agent's identifier to its actual address. Discovery mechanisms include broadcasts, distributed keystores and centralised repositories. Each method has its own drawbacks in query time and consistency. Depending on the frequency of agent discovery operations and actual migrations, one may also consider propagating notifications of topology changes down a hierarchy following a migration, with lower-level agents subscribing to their parent agents and receiving notifications whenever their scopes have been altered.

4   Cost Functions and Metrics

Different configurations vary in the degree of isolation that they offer and the cost required to maintain them. The ability to quantify these factors is essential to the process of provisioning isolation, as it allows configurations to be compared, and enables allocations to be optimised. When comparing system hierarchies containing long-lived processes, one must consider the cost of maintaining a configuration over time, rather than simply comparing a system's instantaneous configuration. Thus, metrics and costs should be evaluated over the $\text{next}_\circlearrowleft^\infty()$ of a given hierarchy.

4.1   Metrics

Several metrics and notions of cost can be defined, including, but not limited to:

Utilisation measures the aggregate usage of a system's capacity. Certain confinements can only contain a number of sub-confinements before the system's overall performance begins to drop. For example, consider the scenario of a process scheduler allocating processes to cores evenly. Given that load(Y) returns the average CPU utilisation of a process Y expressed as a fraction, one can measure CPU utilisation for a hierarchy $\mathcal{C}$ as a dimensionless unit as follows:

$$\text{util}(\mathcal{C}) = \sum_{C:X\,\in^+\,\mathcal{C}} \min\left(\sum_{P:Y\in X} \frac{\text{load}(Y)}{|\{D\mid C:D\in^+\mathcal{C}\wedge Y\in D\}|}\,,\, 1.0\right)$$

$$\approx \sum_{C:X\,\in^+\,\mathcal{C}} \min\left(k\sum_{P:Y\in X} |\!\uparrow\!(Y)|^{-1}\,,\, 1.0\right)$$

The second formula is an approximation that can be computed statically given an average processor usage k and the **P**-to-**C** mapping defined by an agent's $\rightarrow$ structure ($\uparrow()$ is defined in Example 2). The min function caps each **C**'s usage value.

Capacity is the number of confinements of a given type in a configuration, while **total capacity** is the total number of confinements in the hierarchy.

Consolidation factor is defined as **capacity/utilisation**, and represents the ratio between the system's utilisation and the number of confinements of a given type within a hierarchy.

Pairwise co-locations counts the total number of pairs of co-located confinements in a given hierarchy, and is defined as:

$$\text{pairs}(\mathcal{C}) = \frac{1}{2}\left|\left\{\langle X,D,Y\rangle \mid X,Y,D\in^+\mathcal{C}, X\neq Y, X\overset{D}{\leftrightarrow}Y\right\}\right|$$

Containment hierarchies can be topologically sorted, and metrics can be computed by performing a breadth-first search and evaluating each sub-graph, provided that costs are compositional. The evaluation of metrics is complicated by agents' partial system specifications. For example, a tenant can compute pairs() within its own **VM**, yet this will only serve as a lower-bound, and would have to be combined with additional information from the parent confinement.

In a cloud scenario, tenants and the cloud provider may attempt to optimise their configurations with respect to different metrics. For example, a tenant will want to compromise between pairwise co-locations and total capacity. Conversely, while a cloud provider will attempt to maximise consolidation so as to maintain a smaller deployment, it has a lower incentive to minimise a tenant's total capacity if it bills its clients on the basis of committed resources.

Example 4 (Comparing architectures). A system's containments can vary across vendors. To illustrate, we examine two different CPUs, namely an Intel i7-4790 (INTEL) with 8 hardware threads using SMT, and a hex-core AMD Phenom II X6 (AMD). Apart from cache exclusivity, the architectures vary in that the former has two hardware threads to each **L1** containment, whereas the latter has per-core **L1** and **L2** caches. This results in the following models:

$$\text{INTEL} \stackrel{\text{def}}{=} \textbf{L3}{:}0\,[\{\textbf{L2}{:}\text{i}\,[\textbf{L1}{:}\text{i}\,[\textbf{C}{:}\text{i}\,[]\,,\textbf{C}{:}\text{i}{+}4\,[]]]\mid 0 \leq i \leq 3\}]$$

$$\text{AMD} \stackrel{\text{def}}{=} \textbf{L3}{:}0\,[\{\textbf{L2}{:}\text{i}\,[\textbf{L1}{:}\text{i}\,[\textbf{C}{:}\text{i}\,[]]]\mid 0 \leq i \leq 5\}]$$

Consider the case where processes must never be co-located through **L1** or **L2**. For the INTEL hierarchy, this effectively halves the **C** capacity[2]. Assuming that each system divides P processes amongst its **C**s equally, util(AMD) = $\min(k_{\text{AMD}}P/6, 6.0)$, and util(INTEL) = $\min(k_{\text{INTEL}}P/4, 4.0)$. Thus, INTEL's process execution time k_{INTEL} must be two thirds of k_{AMD} in order to have equal utilisation rates. □

4.2 Ongoing and Migration Costs

Configurations offer different security guarantees at different costs. Evaluating costs and metrics on a configuration's $\text{next}_{\hookcirclearrowleft}^{\infty}()$ is a tradeoff between performance and precision, as it avoids recomputing costs after each local migration operation.

Given a static model, a configuration can be progressively modified until it reaches an optimal state with respect to a property of the system. For example, tenants within a cloud have an incentive to use resources efficiently, and cloud providers generally attempt to provide resources to tenants with a minimum of overhead. Thus, if no confinements are created or destroyed by the tenants' agents, a cloud provider can alter the system's configuration incrementally until it reaches its lowest cost state.

---

[2] Disabling hyperthreading was once common amongst cloud providers [33], although Amazon EC2 has recently foregone this practice [5].

(2)**L1**:L_0 [**L1s**:S_0 [], **L1s**:S_1 []] | **L1**:L_1 [P_0, P_1, P_2]

$(2+\alpha)$**L1**:L_0 [**L1s**:S_0 [], **L1s**:S_1 [P_1]] | **L1**:L_1 [P_0, P_2] $(2+\alpha)$**L1**:L_0 [**L1s**:S_0 [P_0], **L1s**:S_1 []] | **L1**:L_1 [P_1, P_2]

$(1+2\alpha)$**L1**:L_0 [**L1s**:S_0 [P_0], **L1s**:S_1 [P_1]] | **L1**:L_1 [P_2]

$(1+2\alpha)$**L1**:L_0 [**L1s**:S_0 [], **L1s**:S_1 [P_0, P_1]] | **L1**:L_1 [P_2] $(1+2\alpha)$**L1**:L_0 [**L1s**:S_0 [P_0, P_1], **L1s**:S_1 []] | **L1**:L_1 [P_2]

(2α)**L1**:L_0 [**L1s**:S_0 [P_0], **L1s**:S_1 [P_1, P_2]] | **L1**:L_1 [] ↔ (2α)**L1**:L_0 [**L1s**:S_0 [P_0, P_2], **L1s**:S_1 [P_1]] | **L1**:L_1 []

(2α)**L1**:L_0 [**L1s**:S_0 [], **L1s**:S_1 [P_0, P_1, P_2]] | **L1**:L_1 [] (2α)**L1**:L_0 [**L1s**:S_0 [P_0, P_1, P_2], **L1s**:S_1 []] | **L1**:L_1 []

Fig. 6. A subset of possible global migrations between configurations.

The fluidity of cloud architectures necessitate a dynamic model, which limits the time allowed for a system to converge to an optimum. More generally, assuming that a system will remain in configuration $\mathcal{C}$ for a duration τ, one should temporarily move to $\mathcal{C}'$ if the cost of $\tau\mathcal{C}$ is greater than that of migrating to and from $\mathcal{C}'$ combined with the cost of maintaining $\tau\mathcal{C}'$. An accurate characterisation of τ enables configurations to be optimised with a minimum of migrations, yet a system in constant flux or with very small values of τ can potentially negate gains in migrating. Cheap migration operations can help offset the effects of τ.

Example 5. Figure 6 models migrations between various $\mathsf{next}_{\cup}^{\infty}()$ states of a system's **L1** caches with three processes, where one of the caches has deployed the soft isolation strategy described in Example 3. Utilisation rates are given in brackets, assuming that (a) each **L1** confinement is shared between two cores and has a total capacity of 2, (b) each process has a utilisation factor of 1, (c) **L1** confinements have zero cost, as they are built into the architecture, and (d) non-empty **L1s** confinements reduce their core's capacity to α (overhead values can reach up to 7 % [37]). Disabling co-scheduling on the partitioned core will cause its capacity to be halved. Utilisation is highest $(2+\alpha)$ when the unmitigated cache is at full capacity, with additional processes running within soft isolations. The configurations with the lowest `pairs()` are obtained for $1 + 2\alpha$. □

Metrics can also be extended to encompass *special purpose confinements* [9] and heterogeneous deployments, with certain configurations being cheaper or more secure to maintain on machines with dedicated hardware.

4.3 Automatically Generating Migration Sequences

The allocation of isolations to locations within a computational hierarchy is ultimately an exercise in scheduling. In its most general form, determining where confinements should be placed within a system is equivalent to bin-packing, thus eluding an efficient solution. The problem of placement is further complicated by the addition of quality of service predicates, which would typically include limits on capacity and utilisation. Finally, the hierarchical nature of the systems being investigated introduces its own nuances. For example, migrating an intermediate node within a containment graph will have a cascading effect on the constraints of its constituents.

The task is thus to determine a sequence of migration operations that will move a system from a configuration C to a new configuration C' that satisfies the isolation and quality of service criteria that are being requested. If C' is known, then one can compute a sequence of migration operations leading to it using a minimum edit distance algorithm for graphs, with migrations corresponding to edit operations that are weighted according to the migration mechanisms' costs. One drawback of such an approach is that the minimum graph edit distance cannot always be calculated efficiently [22]. More crucially, this approach requires that C' be identified beforehand, whereas one typically has to compute both the migration sequence as well as the final configuration.

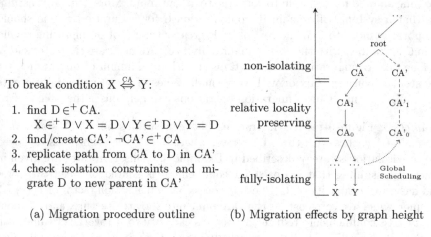

To break condition $X \overset{CA}{\Leftrightarrow} Y$:

1. find $D \in^+ CA$.
   $X \in^+ D \vee X = D \vee Y \in^+ D \vee Y = D$
2. find/create CA'. $\neg CA' \in^+ CA$
3. replicate path from CA to D in CA'
4. check isolation constraints and migrate D to new parent in CA'

(a) Migration procedure outline

(b) Migration effects by graph height

Fig. 7. Computing migration paths for breaking $X \overset{CA}{\Leftrightarrow} Y$.

Figure 7a provides a general outline of the steps required to break the co-location of X and Y via a common ancestor CA within a partially-specified hierarchy described in Fig. 7b. In the absence of efficient and exact oracles, several steps must be approximated by heuristics, as will be discussed in the remainder of this section. Note that the process of releasing or removing isolation constraints is similar to this procedure, with a greater focus on consolidating previously-isolated confinements back into existing confinements so as to lead to a cheaper configuration.

Finding a Source. The impact that the migration of a confinement D will have on a graph's isolation constraints will vary based on the position of D within that graph. For instance, migrating a process from one CPU core to the next will break locality at the core level, but not at the machine level.

When attempting to reconfigure the configuration illustrated by Fig. 7b to comply with the constraint $\neg(X \overset{CA}{\Leftrightarrow} Y)$, one finds that individual migration operations moving confinements outside of CA can take one of three forms, namely: (a) *fully isolating*, where X and Y share no common ancestor up to the depth of CA, (b) *relative locality preserving*, whereby co-location through CA is broken, yet the confinements are still co-located within an intermediate common confinement, and (c) *non-isolating*, where the structures producing co-location through CA are preserved by the migration. Hence, the depth within the graph at which the confinement being migrated exists determines how many co-locations will survive migration. Consequently, for isolation to be achieved, one must migrate a confinement on the containment path leading from CA to X or Y. Note that in the case of multiple separate routes for co-location through CA, one may have to migrate more than one confinement to fulfil a single isolation constraint.

Migrations that preserve relative locality may be insecure and must be performed with caution, as attacks on the locality type of CA may still be viable were one to migrate to a location of the same type (such as the sibling CA'). Conversely, one cannot rely entirely on fully-isolating migrations due to the finiteness of physical infrastructures. In the case of migrations at the same depth, such as when migrating either X or Y, one should ideally choose a migration that results in the lowest cost.

Finding a Target. Given that an appropriate confinement $D \in^+ CA$ has been marked for migration, the next step is to determine a suitable destination. Trivially, this must exist outside of CA. Referring to Fig. 7b, the earliest depth within the graph to which the localities can be migrated is CA', a confinement directly co-located with CA.

Provided that it is of the correct type, any confinement CA'. $\neg(CA' \in^+ CA)$ can serve as a destination confinement, yet a heuristic may find it reasonable to attempt to keep migrations as local as possible. In broad terms, migration amongst smaller localities (**VC** to **C**, or **P** to **C**) can be performed in milliseconds, as opposed to the migration of larger structures (**P** to **OS**, or **VM** to **M**), which can be a thousand times slower, principally due to the involvement of the network layers and shared storage [21].

Creating an Equivalent Environment. When migrating a confinement to a new parent, one would generally have to create a containment graph at the destination that matches the source's nesting structure. In certain cases, it may not be necessary to duplicate the full environment at the destination. For example, when migrating a **VM** that is running within a second **VM**, one may opt to migrate the former directly to bare metal.

Satisfying Constraints. When executing a sequence of migration operations, one must ensure that both the end state as well as the intermediate configurations do not violate any constraints that have previously been placed on the system. Ideally, constraints are checked before any migrations are performed, and migrations are only carried out once it has been established that they respect all isolation constraints. Failing this, transaction semantics must be added to migration sequences, giving the ability to dynamically roll back migration operations and attempt to identify an alternative path.

Backtracking will introduce delays in the servicing of isolation requests, which may not always be tolerable. If the workloads are well characterised, one may determine that certain constraints can be temporarily relaxed. For example, a tenant may tolerate a short-lived dip in performance, which would in turn allow a machine to be temporarily over-provisioned whilst performing a sequence of reconfiguration operations.

5   Applications

The following section investigates various contexts in which the model can be applied, including *runtime enforcement*, as well as in the modelling and analysis of an access-based side-channel and a replication-based timing channel mitigation.

5.1   Runtime Isolation

While co-location properties can be verified for specific scopes, the guarantees may no longer hold after a system has been reconfigured. Runtime monitoring serves to dynamically resolve isolation predicates that depend on confinements at the edges of a configuration's scope. The model can be used to define policies within a runtime monitoring framework, where declarative restrictions on co-locations are used to define invalid configurations. Once a bad state is detected (such as on detecting suspicious memory access patterns [34]), the system can be reconfigured to a correct state using migration, leading to a reactive architecture. Alternatively, the framework can be driven by a system of leases, with isolation being procured before a security-sensitive process executes.

5.2   Pre-emption Rate Limiting

The presented model can be used to reason about attacks at different granularities, which we demonstrate by modelling an access-driven cross-VM side-channel attack developed by Zhang et al. [35], and its scheduler-based mitigation [32]. The attack relies on a PRIME-PROBE cache access pattern, similar to the attack described in Example 2.

Consider a hypervisor managing two virtual machines, namely a victim VM_v and attacker VM_a. Both machines (collectively referred to as $\overrightarrow{V}$) share a core c_0. The hypervisor agent Hyp is defined as:

$$\mathbf{A}{:}\text{Hyp}(\{c^{\text{VM}_v}, c^{\text{VM}_a}, c^{c_0}\})^{\{(\text{VM}_v, c_0), (\text{VM}_a, c_0)\}}_{\{\text{VM}_v, \text{VM}_a, c_0\}} \left[\overrightarrow{V}\right]$$

and implemented as a process Hyp^I defined as:

$$\text{Hyp}^I \equiv \overset{\mathbf{VM}:X \in \vec{V}}{\sqcap} X \curvearrowright C_0.X \curvearrowright \text{Hyp}.\text{Hyp}^I$$

The $\text{next}_U^\infty()$ graph of the system at this coarse level of granularity would reveal that the virtual machines are co-located through C_0, yet the mechanism by which they interfere with each other is not immediately apparent. The hierarchy can be defined at a finer granularity by modelling **L1** as a confinement of N *cache-line sets* (**CLS**), giving **L1**:CLS_0 [{**CLS**:cs_i [] | $0 \le i < N$}]. Cache-lines are invalidated as processes execute within a **VC**. In a fine-grained model, the agent process is modified to map **VC**s to **CLS** confinements, signifying that an operation running within that **VC** has disturbed the cache set in question (more precise models of cache eviction policies may also be defined, yet this is unnecessary for the purposes of this exposition). A process carried out by an agent Ag which schedules a **VC** to a **C**, models the **VM**'s interactions with **CLS** for R times, and then yields control of the scheduler is defined as:

$$\text{run}(\mathbf{A}:\text{Ag}, \mathbf{L1}:L, \mathbf{C}:c, \mathbf{VC}:vc, R) \equiv vc \curvearrowright c.(\overset{\mathbf{CLS}:cs \in L}{\sqcap} vc \curvearrowright cs)^R.vc \curvearrowright \text{Ag}$$

The attack is access-based, where the attacker attempts to determine the pattern of a victim's memory accesses. The attacker achieves this by priming the cache and checking its access times after the victim executes, placing its **VC** VC_a within a cache set previously occupied by vc_v, leading to the sequence:

$$\text{run}(\text{Ag}, \text{CLS}_0, C_0, \text{VC}_a, N).\text{run}(\text{Ag}, \text{CLS}_0, C_0, \text{VC}_v, R)$$

The attacker's resolution of the victim's intermediate cache states is greatly influenced by R. If a victim can be pre-empted frequently, then the attacker can build a more precise memory access model. Conversely, large values of R will increase the probability that other cache regions unrelated to the security-sensitive computation under attack will have been accessed, leading to noise. Thus, the victim VM_v attempts to choose a value of R such that it *maximises* the value of `pairs()` formed over an execution.

A mitigation against this attack [32] places a minimum running time on virtual machines, which stops an attacker from forcing deschedules and limiting its ability to profile a victim. By knowing the number of cache invalidations required to achieve the desired level of isolation and the cost of performing cache operations, one can determine a minimum **VM** scheduling quantum length.

A similar fine-grained cache analysis can be performed for cache colouring [26], where scheduling must guarantee disjoint cache sets. An additional related mitigation is that of the cache cleaning process (Example 3), which is effectively a solution for the same problem using a different scheduling level.

5.3   Timing Channel Elimination

STOPWATCH [27] is a collection of mitigations designed to reduce the information content of timing channels in the cloud. The approach's mitigation centres on the use of *replication* to create R copies of each virtual machine ($R \geq 3$), each of which is placed on a different machine containing other tenants' replicated **VM**s. Clock sources on a **VM** are then modified to report time as a median of its local time and that of the replicas. This ensures that a co-located attacker will observe the same timing behaviour. Several aspects of the mitigation can be modelled, including event synchronisation and OS-level soft isolations. This section will focus on the **VM** replication and placement aspects of STOPWATCH.

Given a network NET of machines, the **VM** placement requirements of STOP-WATCH can be modelled as three invariant conditions, namely:

$$\forall \mathbf{VM}{:}v \in^+ \text{NET}. \left| \left\{ v' \mid \mathbf{VM}{:}v' \in^+ \text{NET}, \text{is\_replica}(v', v) \right\} \right| = R \quad (1)$$

$$\forall \mathbf{VM}{:}v, \mathbf{M}{:}M \in^+ \text{NET}. \left| \left\{ v' \mid \mathbf{VM}{:}v' \in M, \text{tenant}(v') = \text{tenant}(v) \right\} \right| \leq 1 \quad (2)$$

$$\forall \mathbf{VM}{:}v_1, \mathbf{VM}{:}v_2, \mathbf{M}{:}M \in^+ \text{NET}. \ v_1 \neq v_2 \wedge v_1 \overset{M}{\longleftrightarrow} v_2 \rightarrow$$

$$\neg \exists \mathbf{VM}{:}v_3, \mathbf{VM}{:}v_4, \mathbf{M}{:}M' \in^+ \text{NET}. \ v_3 \neq v_4 \wedge v_3 \overset{M'}{\longleftrightarrow} v_4 \wedge M \neq M' \wedge$$

$$\text{tenant}(v_1) = \text{tenant}(v_3) \wedge \text{tenant}(v_2) = \text{tenant}(v_4) \quad (3)$$

The first invariant ensures that there are R replica machines within the network. The second invariant checks that each machine has at most one virtual machine belonging to the same tenant. The final invariant checks that any given pair of tenants can be co-located in at most one machine.

6   Related Work

Ambient Models. A seminal work in modelling hierarchical architectures was the calculus of *mobile ambients* [17], which extended process calculi with the *ambient* process construct. Ambients specify boundaries within which other ambients exist and migrate. Several extensions to the original calculus were subsequently defined, including the ability to define security zones to detect confidentiality breaches [15], as well as to model resource allocation through a system of markers [8]. An additional extension is the *cloud calculus* [25].

Graph Models. Graphs allow the definition of many-to-many relationships between a system's entities. Graph models for **VM** networks can be generated automatically [11,16]. These can then be checked statically [14] to detect violations in operational correctness, failure resilience and isolation. Additional work focuses on making the analysis of dynamic systems more efficient through incremental analysis [13]. The creation and application of deltas is event-driven, triggered using hooks to a hypervisor. Challenges in dynamic monitoring include asynchronous updates, non-atomic actions, unordered events and blocking behaviour introduced by instrumentation [12]. Other approaches group resources into *colours* within which data can be shared, and employ a system of roles that can modify colour groupings and conflict rules [10].

Scheduler-based mitigations. Scheduling policies can be exploited to form illicit channels [32] or steal computational resources [31]. Setting a minimum time between deschedules can undermine a side-channel by obscuring residual cache effects [32]. Global scheduling can be used to reduce contention [31]. Efficiently choosing migration targets is non-trivial, as placement can be constrained by several factors in addition to isolation requirements [30]. The problem can thus be formulated as one of *constraint satisfaction*. Other approaches address placement as a bin-packing problem to guarantee different degrees of isolation whilst upholding a system's functional constraints [6]. The approach is evaluated in terms of a *competitive ratio*, comparing the cost of configurations produced by on-line scheduling against optimal placement, where cost is the number of bins used. Heuristics can aid migration and placement [18]. Another approach uses leases and deadlines to reserve resources and prioritise migrations [4].

Detection and generation. One challenge of policy-based defences is to create policies. Methods have been developed for detecting certain types of leaks through various techniques, including information flow analysis [7], abstract interpretation [20], and data tagging and tracking [29].

7 Conclusions and Future Work

This work has investigated the modelling of temporal and spatial co-location within the context of illicit channels, examining the issues of cost, scoping and migration. It considered the creation of a model that can consistently reason about a variety of heterogeneous systems through a uniform notion of containment. It also examined the challenges in allocating resources within a hierarchical architecture. These concepts were applied to the modelling and analysis of several established attacks and defences, giving insight into their inner workings.

Future work will focus on the automated synthesis of runtime enforcement monitors, and the integration of the model into simulation frameworks.

References

1. CRIU project page, January 2016. http://criu.org/Main_Page
2. Libvirt project page, January 2016. http://libvirt.org/
3. Adams, K., Agesen, O.: A comparison of software and hardware techniques for x86 virtualization. In: Proceedings of the 12th International Conference on Architectural Support for Programming Languages and Operating Systems, pp. 2–13. ASPLOS XII. ACM, New York (2006). http://doi.acm.org/10.1145/1168857.1168860
4. Afoulki, Z., Rouzaud-Cornabas, J.: A security-aware scheduler for virtual machines on IaaS clouds. Technical report LIFO, ENSI de Bourges (2011)
5. Amazon: Amazon EC2 instances, April 2015. https://aws.amazon.com/ec2/instance-types/
6. Azar, Y., Kamara, S., Menache, I., Raykova, M., Shepard, B.: Co-location-resistant clouds. In: Proceedings of the 6th Edition of the ACM Workshop on Cloud Computing Security, pp. 9–20. CCSW 2014. ACM, New York (2014). http://doi.acm.org/10.1145/2664168.2664179

7. Backes, M., Kopf, B., Rybalchenko, A.: Automatic discovery and quantification of information leaks. In: Proceedings of the 2009 30th IEEE Symposium on Security and Privacy, SP 2009, pp. 141–153. IEEE Computer Society, Washington, DC (2009). http://dx.doi.org/10.1109/SP.2009.18

8. Barbanera, F., Bugliesi, M., Dezani-Ciancaglini, M., Sassone, V.: A calculus of bounded capacities. In: Saraswat, V.A. (ed.) ASIAN 2003. LNCS, vol. 2896, pp. 205–223. Springer, Heidelberg (2003)

9. Baumann, A., Peinado, M., Hunt, G.: Shielding applications from an untrusted cloud with haven. In: 11th USENIX Symposium on Operating Systems Design and Implementation (OSDI 2014), pp. 267–283. USENIX Association, Broomfield, October 2014. https://www.usenix.org/conference/osdi14/technical-sessions/presentation/baumann

10. Bijon, K.Z., Krishnan, R., Sandhu, R.: A formal model for isolation management in cloud infrastructure-as-a-service. In: Au, M.H., Carminati, B., Kuo, C.-C.J. (eds.) NSS 2014. LNCS, vol. 8792, pp. 41–53. Springer, Heidelberg (2014)

11. Bleikertz, S., Groß, T., Mödersheim, S.: Automated verification of virtualized infrastructures. In: Proceedings of the 3rd ACM Workshop on Cloud Computing Security Workshop, CCSW 2011, pp. 47–58. ACM, New York (2011). http://doi.acm.org/10.1145/2046660.2046672

12. Bleikertz, S., Groß, T., Mödersheim, S.: Modeling and analysis of dynamic infrastructure clouds. Technical report, IBM Zurich, December 2013

13. Bleikertz, S., Vogel, C., Groß, T.: Cloud radar: near real-time detection of security failures in dynamic virtualized infrastructures. In: Proceedings of the 30th Annual Computer Security Applications Conference, ACSAC 2014, pp. 26–35. ACM, New York (2014). http://doi.acm.org/10.1145/2664243.2664274

14. Bleikertz, S., Gro, T.: A virtualization assurance language for isolation and deployment. In: POLICY, pp. 33–40. IEEE Computer Society (2011). http://dblp.uni-trier.de/db/conf/policy/policy2011.html#BleikertzG11

15. Braghin, C., Cortesi, A., Focardi, R.: Security boundaries in mobile ambients. Comput. Lang. Syst. Struct. 28(1), 101–127 (2002). Computer Languages and Security. http://www.sciencedirect.com/science/article/pii/S0096055102000097

16. Broquedis, F., Clet-Ortega, J., Moreaud, S., Furmento, N., Goglin, B., Mercier,G., Thibault, S., Namyst, R.: hwloc: a generic framework for managing hardware affinities in HPC applications. In: The 18th Euromicro International Conference on Parallel, Distributed and Network-Based Computing, PDP 2010. IEEE, Pisa, February 2010. https://hal.inria.fr/inria-00429889

17. Cardelli, L., Gordon, A.D.: Mobile ambients. In: Proceedings of POPL 1998. ACM Press (1998)

18. Caron, E., Rouzaud-Cornabas, J.: Improving users' isolation in IaaS: virtual machine placement with security constraints. Research report RR-8444, INRIA, January 2014. https://hal.inria.fr/hal-00924296

19. Dolan-Gavitt, B., Leek, T., Hodosh, J., Lee, W.: Tappan zee (north) bridge: mining memory accesses for introspection. In: ACM CCS 2013, pp. 839–850. ACM, New York (2013). http://doi.acm.org/10.1145/2508859.2516697

20. Doychev, G., Feld, D., Köpf, B., Mauborgne, L., Reineke, J.: Cacheaudit: A tool for the static analysis of cache side channels. In: Proceedings of the 22nd USENIX Conference on Security, SEC 2013, pp. 431–446. USENIX Association, Berkeley (2013). http://dl.acm.org/citation.cfm?id=2534766.2534804

21. Falzon, K., Bodden, E.: Dynamically provisioning isolation in hierarchical architectures. In: López, J., Mitchell, C.J. (eds.) ISC 2015. LNCS, vol. 9290, pp. 83–101. Springer, Heidelberg (2015). http://dx.doi.org/10.1007/978-3-319-23318-5_5

22. Gao, X., Xiao, B., Tao, D., Li, X.: A survey of graph edit distance. Pattern Anal. Appl. **13**(1), 113–129 (2010). http://dx.doi.org/10.1007/s10044-008-0141-y

23. Gueron, S.: Intel advanced encryption standard (aes) new instructions set, May 2010. http://www.intel.com/content/dam/doc/white-paper/advanced-encryption-standard-new-instructions-set-paper.pdf

24. Hu, W.M.: Reducing timing channels with fuzzy time. In: Proceedings, 1991 IEEE Computer Society Symposium on Research in Security and Privacy, 1991, pp. 8–20, May 1991

25. Jarraya, Y., Eghtesadi, A., Debbabi, M., Zhang, Y., Pourzandi, M.: Cloud calculus: security verification in elastic cloud computing platform. In: Smari, W.W., Fox, G.C. (eds.) CTS, pp. 447–454. IEEE (2012). http://dblp.uni-trier.de/db/conf/cts/cts2012.html#JarrayaEDZP12

26. Kim, T., Peinado, M., Mainar-Ruiz, G.: Stealthmem: system-level protection against cache-based side channel attacks in the cloud. In: 21st USENIX Conference on Security Symposium. Security 2012. USENIX Association, Berkeley (2012). http://dl.acm.org/citation.cfm?id=2362793.2362804

27. Li, P., Gao, D., Reiter, M.: Mitigating access-driven timing channels in clouds using stopwatch. In: 2013 43rd Annual IEEE/IFIP International Conference on Dependable Systems and Networks (DSN), pp. 1–12, June 2013

28. Osvik, D.A., Shamir, A., Tromer, E.: Cache attacks and countermeasures: the case of AES. In: Pointcheval, D. (ed.) CT-RSA 2006. LNCS, vol. 3860, pp. 1–20. Springer, Heidelberg (2006). http://dx.doi.org/10.1007/11605805_1

29. Priebe, C., Muthukumaran, D., O'Keeffe, D., Eyers, D., Shand, B., Kapitza, R., Pietzuch, P.: Cloudsafetynet: detecting data leakage between cloud tenants. In: ACM Cloud Computing Security Workshop (CCSW). ACM, Scottsdale, November 2014

30. Raj, H., Nathuji, R., Singh, A., England, P.: Resource management for isolation enhanced cloud services. In: Proceedings of the 2009 ACM Workshop on Cloud Computing Security, CCSW 2009, pp. 77–84. ACM, New York (2009). http://doi.acm.org/10.1145/1655008.1655019

31. Varadarajan, V., Kooburat, T., Farley, B., Ristenpart, T., Swift, M.M.: Resource-freeing attacks: improve your cloud performance (at your neighbor's expense). In: Proceedings of the 2012 ACM Conference on Computer and Communications Security, CCS 2012, pp. 281–292. ACM, New York (2012). http://doi.acm.org/10.1145/2382196.2382228

32. Varadarajan, V., Ristenpart, T., Swift, M.: Scheduler-based defenses against cross-vm side-channels. In: 23rd USENIX Security Symposium (USENIX Security 2014), pp. 687–702. USENIX Association, San Diego, August 2014. https://www.usenix.org/conference/usenixsecurity14/technical-sessions/presentation/varadarajan

33. Wu, Z., Xu, Z., Wang, H.: Whispers in the hyper-space: high-speed covert channel attacks in the cloud. In: 21st USENIX Conference on Security Symposium, Security 2012, pp. 159–173. USENIX Association, Berkeley (2012). http://dl.acm.org/citation.cfm?id=2362793.2362802

34. Zhang, Y., Juels, A., Oprea, A., Reiter, M.K.: Homealone: Co-residency detection in the cloud via side-channel analysis. In: IEEE S&P 2011, pp. 313–328. IEEE Computer Society, Washington, DC (2011). http://dx.doi.org/10.1109/SP.2011.31

35. Zhang, Y., Juels, A., Reiter, M.K., Ristenpart, T.: Cross-vm side channels and their use to extract private keys. In: ACM CCS 2012, pp. 305–316. ACM, New York (2012). http://doi.acm.org/10.1145/2382196.2382230

36. Zhang, Y., Juels, A., Reiter, M.K., Ristenpart, T.: Cross-tenant side-channel attacks in paas clouds. In: Proceedings of the 2014 ACM SIGSAC Conference on Computer and Communications Security, CCS 2014, pp. 990–1003. ACM, New York (2014). http://doi.acm.org/10.1145/2660267.2660356
37. Zhang, Y., Reiter, M.K.: Düppel: retrofitting commodity operating systems to mitigate cache side channels in the cloud. In: ACM CCS 2013, pp. 827–838. ACM, New York (2013). http://doi.acm.org/10.1145/2508859.2516741

Correct Audit Logging: Theory and Practice

Sepehr Amir-Mohammadian[1]([✉]), Stephen Chong[2], and Christian Skalka[1]

[1] University of Vermont, Burlington, USA
{samirmoh,ceskalka}@uvm.edu
[2] Harvard University, Cambridge, USA
chong@seas.harvard.edu

Abstract. Retrospective security has become increasingly important to the theory and practice of cyber security, with auditing a crucial component of it. However, in systems where auditing is used, programs are typically instrumented to generate audit logs using manual, ad-hoc strategies. This is a potential source of error even if log analysis techniques are formal, since the relation of the log itself to program execution is unclear. This paper focuses on provably correct program rewriting algorithms for instrumenting formal logging specifications. Correctness guarantees that the execution of an instrumented program produces sound and complete audit logs, properties defined by an information containment relation between logs and the program's logging semantics. We also propose a program rewriting approach to instrumentation for audit log generation, in a manner that guarantees correct log generation even for untrusted programs. As a case study, we develop such a tool for OpenMRS, a popular medical records management system, and consider instrumentation of break the glass policies.

1 Introduction

Retrospective security is the enforcement of security, or detection of security violations, after program execution [33,36,40]. Many real-world systems use retrospective security. For example, the financial industry corrects errors and fraudulent transactions not by proactively preventing suspicious transactions, but by retrospectively correcting or undoing these problematic translations. Another example is a hospital whose employees are trusted to access confidential patient records, but who might (rarely) violate this trust [17]. Upon detection of such violations, security is enforced retrospectively by holding responsible employees accountable [41].

Retrospective security cannot be achieved entirely by traditional computer security mechanisms, such as access control, or information-flow control. Reasons include that detection of violations may be external to the computer system (such as consumer reports of fraudulent transactions, or confidential patient information appearing in news media), the high cost of access denial (e.g., preventing emergency-room physicians from accessing medical records) coupled with high trust of systems users (e.g., users are trusted employees that rarely violate this trust) [42]. In addition, remediation actions to address violations may also be

© Springer-Verlag Berlin Heidelberg 2016
F. Piessens and L. Viganò (Eds.): POST 2016, LNCS 9635, pp. 139–162, 2016.
DOI: 10.1007/978-3-662-49635-0_8

external to the computer system, such as reprimanding employees, prosecuting law suits, or otherwise holding users accountable for their actions [41].

Auditing underlies retrospective security frameworks and has become increasingly important to the theory and practice of cyber security. By maintaining a record of appropriate aspects of a computer system's execution, an audit log (and subsequent examination of the audit log) can enable detection of violations, provide sufficient evidence to hold users accountable for their actions, and support other remediation actions. For example, an audit log can be used to determine *post facto* which users performed dangerous operations, and can provide evidence for use in litigation.

However, despite the importance of auditing to real-world security, relatively little work has focused on the formal foundations of auditing, particularly with respect to defining and ensuring the correctness of audit log generation. Indeed, correct and efficient audit log generation poses at least two significant challenges. First, it is necessary to record sufficient and correct information in the audit log. If a program is manually instrumented, it is possible for developers to fail to record relevant events. Recent work showed that major health informatics systems do not log sufficient information to determine compliance with HIPAA policies [30]. Second, an audit log should ideally not contain more information than needed. While it is straightforward to collect sufficient information by recording essentially *all* events in a computer system, this can cause performance issues, both slowing down the system due to generating massive audit logs, and requiring the handling of extremely large audit logs. Excessive data collection is a key challenge for auditing [14,23,29], and is a critical factor in the design of tools that generate and employ audit logs (e.g., spam filters [15]).

A main goal of this paper is to establish formal conditions for audit logs, that can be used to establish correctness conditions for logging instrumentation. We define a general semantics of audit logs using the theory of *information algebra* [32], and interpret both program execution traces and audit logs as information elements. A *logging specification* defines the intended relation between the information in traces and in audit logs. An audit log is correct if it satisfies this relation. A benefit of this formulation is that it separates logging specifications from programs, rather than burying them in code and implementation details.

Separating logging specifications from programs allows a clean declaration of what instrumentation should accomplish, and enables algorithms for implementing general classes of logging specifications that are provably correct. As we will show, correct instrumentation of logging specifications is a safety property, hence enforceable by security automata [38]. Inspired by related approaches to security automata implementation [21], we focus on program rewriting to automatically enforce correct audit instrumentation. Program rewriting has a number of practical benefits versus, for example, program monitors, such as lower OS process management overhead.

We consider a case study of our approach, a program rewriting algorithm for correct instrumentation of logging specifications in OpenMRS (openmrs.org), a popular open source medical records software system. Our tool allows system administrators to define logging specifications which are automatically instrumented in OpenMRS legacy code. Implementation details and optimizations are handled transparently by the general program rewriting algorithm, not the logging specification. Formal foundations ensure that logging specifications are implemented correctly by the algorithm. In particular, we show how our system can implement "break the glass" auditing policies.

1.1   A Motivating Example from Practice

Although audit logs contain information *about* program execution, they are not just a straightforward selection of program events. Illustrative examples from practice include so-called "break the glass policies" used in electronic medical record systems [35]. These policies use access control to disallow care providers from performing sensitive operations such as viewing patient records, however care providers can "break the glass" in an emergency situation to temporarily raise their authority and access patient records, *with the understanding that subsequent sensitive operations will be logged and potentially audited.* One potential accountability goal is the following:

> *In the event that a patient's sensitive information is inappropriately leaked, determine who accessed a given patient's files due to "breaking the glass."*

Since it cannot be predicted a priori whose information may leak, this goal can be supported by using an audit log that records all reads of sensitive files following glass breaking. To generate correct audit logs, programs must be instrumented for logging appropriately, i.e., to implement the following *logging specification* that we call LS_H:

> LS_H : *Record in the log all patient information file reads following a break the glass event, along with the identity of the user that broke the glass.*

If at some point in time in the future it is determined that a specific patient **P**'s information was leaked, logs thus generated can be analyzed with the following query that we call LQ_H:

> LQ_H : *Retrieve the identity of all users that read **P**'s information files.*

The specification LS_H and the query LQ_H together constitute an auditing policy that directly supports the above-stated accountability goal. Their separation is useful since at the time of execution the information leak is unknown, hence **P** is not known. Thus while it is possible to implement LS_H as part of program execution, LQ_H must be implemented retrospectively.

It is crucial to the enforcement of the above accountability goal that LS_H is implemented correctly. If logging is incomplete then some potential recipients may be missed. If logging is overzealous then bloat is possible and audit logs become "write only". These types of errors are common in practice [30]. To establish formal correctness of instrumentation for audit logs, it is necessary to define a formal language of logging specifications, and establish techniques to guarantee that instrumented programs satisfy logging specifications. That is the focus of this paper. Other work has focused on formalisms for querying logs [18,39], however these works presuppose correctness of audit logs for true accountability.

1.2   Threat Model

With respect to program rewriting (i.e., automatic techniques to instrument existing programs to satisfy a logging specification), we regard the program undergoing instrumentation as untrusted. That is, the program source code may have been written to avoid, confuse, or subvert the automatic instrumentation techniques. We do, however, assume that the source code is well-formed (valid syntax, well-typed, etc.). Moreover, we trust the compiler, the program rewriting algorithm, and the runtime environment in which the instrumented program will ultimately be executed. Confidentiality and non-malleability of generated audit logs, while important, is beyond the scope of this paper.

2   A Semantics of Audit Logging

Our goal in this Section is to formally characterize logging specifications and correctness conditions for audit logs. To obtain a general model, we leverage ideas from the theory of *information algebra* [32], which is an abstract mathematical framework for information systems. In short, we interpret program traces as information, and logging specifications as functions from traces to information. This separates logging specifications from their implementation in code, and defines exactly the information that should be in an audit log. This in turn establishes correctness conditions for audit logging implementations.

Following [38], an *execution trace* $\tau = \kappa_0\kappa_1\kappa_2\ldots$ is a possibly infinite sequence of configurations κ that describe the state of an executing program. We deliberately leave configurations abstract, but examples abound and we explore a specific instantiation for a λ-calculus in Sect. 4. Note that an execution trace τ may represent the partial execution of a program, i.e. the trace τ may be extended with additional configurations as the program continues execution. We use metavariables τ and σ to range over traces.

An *information algebra* contains information elements X (e.g. a set of logical assertions) taken from a set Φ (the algebra). A partial ordering is induced on Φ by the so-called *information ordering* relation $\leq$, where intuitively for $X, Y \in \Phi$ we have $X \leq Y$ iff Y contains at least as much information as X, though its precise meaning depends on the particular algebra. We say that X and Y are *information equivalent*, and write $X = Y$, iff $X \leq Y$ and $Y \leq X$. We assume given a function $\lfloor \cdot \rfloor$ that is an injective mapping from traces to Φ. This mapping *interprets a given trace as information*, where the injective requirement ensures that information is not lost in the interpretation. For example, if σ is a proper prefix of τ and thus contains strictly less information, then formally $\lfloor \sigma \rfloor \leq \lfloor \tau \rfloor$. We intentionally leave both Φ and $\lfloor \cdot \rfloor$ underspecified for generality, though application of our formalism to a particular logging implementation requires instantiation of them. We discuss an example in Sect. 3.

We let LS range over *logging specifications*, which are functions from traces to Φ. As for Φ and $\lfloor \cdot \rfloor$, we intentionally leave the language of specifications abstract, but consider a particular instantiation in Sect. 3. Intuitively, $LS(\tau)$ denotes the information that should be recorded in an audit log during the execution of τ given specification LS, regardless of whether τ actually records any log information, correctly or incorrectly. We call this the semantics of the logging specification LS.

We assume that auditing is implementable, requiring at least that all conditions for logging any piece of information must be met in a finite amount of time. As we will show, this restriction implies that correct logging instrumentation is a safety property [38].

Definition 1. *We require of any logging specification LS that for all traces τ and information $X \leq LS(\tau)$, there exists a finite prefix σ of τ such that $X \leq LS(\sigma)$.*

It is crucial to observe that some logging specifications may *add* information not contained in traces to the auditing process. Security information not relevant to program execution (such as ACLs), interpretation of event data (statistical or otherwise), etc., may be added by the logging specification. For example, in the OpenMRS system, logging of sensitive operations includes a human-understandable "type" designation which is not used by any other code. Thus, given a trace τ and logging specification LS, it is *not* necessarily the case that $LS(\tau) \leq \lfloor \tau \rfloor$. Audit logging is not just a filtering of program events.

2.1 Correctness Conditions for Audit Logs

A logging specification defines what information should be contained in an audit log. In this section we develop formal notions of *soundness* and *completeness* as audit log correctness conditions. We use metavariable $\mathbb{L}$ to range over audit logs. Again, we intentionally leave the language of audit logs unspecified, but assume that the function $\lfloor \cdot \rfloor$ is extended to audit logs, i.e. $\lfloor \cdot \rfloor$ is an injective mapping from audit logs to Φ. Intuitively, $\lfloor \mathbb{L} \rfloor$ denotes the information in $\mathbb{L}$, interpreted as an element of Φ.

An audit log $\mathbb{L}$ is sound with respect to a logging specification LS and trace τ if the log information is contained in $LS(\tau)$. Similarly, an audit log is complete with respect to a logging specification if it contains all of the information in the logging specification's semantics. Crucially, both definitions are independent of the implementation details that generate $\mathbb{L}$.

Definition 2. *Audit log $\mathbb{L}$ is* sound *with respect to logging specification LS and execution trace τ iff $\lfloor \mathbb{L} \rfloor \leq LS(\tau)$. Similarly, audit log $\mathbb{L}$ is* complete *with respect to logging specification LS and execution trace τ iff $LS(\tau) \leq \lfloor \mathbb{L} \rfloor$.*

The relation to log queries. As discussed in Sect. 1.1, we make a distinction between logging specifications such as LS_H which define how to record logs, and log queries such as LQ_H which ask questions of logs, and our notions of soundness and completeness apply strictly to logging specifications. However, any logging query must assume a logging specification semantics, hence a log that is demonstrably sound and complete provides the same answers on a given query that an "ideal" log would. This is an important property that is discussed in previous work, e.g. as "sufficiency" in [6].

2.2 Correct Logging Instrumentation is a Safety Property

In case program executions generate audit logs, we write $\tau \rightsquigarrow \mathbb{L}$ to mean that a finite trace τ generates $\mathbb{L}$, i.e. $\tau = \kappa_0 \ldots \kappa_n$ and $logof(\kappa_n) = \mathbb{L}$ where $logof(\kappa)$ denotes the audit log in configuration κ, i.e. the residual log after execution of the full trace. Ideally, information that *should* be added to an audit log, *is* added to an audit log, immediately as it becomes available. This ideal is formalized as follows.

Definition 3. *For all logging specifications LS, the trace τ is ideally instrumented for LS iff for all finite prefixes σ of τ we have $\sigma \rightsquigarrow \mathbb{L}$ where $\mathbb{L}$ is sound and complete with respect to LS and σ.*

We observe that the restriction imposed on logging specifications by Definition 1, implies that ideal instrumentation of any logging specification is a safety property in the sense defined by Schneider [38][1].

Theorem 1. *For all logging specifications LS, the set of ideally instrumented traces is a safety property.*

This result implies that e.g. edit automata can be used to enforce instrumentation of logging specifications (see our Technical Report [3]). However, theory related to safety properties and their enforcement by execution monitors [4, 38] do not provide an adequate semantic foundation for audit log generation, nor an account of soundness and completeness of audit logs.

2.3 Implementing Logging Specifications with Program Rewriting

The above-defined correctness conditions for audit logs provide a foundation on which to establish correctness of logging implementations. Here we consider program rewriting approaches. Since rewriting concerns specific languages, we introduce abstract notion of programs $\mathfrak{p}$ with an operational semantics that can produce a trace τ. We write $\mathfrak{p} \Downarrow \sigma$ iff program $\mathfrak{p}$ can produce execution trace τ, either deterministically or non-deterministically, and σ is a *finite* prefix of τ.

A rewriting algorithm $\mathcal{R}$ is a (partial) function that takes a program $\mathfrak{p}$ in a source language and a logging specification LS and produces a new program,

---

[1] The proofs of Theorems 1–5 in this text are omitted for brevity, but are available in a related Technical Report [3].

$\mathcal{R}(\mathfrak{p}, LS)$, in a target language.[2] The intent is that the target program is the result of instrumenting $\mathfrak{p}$ to produce an audit log appropriate for the logging specification LS. A rewriting algorithm may be partial, in particular because it may only be intended to work for a specific set of logging specifications.

Ideally, a rewriting algorithm should preserve the semantics of the program it instruments. That is, $\mathcal{R}$ is semantics-preserving if the rewritten program simulates the semantics of the source code, modulo logging steps. We assume given a correspondence relation $:\approx$ on execution traces. A coherent definition of correspondence should be similar to a bisimulation, but it is not necessarily symmetric nor a bisimulation, since the instrumented target program may be in a different language than the source program. We deliberately leave the correspondence relation underspecified, as its definition will depend on the instantiation of the model. We provide an explicit definition of correspondence for λ-calculus source and target languages in Sect. 4.

Definition 4. *Rewriting algorithm $\mathcal{R}$ is* semantics preserving *iff for all programs $\mathfrak{p}$ and logging specifications LS such that $\mathcal{R}(\mathfrak{p}, LS)$ is defined, all of the following hold:*

1. *For all traces τ such that $\mathfrak{p} \Downarrow \tau$ there exists τ' with $\tau :\approx \tau'$ and $\mathcal{R}(\mathfrak{p}, LS) \Downarrow \tau'$.*
2. *For all traces τ such that $\mathcal{R}(\mathfrak{p}, LS) \Downarrow \tau$ there exists a trace τ' such that $\tau' :\approx \tau$ and $\mathfrak{p} \Downarrow \tau'$.*

In addition to preserving program semantics, a correctly rewritten program constructs a log in accordance with the given logging specification. More precisely, if LS is a given logging specification and a trace τ describes execution of a source program, rewriting should produce a program with a trace τ' that corresponds to τ (i.e., $\tau :\approx \tau'$), where the log $\mathbb{L}$ generated by τ' contains the same information as $LS(\tau)$, or at least a sound approximation. Some definitions of $:\approx$ may allow several target-language traces to correspond to source-language traces (as for example in Sect. 4, Definition 10). In any case, we expect that at least one simulation exists. Hence we write $simlogs(\mathfrak{p}, \tau)$ to denote a nonempty set of logs $\mathbb{L}$ such that, given a finite source language trace τ and target program $\mathfrak{p}$, there exists some trace τ' where $\mathfrak{p} \Downarrow \tau'$ and $\tau :\approx \tau'$ and $\tau' \rightsquigarrow \mathbb{L}$. The name *simlogs* evokes the relation to logs resulting from simulating executions in the target language.

The following definitions then establish correctness conditions for rewriting algorithms. Note that satisfaction of either of these conditions only implies condition (1) of Definition 4, not condition (2), so semantics preservation is an independent condition.

Definition 5. *Rewriting algorithm $\mathcal{R}$ is* sound/complete *iff for all programs $\mathfrak{p}$, logging specifications LS, and finite traces τ where $\mathfrak{p} \Downarrow \tau$, for all $\mathbb{L} \in simlogs(\mathcal{R}(\mathfrak{p}, LS), \tau)$ it is the case that $\mathbb{L}$ is sound/complete with respect to LS and τ.*

---

[2] We use metavariable $\mathfrak{p}$ to range over programs in either the source or target language; it will be clear from context which language is used.

3   Languages for Logging Specifications

Now we go into more detail about information algebra and why it is a good foundation for logging specifications and semantics. We use the formalism of information algebras to characterize and compare the information contained in an audit log with the information contained in an actual execution. For a detailed account of information algebra, the reader is referred to a definitive survey paper [32]– available space disallows a detailed account here. In short, in addition to a definition of the elements of Φ, any information algebra Φ includes two basic operators:

- Combination: The operation $X \otimes Y$ *combines* the information in elements $X, Y \in \Phi$.
- Focusing: The operation $X^{\Rightarrow S}$ isolates the elements of $X \in \Phi$ that are relevant to a *sublanguage* S, i.e. the subpart of X specified by S.

Focusing and combination must additionally satisfy certain properties (see our Technical Report [3]). The definitions of elements $X \in \Phi$, sublanguages S, combination, and focusing constitute the definition of the algebra. In all cases, the relation $X \leq Y$ holds iff $X \otimes Y = Y$. Proving that $\otimes$ has been correctly defined for an algebra implies that $\leq$ is a partial order [32].

3.1   Support for Various Approaches

Various approaches are taken to audit log generation and representation, including logical [18], database [1], and probabilistic approaches [43]. Information algebra is sufficiently general to contain relevant systems as instances, so our notions of soundness and completeness can apply broadly. Here we discuss logical and database approaches.

First Order Logic (FOL). Logics have been used in several well-developed auditing systems [10,24], for the encoding of both audit logs and queries. FOL in particular is attractive due to readily available implementation support, e.g. Datalog and Prolog.

Let Greek letters ϕ and ψ range over FOL formulas and let capital letters X, Y, Z range over sets of formulas. We posit a sound and complete proof theory supporting judgements of the form $X \vdash \phi$. In this text we assume without loss of generality a natural deduction proof theory.

Elements of our algebra are sets of formulas closed under logical entailment. Intuitively, given a set of formulas X, the closure of X is the set of formulas that are logically entailed by X, and thus represents all the information contained in X. In spirit, we follow the treatment of sentential logic as an information algebra explored in related foundational work [32], however our definition of closure is syntactic, not semantic.

Definition 6. *We define a closure operation C, and a set Φ_{FOL} of closed sets of formulas:*

$$C(X) = \{\phi \mid X \vdash \phi\} \qquad \Phi_{FOL} = \{X \mid C(X) = X\}$$

Note in particular that $C(\varnothing)$ is the set of logical tautologies.

Let *Preds* be the set of all predicate symbols, and let $S \subseteq$ *Preds* be a set of predicate symbols. We define *sublanguage* L_S to be the set of well-formed formulas over predicate symbols in S (and including boolean atoms T and F, and closed under the usual first-order connectives and binders). We will use sublanguages to define refinement operations in our information algebra. Subset containment induces a lattice structure, denoted $\mathcal{S}$, on the set of all sublanguages, with $\mathcal{F} = L_{Preds}$ as the top element.

Now we can define the focus and combination operators, which are the fundamental operators of an information algebra. Focusing isolates the component of a closed set of formulas that is in a given sublanguage. Combination closes the union of closed sets of formulas. Intuitively, the focus of a closed set of formulas X to sublanguage L is the refinement of the information in X to the formulas in L. The combination of closed sets of formulas X and Y combines the information of each set.

Definition 7. *Define:*

1. *Focusing:* $X^{\Rightarrow S} = C(X \cap L_S)$ *where* $X \in \Phi_{FOL}$, $S \subseteq$ *Preds*
2. *Combination:* $X \otimes Y = C(X \cup Y)$ *where* $X, Y \in \Phi_{FOL}$

These definitions of focusing and combination enjoy a number of properties within the algebra, as stated in the following Theorem, establishing that the construction is a domain-free information algebra [31]. FOL has been treated as an information algebra before, but our definitions of combination and focusing and hence the result are novel.

Theorem 2. *Structure $(\Phi_{FOL}, \mathcal{S})$ with focus operation $X^{\Rightarrow S}$ and combination operation $X \otimes Y$ forms a domain-free information algebra.*

In addition, to interpret traces and logs as elements of this algebra, i.e. to define the function $\lfloor \cdot \rfloor$, we assume existence of a function $toFOL(\cdot)$ that injectively maps traces and logs to sets of FOL formulas, and then take $\lfloor \cdot \rfloor = C(toFOL(\cdot))$. To define the range of $toFOL(\cdot)$, that is, to specify how trace information will be represented in FOL, we assume the existence of *configuration description predicates* P which are each at least unary. Each configuration description predicate fully describes some element of a configuration κ, and the first argument is always a natural number t, indicating the time at which the configuration occurred. A set of configuration description predicates with the same timestamp describes a configuration, and traces are described by the union of sets describing each configuration in the trace. In particular, the configuration description predicates include predicate $\text{Call}(t, f, x)$, which indicates that function f is called at time t with argument x. We will fully define $toFOL(\cdot)$ when we discuss particular source and target languages for program rewriting.

Example 1. We return to the example described in Sect. 1.1 to show how FOL can express break the glass logging specifications. Adapting a logic programming style, the trace of a program can be viewed as a fact base, and the logging specification LS_H performs resolution of a LoggedCall predicate, defined via the following Horn clause we call ψ_H:

$$\forall t, d, s, u.(\text{Call}(t, \mathbf{read}, u, d) \wedge \text{Call}(s, \mathbf{breakGlass}, u) \wedge s < t \wedge \text{PatientInfo}(d))$$
$$\implies \text{LoggedCall}(t, \mathbf{read}, u, d)$$

Here we imagine that **breakGlass** is a break the glass function where u identifies the current user and PatientInfo is a predicate specifying which files contain patient information. The log contains only valid instances of LoggedCall given a particular trace, which specify the user and sensitive information accessed following glass breaking, which otherwise would be disallowed by a separate access control policy.

Formally, we define logging specifications in a logic programming style by using combination and focusing. Any logging specification is parameterized by a sublanguage S that identifies the predicate(s) to be resolved and Horn clauses X that define it/them, hence we define a functional *spec* from pairs (X, S) to specifications LS, where we use λ as a binder for function definitions in the usual manner:

Definition 8. *The function spec is given a pair* (X, S) *and returns a FOL logging specification, i.e. a function from traces to elements of* Φ_{FOL}:

$$spec(X, S) = \lambda \tau.(\lfloor \tau \rfloor \otimes C(X))^{\Rightarrow S}.$$

In any logging specification spec(X, S), *we call* X *the* guidelines.

The above example LS_H would then be formally defined as $spec(\psi_H, \{\text{LoggedCall}\})$.

Relational Database. Relational algebra is a canonical example of an information algebra, though we provide a different formulation than the standard one [32] since the latter is not suited to our purpose here. We define databases D as sets of relations, where a relation X is a set of *tuples*. We write $((a_1 : x_1), ..., (a_n : x_1))$ to denote an n-ary tuple with attributes (aka label) a_i associated with values x_i. Databases are elements of the information algebra, and sublanguages S are collections of sets of attributes. Each set of attributes corresponds to a specific relation. We define focusing as the restriction to particular relations in a database, and combination as the union of databases. Hence, letting $\leq_{RA}$ denote the relational algebra information ordering, $D_1 \leq_{RA} D_2$ iff $D_1 \otimes D_2 = D_2$. We refer to this algebra as Φ_{RA}. The details of our formulation and the proof that it satisfies the required properties is given in our Technical Report [3]. Relational databases are heavily used for storing and querying audit logs, so this formulation is crucial for practical application of our correctness properties, as discussed in Sect. 5.

3.2   Transforming and Combining Audit Logs

Multiple audit logs from different sources are often combined in practice. Also, logging information is often transformed for storage and communication. For example, log data may be generated in common event format (CEF), which is parsed and stored in relational database tables, and subsequently exported and communicated via JSON. In all cases, it is necessary to characterize the effect of transformation (if any) on log information, and relate queries on various representations to the logging specification semantics. Otherwise, it is unclear what is the relation of log queries to log-generating programs.

To address this, information algebra provides a useful concept called *monotone mapping*. Given two information algebras Ψ_1 and Ψ_2 with ordering relations $\leq_1$ and $\leq_2$ respectively, a mapping μ from elements X, Y of Ψ_1 to elements $\mu(X), \mu(Y)$ of Ψ_2 is monotone iff $X \leq_1 Y$ implies $\mu(X) \leq_2 \mu(Y)$. For example, assuming that Ψ_1 is our FOL information algebra while Ψ_2 is relational algebra, we can define a monotone mapping using a *least Herbrand interpretation* [11], denoted $\mathfrak{H}$, and by positing a function *attrs* from n-ary predicate symbols to functions mapping numbers $1, ..., n$ to labels. That is, $attrs(\mathrm{P})(n)$ is the label associated with the nth argument of predicate P. We require that if $\mathrm{P} \neq \mathrm{Q}$ then $attrs(\mathrm{P})(j) \neq attrs(\mathrm{Q})(k)$ for all j, k. To map predicates to tuples we have:

$$tuple(\mathrm{P}(x_1, \ldots, x_n)) = ((attrs(\mathrm{P})(1) : x_1), \ldots, (attrs(\mathrm{P})(n) : x_n))$$

Then to obtain a relation from all valid instances of a particular predicate P given formulas X we define:

$$R_\mathrm{P}(X) = \{tuple(\mathrm{P}(x_1, \ldots, x_n)) \mid \mathrm{P}(x_1, \ldots, x_n) \in \mathfrak{H}(X)\}$$

Now we define the function *rel* which is collection of all relations obtained from X, where $\mathrm{P}_1, ..., \mathrm{P}_n$ are the predicate symbols occurring in X:

$$rel(X) = \{R_{\mathrm{P}_1}(X), \cdots, R_{\mathrm{P}_n}(X)\}$$

Theorem 3. *rel is a monotone mapping.*

Thus, if we wish to generate an audit log $\mathbb{L}$ as a set of FOL formulas, but ultimately store the data in a relational database, we are still able to maintain a formal relation between stored logs and the semantics of a given trace τ and specification LS. E.g., if a log $\mathbb{L}$ is sound with respect to τ and LS, then $rel(\lfloor \mathbb{L} \rfloor) \leq_{RA} rel(LS(\tau))$. While the data in $rel(\lfloor \mathbb{L} \rfloor)$ may very well be broken up into multiple relations in practice, e.g. to compress data and/or for query optimization, the formalism also establishes correctness conditions for the transformation that relate resulting information to the logging semantics $LS(\tau)$ by way of the mapping. We reify this idea in our OpenMRS implementation as discussed in Sect. 5.2.

4   Rewriting Programs with Logging Specifications

Since correct logging instrumentation is a safety property (2.2), there are several possible implementation strategies. For example, one could define an edit automata that enforces the property (see our Technical Report [3]), that could be implemented either as a separate program monitor or using IRM techniques [21]. But since we are interested in program rewriting for a particular class of logging specifications, the approach we discuss here is more simply stated and proven correct than a general IRM methodology.

We specify a class of logging specifications of interest, along with a program rewriting algorithm that is sound and complete for it. We consider a basic λ-calculus that serves as formal setting to establish correctness of a program rewriting approach to correct instrumentation of logging specification. We use this same approach to implement an auditing tool for OpenMRS, described in the next Section. The supported class of logging specifications is predicated on temporal properties of function calls and characteristics of their arguments. This class has practical potential since security-sensitive operations are often packaged as functions or methods (e.g. in medical records software [37]), and the supported class allows complex policies such as break the glass to be expressed. The language of logging specifications is FOL, and we use Φ_{FOL} to define the semantics of logging and prove correctness of the algorithm.

4.1   Source Language

We first define a source language Λ_{call}, including the definitions of configurations, execution traces, and function $toFOL(\cdot)$ that shows how we concretely model execution traces in FOL.

Language Λ_{call} is a simple call-by-value λ-calculus with named functions. A Λ_{call} program is a pair $(e, \mathcal{C})$ where e is an expression, and $\mathcal{C}$ is a *codebase* which maps function names to function definitions. A Λ_{call} configuration is a triple $(e, n, \mathcal{C})$, where e is the expression remaining to be evaluated, n is a timestamp (a natural number) that indicates how many steps have been taken since program execution began, and $\mathcal{C}$ is a codebase. The codebase does not change during program execution.

The syntax of Λ_{call} is as follows.

$$
\begin{aligned}
v &::= x \mid \mathbf{f} \mid \lambda x.\, e & \textit{values} \\
e &::= e\, e \mid v & \textit{expressions} \\
E &::= [\,] \mid E\, e \mid v\, E & \textit{evaluation contexts} \\
\kappa &::= (e, n, \mathcal{C}) & \textit{configurations} \\
\mathfrak{p} &::= (e, \mathcal{C}) & \textit{programs}
\end{aligned}
$$

The small-step semantics of Λ_{call} is defined as follows.

$$\frac{\beta}{((\lambda x.\ e)\ v, n, \mathcal{C}) \to (e[v/x], n+1, \mathcal{C})} \qquad \frac{\mathcal{C}(\mathbf{f}) = \lambda x.\ e}{(\mathbf{f}\ v, n, \mathcal{C}) \to (e[v/x], n+1, \mathcal{C})}\ \beta_{\text{Call}}$$

$$\frac{\text{Context}}{(e, n, \mathcal{C}) \to (e', n', \mathcal{C})}{(E[e], n, \mathcal{C}) \to (E[e'], n', \mathcal{C})}$$

An execution trace τ is a sequence of configurations, and for a program $\mathfrak{p} = (e, \mathcal{C})$ and execution trace $\tau = \kappa_0 \ldots \kappa_n$ we define $\mathfrak{p} \Downarrow \tau$ if and only if $\kappa_0 = (e, 0, \mathcal{C})$ and for all $i \in 1..n$ we have $\kappa_{i-1} \to \kappa_i$.

We now show how to model a configuration as a set of ground instances of predicates, and then use this to model execution traces. We posit predicates Call, App, Value, Context, and Codebase to logically denote run time entities. For $\kappa = (e, n, \mathcal{C})$, we define $toFOL(\kappa)$ by cases, where $\langle\mathcal{C}\rangle_n = \bigcup_{\mathbf{f} \in \text{dom}(\mathcal{C})} \{\text{Codebase}(n, \mathbf{f}, \mathcal{C}(\mathbf{f}))\}$[3].

$$toFOL(v, n, \mathcal{C}) = \{\text{Value}(n, v)\} \cup \langle\mathcal{C}\rangle_n$$
$$toFOL(E[\mathbf{f}\ v], n, \mathcal{C}) = \{\text{Call}(n, \mathbf{f}, v), \text{Context}(n, E)\} \cup \langle\mathcal{C}\rangle_n$$
$$toFOL(E[(\lambda x.\ e)\ v)], n, \mathcal{C}) = \{\text{App}(n, (\lambda x.e), v), \text{Context}(n, E)\} \cup \langle\mathcal{C}\rangle_n$$

We define $toFOL(\tau)$ for a potentially infinite execution trace $\tau = \kappa_0\kappa_1 \ldots$ by defining it over its prefixes. Let $\text{prefix}(\tau)$ denote the set of prefixes of τ. Then, $toFOL(\tau) = \bigcup_{\sigma \in \text{prefix}(\tau)} toFOL(\sigma)$, where $toFOL(\sigma) = toFOL(\kappa_0) \cup \cdots \cup toFOL(\kappa_n)$, for $\sigma = \kappa_0 \ldots \kappa_n$. Function $toFOL(\cdot)$ is injective up to α-equivalence since $toFOL(\tau)$ fully and uniquely describes the execution trace τ.

4.2 Specifications Based on Function Call Properties

We define a class **Calls** of logging specifications that capture temporal properties of function calls, such as those reflected in break the glass policies. We restrict specification definitions to safe Horn clauses to ensure applicability of well-known results and total algorithms such as Datalog [11]. Specifications in **Calls** support logging of calls to a specific function $\mathbf{f}$ that happen after functions $\mathbf{g}_1, \ldots, \mathbf{g}_n$ are called. Conditions on all function arguments, and times of their invocation, can be defined via a predicate ϕ. Hence more precise requirements can be imposed, e.g. a linear ordering on function calls, particular values of functions arguments, etc.

---

[3] While Λ_{call} expressions and evaluation contexts appear as predicate arguments, their syntax can be written as string literals to conform to typical Datalog or Prolog syntax.

Definition 9. Calls *is the set of all logging specifications* $spec(X, \{$ LoggedCall$\})$ *where* X *contains a safe Horn clause of the following form:*

$$\forall t_0, \ldots, t_n, x_0, \ldots, x_n \,.\, \mathrm{Call}(t_0, \mathbf{f}, x_0) \bigwedge_{i=1}^{n} (\mathrm{Call}(t_i, \mathbf{g}_i, x_i) \wedge t_i < t_0) \wedge$$

$$\phi((x_0, t_0), \ldots, (x_n, t_n)) \implies \mathrm{LoggedCall}(t_0, \mathbf{f}, x_0).$$

While set X may contain other safe Horn clauses, in particular definitions of predicates occurring in ϕ, no other Horn clause in X uses the predicate symbols LoggedCall, Value, Context, Call, App, *or* Codebase. *For convenience in the following, we define* Logevent$(LS) = \mathbf{f}$ *and* Triggers$(LS) = \{\mathbf{g}_1, \ldots, \mathbf{g}_n\}$.

We note that specifications in **Calls** clearly satisfy Definition 1, since preconditions for logging a particular call to $\mathbf{f}$ must be satisfied at the time of that call.

4.3   Target Language

The syntax of target language Λ_{log} extends Λ_{call} syntax with a command to track *logging preconditions* (*callEvent*$(\mathbf{f}, v)$), i.e. calls to logging triggers, and a command to emit log entries (*emit*$(\mathbf{f}, v)$). Configurations are extended to include a set X of logging preconditions, and an audit log $\mathbb{L}$.

$$e ::= \ldots \mid callEvent(\mathbf{f}, v); e \mid emit(\mathbf{f}, v); e \qquad\qquad expressions$$
$$\kappa ::= (e, X, n, \mathbb{L}, \mathcal{C}) \qquad\qquad configurations$$

The semantics of Λ_{log} extends the semantics of Λ_{call} with new rules for commands *callEvent*$(\mathbf{f}, v)$ and *emit*$(\mathbf{f}, v)$, which update the set of logging preconditions and audit log respectively. An instrumented program uses the set of logging preconditions to determine when it should emit events to the audit log. The semantics is parameterized by a guideline $X_{Guidelines}$, typically taken from a logging specification. Given the definition of **Calls**, these semantics would be easy to implement using e.g. a Datalog proof engine.

Precondition

$$\overline{(callEvent(\mathbf{f}, v); e, X, n, \mathbb{L}, \mathcal{C}) \to (e, X \cup \{\mathrm{Call}(n-1, \mathbf{f}, v)\}, n, \mathbb{L}, \mathcal{C})}$$

Log

$$\frac{X \cup X_{Guidelines} \vdash \mathrm{LoggedCall}(n-1, \mathbf{f}, v)}{(emit(\mathbf{f}, v); e, X, n, \mathbb{L}, \mathcal{C}) \to (e, X, n, \mathbb{L} \cup \{\mathrm{LoggedCall}(n-1, \mathbf{f}, v)\}, \mathcal{C})}$$

NoLog

$$\frac{X \cup X_{Guidelines} \nvdash \mathrm{LoggedCall}(n-1, \mathbf{f}, v)}{(emit(\mathbf{f}, v); e, X, n, \mathbb{L}, \mathcal{C}) \to (e, X, n, \mathbb{L}, \mathcal{C})}$$

Note that to ensure that these instrumentation commands do not change execution behavior, the configuration's time is not incremented when $callEvent(\mathbf{f}, v)$ and $emit(\mathbf{f}, v)$ are evaluated. That is, the configuration time counts the number of source language computation steps.

The rules Log and NoLog rely on checking whether $X_{Guidelines}$ and logging preconditions X entail $\text{LoggedCall}(n - 1, \mathbf{f}, v)$. For a target language program $\mathfrak{p} = (e, \mathcal{C})$ and execution trace $\tau = \kappa_0 \ldots \kappa_n$ we define $\mathfrak{p} \Downarrow \tau$ if and only if $\kappa_0 = (e, \emptyset, 0, \emptyset, \mathcal{C})$ and for all $i \in 1..n$ we have $\kappa_{i-1} \rightarrow \kappa_i$.

To establish correctness of program rewriting, we need to define a correspondence relation $:\approx$. Source language execution traces and target language execution traces correspond if they represent the same expression evaluated to the same point. We make special cases for when the source execution is about to perform a function application that the target execution will track or log via an $callEvent(\mathbf{f}, v)$ or $emit(\mathbf{f}, v)$ command. In these cases, the target execution may be ahead by one or two steps, allowing time for addition of information to the log.

Definition 10. *Given source language execution trace $\tau = \kappa_0 \ldots \kappa_m$ and target language execution trace $\tau' = \kappa'_0 \ldots \kappa'_n$, where $\kappa_i = (e_i, t_i, \mathcal{C}_i)$ and $\kappa'_i = (e'_i, X_i, t'_i, \mathbb{L}_i, \mathcal{C}'_i)$, $\tau :\approx \tau'$ iff $e_0 = e'_0$ and either*

1. *$e_m = e'_n$ (taking $=$ to mean syntactic equivalence); or*
2. *$e_m = e'_{n-1}$ and $e'_n = callEvent(\mathbf{f}, v); e'$ for some expressions $\mathbf{f}$, v, and e'; or*
3. *$e_m = e'_{n-2}$ and $e'_n = emit(\mathbf{f}, v); e'$ for some expressions $\mathbf{f}$, v, and e'.*

Finally, we need to define $toFOL(\mathbb{L})$ for audit logs $\mathbb{L}$ produced by an instrumented program. Since our audit logs are just sets of formulas of the form $\text{LoggedCall}(t, \mathbf{f}, v)$, we define $toFOL(\mathbb{L}) = \mathbb{L}$.

4.4   Program Rewriting Algorithm

Our program rewriting algorithm $\mathcal{R}_{\Lambda_{\text{call}}}$ takes a Λ_{call} program $\mathfrak{p} = (e, \mathcal{C})$, a logging specification $LS = spec(X_{Guidelines}, \{\text{LoggedCall}\}) \in \mathbf{Calls}$, and produces a Λ_{log} program $\mathfrak{p}' = (e', \mathcal{C}')$ such that e and e' are identical, and $\mathcal{C}'$ is identical to $\mathcal{C}$ except for the addition of $callEvent(\mathbf{h}, v)$ and $emit(\mathbf{h}, v)$ commands. The algorithm is straightforward: we modify the codebase to add $callEvent(\mathbf{h}, v)$ to the definition of any function $\mathbf{h} \in Triggers(LS) \cup \{Logevent(LS)\}$ and add $emit(\mathbf{f}, v)$ to the definition of function $\mathbf{f} = Logevent(LS)$.

Definition 11. *For Λ_{call} program $\mathfrak{p} = (e, \mathcal{C})$ and logging specifications $LS \in$ **Calls**, define:*

$$\mathcal{R}_{\Lambda_{\text{call}}}((e, \mathcal{C}), LS) = (e, \mathcal{C}')$$

where $\mathcal{C}'(\mathbf{f}) =$

$$\begin{cases} \lambda x. callEvent(\mathbf{f}, x); emit(\mathbf{f}, x); e_{\mathbf{f}} & \text{if } \mathbf{f} = Logevent(LS) \text{ and } \mathcal{C}(\mathbf{f}) = \lambda x.e_{\mathbf{f}} \\ \lambda x. callEvent(\mathbf{f}, x); e_{\mathbf{f}} & \text{if } \mathbf{f} \in Triggers(LS) \text{ and } \mathcal{C}(\mathbf{f}) = \lambda x.e_{\mathbf{f}} \\ \mathcal{C}(\mathbf{f}) & \text{otherwise} \end{cases}$$

This algorithm obeys the required properties, i.e. it is both semantics preserving and sound and complete for a given logging specification.

Theorem 4. *Algorithm $\mathcal{R}_{\Lambda_{\mathrm{call}}}$ is semantics preserving (Definition 4).*

Theorem 5 (Soundness and Completeness). *Algorithm $\mathcal{R}_{\Lambda_{\mathrm{call}}}$ is sound and complete (Definitions 5).*

5 Case Study on a Medical Records System

As a case study, we have developed a tool [2] that enables automatic instrumentation of logging specifications for the OpenMRS system. The implementation is based on the formal model developed in Sect. 4 which enjoys a correctness guarantee. The logging information is stored in a SQL database consisting of multiple tables, and the correctness of this scheme is established via the monotone mapping defined in Sect. 3.2. We have also considered how to reduce memory overhead as a central optimization challenge.

OpenMRS is a Java-based open-source web application for medical records, built on the Spring Framework. Previous efforts in auditing for OpenMRS include recording any modification to the database records as part of the OpenMRS core implementation, and logging every function call to a set of predefined records. The latter illustrates the relevance of function invocations as a key factor in logging. Furthermore, function calls define the fundamental unit of "secure operations" in OpenMRS access control [37]. This highlights the relevance of our **Calls** logging specification class, particularly as it pertains to specification of break the glass policies, which are sensitive to authorization.

In contrast to previous auditing solutions for OpenMRS, ours allows security administrators to define logging specifications separately from code. Our tool automatically instruments code to correctly support these specifications. This is more convenient, declarative, and less error prone than direct ad hoc instrumentation of code.

System Architecture Summary. To clarify the following discussion, we briefly summarize the architecture of our system. Logging specifications are made in the style of **Calls** (Definition 9), which can be parsed into JSON objects with a standard form recognized by our system. Instrumentation of legacy code is then accomplished using aspect oriented programming. Parsed specifications are used to identify join points, where the system weaves aspects supporting audit logging into OpenMRS bytecode. These aspects communicate with a proof engine at the joint points to reason about audit log generation, implementing the semantics developed for Λ_{log} in Sect. 4.3. In our deployment logs are recorded in a SQL database, but our architecture supports other approaches via the use of listeners.

5.1 Break the Glass Policies for OpenMRS

Break the glass policies for auditing are intended to retrospectively manage the same security that is proactively managed by access control (before the glass is broken). Thus it is important that we focus on the same resources in auditing as those focused on by access control. The data model of OpenMRS consists of several domains, e.g. "Patient" and "User" domains contain information about the patients and system users respectively, and the "Encounter" domain includes information regarding the interventions of healthcare providers with patients. In order to access and modify the information in different domains, corresponding service-layer functionalities are defined that are accessible through a web interface. These functionalities provide security sensitive operations through which data assets are handled. Thus, OpenMRS authorization mechanism checks user eligibility to perform these operations [37]. Likewise, we identify these functionalities in logging specifications, i.e. triggers and logging events are service-layer methods that provide access to data domains, e.g., the patient and user data.

We adapt the logical language of logging specifications developed above (Definition 9), with the minor extension that we allow logging of methods with more than one argument. We note that logging specifications can include other information specified as safe Horn clauses, e.g. ACLs. Here is a simple example of a break the glass auditing policy specified in this form, which states that if the glass is broken by some low-level user, and subsequently patient information is accessed by that user, the access should be logged. The variable U refers to the user, and the variable P refers to the patient. This specification also defines security levels for two users, alice and admin. The predicate @< defines the usual total ordering on integers.

```
loggedCall(T, getPatient, U, P) :-
  call(T, getPatient, U, P), call(S, breakTheGlass, U),
  @<(S, T), hasSecurityLevel(U, low).

hasSecurityLevel(admin, high).
hassecuritylevel(alice, low).
```

To enable these policies in practice, we have added a "break the glass" button to a user menu in the OpenMRS GUI that can be manually activated on demand. Activation invokes the breakTheGlass method parameterized by the user id. We note that breaking the glass does not turn off access control in our current implementation, which we consider a separate engineering concern that is out of scope for this paper.

5.2   Code Instrumentation

To instrument code for log generation, we leverage the Spring Framework that supports aspect-oriented programming (AOP). AOP is used to rewrite code where necessary with "advice", which in our case is *before* certain method invocations (so-called "before advice"). Our advice checks the invoked method names and implements the semantics given in Sect. 4.3, establishing correctness of audit logging. Join points are automatically extracted from logging specifications, and defined with service-level granularity in a configuration file. Weaving into bytecode is also performed automatically by our system.

For example, in the following excerpt of a configuration file, every interface method of the service `PatientService` is a join point so before invoking each of those methods the advice in `RetroSecurityAdvice` will be woven into the control flow. The `RetroSecurityAdvice` is automatically generated by our system based on the logging specification, but essentially determines whether a method call is a trigger or a logging event and interacts with the proof engine appropriately in each case.

```
<advice>
<point>org.openmrs.api.PatientService</point>
<class>
 org.openmrs.module.retrosecurity.advice.RetroSecurityAdvice
</class>
</advice>
```

Proof Engine. According to the the semantics of $\Lambda_{\log}$, it is necessary to perform logical deduction, in particular resolution of LoggedCall predicates. To this end, we have employed XSB Prolog as a proof engine, due to its reliability and robustness. In order to have a bidirectional communication between the Java application and the engine, InterProlog Java/Prolog SDK [27] is used.

The proof engine is initialized in a separate thread with an interface to the main execution trace. The interface includes methods to define predicates, and to add rules and facts. Asynchrony of the logic engine avoids blocking the "normal" execution trace for audit logging purposes, preserving its original performance. The interface also provides an instant querying mechanism. The instrumented program communicates with the XSB Prolog engine as these interface methods are invoked in advices.

Writing and Storing the Log. Asynchronous communication with the proof engine through multi-threading enables us to modularize the deduction of the information that we need to log, separate from the storage and retainment details. This supports a variety of possible approaches to storing log information– e.g., using a strict transactional discipline to ensure writing to critical log, and/or blocking execution until log write occurs. Advice generated by the system for audit log generation just needs to include event listeners to implement the technology of choice for log storage and retainment.

In our application, the logging information is stored in a SQL database consisting of multiple tables. In case new logging information is derived by the proof engine, the corresponding listeners in the main execution trace are notified and the listeners partition and store the logging information in potentially multiple tables. Correctness of this storage technique is established using the monotone mapping *rel* defined in Sect. 3.2.

Consider the case where a `loggedCall` is derived by the proof engine given the logging specification in Sect. 5.1. Here, the instantiation of U and P are user and patient names, respectively, used in the OpenMRS implementation. However, logged calls are stored in a table called `GetPatL` with attributes `time`, `uid`, and `pid`, where `uid` is the primary key for a `User` table with a `uname` attribute, and `pid` is the primary key for a `Patient` table with a `patient_name` attribute. Thus, for any given logging specification of the appropriate form, the monotonic mapping *rel* of the following `select` statement gives us the exact information content of the logging specification following execution of an OpenMRS session:

```
select time,"getPatient", uname, patient_name
from GetPatL, User, Patient
where GetPatL.uid = User.uid and GetPatL.pid = Patient.pid
```

5.3   Reducing Memory Overhead

A source of overhead in our system is memory needed to store logging preconditions. We observe that a naive implementation of the intended semantics will add all trigger functions to the logging preconditions, regardless of whether they are redundant in some way. To optimize memory usage, we therefore aim to refrain from adding information about trigger invocations if it is unnecessary for future derivations of audit log information. As a simple example, in the following logging specification it suffices to add only the first invocation of $\mathbf{g}$ to the set of logging preconditions to infer the relevant logging information.

$$\forall t_0, t_1, x_0, x_1 . \operatorname{Call}(t_0, \mathbf{f}, x_0) \wedge \operatorname{Call}(t_1, \mathbf{g}, x_1) \wedge t_1 < t_0 \implies \operatorname{LoggedCall}(t_0, \mathbf{f}, x_0).$$

Intuitively, our general approach is to rewrite the body of a given logging specification in a form consisting of different conjuncts, such that the truth valuation of each conjunct is independent of the others. This way, the required information to derive each conjunct is independent of the information required for other conjuncts. Then, if the inference of a LoggedCall predicate needs a conjunct to be derived only once during the program execution, following derivation of that conjunct, triggers in the conjunct are "turned off", i.e. no longer added to logging preconditions when encountered during execution. Otherwise, the triggers are never turned off. This way, we ensure that none of the invocations of the logging event is missed.

Formally, the logging specification is rewritten in the form

$$\forall t_0, \ldots, t_n, x_0, \ldots, x_n . \bigwedge_{i=1}^{n} (t_i < t_0) \bigwedge_{k=1}^{L} Q_k \implies \operatorname{LoggedCall}(t_0, \mathbf{g}_0, x_0),$$

where each Q_k is a conjunct of literals with independent truth valuation resting on disjointness of predicated variables. In what follows, a formal description of the technique is given.

Consider the Definition 9. We define Ψ to be the set of all positive literals in the body of LoggedCall excluding literals $t_i < t_0$ for all $i \in \{1, \cdots, n\}$. Moreover, let's denote the set of free variables of a formula ϕ as $FV(\phi)$, and abuse this notation to represent the set of free variables that exist in a set of formulas. Next, we define the relation $\circledast_{FV}$ over free variables of positive literals in Ψ, which represents whether they are free variables of the same literal, and extend this transitively in the relation $\circledast_{TFV}$.

Definition 12. *Let $\circledast_{FV} \subseteq FV(\Psi) \times FV(\Psi)$ be a relation where $\alpha \circledast_{FV} \beta$ iff there exists some literal $\phi \in \Psi$ such that $\alpha, \beta \in FV(\phi)$. Then, the transitive closure of $\circledast_{FV}$ is denoted by $\circledast_{TFV}$.*

Note that $\circledast_{TFV}$ is an equivalence relation. Let $[\alpha]_{\circledast_{TFV}}$ denote the equivalence class induced by $\circledast_{TFV}$ over $FV(\Psi)$, where $[\alpha]_{\circledast_{TFV}} \triangleq \{\beta \mid \alpha \circledast_{TFV} \beta\}$. Intuitively, each equivalence class $[\alpha]_{\circledast_{TFV}}$ represents a set of free variables in Ψ that are free in a subset of literals of Ψ, transitively. To be explicit about these subsets of literals, we have the following definition (Definition 13). Note that rather than representing an equivalence class using a representative α (i.e., the notation $[\alpha]_{\circledast_{TFV}}$), we may employ an enumeration of these classes and denote each class as C_k, where $k \in 1 \cdots L$. L represents the number of equivalence classes that have partitioned $FV(\Psi)$. In order to map these two notations, we consider a mapping $\omega : FV(\Psi) \to \{1, \cdots, L\}$ where $\omega(\alpha) = k$ if $[\alpha]_{\circledast_{TFV}} = C_k$.

Definition 13. *Let C be an equivalence class induced by $\circledast_{TFV}$. The predicate class $\mathcal{P}_C$ is a subset of literals of Ψ defined as $\mathcal{P}_C \triangleq \{\phi \in \Psi \mid FV(\phi) \subseteq C\}$. We define the independent conjuncts as $Q_C \triangleq \bigwedge_{\phi \in \mathcal{P}_C} \phi$. We also denote $Q_{[\alpha]}$ as Q_k if $\omega(\alpha) = k$. Obviously, $FV(Q_k) = C_k$.*

The above described techniques are used to implement memory overhead mitigation in our OpenMRS retrospective security module– the same mechanism used to perform a `loggedCall` query is used to check whether the independent conjunct Q_C containing a trigger method is satisfiable whenever the trigger is invoked, in which case all triggers in the conjunct are turned off, i.e. no longer added to preconditions when called. In order to prove the correctness of our approach, we have formalized a new calculus $\Lambda'_{\log}$ with memory overhead mitigation capabilities, and shown that the generated log is the same as the log generated in $\Lambda_{\log}$ for the same programs. The reader is referred to our Technical Report [3] for this formalization.

6   Related Work

Previous work by DeYoung et al. has studied audit policy specification for medical (HIPAA) and business (GLBA) processes [19,20]. This work illustrates the effectiveness and generality of a temporal logic foundation for audit policy specification, which is well-founded in a general theory of privacy [18]. Their auditing system has also been implemented in a tool similar to an interactive theorem prover [24]. Their specification language inspired our approach to logging specification semantics. However, this previous work assumes that audit logs are given, and does not consider the correctness of logs. Some work does consider trustworthiness of logs [7], but only in terms of tampering (malleability). In contrast, our work provides formal foundations for the correctness of audit logs, and considers algorithms to automatically instrument programs to generate correct logs.

Other work applies formal methods (including predicate logics [10,16], process calculi and game theory [28]) to model, specify, and enforce auditing and accountability requirements in distributed systems. In that work, audit logs serve as evidence of resource access rights, an idea also explored in Aura [39] and the APPLE system [22]. In Aura, audit logs record machine-checkable proofs of compliance in the Aura policy language. APPLE proposes a framework based on trust management and audit logic with log generation functionality for a limited set of operations, in order to check user compliance.

In contrast, we provide a formal foundation to support a broad class of logging specifications and relevant correctness conditions. In this respect our proposed system is closely related to PQL [34], which supports program rewriting with instrumentation to answer queries about program execution. From a technical perspective, our approach is also related to trace matching in AspectJ [1], especially in the use of logic to specify trace patterns. However, the concern in that work is aspect pointcut specification, not logging correctness, and their method call patterns are restricted to be regular expressions with no conditions on arguments, whereas the latter is needed for the specifications in **Calls**.

Logging specifications are related to safety properties [38] and are enforceable by security automata, as we have shown. Hence IRM rewriting techniques could be used to implement them [21]. However, the theory of safety properties does not address correctness of audit logs as we do, and our approach can be viewed as a logging-specific IRM strategy. Guts et al. [25] develop a static technique to guarantee that programs are properly instrumented to generate audit logs with sufficient evidence for auditing purposes. As in our research, this is accomplished by first defining a formal semantics of auditing. However, they are interested in evidence-based auditing for specific distributed protocols.

Other recent work [23] has proposed log filters as a required improvement to the current logging practices in the industry due to costly resource consumption and the loss of necessary log information among the collected redundant data. This work is purely empirical, not foundational, but provides practical evidence of the relevance of our efforts since logging filters could be defined as logging specifications.

Audit logs can be considered a form of *provenance*: the history of computation and data. Several recent works have considered formal semantics of provenance [8,9]. Cheney [12] presents a framework for provenance, built on a notion of system traces. Recently, W3C has proposed a data model for provenance, called PROV [5], which enjoys a formal description of its specified constraints and inferences in first-order logic, [13], however the given semantics does not cover the relationship between the provenance record and the actual system behavior. The confidentiality and integrity of provenance information is also a significant concern [26].

7   Conclusion

In this paper we have addressed the problem of audit log correctness. In particular, we have considered how to separate logging specifications from implementations, and how to formally establish that an implementation satisfies a specification. This separation allows security administrators to clearly define logging goals independently from programs, and inspires program rewriting tools that support correct, automatic instrumentation of logging specifications in legacy code.

By leveraging the theory of information algebra, we have defined a semantics of logging specifications as functions from program traces to information. By interpreting audit logs as information, we are then able to establish correctness conditions for audit logs via an information containment relation between log information and logging specification semantics. These conditions allow proof of correctness of program rewriting algorithms that automatically instrument general classes of logging specifications.

We define a particular program rewriting strategy for a core functional calculus that supports instrumentation of logging specifications expressed in first order logic, and then prove this strategy correct. This strategy is then applied to develop a practical tool for instrumenting logging specifications in OpenMRS, a popular medical records system. We discuss implementation features of this tool, including optimizations to minimize memory overhead.

Acknowledgement. This work is supported in part by the National Science Foundation under Grant No. 1408801 and Grant No. 1054172, and by the Air Force Office of Scientific Research.

References

1. Allan, C., Avgustinov, P., Christensen, A.S., Hendren, L.J., Kuzins, S., Lhoták, O., de Moor, O., Sereni, D., Sittampalam, G., Tibble, J.: Adding trace matching with free variables to AspectJ. OOPSLA **2005**, 345–364 (2005)
2. Amir-Mohammadian, S., Chong, S., Skalka, C.: Retrospective Security Module for OpenMRS (2015). https://github.com/sepehram/retro-security-openmrs
3. Amir-Mohammadian, S., Chong, S., Skalka, C.: The theory and practice of correct audit logging. Technical report, University of Vermont, October 2015. https://www.uvm.edu/~samirmoh/TR/TR_Audit.pdf
4. Bauer, L., Ligatti, J., Walker, D.: More enforceable security policies. Technical report TR-649-02, Princeton University, June 2002
5. Belhajjame, K., B'Far, R., Cheney, J., Coppens, S., Cresswell, S., Gil, Y., Groth, P., Klyne, G., Lebo, T., McCusker, J., Miles, S., Myers, J., Sahoo, S., Tilmes, C.: PROV-DM: the PROV data model. (2013). http://www.w3.org/TR/2013/REC-prov-dm-20130430. Accessed 07 February 2015
6. Biswas, D., Niemi, V.: Transforming privacy policies to auditing specifications. HASE **2011**, 368–375 (2011)
7. Böck, B., Huemer, D., Tjoa, A.M.: Towards more trustable log files for digital forensics by means of trusted computing. In: AINA 2010, pp. 1020–1027. IEEE Computer Society (2010)
8. Buneman, P., Chapman, A., Cheney, J.: Provenance management in curated databases. SIGMOD **2006**, 539–550 (2006)
9. Buneman, P., Khanna, S., Tan, W.-C.: Why and where: a characterization of data provenance. In: Bussche, J., Vianu, V. (eds.) ICDT 2001. LNCS, vol. 1973, pp. 316–330. Springer, Heidelberg (2000)

10. Cederquist, J.G., Corin, R., Dekker, M.A.C., Etalle, S., den Hartog, J.I., Lenzini, G.: Audit-based compliance control. Int. J. Inf. Secur. **6**(2–3), 133–151 (2007)
11. Ceri, S., Gottlob, G., Tanca, L.: What you always wanted to know about Datalog (and never dared to ask). IEEE Trans. Knowl. Data Eng. **1**(1), 146–166 (1989)
12. Cheney, J.: A formal framework for provenance security. CSF **2011**, 281–293 (2011)
13. Cheney, J.: Semantics of the PROV data model (2013). http://www.w3.org/TR/2013/NOTE-prov-sem-20130430. Accessed 07 February 2015
14. Chuvakin, A.: Beautiful log handling. In: Oram, A., Viega, J. (eds.) Beautiful security: leading security experts explain how they think. O'Reilly Media Inc. (2009)
15. Cook, D., Hartnett, J., Manderson, K., Scanlan, J.: Catching spam before it arrives: domain specific dynamic blacklists. In: AusGrid 2006, pp. 193–202. Australian Computer Society, Inc.(2006)
16. Corin, R., Etalle, S., den Hartog, J.I., Lenzini, G., Staicu, I.: A logic for auditing accountability in decentralized systems. FAST **2004**, 187–201 (2004)
17. CPMC Press Release: Audit finds employee access to patient files without apparent business or treatment purpose (2015). http://www.cpmc.org/about/press/News2015/phi.html. 30 January 2015
18. Datta, A., Blocki, J., Christin, N., DeYoung, H., Garg, D., Jia, L., Kaynar, D., Sinha, A.: Understanding and protecting privacy: formal semantics and principled audit mechanisms. In: Jajodia, S., Mazumdar, C. (eds.) ICISS 2011. LNCS, vol. 7093, pp. 1–27. Springer, Heidelberg (2011)
19. DeYoung, H., Garg, D., Jia, L., Kaynar, D., Datta, A.: Privacy policy specification and audit in a fixed-point logic: How to enforce HIPAA, GLBA, and all that. Technical report CMU-CyLab-10-008, Carnegie Mellon University, April 2010
20. DeYoung, H., Garg, D., Jia, L., Kaynar, D.K., Datta, A.: Experiences in the logical specification of the HIPAA and GLBA privacy laws. WPES **2010**, 73–82 (2010)
21. Erlingsson, Ú.: The inlined reference monitor approach to security policy enforcement. Ph.D. thesis, Cornell University (2003)
22. Etalle, S., Winsborough, W.H.: A posteriori compliance control. SACMAT **2007**, 11–20 (2007)
23. Fu, Q., Zhu, J., Hu, W., Lou, J., Ding, R., Lin, Q., Zhang, D., Xie, T.: Where do developers log? an empirical study on logging practices in industry. ICSE **2014**, 24–33 (2014)
24. Garg, D., Jia, L., Datta, A.: Policy auditing over incomplete logs: theory, implementation and applications. CCS **2011**, 151–162 (2011)
25. Guts, N., Fournet, C., Zappa Nardelli, F.: Reliable evidence: auditability by typing. In: Backes, M., Ning, P. (eds.) ESORICS 2009. LNCS, vol. 5789, pp. 168–183. Springer, Heidelberg (2009)
26. Hasan, R., Sion, R., Winslett, M.: The case of the fake Picasso: preventing history forgery with secures provenance. FAST **2009**, 1–14 (2009)
27. InterProlog Consulting: Logic for your app (2014). http://interprolog.com/. Accessed 27 September 2015
28. Jagadeesan, R., Jeffrey, A., Pitcher, C., Riely, J.: Towards a theory of accountability and audit. In: Backes, M., Ning, P. (eds.) ESORICS 2009. LNCS, vol. 5789, pp. 152–167. Springer, Heidelberg (2009)
29. Kemmerer, R.A., Vigna, G.: Intrusion detection: a brief history and overview. Computer **35**(4), 27–30 (2002)
30. King, J.T., Smith, B., Williams, L.: Modifying without a trace: General audit guidelines are inadequate for open-source electronic health record audit mechanisms. In: IHI 2012, pp. 305–314. ACM (2012)

31. Kohlas, J.: Information Algebras: Generic Structures For Inference. Discrete mathematics and theoretical computer science. Springer, London (2003)
32. Kohlas, J., Schmid, J.: An algebraic theory of information: an introduction and survey. Information **5**(2), 219–254 (2014)
33. Lampson, B.W.: Computer security in the real world. IEEE Computer **37**(6), 37–46 (2004)
34. Martin, M., Livshits, B., Lam, M.S.: Finding application errors and security flaws using PQL: a program query language. In: OOPSLA 2005, pp. 365–383. ACM (2005)
35. Matthews, P., Gaebel, H.: Break the glass. In: HIE Topic Series. Healthcare Information and Management Systems Society (2009). http://www.himss.org/files/himssorg/content/files/090909breaktheglass.pdf
36. Povey, D.: Optimistic security: a new access control paradigm. NSPW **1999**, 40–45 (1999)
37. Rizvi, S.Z., Fong, P.W.L., Crampton, J., Sellwood, J.: Relationship-based access control for an open-source medical records system. SACMAT **2015**, 113–124 (2015)
38. Schneider, F.B.: Enforceable security policies. ACM Trans. Inf. Syst. Secur. **3**(1), 30–50 (2000)
39. Vaughan, J.A., Jia, L., Mazurak, K., Zdancewic, S.: Evidence-based audit. CSF **2008**, 177–191 (2008)
40. Weitzner, D.J.: Beyond secrecy: new privacy protection strategies for open information spaces. IEEE Internet Comput. **11**(5), 94–96 (2007)
41. Weitzner, D.J., Abelson, H., Berners-Lee, T., Feigenbaum, J., Hendler, J.A., Sussman, G.J.: Information accountability. Commun. ACM **51**(6), 82–87 (2008)
42. Zhang, W., Chen, Y., Cybulski, T., Fabbri, D., Gunter, C.A., Lawlor, P., Liebovitz, D.M., Malin, B.: Decide now or decide later? Quantifying the tradeoff between prospective and retrospective access decisions. CCS **2014**, 1182–1192 (2014)
43. Zheng, A.X., Jordan, M.I., Liblit, B., Naik, M., Aiken, A.: Statistical debugging: simultaneous identification of multiple bugs. In: ICML 2006, pp. 1105–1112. ACM (2006)

The Value of Attack-Defence Diagrams

Holger Hermanns[1], Julia Krämer[2(✉)], Jan Krčál[1], and Mariëlle Stoelinga[3]

[1] Saarland University – Computer Science, Saarbrücken, Germany
{hermanns,krcal}@cs.uni-saarland.de
[2] Paderborn University, Paderborn, Germany
juliadk@mail.upb.de
[3] University of Twente, Enschede, The Netherlands
marielle@cs.utwente.nl

Abstract. Success or failure of attacks on high-security systems, such as hacker attacks on sensitive data, depend on various situational conditions, including the timing and success chances of single attack steps, and concurrent countermeasures of the defender. With the existing state-of-the-art modelling tools for attack scenarios, comprehensive considerations of these conditions have not been possible. This paper introduces Attack-Defence Diagrams as a formalism to describe intricate attack-defence scenarios that can represent the above mentioned situational conditions. A diagram's semantics naturally corresponds to a game where its players, the attacker and the defender, compete to turn the game's outcome from undecided into a successful attack or defence, respectively. Attack-Defence Diagrams incorporate aspects of time, probability, and cost, so as to reflect timing of attack steps and countermeasures, their success chances, as well as skills and knowledge of the attacker and defender that may increase over time with lessons learned from previous attack steps. The semantics maps on stochastic timed automata as the underlying mathematical model in a compositional manner. This enables an efficient what-if quantitative evaluation to deliver cost and success estimates, as we demonstrate by a case study from the cyber-security domain.

1 Introduction

Cyber-security is naturally understood as a 2-player game, where the system attacker plays against the defender and where both players try to optimize their interest, often quantified by means of a utility function. Studying such a game provides insight in the interaction and trade-offs between various concrete security measures: which attack scenarios carry the most risk, and what is the most effective defence?

This view point is exploited and elaborated upon in this paper, introducing Attack Defence Diagrams (ADD). ADDs are akin to, but significantly more expressive than attack trees and their variants like attack-defence trees [23], attack countermeasure trees [35], and attack graphs [21]. ADDs are acyclic graphs that express how basic steps can be combined into a game between attacker

© Springer-Verlag Berlin Heidelberg 2016
F. Piessens and L. Viganò (Eds.): POST 2016, LNCS 9635, pp. 163–185, 2016.
DOI: 10.1007/978-3-662-49635-0_9

and defender, competing to swing the game from being undecided (uu) over to either a successful attack, or a successful defence of the system. This genuine game perspective is reflected semantically by the use of three-valued logic (3VL) to characterise the dynamic evolution of the game. In this, the local context determines whether 'true' or 'false' (tt or ff) corresponds to success or defeat of attacker, or dually defender.

The game outcome may crucially depend on aspects of time, probability, and cost, reflecting the timing of attack steps and countermeasures, their success chances, as well as skills, knowledge and budget of attacker and defender. This links to ongoing and substantial [32] activities to develop *cyber threat metrics* that are aimed at providing characteristics of (attacker) moves in terms of cost, time, detection probability or success probability.

To represent these aspects, basic events in ADD are equipped with relevant quantitative information about duration, success probability, and cost. ADD gates then express the dynamics how attacks and defences interact and propagate through the system, gradually determining the game. Apart from standard gates like AND, OR, and their sequential versions, we introduce several new gates and an assembly box for other gates facilitating security modelling. Also cyclic or repetitive behaviour is supported by ADD.

From the expressiveness perspective, ADDs unite and over-arch ADVISE and attack defence trees and graphs. ADVISE [28] is a powerful security analysis framework with analysis capabilities for a wide number of quantitative security metrics. However, ADVISE provides limited syntactic constructs for security modelling. Attack trees and attack graphs do provide such syntactic aids, as well as quantitative analysis methods. However, to the best of our knowledge, none of the approaches thus far provides a comprehensive framework combining cost, probability, time, defences, and choices of players in a game interpretation. Also, we believe that current versions of attack defence trees and graphs lack expressivity when in comes to modelling real defence measures.

The dynamic quantitative interpretation of ADDs is realized via the Modest framework [15], a state-of-the-art stochastic modelling formalism with powerful analysis capabilities and tool support. In the style of [27] we provide a compositional translation from ADD to Modest. That is, we translate each ADD modelling construct into a Modest process and then compose these processes to obtain the entire game model. In this way, we can analyse various security metrics for the ADD model, for example, we can *perform what-if analysis* for fixed strategies for both players and *investigate game-related questions* like best responses to player actions. Section 2.2 presents security metrics in more detail.

Related work. There exists a vast body of work on game-theoretic approaches to security analysis, ranging from games with complete information, to Bayesian games, from competitive to cooperative games, from static to repeated games, and from strategic games to Stackelberg games. We refer to [31] for a comprehensive overview. Many of these approaches are tailored to a specific security setting, such as network security (e.g., [29]), intrusion detection (e.g., [36]), cryptography (e.g. [22]), or the internet-of-things (e.g., [34]).

In contrast to these specific approaches, attack trees and their variants are more generic, application-independent security frameworks. Their game-based interpretations have appeared in [4], deriving Pareto optimal curves for discrete probability and cost; and in [11] computing optimal strategies in attack trees with multiple cost parameters. Time-dependence is not studied in [4,11]. In [6] the return on security investment is computed by transforming attack-defence trees into classical Matrix games. The work [37] computes, by solving a partially observable MDP, the optimal responses to dynamically detected network intrusions modelled as attack-response trees. Quantitative attack-trees analysis is also a popular topic; we refer to [24] for an overview. Papers that consider time-dependent behavior include [33] using Boolean logic driven Markov processes to analyse attack probabilities for attack trees enriched with triggers; [2,3] that develop a compositional approach exploiting symmetry to keep the underlying stochastic models minimal; and the ADVISE framework [28]. Nevertheless, ADD serve as an overarching notation for (at least) attack trees and ADVISE as the essence of both modelling techniques can fully be represented by ADD.

In contrast to attack-defence trees [21,23,26,35], we do not necessarily divide events into events of the attacker and events of the defender. Furthermore, we do not restrict ourselves to directed acyclic graphs as the modelling techniques presented in [24]; we allow cyclic behaviour using special reset edges and trigger edges. In addition, we also allow for an inherited notion of time, probability, and cost, even influencing each other.

Main Contributions. This paper proposes Attack-Defence Diagrams

- as a convenient modelling technique for security-critical systems;
- as a framework that subsumes several other attack-defence notations;
- supporting the main ingredients for security risk assessments: time, probability and costs;
- providing explicit distinction of attacker and defender and considerations of their conflicting intentions and their interplay;
- equipped with a formal and fully compositional semantics in terms of stochastic timed automata;
- where 3VL is used to represent the status of attack and defence steps;
- with illustrative examples demonstrating feasibility of the ADD approach.

STA is a mature formalism for compositional modelling of systems exhibiting randomness, non-determinism as well as real-time aspects. The semantics makes it possible to harvest recent advances on tool support [16,19] for STA, through the Modest Toolset [18]. As a result, we can apply existing tools for simulation as well as for formal symbolic analysis of ADDs. While game-based *analysis* is out of scope of this paper, we provide the conceptual basis for further foundational results as well as advanced analysis techniques.

Organisation of the Paper. Section 2 introduces the syntax of Attack-Defence Diagrams by example. In Sect. 3 we define the syntax formally. Section 5 is the technical core of the paper where we define the semantics of attack-defence graphs in terms of stochastic timed automata, briefly introduced in Sect. 4. We conclude the paper with a case study in Sect. 6 and a short discussion in Sect. 7. The paper is rooted in the thesis [25].

2   A Gentle Introduction to Attack Defence Diagrams

In this section we provide an intuitive discussion of the attack defence diagram formalism using a running example. In addition, we present a variety of principal and practical means to derive security metrics.

2.1   ADD Basics

The central ingredients of ADDs are *events*. The most basic ones, *basic events* (BE), indicate an atomic, unique and significant happening in a real-world system. We distinguish *triggerable* and *non-triggerable* basic events. Triggerable BE causally depend on other events, but non-triggerable ones do not; triggers also appear in [33] to model instantaneous mode switches depending on a Boolean variable. We furthermore distinguish resettable and non-resettable basic events. The latter happen at most once, the earlier might happen several times, or even periodically.

Example 1. As a running example, we consider a scenario where an attacker intends to get access to an email account of a company, so as to write embarrassing emails. In this setting, an attempt to guess the account password can be considered a non-triggerable BE, while the event BE of the attacker logging into the account is a triggerable BE, since it causally depends on obtaining the correct password.

Sending an embarrassing mail can happen only once and cannot be undone after happening. Thus, this event is non-resettable, while checking for malware can be performed repetitively and thus is considered resettable.   □

In the above example, a brute-force random guess of a password has a certain probability of success, takes some time, and involves certain effort. To enable reasoning about such quantitative aspects within ADD, the BE can be decorated with *success probabilities*, with *time* durations, and with *costs* for delaying and executing single steps. The latter may right away represent money, or an abstract measure of skills the attacker or defender need to achieve or invest. The time point in which an event happens, or the time duration to achieve this goal (depending on the interpretation), is determined either randomly by sampling from some probability distribution (*time-driven* BE) or by one of the players (*player-driven* BE), either attacker or defender.

Example 2. A single brute-force attempt of guessing a bit string of length 128 has a success probability of 2^{-128}. Situational conditions may dictate that every attempt causes (estimate) cost of 0.1, and takes on average 0.25 time units to effectuate. If only the average duration T is known, the provably best (and widely used) model for duration is the exponential distribution with rate $1/T$.   □

We use three-valued logic (3VL) to represent the outcome of events. Basic events start with the truth value undefined (uu), and subsequently can execute successfully – changing to true (tt), or unsuccessfully – changing to false (ff).

Example 3. The basic event representing the above attempt executes successfully with probability 2^{-128} and unsuccessfully with the remaining probability, after a delay sampled from an exponential distribution with rate 4.   □

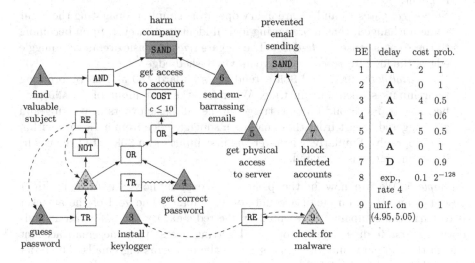

Fig. 1. An ADD representation of an attack on some email account.

Apart from basic events, so-called composed events, or *gates*, form an integral part of an ADD. Gates enable the specification of complex situations, providing means to refine them into simpler events and eventually basic events.

Example 4. Figure 1 displays an ADD for our running example. The solid edges form a directed acyclic graph where basic events are source vertices (triangular shaped) and gates are the remaining vertices (box shaped). If a solid edge points from u to v, we say that u is the input of gate v. Dashed and squiggle edges serve the purpose of resetting and triggering, as will be explained later. The colouring indicates whether the event is driven by or belongs to attacker (red with horizontal stripes), defender (green with vertical stripes), or is driven by time (gray with dots).   □

Gates can roughly be considered as propagators of and operators on 3VL. Their value is ultimately determined by the truth values of basic events. The latter evolve in continuous-time, based on randomness as well as decisions of the players. The following gates are supported:

– *Logical gates* AND, OR, NOT, SWP serve as standard 3VL operators (where NOT swaps tt and ff and SWP swaps tt and uu). The latter is included for functional completeness, meaning that any 3VL operator is in fact supported;

– *Conditional gates* COST and IF propagate the input values ff and uu unchanged. When the input value becomes tt, the gates propagate tt given a side-condition is currently met, and ff, otherwise. This value is propagated as long as the input stays tt no matter how the value of the side-condition changes afterwards. The side-condition of a COST gate is whether one of the costs accumulated so far satisfies a specified cost bound. The side-condition of an IF gate is whether its second input, called *guard* has value tt at the moment.

– *Side-effect* gates TR and RE are unary operators simply propagating the input value unchanged, thus representing logical identity. However, upon becoming tt, these gates cause a *side-effect*. The TR gate *triggers* basic events via squiggle edges, the RE gate *resets* basic events via dashed edges.

– *Sequential gates* SAND and SOR extend the standard AND and OR by ordering their inputs sequentially in time. Whenever the first input of a SAND gate becomes tt, its second input is triggered, i.e. all basic events in its subgraph get triggered (apart from those having a squiggle edge from a TR gate within the subgraph). Similarly, whenever the first input of an SOR gate becomes ff, its second input is triggered.

Example 5. We are now in the position to explain how the ADD in Fig. 1 describes an attack on email accounts of a company. The goal of the attacker is to harm the company, represented by the red sink. By the SAND gate it boils down to *first* finding a juicy topic and getting access to some email account within the company and only *then* sending the embarrassing emails. The order in which the subgoals of AND are met does not matter.

Thanks to the OR gates, the subgoal get access to account can be achieved using three different approaches. All the basic events 3, 4, 5, and 8 are associated with positive execution costs representing the effort necessary to prepare the event. We assume the attacker has limited resources, modelled by the COST gate. It becomes satisfied if its input OR gate becomes satisfied and the accumulated cost at this moment is ≤ 10, i.e. attacker has not tried all possibilities so far.

The computers in the company are nearly periodically checked for malware. Therefore, the time-driven event 9 is executed every ≈ 5 time units. The periodicity is guaranteed by the RE gate that resets the BE right after it executes. The RE gate also implements the effect of the malware check – it removes the keylogger by resetting BE 3. Thanks to a RE gate, also guessing the password may be repeated by the attacker arbitrary many times until it is successful. However, for every such guess, the execution cost is incurred.

The goal of the defender is to prevent sending the email, represented by the green sink. This boils down to blocking all infected accounts before the embarrassing emails can be sent. The accounts can be blocked only after the company notices a suspicious activity in their building.   □

The players can decide to execute their active BE at arbitrary moments of time (except repetitively in zero time). These decisions of the players are based on the evolution of the truth values of all nodes in the ADD. For instance, a player may choose to execute a basic event at the time point when some gate turns tt, at the time point when it turns tt for the third time, or exactly 2 time units after it has turned false ff. The decisions may also use randomization, e.g. executing the basic event after a random delay (uniformly) from [2, 3]. Such a recipe when to drive basic events is called a *strategy* of the player; we formalize strategies in Sect. 5.

2.2   Security Metrics

Metrics provide useful insight in the security level of the system under consideration, allowing security engineers to make design decisions, e.g., where to invest their security budget, or which security solution to implement. The ADD framework provides support for the analysis of various metrics, and their corresponding strategies.

What-if analysis. If we assume to know the strategy of both attacker and defender, i.e. we know exactly which player-driven BE they play and when, then we obtain a model that is fully stochastic, and we can calculate several security metrics. These metrics can involve all quantitative attributes, namely probability, time and cost. Typical examples for the model in Fig. 1 include: *What is the probability of a successful attack?* asking about the probability that an embarrassing email gets sent, or conversely, that it is prevented: *What is the probability of a successful defence?* Due to the information contained in the model it is also straightforward to calculate cost metrics such as *What is the expected cost of a successful attack?* Apart from analyses that focus on the top level nodes, our metrics may involve any of the BE and gates in the ADD, such as BE 8 in Fig. 1: *What is the probability of succeeding by correctly guessing the password? With what frequency are key-loggers removed from the system?* In our running example the latter corresponds to resetting BE 3 from tt to uu. In models that capture the long-run situation with repetitive attack attempts, we can also ask questions such as:

   What is the average number of attacks per year? How much is spent on average per year on defence? What is the expected ratio of defended attacks? Extending recent work on security metrics for attack trees [27] such metrics can be combined and represented as succinct diagrams showing different attack-defence scenarios, so as to show trade-offs among different attack strategies, for instance for the use of an enterprise risk manager to effectively plan defence strategies.

Game related questions. All these metrics can be similarly used in the following game questions:

- If we know the strategy of only one player, but not of its opponent, what is the *best response strategy* of the opponent for a given metrics. Suppose, in Fig. 1 only the defender strategy is given: the defender blocks infected accounts right after the attacker gets physical access to the server. What is the counter-strategy to maximize the probability of a successful attack? And: what is the maximal probability?

– If we leave the strategies open for both players, what are their *optimal strategies*? An optimal strategy maximizes the interest of the player, assuming that the other player always plays a best-response strategy.

With formal preciseness, such questions are often computationally difficult [10], or even undecidable [9]. Nevertheless, we believe that heuristic or statistical approaches [12,13] can provide useful results even for such complex models.

3   Formal Syntax of Attack-Defence Diagrams

To formally define time-driven basic events, we use cumulative distribution functions representing the occurrence probability of a basic event over time. In the following, we call the set of all cumulative distribution functions $\mathcal{F}$.

Definition 1 (Attack-Defence Diagrams). *An attack-defence diagram (ADD) is a tuple* $\mathsf{ADD} = (\mathsf{V}, \mathsf{E}, \mathsf{T}, \mathsf{Pr}, \mathcal{C}, \mathsf{C_E}, \mathsf{C_D}, \mathsf{D}, \mathsf{TEdge}, \mathsf{REdge})$ *where*

– (V, E) *is a directed acyclic graph, with designated goal sink vertices att and def, the source vertices* $\mathsf{BE} \subseteq \mathsf{V}$ *are called* basic events *and all other* $\mathsf{G} := \mathsf{V} \setminus \mathsf{BE}$ *are called* gates; *direct predecessors of each gate are called its inputs;*

– $\mathsf{T} \colon \mathsf{G} \to \mathsf{O}$ *is the type function assigning to each gate one of the operators*

$$\mathsf{O} = \{\mathsf{AND}, \mathsf{OR}, \mathsf{NOT}, \mathsf{SWP}, \mathsf{COST}, \mathsf{IF}, \mathsf{RE}, \mathsf{TR}, \mathsf{SAND}, \mathsf{SOR}\};$$

we require that gates of type $\mathsf{AND}, \mathsf{OR}, \mathsf{IF}, \mathsf{SAND}, \mathsf{SOR}$ *have a left and a right input, other gates have only one input.*

– $\mathsf{Pr} \colon \mathsf{BE} \to [0,1]$ *assigns to each BE the probability of a successful execution,*

– $\mathcal{C}$ *is a finite set of costs,* $\mathsf{C_D} \colon \mathsf{BE} \times \mathcal{C} \to \mathbb{R}$ *specifies all costs of execution of BE, whereas* $\mathsf{C_D} \colon \mathsf{BE} \times \mathcal{C} \to \mathbb{R}$ *specifies all delay cost rates of BE, e.g. the costs incurred per time unit if the execution of BE is delayed; additionally, each vertex v labelled by* COST *is equipped with a bound* $c_v \bowtie_v \mathsf{tresh}_v$ *(applied to cost c_v accumulated so far) where* $\bowtie_v \in \{\leq, <, \geq, >, =, \neq\}$ *and* $\mathsf{tresh}_v \in \mathbb{R}^{\geq 0}$.

Furthermore, each basic event $\mathsf{BE} = \mathsf{BE_A} \uplus \mathsf{BE_D} \uplus \mathsf{BE_T}$ *either belongs to the Attacker or to the Defender or is Time-driven. Finally, we have,*

– $\mathsf{D} \colon \mathsf{BE_T} \to \mathcal{F}$ *that assigns to each time-driven basic event a cumulative distribution function over its positive delay, i.e.* $\mathsf{D}(b)(0) = 0$,

– $\mathsf{TEdge} \subseteq \{v \in \mathsf{G} \mid \mathsf{T}(v) = \mathsf{TR}\} \times \mathsf{BE}$ *are trigger edges from* TR *gates to BE;* $\mathsf{BE_{Tr}} := \{b \in \mathsf{BE} \mid \exists v \in \mathsf{V} : (v, b) \in \mathsf{TEdge}\}$ *denotes the set of triggerable BE;*

– $\mathsf{REdge} \subseteq \{v \in \mathsf{G} \mid \mathsf{T}(v) = \mathsf{RE}\} \times \mathsf{BE}$ *are reset edges from* RE *gates to BE;* $\mathsf{BE_{Tr}} := \{b \in \mathsf{BE} \mid \exists v \in \mathsf{V} : (v, b) \in \mathsf{REdge}\}$ *denotes the set of resettable BE;*

Intuitive Semantic Interpretation. In an ADD, the successful attacks and defences are represented by the goal gates. The goal of the attacker is to turn the att gate (colored red in our example) to tt or to turn the def gate (colored green) to ff. If both players meet their goal at the same time, it is considered a draw. Using logical gates, the successful attacks and defences are decomposed into smaller and smaller parts down to the level of basic events.

All basic events initially are set to the undefined value uu. Triggered basic events start in the *passive* mode, whereas other basic event start in the *active* mode. An active basic event b may *execute* after an arbitrary *positive* delay. If b is player-driven, the delay is chosen by the corresponding player, if b is time-driven, the delay is chosen randomly according to $D(b)$. After the delay, the basic event b changes its truth value to tt with probability $Pr(b)$ and to ff with probability $1 - Pr(b)$. A passive basic event cannot execute. Every time unit of having a basic event b active incurs a cost $C_D(b)$ and every execution of a basic event b incurs a cost $C_E(b)$.

Whenever a value of a basic event changes, all gates switch to a possibly new value in zero time according to the logical rules discussed in Sect. 2.1. Only after this, the possible side-effects of TR and RE take place. This may again change truth values of some basic events, in turn changing truth values of the gates. This again may cause side-effects of some other TR and RE gates and so on. All this happens in zero time and repeats until a fixed-point is reached. A fixed-point is always reached since we assure that a BE never executes in zero time after becoming active.

4   Stochastic Timed Automata

The formal semantics of ADD is based on stochastic timed automata (STA), which are apt for this task as they feature not only non-determinism and probabilism but also cost decorations, as well as clocks and sampling. This all together is needed to properly reflect the dynamics of an ADD model as time passes.

In the following, we consider STAs as defined in [7,17]. Let Var be a set of *real-valued variables*. For simplicity, Boolean, 3VL, and integer variables are assumed to be encoded using real variables. Moreover, $CK \subseteq Var$ is the set of clock variables. A *valuation* is a function $Var \rightarrow \mathbb{R}$, which assigns to each variable a concrete value. The set of all valuations is denoted by $Val(Var)$. For $v \in Val(Var)$ and $t \in \mathbb{R}$ we denote by $v + t$ the valuation, where all clocks are incremented by t, i.e. $(v + t)(x) := v(x) + t$ if $x \in CK$ and $(v + t)(x) := v(x)$ if $x \in Var \setminus CK$.

To express Boolean formulas over variables, we introduce *constraints*. They allow for example to compare clocks to certain points in time or to compare two clock valuations.

Definition 2 (Constraints [17]). *Constraint, denoted* CS, *are*

$$\psi ::= \text{tt} \mid \text{ff} \mid \varphi \wedge \psi \mid \varphi \vee \psi \mid x_1 \bowtie x_2$$

where $x_1, x_2 \in \mathbb{R} \cup Var$ *and* $\bowtie \in \{<, \leq, >, \geq, =, \neq\}$.

Subsequently, we write $\nu \models cs$ if the constraint cs evaluates to *true* under the valuation ν. Furthermore, we consider *variable assignments*, denoted by Asgn, which on their right contain arithmetic expressions or sampling expressions over Var \ CK, e.g.

$$x := x + sample(F), \quad x := 3 + sample(Exp_3), \quad x := x * y * (x > y ? 1 : -1).$$

A sampling expression $sample(F)$ is an instruction, which allows random sampling from an arbitrary probability distribution F (such as exponential with rate 3, or uniform in the interval $[1/2, \pi]$). Specifically, in STAs one can compare clock valuations to sampled values.

Definition 3 (Stochastic Timed Automata [17]**).** *A stochastic timed automaton (STA) is a tuple* Aut $= ($Loc$, \ell_0,$ Act$,$ Var$, \rightarrow)$ *where* Loc *is a finite set of locations,* ℓ_0 *is the initial location,* Act *is a finite set of actions,* Var *is a finite set of (real-valued) variables. We write* CK $\subseteq$ Var *for the set of clock variables.* $\rightarrow \subseteq$ Loc $\times$ Act $\times$ CS $\times$ CS $\times$ dist(Asgn $\times$ Loc) *is a finite transition relation.*

As defined above, a transition in a STA is a tuple of the form (ℓ, a, g, d, μ). This transition starts in location ℓ and leads to a probability distribution μ over assignments and successor locations. The transition labels are threefold, with a being an action label, and g and d being constraints. Here, constraint g plays the role of a *guard* (as in Dijkstra's guarded commands), determining when the transition is enabled, while d is a *deadline* constraining the time by which progress must have been made. This is similar to invariants in classical timed automata [1], but notably, STAs are based on timed automata with deadlines [8].

The dynamic STA behaviour is as follows. The automaton starts in the initial location ℓ_0 with the initial valuation v_0 assigning 0 to all variables. The automaton waits in this location for a *non-deterministically* chosen amount of time t_0 and takes a *non-deterministically* chosen transition $(\ell_0, a_0, g, d, \mu) \in \rightarrow$ such that

- $v_0 + t_0 \models g$, i.e. after the waiting, the *guard* of the transition is satisfied,
- $v_0 + t \not\models d'$ for all $0 \leq t < t_0$ and all d' such that $(\ell_0, a', g', d', \mu') \in \rightarrow$, i.e. no deadline is surpassed in ℓ_0 before time t_0.

Upon taking the transition, a branch of the transition, i.e. an assignment $u \in$ Asgn and next location ℓ_1, is picked *randomly* according to the distribution μ. The STA performs action a_0 and moves into ℓ_1 with valuation v_1 obtained from $v_0 + t_0$ by performing the possibly *random* assignment u. The same process repeats in ℓ_1, and so on, forming an infinite execution $\ell_0 v_0 \ell_1 v_1 \cdots$ of the STA.

In this paper, we use deadlines of transitions only to distinguish *urgent* transitions with $d = g$ from *non-urgent* transitions with $d = $ ff. Similarly to modal transition systems, we depict by solid edges the urgent transitions that *must* occur as soon as the guard is satisfied; and by dashed edges the non-urgent transitions that *may* be arbitrarily delayed.

Every STA defines a timed probabilistic transition system [15] that still captures both the delay non-determinism as well as transition non-determinism.

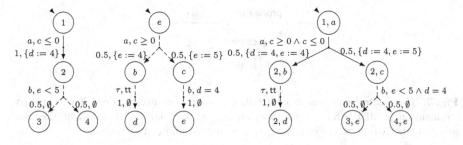

Fig. 2. Two STAs on the left and their parallel composition on the right. Each transition is separated into two parts – the first part is labelled with an action and a guard constraint, whereas the second one is labelled with a pair of probability and assignments.

The non-determinism is then resolved by a *scheduler* yielding purely probabilistic behaviour. For every scheduler σ we thus obtain a probability measure $\mathbb{P}^\sigma$ over the space of all runs of STA.

STAs are *compositional*. That is, one can construct a large STA by putting together smaller STAs, composing them via a parallel composition operator $\|$. We use common alphabet synchronisation in the style of CSP [20] or FSP [30]. An example is given in Fig. 2.

Definition 4 ($\|$ [17]). *Let* $\mathsf{Aut}_i = (\mathsf{Loc}_i, \ell_{0i}, \mathsf{Act}_i, \mathsf{Var}_i, \rightarrow_i)$ *for* $i \in \{1, 2\}$ *be STAs. We call* $\mathsf{Aut}_1 \| \mathsf{Aut}_2 = (\mathsf{Loc}_1 \times \mathsf{Loc}_2, (\ell_{01}, \ell_{02}), \mathsf{Act}_1 \cup \mathsf{Act}_2, \mathsf{Var}_1 \cup \mathsf{Var}_2, \rightarrow)$ *their parallel composition where* $((\ell_1, \ell_2), a, g, d, \mu) \in \rightarrow$ *if and only if*

- *either* $a \notin \mathsf{Act}_1 \cap \mathsf{Act}_2$ *and there is* $(\ell_1, a, g, d, \mu_1) \in \rightarrow_1$ *such that* $\mu = \mu_1 \cdot \delta_{(\emptyset, \ell_2)}$
  or $(\ell_2, a, g, d, \mu_2) \in \rightarrow_2$ *such that* $\mu = \mu_2 \cdot \delta_{(\emptyset, \ell_2)}$;
- *or* $a \in \mathsf{Act}_1 \cap \mathsf{Act}_2$ *and there are* $(\ell_1, a, g_1, d_1, \mu_1) \in \rightarrow_1$, $(\ell_2, a, g_2, d_2, \mu_2) \in \rightarrow_2$ *such that* $g = g_1 \wedge g_2$, $d = d_1 \wedge d_2$ *and* $\mu = \mu_1 \cdot \mu_2$.

Here, the product of distributions μ_1, μ_2 *over* $dist(\mathsf{Asgn} \times \mathsf{Loc})$ *is defined as*

$$(\mu_1 \cdot \mu_2)(A, (\ell_1, \ell_2)) = \sum_{A' \subseteq A} \mu_1(A', \ell_1) \cdot \mu_2(A \setminus A', \ell_2).$$

Common alphabet synchronisation is known to be commutative and associative modulo (timed probabilistic) bisimulation, so brackets are not needed if composing more than two processes.

5   Semantics of Attack-Defence Diagrams

For this section we consider given a fixed Attack-Defence Diagram $\mathsf{ADD} = (V, E, T, \mathsf{Pr}, \mathcal{C}, \mathsf{C_E}, \mathsf{C_D}, D, \mathsf{TEdge}, \mathsf{REdge})$. We shall define the semantics of this ADD by translating each basic event and each gate into a dedicated STA, called a *gadget* in the sequel. Then, we define strategies of the attacker and the defender

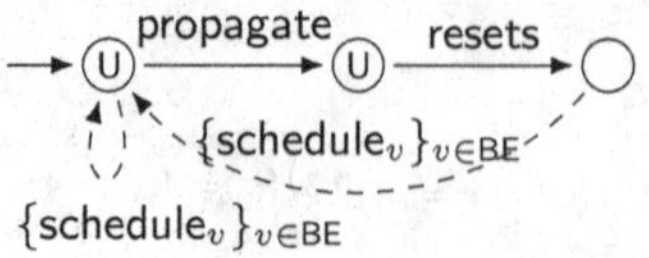

Fig. 3. The Central component controlling the order of propagation. For simplicity, we mention in all the STA in this section only non-trivial guards, probabilities, and assignments. A first round of propagation is always enforced at time 0.

as additional STA components. For a given pair of strategies, the overall STA is then constructed by composing STA of all vertices and of the two strategies. The resulting automaton then uniquely defines the behaviour of the system under the given pair of strategies.

5.1   Gadget Ingredients

The STA gadgets need to make sure that the 3VL values correctly propagate through the ADD whenever the value of at least one basic event changes. In all figures of gadgets, we use background colours to denote the current truth value of the gadget: green for tt, red for ff, and gray for uu. To ease the understanding, we also annotate with U (for *urgent*) those states where no time can pass. For the propagation of truth values, we use several types of synchronization actions:

- for each vertex $v \in V$, we have actions uu_v, tt_v, and ff_v signalling its value is undefined, true, and false, respectively;
- for each *resettable* basic event b, we have a reset action res_b, and for each *triggerable* basic event b, we have a triggering action $trig_b$.

For correctness and unambiguity of the propagation we need a distinguished component STA called Central, depicted in Fig. 3, with a few additional synchronization actions. A new round of propagation of values is started whenever some basic events change their values. Every such basic event b indicates to Central that propagation is needed by its action $schedule_b$. Afterwards, an action propagate informs all BE to initiate the propagation. Asynchronously, every basic event emits its current value, and each gate emits its value as soon as it receives the values from all its inputs. After these values have propagated through the graph underlying the ADD, the trigger gates emit all the $trig_b$ messages and so do the reset gates, emitting res_b messages. To guarantee unambiguous behaviour, triggers occur before resets. Thus, all TR and RE gates synchronize with Central by an action resets that separates triggers from resets.

Translating Basic Events. In Fig. 4 on the left, we depict the STA for a simple player-driven BE that is neither triggerable, nor resettable. The BE v is active in its initial state; at any (positive) moment of time it may choose to execute$_v$ and

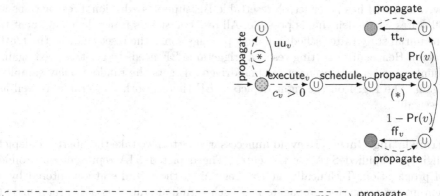

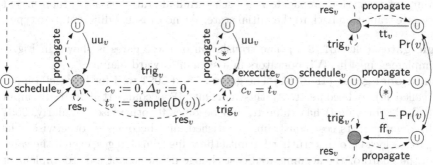

Fig. 4. Translation of a basic event v. On the right, we depict the STA for a simple player-driven BE. Below, we have the STA for a time-driven BE that is also both triggerable and resettable. For clarity, we mark states which represent that the gate is tt with red (with horizontal stripes), ff with green (with vertical stripes), and uu with gray (with dots). The symbol $(*)$ stands for a set of updates that update each cost variable $c \in C$ by $c := c + C_E(v)(c) + \Delta_v C_D(v)(c)$ and reset $\Delta_v := 0$ where Δ_v is a local clock to measure the time since the last propagation.

also indicate to Central by the schedule$_v$ action that new truth values need to get propagated. After it receives the propagate signal, it probabilistically chooses the new truth value and sends it out. Any later propagation results in the same truth value. During every propagation, we also need to update the cost variables by all the costs incurred during the time since the last propagation, measured by a clock Δ_v.

The main difference between a time-driven and a player-driven BE is in the guard on the executing transition as shown in Fig. 4 on the right. The guard guarantees that the BE executes after a delay randomly chosen according to the distribution $D(v)$. Technically, the delay is sampled to a variable t_v when becoming active, along with resetting a clock c_v (and Δ_v). At the moment when $t_v = c_v$, the delay is over and the execution of the BE must get scheduled.

A triggerable BE starts in a passive mode and enters the active mode by a non-urgent trig$_v$ action. Any further triggering when the BE is already active or even executed has no effect. A resettable BE supports additional res_v actions in all states where delaying is possible. All res_v transitions bring the component to the initial state (after scheduling new propagation if the reset changes the truth value). Hence, after getting reset, a triggerable BE needs to get triggered again. Similarly, after getting reset, a time-driven BE gets the random delay sampled again. The Fig. 4 on the right depicts a BE that is both triggerable as well as resettable.

Translating Gates. To avoid unnecessary clutter, we take the liberty to depict slightly simplified STA for the gates. The depicted STA represent one round of propagation. Technically, at the beginning, the initial state is entered by a non-urgent transition propagate and each terminal state has also a non-urgent propagate transition back to the initial state. We now discuss different gate types.

Logic gates (OR, NOT, SWP) The translation of these gates is shown in Fig. 5, implementing the 3VL operators in a straightforward manner.

Conditional gates (IF, COST) The gates IF and COST wait for heir (left) input (called in) to become tt. At this moment, IF becomes tt if its right input (called g or *guard*) has value tt, and becomes ff, otherwise. Similarly, COST becomes tt if its cost constraint is satisfied, and becomes ff, otherwise. The gates is locked to this truth value until the value of in changes, even if the value of the guard or the accumulated cost change in the meantime. To implement this behaviour, the gate v stores the value it is locked to in a (local) variable 1_v (initially being uu). The gates are depicted in Fig. 6.

Side-effect gates (TR, RE) In the logical sense, the gate TR (RE) serves as an identity, only echoing the truth value of its input. Whenever the gate is becoming tt, it triggers (resets) all the basic events $b_1, \ldots, b_n$ it is connected to by the trigger (reset) edges. No further triggering or resetting is performed before the input changes its truth value to ff or uu, again implemented by storing the last value in a local variable 1_{in}. The translations are in Fig. 7.

Derivable gates (AND, SAND, SOR) We omit the explicit translations of these gates as they can be equivalently expressed by other operators, as depicted in Fig. 8. For the sake of efficient analysis, one may instead resort to explicit translations of these gates into gadgets.

5.2   Strategies of the Players

To enable analyses that treat the ADD as a game between the attacker and the defender, we need to formalize *strategies* that prescribe the behaviour of these two players.

In this paper we focus on strategies that base their decisions on finite memory about the past events. In the context of continuous-time systems, finite memory is usually expressed by a finite-state timed automaton (as in, e.g., [10,14]). We express a strategy of each player by a finite-state *stochastic* timed automaton.

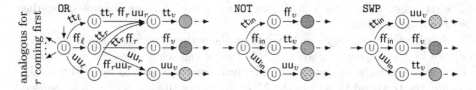

Fig. 5. Translation of the gate OR with inputs l and r, and gates NOT and SWP with input in. Before each propagation, the gadget moves to the initial state; after the propagation, the colour represents the new truth value. For the gate OR we depict only one half of the gadget (where the left input comes before the right input). The other half is analogous.

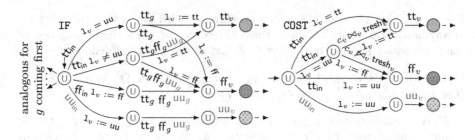

Fig. 6. Translation of the gate IF and the gate COST. For the gate IF, we again depict only a half of the gadget where the truth value of in comes before the truth value of g.

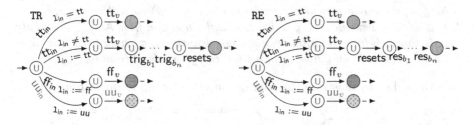

Fig. 7. Translation of the Gate RE and the Gate TR.

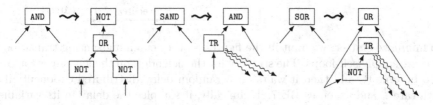

Fig. 8. Encoding operators AND, SAND, and SOR. The gate AND is easily expressed using the 3VL version of the De Morgan rule. The gate SAND can be encoded using AND and a TR gate: Whenever the left input becomes tt, the TR gate triggers all basic events in the subtree of the right input (apart from those having a trigger edge incoming from within the subgraph). Similarly, the gate SOR is encoded with such a TR gate and an OR gate. Here, the TR gate performs the triggering whenever the left input turns ff.

The strategies then serve as additional components that are composed together with all the gadgets.

Intuitively, a strategy synchronizes on the actions executing the basic events *driven* by the respective player. In this way, it can select the time at which the basic events is to be executed. The STA furthermore is able to *sense* actions signalling the truth values within the ADD. We define these sets of actions (sensed, respectively driven) of player $\mathbf{P} \in \{\mathbf{A}, \mathbf{D}\}$ by

$$\mathsf{Act_{sense}} := \{\mathsf{tt}_v, \mathsf{ff}_v, \mathsf{uu}_v \mid v \in V\} \cup \{\mathsf{trig}_b, \mathsf{res}_b \mid b \in \mathsf{BE}\}$$
$$\mathsf{Act_{drive}^P} := \{\mathsf{execute}_b \mid b \in \mathsf{BE_P}\}$$

We require that the component can synchronize with any action from $\mathsf{Act_{sense}}$ at any moment of time. This way, the strategy cannot block the propagation of the truth values and can only react to it. Let us give a formal definition.

Definition 5 (Strategy). *A strategy of player* $\mathbf{P} \in \{\mathbf{A}, \mathbf{D}\}$ *is an STA* $\mathcal{P} = (\mathsf{Loc}, \ell_0, \mathsf{Act_{sense}} \cup \mathsf{Act_{drive}^P}, \mathsf{Var}, \rightarrow)$ *such that*

- $\mathcal{P}$ *is transition-deterministic, i.e. in each state* ℓ *there is always at most one enabled transition for each action* a. *Precisely, for any transitions* $(\ell, a, g_1, d_1, \mu_1)$ *and* $(\ell, a, g_2, d_2, \mu_2)$ *there is no valuation* v *where both* $v \models g_1$ *and* $v \models g_2$;
- $\mathcal{P}$ *is sense-enabled, i.e. for each state* ℓ, *valuation* v, *and input action* $a \in \mathsf{Act_{sense}}$, *there is a non-urgent transition* $(\ell, a, g, \mathsf{ff}, \mu)$ *such that* $v \models g$;
- $\mathcal{P}$ *is drive-urgent, i.e. every transitions with an action from* $\mathsf{Act_{drive}^P}$ *is urgent;*
- $\mathcal{P}$ *is timelock-free, i.e. after taking a* res_b *transition,* σ *cannot reach in zero time a state with an outgoing transition carrying a label from* $\mathsf{Act_{drive}^P}$.

Example 6. Let us illustrate the concept on our running example from Fig. 1.

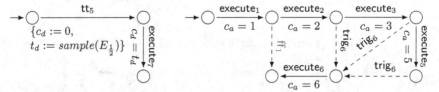

To minimize clutter, we omit in the figures all the remaining sensing transitions that are simply self-loops. The strategy for the defender, on the left, waits for BE 5 to become tt, and then it waits for a random delay distributed exponentially with rate $\frac{1}{2}$ and executes BE 7. Technically, it samples the delay in its variable t_d which is then compared with its clock variable c_d.

The strategy for the attacker, depicted on the right, times its executions relative to clock variable c_a that is never reset. It keeps in memory whether BE 1 has failed and whether BE 6 has already been triggered. □

5.3   Behaviour of an Attack Defence Diagram

As the final step, we explain how the individual STA components are connected into the overall STA that defines the semantics of ADD and thus determine the probabilities of the observed behaviour.

Definition 6 (Semantics of ADD). *Let us fix a strategy $\mathcal{A}$ of the attacker and $\mathcal{D}$ of the defender. Further, let P_1 to P_n be the gadgets of all the vertices of ADD in an arbitrary order. The semantics of ADD with strategies $\mathcal{A}$ and $\mathcal{D}$ is an STA*

$$[\![ADD]\!]^{\mathcal{A},\mathcal{D}} = (\; P_1 \parallel P_2 \parallel \cdots \parallel P_n \parallel \mathsf{Central} \parallel \mathcal{A} \parallel \mathcal{D} \;).$$

Intuitively, the STA semantics of an ADD is a multi-way synchronization of all stochastic timed automata resulting from the vertex-wise translation.

To express properties in ADD, we define *traces* that capture observable behaviour of the resulting STA. First, we define for each state ℓ of the automaton $[\![ADD]\!]^{\mathcal{A},\mathcal{D}}$ its *truth observation* $\theta(\ell) : V \to \{\mathsf{tt}, \mathsf{ff}, \mathsf{uu}, \bot\}$. We set $\theta(\ell)(v)$ to the respective truth value if the gadget of v is in a state of the respective colour and to $\bot$, otherwise. For each run $\rho = \ell_0 v_0 \ell_1 v_1 \cdots$ of the automaton, we take the sequence $o_0 t_0 o_1 t_1 \cdots$ where each t_i is the absolute time when (ℓ_i, v_i) is entered and $o_i := \theta(\ell_i)$. From this sequence we obtain *trace* $\theta(\rho)$ by first removing observations containing $\bot$, i.e. removing all pairs $o\,t$ such that $o(v) = \bot$ for some v, and then removing stuttering, i.e. replacing each maximal subsequence of the form $o t o t \cdots o t$ by $o t$.

By construction of the gadgets and due to the properties of the strategy automata, the resulting semantic automaton does not contain any *real* remaining non-determinism that would influence the observed truth values.

Lemma 1. *Let T be a measurable set[1] of traces and $\theta^{-1}(T) = \{\mathrm{run}\rho \mid \theta(\rho) \in T\}$ be the corresponding runs. For any schedulers σ, σ' in $[\![ADD]\!]^{\mathcal{A},\mathcal{D}}$ we have*

$$\mathbb{P}^{\sigma}_{[\![ADD]\!]^{\mathcal{A},\mathcal{D}}}(\theta^{-1}(T)) = \mathbb{P}^{\sigma'}_{[\![ADD]\!]^{\mathcal{A},\mathcal{D}}}(\theta^{-1}(T)).$$

Thus, we omit schedulers and denote such unique probabilities by $\mathbb{P}^{\mathcal{A},\mathcal{D}}_{\mathsf{ADD}}(T)$. The proof of Lemma 1 follows the same line as in [25].

What-If Analysis for Fixed Strategies $\mathcal{A}$ and $\mathcal{D}$. The operational semantics allow us to formally capture the properties of interest, for instance

- the *probability of successful attack* $\mathbb{P}^{\mathcal{A},\mathcal{D}}_{\mathsf{ADD}}(T_{\mathbf{A}})$ where $T_{\mathbf{A}}$ is the set of traces $\{o_0 t_0 \cdots \mid \exists i : o_i(\mathsf{att}) = \mathsf{tt} \wedge \forall j \le i : o_j(\mathsf{def}) \ne \mathsf{tt}\}$ where the attacker wins,
- the *expected cost of a successful attack* $\mathbb{E}^{\mathcal{A},\mathcal{D}}_{\mathsf{ADD}}(C_c) / \mathbb{P}^{\mathcal{A},\mathcal{D}}_{\mathsf{ADD}}(T_{\mathbf{A}})$ where $\mathbb{E}^{\mathcal{A},\mathcal{D}}_{\mathsf{ADD}}$ is the expectation w.r.t. $\mathbb{P}^{\mathcal{A},\mathcal{D}}_{\mathsf{ADD}}$ and C_c is a random variable assigning to every trace the cost c accumulated before attacker wins or 0 if it does not win, or

---

[1] The measurable space over traces is defined by the standard cylinder construction as for finite state continuous time Markov chains, see e.g. [5].

– the *mean time to attack* $\mathbb{E}_{\mathsf{ADD}}^{\mathcal{A},\mathcal{D}}(W)/\mathbb{P}_{\mathsf{ADD}}^{\mathcal{A},\mathcal{D}}(T_{\mathbf{A}})$ where W similarly returns the time until a successful attack or 0 if the attacker does not win.

Lemma 1 then gives us a straightforward way to perform the analysis. Owing to this result, we can apply an arbitrary scheduler (such as an as-soon-as-possible uniform scheduler) and analyse the probabilities in the resulting stochastic process by stochastic model checking or simulation.

Game Related Questions. Following the discussions in Sects. 1 and 2.2, let us illustrate how the semantics of the ADD framework allows us to capture the game related questions more formally. For this aim, we pick the fundamental probability of a successful attack.

For a fixed strategy $\mathcal{D}$, we define the *best response* probability by

$$\sup_{\mathcal{A}} \mathbb{P}_{\mathsf{ADD}}^{\mathcal{A},\mathcal{D}}(T_{\mathbf{A}}) \qquad \text{or dually} \qquad \inf_{\mathcal{D}} \mathbb{P}_{\mathsf{ADD}}^{\mathcal{A},\mathcal{D}}(T_{\mathbf{A}}) \qquad \text{if we fix } \mathcal{A}, \text{ instead.}$$

One possibility, how to approximate this metric algorithmically is as follows. We obtain a conservative approximation by omitting the unknown strategy $\mathcal{A}$ in the composition in Definition 6. This way, we obtain an STA that still contains substantial non-determinism (of the attacker). Finally, we can approximate [16] the maximum probability of the set of traces $T_{\mathbf{A}}$.

When no strategy is fixed, we define the Stackelberg value by

$$\inf_{\mathcal{D}} \sup_{\mathcal{A}} \mathbb{P}_{\mathsf{ADD}}^{\mathcal{A},\mathcal{D}}(T_{\mathbf{A}}).$$

This value corresponds to the probability of a successful attack in the situation when the defender first chooses publicly its strategy $\mathcal{D}$ and then the attacker reacts by its best-response to this fixed strategy $\mathcal{D}$.

Existing algorithms for STA so far do not allow us to compute this value or optimal strategies of the players. This urges for application of heuristic analysis techniques or for further fundamental research on games over non-Markovian stochastic processes (in the spirit of [9,10]). In particular, understanding of structure of optimal or ε-optimal strategies is vital for obtaining analysis algorithms.

6   Case Study

In this section, we further illustrate the potential of ADD on a toy problem from the domain of cyber-security. We also show what analysis results can be obtained with the tool support currently available.

The Attack-Defence Diagram in Fig. 9 models a student who intends to steal an exam, and a professor who wants to identify and report any such attempt. This model captures three possibilities to steal an exam: to threat or to bribe the professor's secretary, to get access to the server at which the exam is stored, or to steal a printout of the exam from the professor's office. Each of these subgoals is refined further.

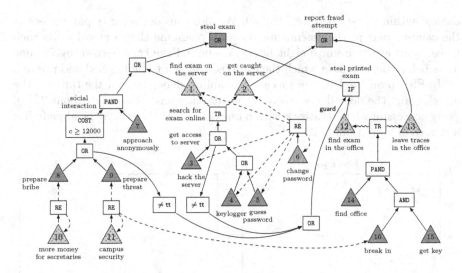

Fig. 9. Attack-Defence Diagram for the Scenario "Steal Exam"

The gate $\neq$ tt evaluates to tt unless its input equals tt, and otherwise to uu. Encoding this gate in 3VL is straightforward (thereby demonstrating the practical benefits of completeness with respect to 3VL). The PAND gate (priority AND) becomes true if the first input turns to tt before the second one, and false if this happens in reverse order. Otherwise, this gate is undefined (uu). Encoding this behaviour using 3VL and an IF gate is straightforward.

We specified the model in a specialized DOT-file format for which have developed a prototypical tool to automatically translate such an ADD to Modest [7,15]. The analysis is then performed using the Modest toolset [18], using the *modes* tool for statistical model checking. Due to Lemma 1, the resolution of non-determinism does not matter (we applied "as-soon-as-possible"-schedulers with uniform resolution of non-deterministic choice). We performed 17,000 simulation runs per configuration considered in order to achieve a significance level below 0.01.

For this case, our analysis focus is on a what-if analysis of the success probability of the attacker (student), and the defender (i.e. the professor). We consider the following fixed strategy of the attacker:

- The attacker first tries to get a digital copy of the exam. He tries to hack the server after three hours and tries to guess the password four hours later.
- He starts to prepare a bribe one day after.
- He tries to break into the office again a day later. He tries to find the office at day, and waits for the night three time units later to get the key and to break shortly after into the office.

As the baseline strategy of the defender, we check whether it is enough for a professor to only change his password every two weeks (which amounts to no change within the studied time frame). We also consider security parameters at the campus part of the defence measures: We assume that a guard visits each place about every seven to eight hours. We bound the time horizon by 72 time units before the exam, in which the exam is assumed to be finished and printed.

In Fig. 10 on the left, the success probability depending on the time for the attacker and the defender is plotted. The attacker has a chance of about 2 % of being successful with his attack within one day. After three days, he already has a chance of more than 5 %.

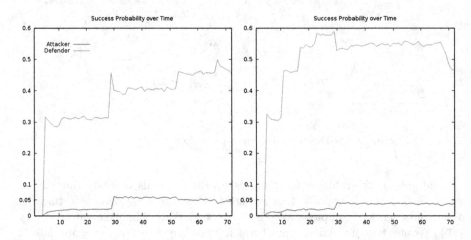

Fig. 10. Development of success probability over time for Defender and Attacker in the original scenario (on the left) and after applying the countermeasures (on the right). Thus, the graphs plot the probability that the player's top gate evaluates to tt at time t.

In the following, we discuss the possibilities how to increase the security of the system. As a countermeasure, we analyse a more regularly change of the password for the server. The professor now updates the password every six hours in the last three days before the exam takes place. In addition, we consider stronger campus security; the guards visit each place every four to five hours instead of every seven to eight hours.

The resulting success probabilities for attacker and defender depending on time can be found in Fig. 10 on the right. The plot shows a significant increase in the success probability of the defender and a slight decrease in the success probability of the attacker – it now never reaches 5 %. The latter is thus not significantly decreased: Neither countermeasures directly influence the probability of getting the correct exam, only the time frame to find the exam shortens. That is why the probability that *only* the intruder leaves traces in the office increases. To decrease the success probability of the attacker even further, a countermeasure must be applied which makes it harder to get the correct exam. For example, not to store the exam in the office or not to save its digital copy on a server.

7   Discussion

In this paper, we have introduced Attack-Defence Diagrams as a convenient and very expressive modelling technique for the conflicting interests of attackers and defenders of security-critical systems. ADDs come with an easy-to-use graph-based syntax which is equipped with a compositional semantics mapping on stochastic timed automata. This semantics is natural to interpret as a game played between attacker and defender, where three-valued logic echoes the trichotomy of the basic game steps being either undecided, or being won by either attacker or defender. The formal link to STA makes ADDs amenable for model checking via the Modest Toolset. Indeed, a modelling study has demonstrated the modelling power of ADDs, and the principal effectiveness of the approach, if fixing particular player strategies. This enables the study of what-if questions as well as the derivation of many other useful metrics.

As already indicated there is a large spectrum of research question that arise especially with respect to the power that players may have, if one ranges over whole families of strategies. The ADD formalism can be seen as the semantic nucleus for meaningful discussions and results in this respect.

Acknowledgements. This work is supported by the EU 7th Framework Programme projects 295261 (MEALS), 318490 (SENSATION), and 318003 (TREsPASS); by the Czech Science Foundation project P202/12/G061; the DFG Transregional Collaborative Research Centre SFB/TR 14 AVACS; the CDZ project 1023 (CAP); the NWO project 612001303 (BEAT); and by the STW and ProRail project 12238 (ArRangeer).

References

1. Alur, R., Dill, D.L.: A theory of timed automata. Theor. Comput. Sci. **126**(2), 183–235 (1994)
2. Arnold, F., Guck, D., Kumar, R., Stoelinga, M.: Sequential and parallel attack tree modelling. In: Koornneef, F., van Gulijk, C. (eds.) SAFECOMP 2015 Workshops. LNCS, vol. 9338, pp. 291–299. Springer, Heidelberg (2015)
3. Arnold, F., Hermanns, H., Pulungan, R., Stoelinga, M.: Time-dependent analysis of attacks. In: Abadi, M., Kremer, S. (eds.) POST 2014 (ETAPS 2014). LNCS, vol. 8414, pp. 285–305. Springer, Heidelberg (2014)
4. Aslanyan, Z., Nielson, F.: Pareto efficient solutions of attack-defence trees. In: Focardi, R., Myers, A. (eds.) POST 2015. LNCS, vol. 9036, pp. 95–114. Springer, Heidelberg (2015)
5. Baier, C., Haverkort, B., Hermanns, H., Katoen, J.-P.: Model-checking algorithms for continuous-time Markov chains. IEEE Trans. Softw. Eng. **29**(6), 524–541 (2003)
6. Bistarelli, S., Dall'Aglio, M., Peretti, P.: Strategic games on defense trees. In: Dimitrakos, T., Martinelli, F., Ryan, P.Y.A., Schneider, S. (eds.) FAST 2006. LNCS, vol. 4691, pp. 1–15. Springer, Heidelberg (2007)
7. Bohnenkamp, H., D'Argenio, P.R., Hermanns, H., Katoen, J.-P.: MODEST: a compositional modeling formalism for hard and softly timed systems. IEEE Trans. Softw. Eng. **32**(2), 812–830 (2006)

8. Bornot, S., Sifakis, J.: An algebraic framework for urgency. Inf. Comput. **163**(1), 172–202 (2000)

9. Bouyer, P., Forejt, V.: Reachability in stochastic timed games. In: Albers, S., Marchetti-Spaccamela, A., Matias, Y., Nikoletseas, S., Thomas, W. (eds.) ICALP 2009, Part II. LNCS, vol. 5556, pp. 103–114. Springer, Heidelberg (2009)

10. Brázdil, T., Krčál, J., Křetínský, J., Kučera, A., Řehák, V.: Stochastic real-time games with qualitative timed automata objectives. In: Gastin, P., Laroussinie, F. (eds.) CONCUR 2010. LNCS, vol. 6269, pp. 207–221. Springer, Heidelberg (2010)

11. Buldas, A., Laud, P., Priisalu, J., Saarepera, M., Willemson, J.: Rational choice of security measures via multi-parameter attack trees. In: López, J. (ed.) CRITIS 2006. LNCS, vol. 4347, pp. 235–248. Springer, Heidelberg (2006)

12. Coulom, R.: Efficient selectivity and backup operators in Monte-Carlo tree search. In: Computers and Games (CG), pp. 72–83 (2006)

13. David, A., Jensen, P., Larsen, K., Mikučionis, M., Taankvist, J.: UPPAAL STRATEGO. In: Baier, C., Tinelli, C. (eds.) TACAS 2015. LNCS, vol. 9035, pp. 206–211. Springer, Heidelberg (2015)

14. David, A., Fang, H., Larsen, K.G., Zhang, Z.: Verification and performance evaluation of timed game strategies. In: Legay, A., Bozga, M. (eds.) FORMATS 2014. LNCS, vol. 8711, pp. 100–114. Springer, Heidelberg (2014)

15. Hahn, E.M., Hartmanns, A., Hermanns, H., Katoen, J.P.: A compositional modelling and analysis framework for stochastic hybrid systems. Formal Methods in System Design **43**(2), 191–232 (2013)

16. Hahn, E.M., Hartmanns, A., Hermanns, H.: Reachability and reward checking for stochastic timed automata. ECEASST 70 (2014)

17. Hartmanns, A.: Model-checking and simulation for stochastic timed systems. In: Aichernig, B.K., de Boer, F.S., Bonsangue, M.M. (eds.) Formal Methods for Components and Objects. LNCS, vol. 6957, pp. 372–391. Springer, Heidelberg (2011)

18. Hartmanns, A., Hermanns, H.: The modest toolset: an integrated environment for quantitative modelling and verification. In: Ábrahám, E., Havelund, K. (eds.) TACAS 2014 (ETAPS). LNCS, vol. 8413, pp. 593–598. Springer, Heidelberg (2014)

19. Hartmanns, A., Hermanns, H.: Explicit model checking of very large mdp using partitioning and secondary storage. In: Finkbeiner, B., Pu, G., Zhang, L. (eds.) ATVA 2015. LNCS, vol. 9364, pp. 131–147. Springer, Heidelberg (2015)

20. Hoare, C.A.R.: Communicating Sequential Processes. Prentice-Hall, London (1985)

21. Ingols, K., Chu, M., Lippmann, R., Webster, S., Boyer, S.: Modeling modern network attacks and countermeasures using attack graphs. In: Annual Conference on Computer Security Applications ACSAC 2009, pp. 117–126, December 2009

22. Katz, J.: Bridging game theory and cryptography: recent results and future directions. In: Canetti, R. (ed.) TCC 2008. LNCS, vol. 4948, pp. 251–272. Springer, Heidelberg (2008)

23. Kordy, B., Mauw, S., Radomirović, S., Schweitzer, P.: Foundations of attack–defense trees. In: Degano, P., Etalle, S., Guttman, J. (eds.) FAST 2010. LNCS, vol. 6561, pp. 80–95. Springer, Heidelberg (2011)

24. Kordy, B., Pietre-Cambacedes, L., Schweitzer, P.: DAG-based attack and defense modeling: Don't miss the forest for the attack trees. CoRR **13–14**, 1–38 (2013)

25. Krämer, J.: Attack-Defence Graphs - On the Formalisation of Security-Critical Systems. Master's thesis, Saarland University, Saarbrücken, Germany (2015)

26. Kumar, R., Guck, D., Stoelinga, M.I.A.: Time dependent analysis with dynamic counter measure trees (2015)

27. Kumar, R., Ruijters, E., Stoelinga, M.: Quantitative attack tree analysis via priced timed automata. In: Sankaranarayanan, S., Vicario, E. (eds.) FORMATS 2015. LNCS, vol. 9268, pp. 156–171. Springer, Heidelberg (2015)

28. LeMay, E., Ford, M.D., Keefe, K., Sanders, W.H., Muehrcke, C.: Model-based security metrics using adversary view security evaluation (ADVISE). In: QEST, pp. 191–200, Washington, DC, USA, IEEE (2011)

29. Lye, K.-W., Wing, J.M.: Game strategies in network security. Int. J. Inf. Sec. 4(1–2), 71–86 (2005)

30. Magee, J., Kramer, J.: Concurrency - state models and Java programs, 2nd edn. Wiley, New York (2006)

31. Manshaei, M.H., Zhu, Q., Alpcan, T., Bacşar, T., Hubaux, J.-P.: Game theory meets network security and privacy. ACM Comput. Surv. 45(3), 1–39 (2013)

32. Mateski, M., Trevino, C.M., Veitch, C.K., Michalski, J., Harris, J.M., Maruoka, S., Frye, J.: Cyber threat metrics. Technical report SAND2012-2427, Sandia National Laboratories, March 2012

33. Pietre-Cambacedes, L., Bouissou, M.: Beyond attack trees: dynamic security modeling with boolean logic driven markov processes (BDMP). In: Dependable Computing Conference (EDCC), 2010 European, pp. 199–208, April 2010

34. Rontidis, G., Panaousis, E.A., Laszka, A., Dagiuklas, T., Malacaria, P., Alpcan, T.: A game-theoretic approach for minimizing security risks in the internet-of-things. In : IEEE International Conference on Communication, Workshop Proceedings, pp. 2639–2644 (2015)

35. Roy, A., Kim, D.S., Trivedi, K.S.: Attack countermeasure trees (ACT): towards unifying the constructs of attack and defense trees. Sec. Commun. Netw. 5(8), 929–943 (2012)

36. Zhu, Q., Fung, C.J., Boutaba, R., Barsar, T.: A game-theoretic approach to knowledge sharing in distributed collaborative intrusion detection networks: fairness. incentives and security, In: CDC (2011)

37. Zonouz, S.A., Khurana, H., Sanders, W.H., Yardley, T.M.: Rre: a game-theoretic intrusion response and recovery engine. IEEE Trans. Parallel Distrib. Syst. 25(2), 395–406 (2014)

Protocols

Composing Protocols with Randomized Actions

Matthew S. Bauer[1]([✉]), Rohit Chadha[2], and Mahesh Viswanathan[1]

[1] University of Illinois at Urbana-Champaign, Champaign, USA
{msbauer2,vmahesh}@illinois.edu
[2] University of Missouri, Columbia, USA
chadhar@missouri.edu

Abstract. Recently, several composition results have been established, showing that two cryptographic protocols proven secure against a Dolev-Yao attacker continue to afford the same security guarantees when composed together, provided the protocol messages are tagged with the information of which protocol they belong to. The key technical tool used to establish this guarantee is a separation result which shows that any attack on the composition can be mapped to an attack on one of the composed protocols running in isolation. We consider the composition of protocols which, in addition to using cryptographic primitives, also employ randomization within the protocol to achieve their goals. We show that if the protocols never reveal a secret with a probability greater than a given threshold, then neither does their composition, given that protocol messages are tagged with the information of which protocol they belong to.

1 Introduction

The design of correct cryptographic protocols is a highly non-trivial task, and security flaws are often subtle. Attacks on many protocols that were previously "proved" secure by hand, have been discovered. One approach that improves the confidence in the correctness of security protocols is formal analysis. In order to make the analysis amenable to automation, usually the assumption of perfect cryptography is made. In this "Dolev-Yao" framework, protocol messages are symbolic terms identified modulo an equational theory (and not bit-strings) that model cryptographic operations. Security is then proven in the presence of an omnipotent attacker that can read all messages sent on public channels by protocol participants, remember the (potentially unbounded) communication history, and (non deterministically) inject new messages in the network addressed to particular participants while remaining anonymous. This Dolev-Yao model has shown to be very successful in identifying security flaws.

Cryptographic protocols are often proven secure in isolation. In practice, however, they may be executing concurrently or sequentially, in a modular fashion, with other protocols. For example, a number of security protocols involve

---

M.S. Bauer and M. Viswanathan—Partially supported by grant NSF CNS 1314485.
R. Chadha—Partially supported by grant NSF CNS 1314338.

F. Piessens and L. Viganò (Eds.): POST 2016, LNCS 9635, pp. 189–210, 2016.
DOI: 10.1007/978-3-662-49635-0_10

a sub-protocol in which short-term secret keys are exchanged. While analyzing such protocols, often the sub-protocol is abstracted away by assuming that the protocol participants have successfully shared secrets. However, two cryptographic protocols proven secure independently may not remain secure if they are executed compositionally. The central problem is that these protocols may share some secret data, as in the key exchange situation described above.

Hence, a number of recent papers have identified sufficient conditions under which such protocol compositions can be proven secure — safety properties are considered in [2,3,5,16–20,22,28–31] and indistinguishability properties in [3,4], while [20,28,30] provide a general framework for proving that protocols compose securely. Other papers [2,29] essentially show that protocol compositions are secure if messages from one protocol cannot be confused with messages from another protocol. [11] shows that this continues to be the case even when dishonest participants do not tag their messages properly. This can be ensured if certain protocol transformations are made (see for example [4,17,18,22]). Essentially, these protocol transformations require that all protocol messages are *tagged* with the protocol name and protocol instance to which they belong. The exact choice of tagging scheme depends on the desired security property; incorrect tagging can actually make a secure protocol insecure [22]. In the computational model, the problem of composing protocols securely has been studied in [9,10].

The focus of this paper is to extend this work on secure protocol composition to protocols that employ randomization. Randomization plays a key role in the design of algorithmic solutions to problems arising in security. For example, randomization is essential in implementing cryptographic primitives such as encryption and key generation. Randomization is also used in cryptographic protocols to achieve security guarantees such as fair exchange (see [7,23]), anonymity (see [14,25,32]), voter privacy in electronic voting (see [33]) and denial of service prevention (see [27]).

We study the problem of when the composition of a (randomized) sub-protocol P followed by (randomized) sub-protocol Q is secure. For non-randomized protocols, this problem was studied in [19]. Our composition framework generalizes that of [19] to handle sequential, parallel and a form of vertical composition while extending to randomized protocols. They show that if one can prove P and Q do not reveal shared secrets when run in isolation (in that case Q is assumed to generate fresh secret keys), then the sequential composition of P and Q does not reveal any secret of Q if the protocol messages are tagged with the information of which protocol they belong to. The key technical tool used to establish this guarantee is a separation result which shows that any attack on the composition can be mapped to an attack on one of P or Q. This is achieved by first showing that, as the protocol messages are tagged, messages from one protocol cannot be confused with the messages of the other protocol. Then an attack trace can be simply separated into traces of P and Q. We study the same problem for the case when P and Q are randomized protocols. Our composition framework generalizes that of [19] to handle sequential, parallel and a form of vertical composition while extending to randomized protocols. The protocols themselves are expressed in a variant of the probabilistic applied-pi calculus [26] which is an extension of applied pi-calculus [1]. The Probabilistic applied-pi calculus is a convenient formalism to describe and analyze randomized security protocols in the Dolev-Yao model.

Contributions: Our first composition result is for the composition of one session of P and one session of Q. We show that if P (in isolation) is secure with probability at least p (i.e., the shared secrets are not leaked) and Q is secure with probability at least q, then the composed protocol is secure with probability at least pq, provided the protocol messages are tagged with the information of the protocol to which they belong. Although we exploit some techniques used in [19] to establish this result, there are important differences. First, the separation result in [19] does not carry over to the randomized setting. This is because an attack on the composition of P and Q is no longer a trace, but is instead a tree, as the protocol itself makes random choices. As a consequence, in different branches representing different resolutions of the randomized coin tosses, it is possible that the attacker may choose to send different messages (See Example 4). In such a case, an attack on the composition of P and Q cannot be separated into an attack on P and an attack on Q. Instead, we show that if there is an attack on the composition of P and Q then either we can extract an attack on P which succeeds with probability $> p$ or there is an attack on Q which succeeds with probability $> q$.

Another challenge manifested in the context of randomized protocols is that one must consider adversaries whose actions do not depend on the result of private coin tosses made by protocol participants, as observed in [8,12,13,15,21,24]. In order to faithfully model the privacy of coin tosses, we mandate that an attacker always take the same actions in any two different probabilistic branches in a run of a protocol if its views of the protocol run in the two branches is exactly the same. This restriction is adopted from [8,12,13,15,21,24], and is the first formalization of this concept within the applied-pi calculus. As demonstrated in Example 3, this class of attackers allows privacy guarantees, typically modeled as indistinguishability properties, to instead be modeled as reachablility properties. Considering a more restricted class of attackers imposes additional challenges in our setting, as membership in this sub-class of attackers must be maintained when mapping attack traces on composed protocols to attacks traces on the individual protocols constituting the composition.

Our second composition result concerns multiple sessions of the composed protocol. Here, we would like to show that if n sessions of P are secure with probability at least p and n sessions of Q are secure with probability at least q then n sessions of the composed protocol are secure with probability at least pq, provided the protocol messages are tagged with the information of which protocol they belong to. Indeed, a similar result is claimed in [19] for the non-randomized protocols. Unfortunately, this result is not valid even for nonrandomized protocols and we exhibit a simple example which contradicts this desired result (See Example 6). Essentially, the reason for this failure is that, in the claimed result, the n sessions of Q are assumed to generate fresh shared secrets in every session;

but P may not be guaranteeing this freshness. Thus, messages of one session can get confused with messages of other sessions. We establish a weaker composition result in which we assume that the messages of each session of Q are tagged with a *unique* session identifier in addition to the protocol identifier. The use of session identifiers ensures that the messages of one session cannot be confused with other sessions.

Finally, we also consider the case for protocols containing an unbounded number of sessions. For this case, we observe that a composition result is only possible when P and Q are secure with probability exactly 1. This is because if m sessions of a protocol leak a secret with probability $r > 0$ then by running mk sessions we can amplify the probability of leaking the secret. This probability approaches 1 as we increase k. We show that if an unbounded number of sessions of P are secure with probability 1 and an unbounded number of sessions of Q are secure with probability 1 then an unbounded number of sessions of the composed protocol are secure with probability 1, if the protocol messages are tagged with the information of which protocol they belong to and the messages of each session of Q are tagged with a *unique* session identifier.

The paper is organized as follows. In Sect. 2 we give relevant background information. Section 3 presents our processes algebra for randomized protocols and Sect. 4 gives our main composition results. Section 5 shows how this result can be extended to protocols with multiple sessions.

2   Preliminaries

We will start by discussing some standard notions from probability theory, Markov Chains and Markov Decision Processes. A process algebra for modeling security protocols with coin tosses will then be presented in Sect. 3. This process algebra closely resembles that of [26], which extends the applied π-calculus by the inclusion of a new operator for probabilistic choice. Following [19], our process calculus will also include several limitations necessary to achieve our results. In particular, conditionals no longer include else branches and we consider only a single public channel.

2.1   Probability Spaces, Markov Chains

We will assume the reader is familiar with probability spaces and Markov chains and give only the necessary definitions. A (sub)-probability space on S is a tuple $\Omega = (X, \Sigma, \mu)$ where Σ is a σ-algebra on X and $\mu : \Sigma \to [0, 1]$ is a countably additive function such that $\mu(\emptyset) = 0$ and $\mu(X) \le 1$. The set Σ is said to be the set of events and μ the (sub)-probability measure of Ω. For $F \in \Sigma$, the quantity $\mu(F)$ is said to be the probability of the event F. If $\mu(X) = 1$ then we call μ a probability measure. Given two (sub)-probability measures μ_1 and μ_2 on a measure space (S, Σ) as well as a real number $p \in [0, 1]$, the convex combination $\mu_1 +_p \mu_2$ is the (sub)-probability measure μ such that for each set $F \in \Sigma$ we have $\mu(F) = p \cdot \mu_1(F) + (1 - p) \cdot \mu_2(F)$. The set of all discrete probability distributions over S

will be denoted by $\mathsf{Dist}(S)$. Given any $x \in S$, the *Dirac measure* on S, denoted δ_x, is the discrete probability measure μ such that $\mu(x) = 1$.

A discrete-time Markov chain (DTMC) is used to model systems which exhibit probabilistic behavior. Formally, a DTMC is a tuple $\mathcal{M} = (Z, z_s, \Delta)$ where Z is a countable set of *states*, z_s the *initial* state and $\Delta : Z \hookrightarrow \mathsf{Dist}(Z)$ is the (partial) *transition function* which maps Z to a (discrete) probability distribution over Z. Informally, the process modeled by $\mathcal{M}$ evolves as follows. The process starts in the state z_s. After i execution steps, if the process is in the state z, the process moves to state z' at execution step $(i + 1)$ with probability $\Delta(z)(z')$. For the rest of the paper, we will assume that for each state z, if $\Delta(z)$ is defined, then the set $\{z' \mid \Delta(z)(z') > 0\}$ is finite. An execution of $\mathcal{M}$ is a (finite or infinite) sequence $z_0 \to z_1 \to z_2 \cdots$ such that $z_0 = z_s$ and for each $i \geq 0$, $\Delta(z_i)(z_{i+1}) > 0$. The function Δ can be extended to a probability measure on the σ-algebra genereted by the set of all executions of $\mathcal{M}$.

2.2 Partially Observable Markov Decision Processes (POMDP)s

POMDPs are used to model processes which exhibit both probabilistic and non-deterministic behavior, where the states of the system are only partially observable. Formally, an POMDP is a tuple $\mathcal{M} = (Z, z_s, Act, \Delta, \equiv)$ where Z is a countable set of *states*, $z_s \in Z$ is the *initial* state, Act is a (countable) set of *actions*, $\Delta : Z \times Act \hookrightarrow \mathsf{Dist}(Z)$ is a partial function called the *probabilistic transition relation* and $\equiv$ is an equivalence relation on Z. Furthermore, we assume that for any action α and two states z_1 and z_2 such that $z_1 \equiv z_2$, $\Delta(z_1, \alpha)$ is defined iff $\Delta(z_2, \alpha)$ is defined. As a matter of notation, we shall write $z \xrightarrow{\alpha} \mu$ whenever $\Delta(z, \alpha) = \mu$. A POMDP is like a DTMC except that at each state z, there is a choice amongst several possible probabilistic transitions. The choice of which probabilistic transition to *trigger* is resolved by an *attacker*. Informally, the process modeled by $\mathcal{M}$ evolves as follows. The process starts in the state z_s. After i execution steps, if the process is in the state z, then the attacker chooses an action α such that $z \xrightarrow{\alpha} \mu$ and the process moves to state z' at the $(i + 1)$-st step with probability $\mu(z')$. The choice of which action to take is determined by the view of the execution observed by the attacker thus far.

An *execution* ρ in the POMDP $\mathcal{M}$ is a (finite or infinite) sequence $z_0 \xrightarrow{\alpha_1} z_1 \xrightarrow{\alpha_2} z_2 \cdots$ such that $z_0 = z_s$ and for each $i \geq 0$, $z_i \xrightarrow{\alpha_{i+1}} \mu_{i+1}$ and $\mu_{i+1}(z_{i+1}) > 0$. The set of all finite executions of $\mathcal{M}$ will be denoted by $\mathsf{Exec}(\mathcal{M})$ and the set of all infinite executions will be denoted by $\mathsf{Exec}^\infty(\mathcal{M})$. If $\rho = z_0 \xrightarrow{\alpha_1} z_1 \xrightarrow{\alpha_2} z_2 \cdots \xrightarrow{\alpha_m} z_m$ is a finite execution then we write $last(\rho) = z_m$ and say the length of ρ, denoted $|\rho|$ is m. An execution ρ_1 is said to be a *one-step extension* of the execution $\rho = z_0 \xrightarrow{\alpha_1} z_1 \xrightarrow{\alpha_2} z_2 \cdots \xrightarrow{\alpha_m} z_m$ if there exists α_{m+1} and z_{m+1} such that $\rho_1 = z_0 \xrightarrow{\alpha_1} z_1 \xrightarrow{\alpha_2} z_2 \cdots \xrightarrow{\alpha_m} z_m \xrightarrow{\alpha_{m+1}} z_{m+1}$. In this case, we say that ρ_1 extends ρ by (α_{m+1}, z_{m+1}). An execution is called maximal if it is infinite or if it is finite and has no one-step extension. For an execution $\rho = z_0 \xrightarrow{\alpha_1} z_1 \xrightarrow{\alpha_2} z_2 \cdots \xrightarrow{\alpha_m} z_m$ we write $tr(\rho)$ to represent the *trace* of ρ, defined as the sequence

$z_0/\equiv \xrightarrow{\alpha_1} z_1/\equiv \xrightarrow{\alpha_2} z_2/\equiv \cdots \xrightarrow{\alpha_m} z_m/\equiv$. The set of all traces is denoted $\mathsf{Trace}(\mathcal{M})$. Informally, a trace models the view of the attacker.

As discussed above, the choice of which transition to take in an execution is resolved by an attacker. Formally, an *attacker* $\mathcal{A} : \mathsf{Trace}(M) \hookrightarrow Act$ is a partial function. An attacker $\mathcal{A}$ resolves all non-determinism and the resulting behavior can be described by a DTMC $\mathcal{M}^{\mathcal{A}} = (\mathsf{Exec}(\mathcal{M}), z_s, \Delta^{\mathcal{A}})$ where for each $\rho \in \mathsf{Exec}(\mathcal{M})$, $\Delta^{\mathcal{A}}(\rho)$ is the discrete probability distribution on $\mathsf{Exec}(\mathcal{M})$ such that $\Delta^{\mathcal{A}}(\rho)$ is defined if and only if $\Delta(last(\rho), \mathcal{A}(\rho))$ is defined. If defined then

$$\Delta^{\mathcal{A}}(\rho)(\rho_1) = \begin{cases} \Delta(last(\rho), \alpha)(z) & \begin{aligned} &\alpha = \mathcal{A}(\rho), z = last(\rho_1), \\ &\text{and } \rho_1 \text{ extends } \rho \text{ by } (\alpha, z). \end{aligned} \\ 0 & \text{otherwise} \end{cases}$$

POMDPs and State-Based Safety Properties. Given a POMDP $\mathcal{M} = (Z, z_s, Act, \Delta, \equiv)$, a set $\Psi \subseteq Z$ is said to be a *state-based safety property*. An execution $\kappa \in \mathsf{Exec}(\mathcal{M}^{\mathcal{A}})$ is said to satisfy Ψ if for each state $\rho = z_0 \xrightarrow{\alpha_1} z_1 \xrightarrow{\alpha_2} z_2 \cdots \xrightarrow{\alpha_m} z_m$ in κ is such that $z_j \in \Psi$ for all $0 \le j \le m$. We say $\mathcal{M}$ satisfies Ψ with probability $\ge p$ against the attacker $\mathcal{A}$ (written $\mathcal{M}^{\mathcal{A}} \models_p \Psi$) if the measure of the set $\{\kappa \mid \kappa$ is an execution of $\mathcal{M}^{\mathcal{A}}$ and $\kappa \not\models \Psi\}$ in the DTMC $\mathcal{M}^{\mathcal{A}}$ is $> 1 - p$. We say that $\mathcal{M}$ satisfies Ψ with probability $\ge p$ (written $\mathcal{M} \models_p \Psi$) if for all adversaries $\mathcal{A}, \mathcal{M}^{\mathcal{A}} \models_p \Psi$.

2.3 Equational Theories and Frames

A signature $\mathcal{F}$ contains a finite set of function symbols, each with an associated arity. We assume a countably infinite set of special constant symbols $\mathcal{N}$, which we call names and use to represent data generated freshly during a protocol execution. Variable symbols are the union of two disjoint sets $\mathcal{X}$ and $\mathcal{X}_w$ which will be used as protocol and frame variables, respectively. It is required that variable symbols are disjoint from $\mathcal{F}$. Terms are built by the application of function symbols to variables and terms in the standard way. Given a signature $\mathcal{F}$ and $\mathcal{Y} \subseteq \mathcal{X} \cup \mathcal{X}_w$, we use $\mathcal{T}(\mathcal{F}, \mathcal{Y})$ to denote the set of terms built over $\mathcal{F}$ and $\mathcal{Y}$. The set of variables occurring in a term is denoted by $vars(t)$. A ground term is one that contains no free variables.

A substitution σ is a function that maps variables to terms. The set $dom(\sigma) = \{x \in \mathcal{X} \cup \mathcal{X}_w \mid \sigma(x) \ne x\}$ is said to be the *domain* of the substitution σ. For the rest of the paper, each substitution will have a finite domain. A substitution σ with domain $\{x_1, ..., x_k\}$ will be denoted as $\{x_1 \mapsto t_1, ..., x_k \mapsto t_k\}$ if $\sigma(x_i) = t_i$. The set $\{t_1, .., t_k\}$ shall be denoted by $ran(\sigma)$. A substitution σ is said to be ground if every term in $ran(\sigma)$ is ground and a substitution with an empty domain shall be denoted as $\emptyset$. A substitution can be extended to terms in the usual way. We shall write $t\sigma$ for the term obtained by applying the substitution σ to the term t.

Our process algebra is parameterized by a non-trivial equational theory $(\mathcal{F}, E)$, where E is a set of $\mathcal{F}$-Equations. By a $\mathcal{F}$-Equation, we mean a pair

$l = r$ where $l, r \in \mathcal{T}(\mathcal{F} \setminus \mathcal{N}, \mathcal{X})$ are terms that do not contain names. Two terms s and t are said to be equal with respect to an equational theory $(\mathcal{F}, E)$, denoted $s =_E t$, if $E \vdash s = t$ in the first order theory of equality. For equational theories defined in the preceding manner, if two terms containing names are equivalent, they will remain equivalent when the names are replaced by arbitrary terms. We often identify an equational theory $(\mathcal{F}, E)$ by E when the signature is clear from the context. Processes are executed in an environment that consists of a frame φ and a binding substitution σ. Formally, $\sigma : \mathcal{X} \to \mathcal{T}(\mathcal{F})$ is a binding substitution that binds the variables of the processes and $\varphi : \mathcal{X}_w \to \mathcal{T}(\mathcal{F})$ is called a frame.

Two frames φ_1 and φ_2 are said to be statically equivalent if $dom(\varphi_1) = dom(\varphi_2)$ and for all $r_1, r_2 \in \mathcal{T}(\mathcal{F} \setminus \mathcal{N}, \mathcal{X}_w)$ we have $r_1\varphi_1 =_E r_2\varphi_1$ iff $r_1\varphi_2 =_E r_2\varphi_2$. Intuitively, two frames are statically equivalent if an attacker cannot distinguish between the information they contain. A term $t \in \mathcal{T}(\mathcal{F})$ is deducible from a frame φ with recipe $r \in \mathcal{T}(\mathcal{F} \setminus \mathcal{N}, dom(\varphi))$ in equational theory E, denoted $\varphi \vdash_E^r t$, if $r\varphi =_E t$. We often omit r and E and write $\varphi \vdash t$ if they are clear from the context.

For the rest of the paper, $\mathcal{F}_b$ and $\mathcal{F}_c$ are signatures with disjoint sets of function symbols and $(\mathcal{F}_b, E_b)$ and $(\mathcal{F}_c, E_c)$ are non-trivial equational theories. The combination of these two theories will be $(\mathcal{F}, E) = (\mathcal{F}_b \cup \mathcal{F}_c, E_b \cup E_c)$.

3   Process Syntax and Semantics

Our process syntax and semantics is similar to that of [19] with the addition of an operator for probabilistic choice. It can also been seen as a variant of [26].

Process Syntax: For technical reasons, we assume a countably infinite set of labels $\mathcal{L}$ and an equivalence relation $\sim$ on $\mathcal{L}$ that induces a countably infinite set of equivalence classes. For $l \in \mathcal{L}$, $[l]$ denotes the equivalence class of l. We use $\mathcal{L}_b$ and $\mathcal{L}_c$ to range over subsets of $\mathcal{L}$ such that $\mathcal{L}_b \cap \mathcal{L}_c = \emptyset$ and both $\mathcal{L}_b$ and $\mathcal{L}_c$ are closed under $\sim$. We assume each equivalence class contains a countably infinite number of labels. Each connective in our grammar will come with a label from $\mathcal{L}$, which will later be used to identify the process performing a protocol step after a composition takes place. The equivalence relation will be used to mask the information an attacker can obtain from the internal actions of a process, in the sense that, when an action with label l is executed, the attacker will only be able to infer $[l]$.

The syntax of processes is introduced in Fig. 1. It begins by introducing what we call basic processes, which we will denote by $B, B_1, B_2, ...B_n$. In the definition of basic processes, $p \in [0, 1]$, $l \in \mathcal{L}$, $x \in \mathcal{X}$ and $c_i \in \{\top, s = t\} \forall i \in \{1, ..., k\}$ where $s, t \in \mathcal{T}(\mathcal{F} \setminus \mathcal{N}, \mathcal{X})$. In the case of the assignment rule $(x := t)^l$, we additionally require that $x \notin vars(t)$. Intuitively, basic processes will be used to represent the actions of a particular protocol participant. 0^l is a process that does nothing and νx^l is the process that creates a fresh name and binds it to x. The process $(x := t)^l$ assigns the term t to the variable x. The test process $[c_1 \wedge ... \wedge c_k]^l$ terminates if c_i is $\top$ or c_i is $s = t$ where $s =_E t$ for all $i \in \{1, ..., k\}$ and otherwise, if some c_i is $s = t$ and $s \neq_E t$, the process deadlocks. The process $in(x)^l$ reads a term t from the public channel and binds it to x and the process $out(t)^l$ outputs a

---

Basic Processes
$$B ::= 0^l \,|\, \nu x^l \,|\, (x := t)^l \,|\, [c_1 \wedge ... \wedge c_k]^l \,|\, in(x)^l \,|\, out(t)^l \,|\, (B \cdot^l B) \,|\, (B \oplus^l_p B)$$

Basic Contexts
$$D[\square] ::= \square \,|\, B \,|\, D[\square] \cdot^l B \,|\, B \cdot^l D[\square] \,|\, D[\square] \oplus^l_p D[\square]$$

Contexts $[a_i \in \{\nu x, (x := t)\}]$
$$C[\square_1, ..., \square_m] ::= a_1^{l_1} \cdot ... \cdot a_n^{l_n} \cdot (D_1[\square_1] |^{l_{n+1}} D_2[\square_2] |^{l_{n+2}} ... |^{l_{n+m-1}} D_m[\square_m])$$

Fig. 1. Process Syntax

term on the public channel. The processes $P \cdot^l Q$ sequentially executes P followed by Q whereas the process $P \oplus^l_p Q$ behaves like P with probability p and like Q with probability $1 - p$.

In Fig. 1, basic processes are extended to include a special process variable $\square$ and $\square_1, ..., \square_m$ are used to represent distinct processes variables. The resulting object is a basic context, which we will denote by $D[\square]$, $D_1[\square]$, $D_2[\square]$, ..., $D_n[\square]$. Notice that only a single process variable can appear in a basic context. $D_1[B_1]$ denotes the process that results from replacing every occurrence of $\square$ in D_1 by B_1. A context is then a sequential composition of fresh variable creations and variable assignments followed by the parallel composition of a set of basic contexts. The prefix of variable creations and assignments is used to instantiate data common to one or more basic contexts. In the definition of contexts, $a \in \{\nu x, (x := t)\}$. A process is nothing but a context that does not contain any process variables. We will use $C, C_1, C_2, ..., C_n$ to denote contexts and P, Q or R to denote processes. For a context $C[\square_1, ..., \square_m]$ and basic processes $B_1, ..., B_m$, $C[B_1, ..., B_m]$ denotes the process that results from replacing the each process variable $\square_i$ by B_i. The binding constructs in a process are assignment, input and fresh name creation. When a variable is bound in B_1, all occurrences of the variable in B_2 are bound in $B_1 \cdot B_2$. However, in $B_1 \oplus_p B_2$, a variable can occur free in B_1 and bound in B_2, or vice versa. A process containing no free variables is called ground.

Definition 1. *A context* $C[\square_1, ..., \square_m] = a_1 \cdot ... \cdot a_n \cdot (D_1[\square_1]|...|D_m[\square_m])$ *is said to be well-formed if every operator has a unique label and for any labels* l_1 *and* l_2 *occurring in* D_i *and* D_j *for* $i, j \in \{1, 2, ..., m\}$, $i \neq j$ *iff* $[l_1] \neq [l_2]$.

For the remainder of this paper, contexts are assumed to be well-formed. A process that results from replacing process variables in a context by basic processes is also assumed to be well-formed. Unless otherwise stated, we will always assume that all of the labels from a basic process come from the same equivalence class.

Convention 1. *For readability, we will omit process labels when they are not relevant in a particular setting. Whenever new actions are added to a process, their labels are assumed to be fresh and not equivalent to any existing labels of that process.*

The following example illustrates how protocol with randomized actions can be modeled using our process syntax.

Example 1. In a simple DC-net protocol, two parties Alice and Bob want to anonymously publish two confidential bits m_A and m_B, respectively. To achieve this, Alice and Bob agree on three private random bits k_0, k_1 and s_b and output a pair of messages according to the following scheme. In our specification of the protocol, all of the private bits will be generated by Alice.

$$
\begin{array}{llll}
\text{If } s_b = 0 & \text{Alice: } M_{A,0} = k_0 \oplus m_A, & M_{A,1} = k_1 \\
& \text{Bob: } M_{B,0} = k_0, & M_{B,1} = k_1 \oplus m_B \\
\text{If } s_b = 1 & \text{Alice: } M_{A,0} = k_0, & M_{A,1} = k_1 \oplus m_A \\
& \text{Bob: } M_{B,0} = k_0 \oplus m_B, & M_{B,1} = k_1
\end{array}
$$

From the protocol output, the messages m_A and m_B can be retrieved as $M_{A,0} \oplus M_{B,0}$ and $M_{A,1} \oplus M_{B,1}$. The party to which the messages belong, however, remains unconditionally private, provided the exchanged secrets are not revealed. This protocol can be modeled using the following equational theory.

$$
\begin{array}{lll}
\mathcal{F}_b = \{0, 1, \oplus, enc, dec, \langle, \rangle, fst, snd\} \\
E_b = \{dec(enc(m, k), k) = m, & x \oplus 0 = x & x \oplus x = 0 \\
\quad x \oplus y = y \oplus x & (x \oplus y) \oplus z = x \oplus (y \oplus z) \\
\quad fst(\langle x, y \rangle) = x & snd(\langle x, y \rangle) = y\}
\end{array}
$$

The role of Alice in this protocol is defined in our process syntax as

$$
\begin{aligned}
A &= A_0 \cdot (m_A := 0 \oplus_{\frac{1}{2}} m_A := 1) \cdot \\
&\quad ((s_b := 0) \cdot out(enc(s_b, k)) \cdot out(\langle k_0 \oplus m_A, k_1 \rangle) \oplus_{\frac{1}{2}} \\
&\quad (s_b := 1) \cdot out(enc(s_b, k)) \cdot out(\langle k_0, k_1 \oplus m_A \rangle)) \\
A_0 &= (k_0 = 0 \oplus_{\frac{1}{2}} k_0 = 1) \cdot (k_1 = 0 \oplus_{\frac{1}{2}} k_1 = 1) \cdot out(enc(\langle k_0, k_1 \rangle, k))
\end{aligned}
$$

We now give the specification of Bob's protocol $B_1 \mid B_2$ below.

$$
\begin{aligned}
B_0 &= in(z_0) \cdot in(z_1) \cdot (k_0 = fst(dec(z_0, k))) \cdot \\
&\quad (k_1 = snd(dec(z_1, k))) \cdot (s_b = dec(z_1, k)) \\
B_1 &= B_0 \cdot (m_B = 0 \oplus_{\frac{1}{2}} m_B = 1) \cdot out(enc(m_B, k)) \cdot [s_b = 0] \cdot out(\langle k_0, k_1 \oplus m_B \rangle) \\
B_2 &= B_0 \cdot in(z_2) \cdot (m_B = dec(z_2, k)) \cdot [s_b = 1] \cdot out(\langle k_0 \oplus m_B, k_1 \rangle)
\end{aligned}
$$

Notice that the output of Bob depends on the value of Alice's coin flip. Because our process calculus does not contain else branches, the required functionality is simulated using the parallel and test operators. Also notice that the communication between Alice and Bob in the above specification requires a pre-established secret key k. This key can be established by first running some key exchange protocol, which in our case, will be modeled by a context $C[\Box_1, \Box_2, \Box_3] = \nu k \cdot (\Box_1 | \Box_2 | \Box_3)$.

$$
\begin{array}{ll}
\text{INPUT} & \dfrac{r \in \mathcal{T}(\mathcal{F} \setminus \mathcal{N}, \mathcal{X}) \quad \varphi \vdash^r t \quad x \notin dom(\sigma)}{(in(x)^l, \varphi, \sigma) \xrightarrow{(r,[l])} \delta_{(0,\varphi,\sigma \cup \{x \mapsto t\})}} \\[3mm]
\text{NEW} & \dfrac{x \notin dom(\sigma) \quad n \text{ is a fresh name}}{(\nu x^l, \varphi, \sigma) \xrightarrow{(\tau,[l])} \delta_{(0,\varphi,\sigma \cup \{x \mapsto n\})}} \\[3mm]
\text{OUTPUT} & \dfrac{vars(t) \subseteq dom(\sigma)}{(out(t)^l, \varphi, \sigma) \xrightarrow{(\tau,[l])} \delta_{(0,\varphi \cup \{w_{(|dom(\varphi)|+1,[l])} \mapsto t\sigma\}, \sigma)}} \\[3mm]
\text{TEST} & \dfrac{\forall i \in \{1,...,n\}, c_i \text{ is } \top \text{ or } c_i \text{ is } s = t \text{ where } vars(s,t) \subseteq dom(\sigma) \text{ and } s\sigma =_E t\sigma}{([c_1 \wedge ... \wedge c_n]^l, \varphi, \sigma) \xrightarrow{(\tau,[l])} \delta_{(0,\varphi,\sigma)}} \\[3mm]
\text{ASSIGN} & \dfrac{vars(t) \subseteq dom(\sigma) \quad x \notin dom(\sigma)}{((x := t)^l, \varphi, \sigma) \xrightarrow{(\tau,[l])} \delta_{(0,\varphi,\sigma \cup \{x \mapsto t\sigma\})}} \\[3mm]
\text{NULL} & \dfrac{(Q_0, \varphi, \sigma) \xrightarrow{\alpha} \mu}{(0 \cdot^l Q_0, \varphi, \sigma) \xrightarrow{\alpha} \mu} \\[3mm]
\text{SEQUENCE} & \dfrac{Q_0 \neq 0 \quad (Q_0, \varphi, \sigma) \xrightarrow{\alpha} \mu}{(Q_0 \cdot^l Q_1, \varphi, \sigma) \xrightarrow{\alpha} \mu \cdot^l Q_1} \\[3mm]
\text{PBRANCH} & \dfrac{}{(Q_1 \oplus_p^l Q_2, \varphi, \sigma) \xrightarrow{(\tau,[l])} \delta_{(Q_1,\varphi,\sigma)} +_p \delta_{(Q_2,\varphi,\sigma)}} \\[3mm]
\text{PARALLEL}_L & \dfrac{(Q_0, \varphi, \sigma) \xrightarrow{\alpha} \mu}{(Q_0|^l Q_1, \varphi, \sigma) \xrightarrow{\alpha} \mu|^l Q_1} \\[3mm]
\text{PARALLEL}_R & \dfrac{((Q_1, \varphi, \sigma) \xrightarrow{\alpha} \mu}{(Q_0|^l Q_1, \varphi, \sigma) \xrightarrow{\alpha} Q_0|^l \mu}
\end{array}
$$

Fig. 2. Process semantics

Process Semantics: Given a process P, an extended process is a 3-tuple (P, φ, σ) where φ is a frame and σ is a binding substitution. Semantically, a ground process P is a POMDP $[\![P]\!] = (Z, z_s, Act, \Delta, \equiv)$, where Z is the set of all extended processes, z_s is $(P, \emptyset, \emptyset)$, $Act = (\mathcal{T}(\mathcal{F} \setminus \mathcal{N}, \mathcal{X}_w) \cup \{\tau\}, \mathcal{L}/\sim)$ and Δ is a partial function from extended processes to Act. We now give some additional notation preceding our formal definitions of Δ and $\equiv$. By $\mu \cdot^l Q$, we mean the distribution μ_1 such that $\mu_1(P', \varphi, \sigma) = \mu(P, \varphi, \sigma)$ if P' is $P \cdot^l Q$ and 0 otherwise. The distributions $\mu|^l Q$ and $Q|^l \mu$ are defined analogously. The definition of Δ is given in Fig. 2. Observe that we write $(P, \varphi, \sigma) \xrightarrow{\alpha} \mu$ if $\Delta((P, \varphi, \sigma), \alpha) = \mu$. Δ is well-defined, as basic processes are deterministic and each equivalence class on $\mathcal{L}$ identifies a unique basic process. Given an extended process η, let $enabled(\eta)$ denote the set of all $(\S, [l])$ such that

$(P, \varphi, \sigma) \xrightarrow{(\S, [l])} \mu, \S \in \mathcal{T}(\mathcal{F} \setminus \mathcal{N}, \mathcal{X}_w) \cup \{\tau\}$ and l is the label of an input or output action. Using this, we lift our notion of equivalence on frames from Sect. 2.3 to an equivalence $\equiv$ on extended processes by requiring that two extended processes $\eta = (P, \varphi, \sigma)$ and $\eta' = (P', \varphi', \sigma')$ are equivalent if $enabled(\eta) = enabled(\eta')$ and $\varphi =_E \varphi'$.

Definition 2. *An extended process* (Q, φ, σ) *preserves the secrecy of* $x \in vars(Q)$ *in the equational theory* $(\mathcal{F}, E)$, *denoted* $(Q, \varphi, \sigma) \models_E x$, *if there is no* $r \in \mathcal{T}(\mathcal{F} \setminus \mathcal{N}, dom(\varphi))$ *such that* $\varphi \vdash_E^r x\sigma$. *We write* $\mathsf{Secret}(x)$, *for* $x \in vars(Q)$, *to represent the set of states of* $[\![Q]\!]$ *that preserve the secrecy of* x. *We also write* $\mathsf{Secret}(\{x_1, ..., x_n\})$ *to denote* $\mathsf{Secret}(x_1) \cap ... \cap \mathsf{Secret}(x_n)$. *We will often omit the braces* $\{,\}$ *for ease of notation.*

Notation 1. Note that for process P and variables $x_1, ..., x_n \in vars(P)$, $\mathsf{Secret}(\{x_1, ..., x_n\})$ is a safety property of $[\![P]\!]$. We shall write $P \models_{E,p} \mathsf{Secret}(\{x_1, ..., x_n\})$ whenever $[\![P]\!] \models_p \mathsf{Secret}(\{x_1, ..., x_n\})$.

Example 2. Consider the DC-net protocol defined in Example 1. The correctness property of the protocol is that, after the completion of the protocol, the origin of the participants messages can be determined with probability at most $\frac{1}{2}$. That is, an attacker can do no better than guess which position Alice's message appears in. This is the same as asserting that an attacker cannot infer the value of the secret bit s_b. In our process semantics, this can be modeled as a secrecy property as follows. Let $A' = A \cdot S$ where $S = in(z) \cdot [z = s_b] \cdot \nu s \cdot out(s)$ and define $C = \nu k \cdot (A' | B_1 | B_2)$. The inclusion of S in Alice's specification requires an attacker to correctly identify the message that belongs to Alice to derive the secret value s. Therefore, if the statement $\nu k \cdot (A' | B_1 | B_2) \models_{E_b, \frac{1}{2}} \mathsf{Secret}(s)$ is valid, no attacker can do better than guess which message belongs to Alice.

4   Composition Results for Single Session Protocols

We are now ready to present our first composition results. Our focus here will begin with the scenario where two principals run a key establishment protocol over the signature $\mathcal{F}_c$ after which each principal uses the established secret to communicate in a protocol over the signature $\mathcal{F}_b$. We will then show how this result can be extended to protocols operating over the same signature, provided the messages of each protocol are tagged. Before formalizing our first result, we show how a simple DC-net protocol using Diffie-Hellman (DH) for key exchange can be modeled in our composition framework. Using the results from Theorem 1, the security guarantees of each sub-protocol are achieved for the full protocol.

Example 3. Consider the processes A', B_1 and B_2, as defined in Example 2. Recall that these processes describe a simple DC-net protocol designed to guarantee the anonymity of the protocol's participants. Further recall that the sub-protocols for Alice (A') and Bob (B_1, B_2) require a pre-established shared symmetric key k. A formal specification of the DH key exchange protocol to establish this key is given below. This process is parameterized by the signature $\mathcal{F}_c = \{g\}$ and equations $E_c = \{(g^x)^y = (g^y)^x\}$.

$$C[\square_0, \square_1, \square_2] = \nu y \cdot in(a) \cdot (A_k \cdot \square_0 | (k := a^y) \cdot \square_1 | (k := a^y) \cdot \square_2 | out(g^y))$$
$$A_k = \nu x \cdot out(g^x) \cdot in(b) \cdot (k := b^x)$$

Now if $C[[\top], [\top], [\top]]$ preserves the secrecy of the shared key k and $\nu k \cdot (A'|B_1|B_2)$ preserves the secrecy of k and s with probability at least $\frac{1}{2}$, then the composed protocol $C[A', B_1, B_2]$ preserves the secrecy of s with probability at least $\frac{1}{2}$. That is, if the DC-net specification does not reveal which message belongs to Alice, then neither does the DC-net protocol using DH key exchange to establish a secret communication channel between Alice and Bob.

We now give our main result.

Theorem 1. Let $C[\square_1, ..., \square_n] = \nu k_1 \cdot ... \cdot \nu k_m \cdot (D_1[\square_1] | D_2[\square_2] | ... | D_n[\square_n])$ be a context over $\mathcal{F}_c$ with labels from $\mathcal{L}_c$, $B_1, B_2, ..., B_n$ be basic processes over $\mathcal{F}_b$ with labels from $\mathcal{L}_b$, $q_1, q_2 \in [0, 1]$ and $x_s \in \bigcup_{i=1}^{n} vars(B_i) \setminus vars(C)$ such that:

1. $fv(C) = \emptyset$ and $fv(B_i) \subseteq \{x_i\}$
2. $vars(C) \cap vars(B_i) \subseteq \{x_i\}$ for $i \in \{1, ..., n\}$
3. $C[B_1, ..., B_n]$ is ground
4. $C[[\top]^{l_0}, ..., [\top]^{l_n}] \models_{E_c, q_1}$ Secret$(x_1, ..., x_n)$ where $l_0, ..., l_n \in \mathcal{L}_b$
5. $\nu k \cdot (x_1 := k) \cdot ... \cdot (x_n := k) \cdot (B_1 | ... | B_n) \models_{E_b, q_2}$ Secret$(x_1, ..., x_n, x_s)$

Then $C[B_1, ..., B_n] \models_{E, q_1 q_2}$ Secret(x_s).

Before describing the proof ideas behind Theorem 1, we highlight some of the proof challenges in the following example.

Example 4. Consider the signatures $\mathcal{F}_a = \{c\}$ and $\mathcal{F}_b = \{h\}$ where c is a constant and h is a 1-ary function symbol. Let $E_a = E_b = \emptyset$ and $C[\square_1, \square_2] = C_1 \cdot \square_1 | C_2 \cdot \square_2$ be the context such that:

$$C_1 = \nu x_k \cdot (out^1(x_k) \oplus_{\frac{1}{2}} out^2(c))$$
$$C_2 = \nu y_k \cdot (out^3(y_k) \oplus_{\frac{1}{2}} out^4(c))$$

Essentially C_1 generates x_k and with probability $\frac{1}{2}$ decides to reveal it. C_2 generates y_k and with probability $\frac{1}{2}$ decides to reveal it. In both cases, when the fresh values are not revealed, a constant is output in its place. Consider the basic processes B_1 and B_2 defined as follows

$$B_1 = in^5(x) \cdot [x = x_k] \cdot \nu x_s \cdot out^6(x_s)$$
$$B_2 = in^7(y) \cdot [y = h(y_k)] \cdot \nu x_s \cdot out^8(x_s)$$

Consider the process $P = C[B_1, B_2]$ and let $C_1', C_2', \sigma, , \varphi_1, \varphi_2, \varphi_{12}, \sigma^f, \varphi_1^f, \varphi_2^f$ and φ_{12}^f be defined as follows:

$$C_1' = out^1(x_k) \oplus_{\frac{1}{2}} out^2(c)$$
$$\varphi_{12} = \{w_1 \to k_1, w_2 \to k_2\}$$
$$C_2' = out^3(y_k) \oplus_{\frac{1}{2}} out^4(c)$$
$$\varphi_{02} = \{w_1 \to k_1, w_2 \to c\}$$
$$\sigma = \{x_k \mapsto k_1, y_k \mapsto k_2\}$$
$$\sigma_1^f = \{x_k \mapsto k_1, y_k \mapsto k_2, x \mapsto k_1, x_s \mapsto k_3\}$$
$$\varphi_0 = \{w_1 \to c\}$$
$$\sigma_2^f = \{x_k \mapsto k_1, y_k \mapsto k_2, y \mapsto h(k_1), x_s \mapsto k_3\}$$
$$\varphi_1 = \{w_1 \to k_1\}$$
$$\varphi_1^f = \{w_1 \to k_1, w_2 \to c, w_4 \mapsto k_3\}$$
$$\varphi_2 = \{w_1 \to c, w_2 \to k_2\}$$
$$\varphi_2^f = \{w_1 \to c, w_2 \to k_2, w_6 \mapsto k_3\}$$
$$\varphi_{00} = \{w_1 \to c, w_2 \to c\}$$
$$\varphi_{12}^f = \{w_1 \to k_1, w_2 \to k_2, w_4 \mapsto k_3\}$$
$$\varphi_{10} = \{w_1 \to k_1, w_2 \to c\}$$

The execution of P shown in Fig. 3 reveals x_s with probability $\frac{3}{4}$. Observe that the transitions out of the states labeling $(B_1|B_2, \varphi_1, \sigma)$ involve transitions of B_1 while the transitions out of $(B_1|B_2, \varphi_2, \sigma)$ involve transitions of B_2. If we try to fire the same transitions out of $(B_1|B_2, \varphi_2, \sigma)$ as in $(B_1|B_2, \varphi_1, \sigma)$ the process will deadlock because the attacker cannot deduce x_k in φ_2. From this, it is easy to see that the execution shown in Fig. 3 cannot be written as an interleaving of one execution of $C_1|C_2$ and one execution of $B_1|B_2$. As a result, the proof technique of [19] is not immediately applicable. Nevertheless, we will be able to show that P keeps x_s secret with probability at least $\frac{1}{4}$.

In the execution of P shown in Fig. 3, the attacker performs different actions depending of the result of coin toss made by C_1. When C_1 outputs a nonce, B_1 is scheduled before B_2. When C_1 outputs the constant c, B_2 is executed first. Such an attack is valid, even when considering our restricted class of adversaries. The reason is that the attacker can infer the result of the coin toss in C_1 by observing what is output.

The proof of Theorem 1 will utilize an extension of the seperation result from [19], which intuitively says that for a context C and a basic process B, if the composition $C[B]$, where C and B are over disjoint signatures and derive a set of variables with probability q, can be transformed into the composition $C'[B']$, where C' and B' represent α-renamings of C and B, such that $vars(C') \cap vars(B') = \emptyset$ and the same secret derivation guarantees are achieved. Given this result, an attacker for a composition of $C[B]$ can be transformed into an attacker for a composition of two protocols C' and B' over disjoint variables. From this attacker $\mathcal{A}$, we need to construct and an attacker $\mathcal{A}'$ for one of the sub-protocols C' or B'. Because C' and B' are simply α-renamings of C and B, $\mathcal{A}'$ is sufficient for contradicting a secrecy guarantee about one of the sub-protocols C or B. One of the challenges in constructing $\mathcal{A}'$ is that the attacker A may use terms over $\mathcal{F}_b \cup \mathcal{F}_c$. That is, it may construct inputs using terms output by both of the sub-protocols C' and B'. Our technique is to transform $\mathcal{A}$ into what we call a "pure" attacker, that constructs its inputs for actions of C' (resp B') using only terms output by actions of C' (resp B'). We define this concept formally. Given a set of labels L closed under $\sim$, let $\mathcal{X}_w^L = \{w_{i,[l]} \mid w_{i,[l]} \in \mathcal{X}_w \land l \in L \land i \in \mathbb{N}\}$

Definition 3. *Let L be a set of labels closed under $\sim$ and $\mathcal{F}$ be a signature. An attacker $\mathcal{A}$ for a process P is said to be pure with respect to $(L, \mathcal{F})$ if whenever $\mathcal{A}$ chooses the action $(r, [l])$ we have $r \in \mathcal{T}(\mathcal{F}, \mathcal{X}_w^L)$.*

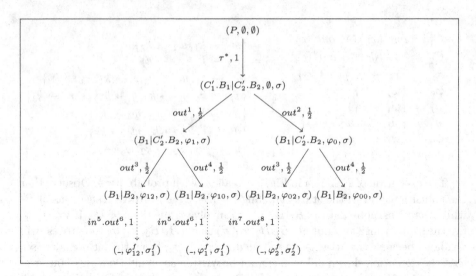

Fig. 3. Execution of P. The solid edges are transitions of the context C and dotted edges are transitions of the basic processes B_1, B_2. For convenience, the edges in the drawn execution tree may compose of more than 1 action. The recipes used in in^3 and in^5 are w_1 and $h(w_2)$ respectively. The transition probabilities also label the edges.

For the kind of compositions we consider in Theorem 1, for example $C'[B']$, an attacker can be transformed into one that is pure with respect to both of the sub-protocols $C'[\top]$ and B'. This construction follows from the techniques outlined in [19].

We are now ready to describe the crux of our composition theorem. The fundamental technical challenge of this result is to show that, for some context $C[\Box]$, process B and set of secrets S, if $C[[\top]] \models_{q_1} \mathsf{Secret}(S)$ and $B \models_{q_2} \mathsf{Secret}(S)$, then $C[B] \models_{q_1 q_2} \mathsf{Secret}(S)$. In light of the preceding results, one must transform a pure attacker for a composed protocol $C[B]$ that reveals some secret values with probability $\geq 1 - q_1 q_2$ into an attacker for one of the sub-protocols C or B that derives the secret values with probability at least $1 - q_1$ or $1 - q_2$, respectively. This essentially boils down to proving that an attacker for the asynchronous product of two POMDP's M_1 and M_2, denoted $M_1 \otimes M_2$, can be transformed into an attacker for either M_1 or M_2. This is achieved by transforming the attacker $\mathcal{A}$ for $M_1 \otimes M_2$ into attacker $\mathcal{A}'$ with the following two properties:

- $\mathcal{A}'$ executes all of the actions from M_1 before executing any actions from M_2.
- For any two executions $\rho, \rho' \in \mathsf{Exec}((M_1 \otimes M_2)^{\mathcal{A}'})$, if the projection of ρ and ρ' onto their components from M_i (for $i \in \{1, 2\}$) produces two equivalent traces and $\mathcal{A}'$ picks an action from M_i, then $\mathcal{A}'(tr(\rho)) = \mathcal{A}'(tr(\rho'))$.
- $\mathcal{A}'$ derives the secret values in S with probability greater than or equal to that of the attacker $\mathcal{A}$.

The details of this construction are quite involved, and can be found in the accompanying technical report [6]. As a result of Theorem 1, one can reason about protocols composed sequentially by taking a context with a single basic context where a single hole appears at the end. The same is true for protocols composed in parallel, as given by Corollary 1. In this setting, one considers a context built over two basic contexts. One basic context contains only a hole, while the other contains no holes.

Corollary 1. *Let C be a basic process over $\mathcal{F}_c$ with labels from $\mathcal{L}_c$ and B be a basic processes over $\mathcal{F}_b$ with labels from $\mathcal{L}_b$ and $q_1, q_2 \in [0, 1]$ such that:*

1. *$vars(C) \cap vars(B) = \emptyset$*
2. *$C \models_{E_c, q_1}$ Secret(x_c) for $x_c \in vars(C)$*
3. *$B \models_{E_b, q_2}$ Secret(x_b) for $x_b \in vars(B)$*

Then $(C|B) \models_{E, q_1 q_2}$ Secret(x_b, x_c).

It is important to point out that the security guarantees of the composed process may in fact be stronger than what we can prove utilizing Theorem 1. This is because we always assume the worst case in that context assigns the same secret values to each basic process. As a result, our composition result will in some cases lead to only an under-approximation on the probability that a set of variables is kept secret, as shown by the following example:

Example 5. Consider the signatures $\mathcal{F}_b = \{h\}$ and $\mathcal{F}_c = \{\}$ with empty equational theories and the context defined as follows:

$$C[\Box_1, \Box_2] = \nu k_1 \cdot \nu k_2 \cdot (([x_1 := k_1] \oplus_{\frac{1}{2}} [x_1 := k_2]) \cdot \Box_1 \mid [x_2 := k_2] \cdot \Box_2)$$

Essentially, the context generates shared secrets x_1 and x_2 for two sub-protocols $\Box_1$ and $\Box_2$ to be run in parallel. For the sub-protocol $\Box_1$, it sets the secret x_1 to k_1 with probability $\frac{1}{2}$ and to k_2 with probability $\frac{1}{2}$. In the second sub-protocol, the shared secret x_2 is set to k_2. Now consider the sub-protocols B_1 and B_2 defined as follows:

$$B_1 = out(h(x_1)) \oplus_{\frac{1}{2}} 0$$
$$B_2 = in(z) \cdot [z = h(x_2)] \cdot \nu x_s \cdot out(x_s)$$

B_1 outputs $h(x_1)$ with probability $\frac{1}{2}$ and with probability $\frac{1}{2}$ does nothing. B_2 checks if the attacker can construct $h(x_2)$ before revealing x_s. It is easy to see that $C[B_1, B_2]$ reveals x_s with probability $\frac{1}{4}$. This is because the attacker can construct $h(x_2)$ when x_1 and x_2 are equal (which happens with probability $\frac{1}{2}$) and when B_1 reveals $h(x_1)$ (which also happens with probability $\frac{1}{2}$). In-fact, we can easily show that $C[B_1, B_2]$ keeps x_s secret with probability exactly $\frac{3}{4}$. However, Theorem 1 can only show $C[B_1, B_2]$ keeps x_s secret with probability $\frac{1}{2}$, since in our composition results, we assume that x_1 and x_2 get the same secret name.

It is often necessary for protocols to share basic cryptographic primitives, such as functions for encryption, decryption and hashing. We extend our composition result to such protocols. The key ingredient for composition in this context is tagging, a syntactic transformation of a protocol and its signature, designed to ensure secure composition. Essentially, tagging a protocol appends a special identifier to each of the messages that it outputs. When the protocol performs an input, it will recursively test all subterms in the input message to verify their tags are consistent with the protocol's tag. One limitation with tagging is that its correctness largely depends on the signature in question. As in [19], we will limit the class of cryptographic primitives we consider to symmetric encryption and a hash function, with the understanding that our results can be extended to primitives for asymmetric encryption.

Let C be a context and B be a basic process, both over the equational theory $(\mathcal{F}_{enc}, E_{enc})$ where $\mathcal{F}_{enc} = \{enc, dec, h\}$ and $E_{enc} = \{dec(enc(m, rn, k), k) = m\}$. To securely compose C and B, the terms occurring in each protocol must be tagged by function symbols from disjoint equational theories. The tagging of two protocols will be done in two steps. To begin, a signature renaming function $\_^d$ will be applied to each of C and B with distinct values of $d \in \{b, c\}$. The function $\_^d$ transforms a context C over the signature $(\mathcal{F}_{enc}, E_{enc})$ to a context C^d by replacing every occurrence of the function symbols enc, dec and h in C by enc_d, dec_d and h_d, respectively. The resulting context C^d is over the signature $(\mathcal{F}^d_{enc}, E^d_{enc})$, for $\mathcal{F}^d_{enc} = \{enc_d, dec_d, h_d\}$ and $E^d_{enc} = \{dec_d(enc_d(m, rn, k), k) = m\}$. Given C^c and B^b over the disjoint signatures $\mathcal{F}^c_{enc}$ and $\mathcal{F}^b_{enc}$, the tagging function $\lceil \_ \rceil$ is then applied to C^c and B^b, generating the the tagged versions of C and B. We omit the details of this function but note that our tagging scheme is similar to that of [4]. The full details can be found in the technical report [6].

Essentially the tagging scheme enforces the requirement that, whenever a protocol manipulates a term, that term should be tagged with the identifier of the protocol. This is achieving by prefixing every atomic action in a tagged protocol with a conjunction of tests such that, if the terms manipulated by the atomic action meet the aforementioned requirement, the tests will pass. Otherwise, the tests will fail and further protocol actions will be blocked. Tagging is a means to enforce the disjointness condition on the context and basic process signatures in Theorem 1. In particular, we can show that an attack on a composition of two tagged protocols originating from the same signature can be mapped to an attack on the composition of the protocols when the signatures are explicitly made disjoint. Given this, we can prove an analogous result to Theorem 1 for tagged protocols.

Theorem 2. Let $C[\Box_1, ..., \Box_n] = \nu k_1 \cdot ... \cdot \nu k_m \cdot (D_1[\Box_1] \mid D_2[\Box_2] \mid ... \mid D_n[\Box_n])$ be a context over $\mathcal{F}_{enc}$ with labels from $\mathcal{L}_c$, $B_1, B_2, ..., B_n$ be basic processes over $\mathcal{F}_{enc}$ with labels from $\mathcal{L}_b$, $q_1, q_2 \in [0, 1]$ and $x_s \in \bigcup_{i=1}^n vars(B_i) \setminus vars(C)$ such that:

- $fv(C) = \emptyset$ and $fv(B_i) \subseteq \{x_i\}$
- $vars(C) \cap vars(B_i) \subseteq \{x_i\}$ for $i \in \{1, ..., n\}$
- $C[B_1, ..., B_n]$ is ground

– $C[[\top]^{l_0}, ..., [\top]^{l_n}] \models_{E_{enc}, q_1} \mathsf{Secret}(x_1, ..., x_n)$ *where* $l_0, ..., l_n \in \mathcal{L}_b$
– $\nu k \cdot (x_1 := k) \cdot ... \cdot (x_n := k) \cdot (B_1|...|B_n) \models_{E_{enc}, q_2} \mathsf{Secret}(x_1, ..., x_n, x_s).$

Then $\lceil C^c[B_1^b, ..., B_n^b] \rceil \models_{E_{enc} \cup E_{tag}, q_1 q_2} \mathsf{Secret}(x_s).$

5   Replication

In this section, we extend our composition result to protocols that can run multiple sessions.[1] We will begin by considering processes that contain only a bounded version of the replication operator. The bounded replication operator has an explicit bound that limits the number of times a process can replicate. We limit ourselves to processes that contain only a single occurrence of this replication operator. This restriction is not limiting for the applications we consider and it will simplify the proofs. It is, however, possible to extends our results to a more general setting in which a process can contain multiple occurrences of the replication operator.

We will start by showing that if the protocols $C = \nu k_1 \cdot ... \cdot \nu k_m$ $\cdot !_n(C[\square_1]|...|C[\square_l])$ and $!_n(B_1|...|B_l)$ are proven secure with probability at least p and q, respectively, then the composition $\nu k_1 \cdot ... \cdot \nu k_m \cdot !_n(C[B_1]|...|C[B_l])$ is secure with probability at least pq, provided the protocol messages are tagged with both a protocol identifier and a unique session identifier. A similar result (with the absence of the session identifier), has been claimed in [19] for nonrandomized protocols (with p and q both being 1). However, we discovered a simple counterexample, which works for the case of two sessions. Essentially the reason for this attack is that protocol messages from one session can be confused with messages from the other session.

Example 6. Consider the signatures $\mathcal{F}_b = \{h, c\}$ and $\mathcal{F}_a = \{\}$ where c is a constant, h is a 1-ary function symbol and $E = E_a \cup E_b = \emptyset$. We will consider two sessions of the composed protocol.

Let P be the process defined as:

$$P = \nu k_1 \cdot \nu k_2 \cdot !_2(P_1|P_2)$$

where $P_1 = (x_k := k_1)$ and $P_2 = (y_k := k_2)$. Let Q be the process defined as:

$$Q = !_2(\nu k \cdot ((x_k := k) \cdot Q_1|(y_k := k) \cdot Q_2))$$
$$Q_1 = (in(y) \cdot ([y = c] \cdot out^l(h(x_k))|[y = h(x_k)] \cdot \nu x_s \cdot out^{l'}(x_s))$$
$$Q_2 = 0.$$

Clearly, P keeps x_k and y_k secret with probability 1 and Q keeps x_k, y_k and x_s secret with probability 1. Theorem 3 from [19] would imply that x_s is kept secret by $W = \nu k_1 \cdot \nu k_2 \cdot !_2(P_1 \cdot Q_1 \mid P_2 \cdot Q_2)$ in both sessions of the protocol. However, we can show that this is not the case. The reason is as follows. In both sessions of the

---

[1] n sessions of P will be denoted by $!_n P$.

composed protocol, x_k gets the same value. In the first session of the composed protocol, when y is input by Q_1, attacker sends the constant c. Thereafter, the attacker learns $h(x_k)$ because Q_1 outputs it. In the second session of the composed protocol, the attacker sends $h(x_k)$ to Q_1; the check $[y = h(x_k)]$ succeeds and the attacker learns x_s in this session.

In process calculus terms, this attack can be realized by the execution:

$$(W, \emptyset, \emptyset) \to^* (W', \emptyset, \sigma') \to^* (W'', \varphi'', \sigma'')$$

where

$$\begin{aligned}
W' &= (Q_1^1 | Q_1^2) \\
\sigma' &= \{k_1 \mapsto n_1, k_2 \mapsto n_2, x_k^1 \mapsto n_1, y_k^1 \mapsto n_2, \\
&\quad\ x_k^2 \mapsto n_1, y_k^2 \mapsto n_2\} \\
W'' &= 0 \\
\sigma'' &= \sigma' \cup \{y^1 \mapsto c, y^2 \mapsto h(n_1), x_s^2 \mapsto n_3\} \\
\varphi'' &= \{w_l \mapsto h(n_1), w_{l'} \mapsto n_3\}
\end{aligned}$$

Note above that we have used superscripts on variables x_k, y_k, y and x_s in the substitutions to indicate their values in different sessions. Essentially in this execution in $(W', \emptyset, \sigma')$, P is finished in both sessions and assigned x_k and y_k the same values in both sessions. The role Q_2 is also finished in both sessions. Q_1^1 is the first session of Q_1 and Q_1^2 is the second session of Q_1. Now in Q_1^1, the attacker inputs c for y resulting in Q_1^1 leaking $h(n_1)$. In Q_1^2, the attacker can input $h(n_1)$ and learn the value of x_s generated.

Formally, a context containing bounded replication is defined as

$$C[\square_1, ..., \square_m] ::= a_1^{l_1} \cdot ... \cdot a_n^{l_n} \cdot !_n^l (D_1[\square_1]|^{l_{n+1}} D_2[\square_2]|^{l_{n+2}} ... |^{l_{n+m-1}} D_m[\square_m])$$

where $a \in \{\nu x, (x := t)\}$ and $n \geq 2$ is a natural number. The semantics for this bounded replication operator is given in Fig. 4, where $i, j \in \mathbb{N}$ are used to denoted the smallest previously unused indices. We will use $P(i)$ to denote that process that results from renaming each occurrence of $x \in vars(P)$ to x^i for $i \in \mathbb{N}$. When $P(i)$ or $P(j)$ is relabeled freshly as in Fig. 4, the new labels must all belong to the same equivalence class (that contains only those labels). The notation x^* denotes the infinite set $\{x^0, x^1, x^2, ...\}$.

Our semantics imposes an explicit variable renaming with each application of a replication rule. The reason for this is best illustrated through an example. Consider the process $!_m in(x) \cdot P$ and the execution

$$(!_m in(x) \cdot P, \emptyset, \emptyset) \to^* (in(x) \cdot P | !_{m-1} in(x) \cdot P, \varphi, \{x \mapsto t\} \cup \sigma)$$

where variable renaming does not occur. This execution corresponds to the attacker replicating $!_m in(x) \cdot P$, running one instance of $in(x) \cdot P$ and then replicating $!_m in(x) \cdot P$ again. Note that, because x is bound at the end of the above execution, the semantics of the input action cause the process to deadlock at

	$n > 2$ l' is a fresh label $P(i)$ is relabeled freshly
B-REPLICATION	$(!_n^l P, \varphi, \sigma) \xrightarrow{(\tau,[l])} \delta_{(P(i)|l'!_{n-1}^l P, \varphi, \sigma)}$

	l' is a fresh label $P(i), P(j)$ are relabeled freshly
B-REPLICATION$_{n=2}$	$(!_2^l P, \varphi, \sigma) \xrightarrow{(\tau,[l])} \delta_{(P(i)|l' P(j), \varphi, \sigma)}$

Fig. 4. Bounded Replication semantics

$in(x)$. In other words, an attacker can only effective run one copy of $!_m in(x) \cdot P$ for any process of the form $!_m in(x) \cdot P$. It is also convenient to consider this restricted version of α-renaming in view of secrecy. In particular, if a variable is α-named arbitrarily with each application of "B-REPLICATION", then the definition of $!_n^l P$ keeping $x \in vars(P)$ secret becomes unclear, or at least more complicated.

As mentioned in Example 6, our composition result must prevent messages from one session of a process with bounded replication from being confused with messages from another sessions. We achieve this in the following way. Our composed processes will contain an occurrence of $\nu\lambda$ directly following the occurrence of a bounded replication operator. This freshly generated "session tag" will then be used to augment tags occurring in the composed processes. We have the following result.

Theorem 3. *Let* $C[\square_1, ..., \square_n] = \nu k_1 \cdot ... \cdot \nu k_m \cdot !_u \nu\lambda \cdot (D_1[\square_1] | D_2[\square_2] | ... | D_n[\square_n])$ *be a context over* $\mathcal{F}_{enc}$ *with labels from* $\mathcal{L}_c$, $B_1, B_2, ..., B_n$ *be basic processes over* $\mathcal{F}_{enc}$ *with labels from* $\mathcal{L}_b$, $q_1, q_2 \in [0,1]$ *and* $x_s \in \bigcup_{i=1}^n vars(B_i) \setminus vars(C)$ *such that:*

- $fv(C) = \emptyset$ *and* $fv(B_i) \subseteq \{x_i\}$
- $vars(C) \cap vars(B_i) \subseteq \{x_i\}$ *for* $i \in \{1, ..., n\}$
- $\lambda \notin vars(P) \cup vars(Q)$
- $C[B_1, ..., B_n]$ *is ground*
- $C[[\top]^{l_0}, ..., [\top]^{l_n}] \models_{\mathcal{E}_{enc}, q_1}$ Secret$(x_1, ..., x_n)$ *where* $l_0, ..., l_n \in \mathcal{L}_b$
- $\nu k \cdot (x_1 := k) \cdot ... \cdot (x_n := k) \cdot !_m(B_1 | ... | B_n) \models_{\mathcal{E}_{enc}, q_2}$ Secret$(x_1, ..., x_n, x_s^*)$

Then $\lceil \nu k_1 \cdot ... \cdot \nu k_m \cdot !_u \nu\lambda \cdot (D_1^c[B_1^{(b,\lambda)}] | D_2^c[B_2^{(b,\lambda)}] | ... | D_n^c[B_n^{(b,\lambda)}]) \rceil \models_{\mathcal{E}_{enc} \cup \mathcal{E}_{tag}, q_1 q_2}$ Secret(x_s^*).

As a final result, we will show how protocols containing unbounded replication can be composed. That is, we will consider processes over the following grammar.

$$C[\square_1, ..., \square_m] :: = a_1^{l_1} \cdot ... \cdot a_n^{l_n} \cdot !^l (D_1[\square_1]|^{l_{n+1}} D_2[\square_2]|^{l_{n+2}} ...|^{l_{n+m-1}} D_m[\square_m])$$

where $a \in \{\nu x, (x := t)\}$. The semantics of this new replication operator are given in Fig. 5, where again, $i \in \mathbb{N}$ is the smallest previously unused index.

l' is a fresh label $P(i)$ is relabeled freshly

REPLICATION$_N$ $(!^l P, \varphi, \sigma) \xrightarrow{(r,l)} \delta_{(P(i)|^{l'}!^l P, \varphi, \sigma)}$

Fig. 5. Replication semantics

As before, when $P(i)$ is relabeled freshly, the new labels must all belong to the same equivalence class.

As previously eluded to, we cannot state a result in the style of Theorem 3 with non-trivial probabilities. This is because, in the unbounded setting, a attacker can always amplify the probability of deriving a secret by running an attack on more sessions of a protocol. Such a restriction makes our result for unbounded processes almost identical to that of Theorem 6 from [19]. Our result, however, has two main advantages. It eliminates the still applicable attack of Example 6 while considering a richer class of processes.

Theorem 4. *Let* $C[\Box_1, ..., \Box_n] = \nu k_1 \cdot ... \cdot \nu k_m \cdot !\nu \lambda \cdot (D_1[\Box_1] \mid D_2[\Box_2] \mid ... \mid D_n[\Box_n])$ *be a context over* $\mathcal{F}_{enc}$ *with labels from* $\mathcal{L}_c$, $B_1, B_2, ..., B_n$ *be basic processes over* $\mathcal{F}_{enc}$ *with labels from* $\mathcal{L}_b$ *and* $x_s \in \bigcup_{i=1}^n vars(B_i) \setminus vars(C)$ *such that:*

- $fv(C) = \emptyset$ *and* $fv(B_i) \subseteq \{x_i\}$
- $vars(C) \cap vars(B_i) \subseteq \{x_i\}$ *for* $i \in \{1, ..., n\}$
- $\lambda \notin vars(P) \cup vars(Q)$
- $C[B_1, ..., B_n]$ *is ground*
- $C[[\top]^{l_0}, ..., [\top]^{l_n}] \models_{E_{enc},1} \mathsf{Secret}(x_1, ..., x_n)$ *where* $l_0, ..., l_n \in \mathcal{L}_b$
- $\nu k \cdot (x_1 := k) \cdot ... \cdot (x_n := k) \cdot !_m (B_1|...|B_n) \models_{E_{enc},1} \mathsf{Secret}(x_1, ..., x_n, x_s^*)$

Then $\lceil \nu k_1 \cdot ... \cdot \nu k_m \cdot !\nu \lambda \cdot (D_1^c[B_1^{(b,\lambda)}] \mid D_2^c[B_2^{(b,\lambda)}] \mid ... \mid D_n^c[B_n^{(b,\lambda)}]) \rceil \models_{E_{enc} \cup E_{tag},1}$ $\mathsf{Secret}(x_s^*)$.

6   Conclusions

We have studied the problem of securely composing two randomized security protocols. For one session, we show that if P is secure with probability p and Q is secure with probability q then the composed protocol is secure with probability at least pq if the protocol messages are tagged with the information of which protocol they belong to. The same result applies to multiple sessions except that in addition the protocol messages of Q also need to be tagged with session identifiers. The focus of this work has been secrecy properties. In terms of future work, we plan to investigate when composition of randomized security protocols preserve indistinguishability properties.

References

1. Abadi, M., Fournet, C.: Mobile values, new names, and secure communication. In: 28th ACM Symposium on Principles of Programming Languages (POPL 2001), pp. 104–115 (2001)
2. Andova, S., Cremers, C.J.F., Gjøsteen, K., Mauw, S., Mjølsnes, S.F., Radomirovic, S.: A framework for compositional verification of security protocols. Inform. Comput. **206**(2–4), 425–459 (2008)
3. Arapinis, M., Cheval, V., Delaune, S.: Composing security protocols: from confidentiality to privacy. http://arxiv.org/pdf/1407.5444v3.pdf
4. Arapinis, M., Cheval, V., Delaune, S.: Verifying privacy-type properties in a modular way. In: 25th IEEE Computer Security Foundations Symposium (CSF 2012), pp. 95–109. IEEE Computer Society Press, Cambridge (2012)
5. Arapinis, M., Delaune, S., Kremer, S.: From one session to many: dynamic tags for security protocols. In: Cervesato, I., Veith, H., Voronkov, A. (eds.) LPAR 2008. LNCS (LNAI), vol. 5330, pp. 128–142. Springer, Heidelberg (2008)
6. Bauer, M.S., Chadha, R., Viswanathan, M.: Composing Protocol with Randomized Actions. Technical report, University of Illinois at Urbana-Champaign, Department of Computer Science (2016)
7. Ben-Or, M., Goldreich, O., Micali, S., Rivest, R.L.: A fair protocol for signing contracts. IEEE Trans. Inf. Theory **36**(1), 40–46 (1990)
8. Canetti, R., Cheung, L., Kaynar, D., Liskov, M., Lynch, N., Pereira, P., Segala, R.: Task-structured probabilistic I/O automata. In: Workshop on Discrete Event Systems (2006)
9. Canetti, R.: Universally composable security: a new paradigm for cryptographic protocols. In: Naor, M. (ed.) 42nd IEEE Symposium on Foundations of Computer Science (FOCS 2001), pp. 136–145. IEEE Computer Society Press (2001)
10. Canetti, R., Herzog, J.C.: Universally composable symbolic analysis of mutual authentication and key-exchange protocols. In: Halevi, S., Rabin, T. (eds.) TCC 2006. LNCS, vol. 3876, pp. 380–403. Springer, Heidelberg (2006)
11. Carbone, M., Guttman, J.D.: Sessions and separability in security protocols. In: Basin, D., Mitchell, J.C. (eds.) POST 2013 (ETAPS 2013). LNCS, vol. 7796, pp. 267–286. Springer, Heidelberg (2013)
12. Chadha, R., Sistla, A.P., Viswanathan, M.: Model checking concurrent programs with nondeterminism and randomization. In: the International Conference on Foundations of Software Technology and Theoretical Computer Science, pp. 364–375 (2010)
13. Chatzikokolakis, K., Palamidessi, C.: Making random choices invisible to the scheduler. Information and Computation (2010) to appear
14. Chaum, D.: The dining cryptographers problem: Unconditional sender and recipient untraceability. J. Cryptology **1**(1), 65–75 (1988)
15. Cheung, L.: Reconciling Nondeterministic and Probabilistic Choices. PhD thesis, Radboud University of Nijmegen (2006)
16. Chevalier, C., Delaune, S., Kremer, S.: Transforming password protocols to compose. In: 31st Conference on Foundations of Software Technology and Theoretical Computer Science, Leibniz International Proceedings in Informatics, pp. 204–216. Leibniz-Zentrum für Informatik (2011)
17. Cortier, V., Delaitre, J., Delaune, S.: Safely composing security protocols. In: Arvind, V., Prasad, S. (eds.) FSTTCS 2007. LNCS, vol. 4855, pp. 352–363. Springer, Heidelberg (2007)

18. Cortier, V., Delaune, S.: Safely composing security protocols. Formal Methods in System Design **34**(1), 1–36 (2009)
19. Ciobâcă, Ş., Cortier, V.: Protocol composition for arbitrary primitives. In: Proceedings of the 23rd IEEE Computer Security Foundations Symposium, CSF, Edinburgh, July 17–19, 2010, pp. 322–336 (2010)
20. Datta, A., Derek, A., Mitchell, J.C., Pavlovic, D.: A derivation system and compositional logic for security protocols. J. Comput. Secur. **13**(3), 423–482 (2005)
21. de Alfaro, L.: The verification of probabilistic systems under memoryless partial information policies is hard. In: PROBMIV (1999)
22. Delaune, S., Kremer, S., Ryan, M.D.: Composition of password-based protocols. In: Proceedings of the 21st IEEE Computer Security Foundations Symposium (CSF 2008), pp. 239–251. IEEE Computer Society Press, June 2008
23. Even, S., Goldreich, O., Lempel, A.: A randomized protocol for signing contracts. Commun. ACM **28**(6), 637–647 (1985)
24. Garcia, F.D., van Rossum, P., Sokolova, A.: Probabilistic Anonymity and Admissible Schedulers. CoRR, abs/0706.1019 (2007)
25. Goldschlag, D.M., Reed, M.G., Syverson, P.F.: Onion routing. Commun. ACM **42**(2), 39–41 (1999)
26. Goubault-Larrecq, J., Palamidessi, C., Troina, A.: A probabilistic applied pi-calculus. In: Shao, Z. (ed.) APLAS 2007. LNCS, vol. 4807, pp. 175–190. Springer, Heidelberg (2007)
27. Gunter, C.A., Khanna, S., Tan, K., Venkatesh, S.S.: Dos protection for reliably authenticated broadcast. In: NDSS (2004)
28. Guttman, J.D.: Authentication tests and disjoint encryption: a design method for security protocols. J. Comput. Secur. **12**(3–4), 409–433 (2004)
29. Guttman, J.D.: Cryptographic protocol composition via the authentication tests. In: de Alfaro, L. (ed.) FOSSACS 2009. LNCS, vol. 5504, pp. 303–317. Springer, Heidelberg (2009)
30. He, C., Sundararajan, M., Datta, A., Derek, A., Mitchell, J.C.: A modular correctness proof of ieee 802.11i and TLS. In: Atluri, V., Meadows, C., Juels, A. (eds.) the 12th ACM Conference on Computer and Communications Security, (CCS), pp. 2–15. ACM (2005)
31. Mödersheim, S., Viganò, L.: Sufficient conditions for vertical composition of security protocols. In: Proceedings of the 9th ACM Symposium on Information, Computer and Communications Security, ASIA CCS 2014, pp. 435–446. ACM, New York (2014)
32. Reiter, M.K., Rubin, A.D.: Crowds: anonymity for web transactions. ACM Trans. Inf. Syst. Secur. **1**(1), 66–92 (1998)
33. Ryan, P.Y.A., Bismark, D., Heather, J., Schneider, S., Xia, Z.: Prêt à voter: a voter-verifiable voting system. IEEE Trans. Inform. Forensics Secur. **4**(4), 662–673 (2009)

Bounding the Number of Agents, for Equivalence Too

Véronique Cortier[1], Antoine Dallon[1,2(✉)], and Stéphanie Delaune[2]

[1] LORIA, CNRS, Nancy, France
dallon@lsv.fr
[2] LSV, CNRS and ENS Cachan, Université Paris-Saclay, Cachan, France

Abstract. Bounding the number of agents is a current practice when modeling a protocol. In 2003, it has been shown that one honest agent and one dishonest agent are indeed sufficient to find all possible attacks, for secrecy properties. This is no longer the case for equivalence properties, crucial to express many properties such as vote privacy or untraceability.

In this paper, we show that it is sufficient to consider two honest agents and two dishonest agents for equivalence properties, for deterministic processes with standard primitives and without else branches. More generally, we show how to bound the number of agents for arbitrary constructor theories and for protocols with simple else branches. We show that our hypotheses are tight, providing counter-examples for non action-deterministic processes, non constructor theories, or protocols with complex else branches.

1 Introduction

Many decision procedures and tools have been developed to automatically analyse cryptographic protocols. Prominent examples are ProVerif [8], Avispa [3], Scyther [18], or Tamarin [21], which have been successfully applied to various protocols of the literature. When modeling a protocol, it is common and necessary to make some simplifications. For example, it is common to consider a fix scenario with typically two honest and one dishonest agents. While bounding the number of sessions is known to be an unsound simplification (attacks may be missed), bounding the number of agents is a common practice which is typically not discussed. In 2003, it has been shown [15] that bounding the number of agents is actually a safe practice for trace properties. One honest agent and one dishonest agent are sufficient to discover all possible attacks against secrecy (for protocols without else branches). The reduction result actually holds for a large class of trace properties that encompasses authentication: if there is an attack

The research leading to these results has received funding from the European Research Council under the European Union's Seventh Framework Programme (FP7/2007-2013)/ERC grant agreement $n°$ 258865, project ProSecure, the ANR project JCJC VIP $n°$ 11 JS02 006 01, and the DGA.

F. Piessens and L. Viganò (Eds.): POST 2016, LNCS 9635, pp. 211–232, 2016.
DOI: 10.1007/978-3-662-49635-0_11

then there is an attack with $b + 1$ agents where b is the number of agents used to *state* the security property.

Trace properties are typically used to specify standard properties such as confidentiality or authentication properties. However, privacy properties such as vote privacy [19] or untraceability [2], or simply properties inherited from cryptographic games [16] (*e.g.* strong secrecy) are stated as equivalence properties. For example, Alice remains anonymous if an attacker cannot distinguish between a session with Alice from a session with Bob. When studying equivalence properties, the practice of bounding the number of agents has been continued. For example, most of the example files provided for equivalence in the ProVerif development [6] model only two or three agents.

The objective of this paper is to characterise when it is safe to bound the number of agents, for equivalence properties. In case of secrecy expressed as a trace property, bounding the number of agents is rather easy. If there is an attack then there is still an attack when projecting all honest agents on one single honest agent, and all dishonest agents on one single dishonest agent. This holds because the protocols considered in [15] do not have else branches: the conditionals only depend on equality tests that are preserved by projection.

Such a proof technique no longer works in case of equivalence. Indeed, an attack against an equivalence property may precisely rely on some disequality, which is not preserved when projecting several names on a single one. Consider for example a simple protocol where A authenticates to B by sending him her name, a fresh nonce, and a hash of these data.

$$A \rightarrow B : A, B, N, \mathsf{h}(A, N)$$

Let's denote this protocol by $P(A, B)$. This is clearly a wrong authentication protocol but let assume we wish to know whether it preserves A's privacy. In other words, is it possible for the attacker to learn whether A or A' is talking? That is, do we have $P(A, B)$ equivalent to $P(A', B)$? We need $A \neq A'$ to observe an attack, otherwise the two processes are identical. This example shows in particular that it is not possible to consider one honest agent and one dishonest agent as for trace properties.

Another issue comes from non deterministic behaviours. Non equivalence between P and Q is typically due to some execution that can be run in P and not in Q due to some failed test, that is, some disequality. Even if we maintain this disequality when projecting, maybe the projection enables new behaviours for Q, rendering it equivalent to P. Since non-determinism is usually an artefact of the modelling (in reality most protocols are perfectly deterministic), we assume in this paper *action-deterministic* protocols: the state of the system is entirely determined by the behaviour of the attacker. Such determinacy hypotheses already appear in several papers, in several variants [5,10,11].

Our Contribution. We show that for equivalence, four agents are actually sufficient to detect attacks, for action-deterministic protocols without else branches and for the standard primitives. We actually provide a more general result, for arbitrary constructor theories and for protocols with (some) else branches.

Equational theories are used to model cryptographic primitives, from standard ones (*e.g.* encryption, signature, or hash) to more subtle ones such as blind signatures [19] or zero-knowledge proofs [4]. The notion of constructor theories (where agents can detect when decryption fails) has been introduced by Blanchet [7]. It captures many cryptographic primitives and in particular all the aforementioned ones, although associative and commutative properties (*e.g.* exclusive or) are out of their scopes since we assume the exchanged messages do not contain destructors. Else branches are often ignored when studying trace properties since most protocols typically abort when a test fails. However, a privacy breach may precisely come from the observation of a failure or from the observation of different error messages. A famous example is the attack found on the biometric French passport [12]. We therefore consider protocols with simple else branches, where error messages may be emitted in the else branches.

Our general reduction result is then as follows. We show that, for arbitrary constructor theories and action-deterministic protocols with simple else branches, we may safely bound the number of agents to $4b + 2$ where b is the *blocking factor* of the theory under consideration. Any theory has a (finite) blocking factor and the theories corresponding to standard primitives have a blocking factor of 1. Moreover, in case protocols do not have else branches, then the number of agents can be further reduced to $2b + 2$ ($b + 1$ honest agents and $b + 1$ dishonest agents), yielding a bound of 2 honest agents and 2 dishonest agents for protocols using standard primitives.

We show moreover that our hypotheses are tight. For example, and rather surprisingly, it is not possible to bound the number of agents with the pure equational theory $\mathsf{dec}(\mathsf{enc}(x, y), y)$ (assuming the function symbol dec may occur in messages as well). Similarly, we provide counter-examples when processes are not action-deterministic or when processes have non simple else branches.

Due to lack of space, the reader is referred to the companion technical report [17] for the missing proofs and additional details.

Related Work. Compared to the initial work of [15] for trace properties, we have considered the more complex case of equivalence properties. Moreover, we consider a more general framework with arbitrary constructor theories and protocols with (simple) else branches. Our proof technique is inspired from the proof of [14], where it is shown that if there is an attack against equivalence for arbitrary nonces, then there is still an attack for a fix number of nonces. Taking advantage of the fact that we bound the number of agents rather than the number of nonces, we significantly extend the result: (simple) else branches; general constructor theories with the introduction of the notion of b-blocking factor; general action-deterministic processes (instead of the particular class of simple protocols, which requires a particular structure of the processes); and protocols with phase (to model more game-based properties).

2   Model for Security Protocols

Security protocols are modelled through a process algebra inspired from the applied pi calculus [1]. Participants in a protocol are modelled as processes, and the communication between them is modelled by means of the exchange of messages that are represented by terms.

2.1   Term Algebra

We consider two infinite and disjoint sets of names: $\mathcal{N}$ is the set of *basic names*, which are used to represent keys, nonces, whereas $\mathcal{A}$ is the set of *agent names*, *i.e.* names which represent the agents identities. We consider two infinite and disjoint sets of variables, denoted $\mathcal{X}$ and $\mathcal{W}$. Variables in $\mathcal{X}$ typically refer to unknown parts of messages expected by participants while variables in $\mathcal{W}$ are used to store messages learnt by the attacker. Lastly, we consider two disjoint sets of *constant symbols*, denoted Σ_0 and Σ_{error}. Constants in Σ_0 will be used for instance to represent nonces drawn by the attacker and this set is assumed to be infinite, while constants in Σ_{error} will typically refer to error messages. We assume a *signature* Σ, *i.e.* a set of function symbols together with their arity. The elements of Σ are split into *constructor* and *destructor* symbols, *i.e.* $\Sigma = \Sigma_c \uplus \Sigma_d$. We denote $\Sigma^+ = \Sigma \uplus \Sigma_0 \uplus \Sigma_{\mathsf{error}}$, and $\Sigma_c^+ = \Sigma_c \uplus \Sigma_0 \uplus \Sigma_{\mathsf{error}}$.

Given a signature $\mathcal{F}$, and a set of atomic data A, we denote by $\mathcal{T}(\mathcal{F}, \mathsf{A})$ the set of *terms* built from atomic data A by applying function symbols in $\mathcal{F}$. Terms without variables are called *ground*. We denote by $\mathcal{T}(\Sigma_c^+, \mathcal{N} \cup \mathcal{A} \cup \mathcal{X})$ the set of *constructor terms*. The set of *messages* $\mathcal{M}_\Sigma$ is some subset of ground constructor terms. Given a set of atomic data A, an A-*renaming* is a function ρ such that $dom(\rho) \cup img(\rho) \subseteq A$. We assume $\mathcal{M}_\Sigma$ as well as $\mathcal{T}(\Sigma_c^+, \mathcal{N} \cup \mathcal{A} \cup \mathcal{X}) \backslash \mathcal{M}_\Sigma$ to be stable under any $\mathcal{A}$-renaming and $(\Sigma_0 \cup \Sigma_{\mathsf{error}})$-renaming. Intuitively, being a message or not should not depend on a particular constant or name.

Example 1. The standard primitives (symmetric and asymmetric encryption, signature, pair, and hash) are typically modelled by the following signature.

$$\Sigma_{\mathsf{std}} = \{\mathsf{enc}, \mathsf{dec}, \mathsf{shk_s}, \mathsf{aenc}, \mathsf{adec}, \mathsf{pub}, \mathsf{priv}, \mathsf{sign}, \mathsf{checksign}, \mathsf{h}, \langle \rangle, \mathsf{proj_1}, \mathsf{proj_2}, \mathsf{eq}\}.$$

The symbols enc and dec (resp. aenc and adec) of arity 2 represent symmetric (resp. asymmetric) encryption and decryption whereas $\mathsf{shk_s}, \mathsf{pub}, \mathsf{priv}$ are constructor keys of arity 1. Pairing is modelled using $\langle \rangle$ of arity 2, whereas projection functions are denoted $\mathsf{proj_1}$ and $\mathsf{proj_2}$ (both of arity 1). Signatures are represented by sign of arity 2 with an associated verification operator $\mathsf{checksign}$ of arity 3. Hash functions are modelled by h, of arity 1. Finally, we consider the function symbol eq to model equality test. This signature is split into two parts: we have that $\Sigma_c = \{\mathsf{enc}, \mathsf{aenc}, \mathsf{h}, \mathsf{sign}, \mathsf{shk_s}, \mathsf{pub}, \mathsf{priv}, \langle \rangle\}$ and $\Sigma_d = \Sigma_{\mathsf{std}} \backslash \Sigma_c$.

We denote $vars(u)$ the set of variables that occur in a term u. The application of a substitution σ to a term u is written $u\sigma$, and we denote $dom(\sigma)$ its *domain*. The *positions* of a term are defined as usual. The properties of cryptographic primitives are modelled through a rewriting system, *i.e.* a set of rewriting rules of the form $g(t_1, \ldots, t_n) \to t$ where g is a destructor, and $t, t_1, \ldots, t_n$ are constructor terms. A term u can be rewritten in v if there is a position p in u, and a rewriting rule $g(t_1, \ldots, t_n) \to t$ such that $u|_p = g(t_1, \ldots, t_n)\theta$ for some substitution θ. Moreover, we assume that $t_1\theta, \ldots, t_n\theta$ as well as $t\theta$ are *messages*. We only consider sets of rewriting rules that yield a convergent rewriting system. We denote $u\!\downarrow$ the *normal form* of a given term u.

A *constructor theory* $\mathcal{E}$ is given by a signature Σ together with a notion of messages $\mathcal{M}_\Sigma$, and a finite set of rewriting rules $\mathcal{R}$ (as decribed above) that defines a convergent rewriting system.

Example 2. The properties of the standard primitives are reflected through the theory $\mathcal{E}_{\mathsf{std}}$ induced by the following convergent rewriting system:

$$
\begin{array}{ll}
\mathsf{dec}(\mathsf{enc}(x, y), y) \to x & \mathsf{proj}_i(\langle x_1, x_2 \rangle) \to x_i \text{ with } i \in \{1, 2\}. \\
\mathsf{adec}(\mathsf{aenc}(x, \mathsf{pub}(y)), \mathsf{priv}(y)) \to x & \mathsf{checksign}(\mathsf{sign}(x, \mathsf{priv}(y)), x, \mathsf{pub}(y)) \to \mathsf{ok} \\
\mathsf{eq}(x, x) \to \mathsf{ok}
\end{array}
$$

We may consider $\mathcal{M}_\Sigma$ to be $\mathcal{T}(\Sigma_c^+, \mathcal{N} \cup \mathcal{A})$ the set of all ground constructor terms. We may as well consider only terms with atomic keys for example.

Constructor theories are flexible enough to model all standard primitives. However, such a setting does not allow one to model for instance a decryption algorithm that never fails and always returns a message (*e.g.* $\mathsf{dec}(m, k)$).

For modelling purposes, we split the signature Σ into two parts, namely Σ_{pub} and Σ_{priv}, and we denote $\Sigma_{\mathsf{pub}}^+ = \Sigma_{\mathsf{pub}} \uplus \Sigma_0 \uplus \Sigma_{\mathsf{error}}$. An attacker builds his own messages by applying public function symbols to terms he already knows and that are available through variables in $\mathcal{W}$. Formally, a computation done by the attacker is a *recipe*, *i.e.* a term in $\mathcal{T}(\Sigma_{\mathsf{pub}}^+, \mathcal{W})$.

2.2   Process Algebra

We assume an infinite set $Ch = Ch_0 \uplus Ch^{\mathsf{fresh}}$ of channels used to communicate, where Ch_0 and Ch^{fresh} are infinite and disjoint. Intuitively, channels of Ch^{fresh} are used to instantiate channels when they are generated during the execution of a protocol. They should not be part of a protocol specification. Protocols are modelled through processes using the following grammar:

$$
\begin{array}{llll}
P, Q = 0 & \mid\; \mathsf{let}\; x = v \;\mathsf{in}\; P \;\mathsf{else}\, 0 & \mid\; \mathsf{new}\; n.P \\
\mid\; \mathsf{in}(c, u).P & \mid\; \mathsf{let}\; x = v \;\mathsf{in}\; P \;\mathsf{else}\, \mathsf{out}(c, \mathsf{err}) & \mid\; (P \mid Q) \\
\mid\; \mathsf{out}(c, u).P & \mid\; !\, \mathsf{new}\; c'.\mathsf{out}(c, c').P & \mid\; i \colon P
\end{array}
$$

where $c, c' \in Ch$, $x \in \mathcal{X}$, $n \in \mathcal{N}$, $\mathsf{err} \in \Sigma_{\mathsf{error}}$, and $i \in \mathbb{N}$. We have that u is a constructor term, *i.e.* $u \in \mathcal{T}(\Sigma_c^+, \mathcal{N} \cup \mathcal{A} \cup \mathcal{X})$ whereas v can be any term in $\mathcal{T}(\Sigma^+, \mathcal{N} \cup \mathcal{A} \cup \mathcal{X})$.

Most of the constructions are rather standard. We may note the special construct $!\,\mathsf{new}\; c'.\mathsf{out}(c, c').\; P$ that combines replication with channel restriction. The goal of this construct, first introduced in [5], is to support replication while preserving some form of determinism, as formally defined later.

Our calculus allows both message filtering in input actions as well as explicit application of destructor symbols through the let construction. The process "let $x = v$ in P else Q" tries to evaluate v and in case of success the process P is executed; otherwise the process is blocked or an error is emitted depending on what is indicated in Q. The let instruction together with the eq theory introduced in Example 2 can encode the usual "if then else" construction. Indeed, the process if $u = v$ then P else Q can be written as let $x = \mathsf{eq}(u, v)$ in P else Q. Since P can be executed only if no destructor remains in the term $\mathsf{eq}(u, v)$, this implies that u and v must be equal. Our calculus also introduces a *phase* instruction, in the spirit of [9], denoted $i: P$. Some protocols like e-voting protocols may proceed in phase. More generally, phases are particularly useful to model security requirements, for example in case the attacker interacts with the protocol before being given some secret.

We denote by $fv(P)$ (resp. $fc(P)$) the set of free variables (resp. channels) that occur in a process P, *i.e.* those that are not in the scope of an input or a let construction (resp. new construction). A *basic process built on a channel c* is a process that contains neither | (parallel) nor ! (replication), and such that all its inputs/outputs take place on the channel c.

Example 3. The Denning Sacco protocol [20] is a key distribution protocol relying on symmetric encryption and a trusted server. It can be described informally as follows, in a version without timestamps:

$$1.\ A \rightarrow S:\ A, B$$
$$2.\ S \rightarrow A:\ \{B, K_{ab}, \{K_{ab}, A\}_{K_{bs}}\}_{K_{as}}$$
$$3.\ A \rightarrow B:\ \{K_{ab}, A\}_{K_{bs}}$$

where $\{m\}_k$ denotes the symmetric encryption of a message m with key k. Agent A (resp. B) communicates to a trusted server S, using a long term key K_{as} (resp. K_{bs}), shared with the server. At the end of a session, A and B should be authenticated and should share a session key K_{ab}.

We model the Denning Sacco protocol as follows. Let k be a name in $\mathcal{N}$, whereas a and b are names from $\mathcal{A}$. We denote by $\langle x_1, \ldots, x_{n-1}, x_n \rangle$ the term $\langle x_1, \langle \ldots \langle x_{n-1}, x_n \rangle \rangle \rangle$. The protocol is modelled by the parallel composition of three basic processes P_A, P_B, and P_S built respectively on c_1, c_2, and c_3. They correspond respectively to the roles of A, B, and S.

$$P_{DS} = !\,\mathsf{new}\ c_1.\mathsf{out}(c_A, c_1).P_A \mid !\,\mathsf{new}\ c_2.\mathsf{out}(c_B, c_2).P_B \mid !\,\mathsf{new}\ c_3.\mathsf{out}(c_S, c_3).P_S$$

where processes P_A, P_B, and P_S are defined as follows.

- $P_A = \mathsf{out}(c_1, \langle a, b \rangle).\mathsf{in}(c_1, \mathsf{enc}(\langle b, x_{AB}, x_B \rangle, \mathsf{shk}_\mathsf{s}(a))).\mathsf{out}(c_1, x_B)$
- $P_B = \mathsf{in}(c_2, \mathsf{enc}(\langle y_{AB}, a \rangle, \mathsf{shk}_\mathsf{s}(b)))$
- $P_S = \mathsf{in}(c_3, \langle a, b \rangle).\ \mathsf{new}\ k.\mathsf{out}(c_3, \mathsf{enc}(\langle b, k, \mathsf{enc}(\langle k, a \rangle, \mathsf{shk}_\mathsf{s}(b)) \rangle, \mathsf{shk}_\mathsf{s}(a))).$

2.3   Semantics

The operational semantics of a process is defined using a relation over configurations. A configuration is a tuple $(\mathcal{P}; \phi; i)$ with $i \in \mathbb{N}$, and such that:

- $\mathcal{P}$ is a multiset of ground processes;
- $\phi = \{\mathsf{w}_1 \triangleright m_1, \ldots, \mathsf{w}_n \triangleright m_n\}$ is a *frame*, *i.e.* a substitution where $\mathsf{w}_1, \ldots, \mathsf{w}_n$ are variables in $\mathcal{W}$, and $m_1, \ldots, m_n$ are messages, *i.e.* terms in $\mathcal{M}_\Sigma$.

Intuitively, i is an integer that indicates the current phase; $\mathcal{P}$ represents the processes that still remain to be executed; and ϕ represents the sequence of messages that have been learnt so far by the attacker.

We often write P instead of $0\colon P$ or $(\{0\colon P\}; \emptyset; 0)$. The operational semantics of a process P is induced by the relation $\xrightarrow{\alpha}$ over configurations as defined in Fig. 1.

IN $\qquad (i\colon \mathsf{in}(c, u).P \cup \mathcal{P}; \phi; i) \xrightarrow{\mathsf{in}(c,R)} (i\colon P\sigma \cup \mathcal{P}; \phi; i) \qquad$ where R is a recipe such that $R\phi{\downarrow}$ is a message, and $R\phi{\downarrow} = u\sigma$ for σ with $dom(\sigma) = vars(u)$.

CONST
$\qquad (i\colon \mathsf{out}(c, \mathsf{cst}).P \cup \mathcal{P}; \phi; i) \xrightarrow{\mathsf{out}(c,\mathsf{cst})} (i\colon P \cup \mathcal{P}; \phi; i) \qquad$ with $\mathsf{cst} \in \Sigma_0 \cup \Sigma_{\mathsf{error}}$.

OUT $\qquad (i\colon \mathsf{out}(c, u).P \cup \mathcal{P}; \phi; i) \xrightarrow{\mathsf{out}(c,\mathsf{w})} (i\colon P \cup \mathcal{P}; \phi \cup \{\mathsf{w} \triangleright u\}; i)$
$\qquad\qquad$ with w a fresh variable from $\mathcal{W}$, and $u \in \mathcal{M}_\Sigma \setminus (\Sigma_0 \cup \Sigma_{\mathsf{error}})$.

SESS
$(i\colon\,! \, \mathsf{new}\, c'.\mathsf{out}(c, c').P \cup \mathcal{P}; \phi; i) \xrightarrow{\mathsf{sess}(c,ch)} (i\colon P\{^{ch}/_{c'}\} \cup i\colon\,!\,\mathsf{new}\,c'.\mathsf{out}(c, c').P \cup \mathcal{P}; \phi; i)$
$\qquad\qquad\qquad\qquad$ with ch a fresh name from $\mathcal{C}h^{\mathsf{fresh}}$.

LET $\qquad (i\colon \mathsf{let}\, x = v \,\mathsf{in}\, P \,\mathsf{else}\, Q \cup \mathcal{P}; \phi; i) \xrightarrow{\tau} (i\colon P\{^{v\downarrow}/_x\} \cup \mathcal{P}; \phi; i) \quad$ when $v{\downarrow} \in \mathcal{M}_\Sigma$.

LET-FAIL $\quad (i\colon \mathsf{let}\, x = v \,\mathsf{in}\, P \,\mathsf{else}\, Q \cup \mathcal{P}; \phi; i) \xrightarrow{\tau} (i\colon Q \cup \mathcal{P}; \phi; i) \qquad$ when $v{\downarrow} \notin \mathcal{M}_\Sigma$.

NULL $\qquad (i\colon 0 \cup \mathcal{P}; \phi; i) \xrightarrow{\tau} (\mathcal{P}; \phi; i)$

PAR $\qquad (i\colon (P \mid Q) \cup \mathcal{P}; \phi; i) \xrightarrow{\tau} (i\colon P \cup i\colon Q \cup \mathcal{P}; \phi; i)$

NEW $\qquad (i\colon \mathsf{new}\, n.P \cup \mathcal{P}; \phi; i) \xrightarrow{\tau} (i\colon P\{^{n'}/_n\} \cup \mathcal{P}; \phi; i) \quad$ with n' a fresh name from $\mathcal{N}$.

MOVE $\qquad\qquad (\mathcal{P}; \phi; i) \xrightarrow{\mathsf{phase}\ i'} (\mathcal{P}; \phi; i') \qquad\qquad$ with $i' > i$.

PHASE $\qquad (i\colon i'\colon P \cup \mathcal{P}; \phi; i) \xrightarrow{\tau} (i'\colon P \cup \mathcal{P}; \phi; i)$

CLEAN $\qquad (i\colon P \cup \mathcal{P}; \phi; i') \xrightarrow{\tau} (\mathcal{P}; \phi; i') \qquad$ when $i' > i$.

Fig. 1. Semantics for processes

The rules are quite standard and correspond to the intuitive meaning of the syntax given in the previous section. When a process emits a message m, we distinguish the special case where m is a constant (CONST rule), in which case the constant m appears directly in the trace instead of being stored in the frame. This has no impact on the intuitive behaviour of the process but is quite handy in the proofs. Regarding phases (rules MOVE, PHASE, and CLEAN), the adversary may move to a subsequent phase whenever he wants while processes may move to the next phase when they are done or simply disappear if the phase is over.

Given a sequence of actions $\alpha_1 \ldots \alpha_n$, the relation $\xrightarrow{\alpha_1 \ldots \alpha_n}$ between configurations is defined as the transitive closure of $\xrightarrow{\alpha}$. Given a sequence of observable action tr, we denote $\mathcal{C} \overset{\text{tr}}{\Rightarrow} \mathcal{C}'$ when there exists a sequence $\alpha_1, \ldots, \alpha_n$ for some n such that $\mathcal{C} \xrightarrow{\alpha_1 \ldots \alpha_n} \mathcal{C}'$, and tr is obtained from this sequence by removing all the unobservable τ actions.

Definition 1. *Given a configuration* $\mathcal{C} = (\mathcal{P}; \phi; i)$, *we denote* trace$(\mathcal{C})$ *the set of traces defined as follows:*

$$\text{trace}(\mathcal{C}) = \{(\text{tr}, \phi') \mid \mathcal{C} \overset{\text{tr}}{\Rightarrow} (\mathcal{P}; \phi'; i') \text{ for some configuration } (\mathcal{P}; \phi'; i')\}.$$

Example 4. Let $\mathcal{C}_{\mathsf{DS}} = (P_{\mathsf{DS}}; \emptyset; 0)$ with P_{DS} as defined in Example 3. We have that $(\text{tr}, \phi) \in \text{trace}(\mathcal{C}_{\mathsf{DS}})$ where tr, and ϕ are as described below:

- tr = sess(c_A, ch_1).sess(c_B, ch_2).sess(c_S, ch_3).out(ch_1, w_1).in(ch_3, w_1). out(ch_3, w_2).in(ch_1, w_2).out(ch_1, w_3).in(ch_2, w_3); and
- $\phi = \{\mathsf{w}_1 \triangleright \langle a, b\rangle,\ \mathsf{w}_2 \triangleright \mathsf{enc}(\langle b, k, \mathsf{enc}(\langle k, a\rangle, \mathsf{shk}_s(b))\rangle, \mathsf{shk}_s(a)),$ $\mathsf{w}_3 \triangleright \mathsf{enc}(\langle k, a\rangle, \mathsf{shk}_s(b))\}$.

This trace corresponds to a normal execution of the Denning Sacco protocol.

2.4 Action-Determinism

As mentioned in introduction, we require processes to be deterministic. We provide in Sect. 4.3 an example showing why the number of agents may not be bound when processes are not deterministic. We consider a definition similar to the one introduced in [5], extended to process with phase.

Definition 2. *A configuration* $\mathcal{C}$ *is* action-deterministic *if whenever* $\mathcal{C} \xrightarrow{\text{tr}}$ $(\mathcal{P}; \phi; i)$, *and* $i : \alpha.P$ *and* $i : \beta.Q$ *are two elements of* $\mathcal{P}$ *with* α, β *instruction of the form* in(c, u), out(c, u) *or* new c'.out(c, c') *then either the underlying channels* c *differ or the instructions are not of the same nature (that is,* α, β *are not both an input, nor both an output, nor both channel creations).*

A process P is action-deterministic if $\mathcal{C} = (P; \phi; 0)$ is action-deterministic for any frame ϕ.

For such protocols, the attacker knowledge is entirely determined (up to α-renaming) by its interaction with the protocol.

Lemma 1. *Let $\mathcal{C}$ be an action-deterministic configuration such that $\mathcal{C} \overset{\text{tr}}{\Rightarrow} \mathcal{C}_1$ and $\mathcal{C} \overset{\text{tr}}{\Rightarrow} \mathcal{C}_2$ for some* tr, $\mathcal{C}_1 = (\mathcal{P}_1; \phi_1; i_1)$, *and* $\mathcal{C}_2 = (\mathcal{P}_2; \phi_2; i_2)$. *We have that $i_1 = i_2$, and ϕ_1 and ϕ_2 are equal modulo α-renaming.*

2.5 Trace Equivalence

Many privacy properties such as vote-privacy or untraceability are expressed as trace equivalence [2,19]. Intuitively, two configurations are trace equivalent if an attacker cannot tell with which of the two configurations he is interacting. We first introduce a notion of equivalence between frames.

Definition 3. *Two frames ϕ_1 and ϕ_2 are in* static inclusion, *written $\phi_1 \sqsubseteq_s \phi_2$, when $dom(\phi_1) = dom(\phi_2)$, and:*

- *for any recipe $R \in \mathcal{T}(\Sigma_{pub}^+, \mathcal{W})$, we have that $R\phi_1\downarrow \in \mathcal{M}_\Sigma$ implies that $R\phi_2\downarrow \in \mathcal{M}_\Sigma$; and*
- *for any recipes $R, R' \in \mathcal{T}(\Sigma_{pub}^+, \mathcal{W})$ such that $R\phi_1\downarrow, R'\phi_1\downarrow \in \mathcal{M}_\Sigma$, we have that: $R\phi_1\downarrow = R'\phi_1\downarrow$ implies $R\phi_2\downarrow = R'\phi_2\downarrow$.*

They are in static equivalence, *written $\phi_1 \sim \phi_2$, if $\phi_1 \sqsubseteq_s \phi_2$ and $\phi_2 \sqsubseteq_s \phi_1$.*

An attacker can see the difference between two sequences of messages if he is able to perform some computation that succeeds in ϕ_1 and fails in ϕ_2; or if he can build a test that leads to an equality in ϕ_1 and not in ϕ_2 (or conversely).

Example 5. Consider $\phi_1 = \phi \cup \{w_4 \triangleright enc(m_1, k)\}$ and $\phi_2 = \phi \cup \{w_4 \triangleright enc(m_2, k')\}$ where ϕ has been introduced in Example 4. The terms m_1, m_2 are public constants in Σ_0, and k' is a fresh name in $\mathcal{N}$. We have that the two frames ϕ_1 and ϕ_2 are statically equivalent. Intuitively, at the end of a normal execution between honest participants, an attacker can not make any distinction between a public constant m_1 encrypted with the session key, and another public constant m_2 encrypted with a fresh key k' that has never been used.

Trace equivalence is the active counterpart of static equivalence. Two configurations are trace equivalent if, however they behave, the resulting sequences of messages observed by the attacker are in static equivalence.

Definition 4. *Let $\mathcal{C}$ and $\mathcal{C}'$ be two configurations. They are in* trace equivalence, *written $\mathcal{C} \approx \mathcal{C}'$, if for every $(tr, \phi) \in$ trace$(\mathcal{C})$, there exist $(tr', \phi') \in$ trace$(\mathcal{C}')$ such that $tr = tr'$, and $\phi \sim \phi'$ (and conversely).*

Note that two trace equivalent configurations are necessary at the same phase. Of course, this is not a sufficient condition.

Example 6. The process P_{DS} presented in Example 3 models the Denning Sacco protocol. Strong secrecy of the session key, as received by the agent B, can be expressed by the following equivalence: $P_{DS}^1 \approx P_{DS}^2$, where P_{DS}^1 and P_{DS}^2 are defined as follows. Process P_{DS}^1 is process P_{DS} with the instruction $1: out(c_2, enc(m_1, y_{AB}))$ added at the end of the process P_B; and P_{DS}^2 is as the protocol P_{DS} with the instruction $1: new\, k.out(c_2, enc(m_2, k))$ at the end of P_B. The terms m_1 and m_2 are two public constants from Σ_0, and we use the phase instruction to make a separation between the protocol execution, and the part of the process that encodes the security property.

While the key received by B cannot be learnt by an attacker, strong secrecy of this key is not guaranteed. Indeed, due to the lack of freshness, the same key can be sent several times to B, and this can be observed by an attacker. Formally, the attack is as follows. Consider the sequence:

$$tr' = tr.sess(c_B, ch_4).in(ch_4, w_3).phase\ 1.out(ch_2, w_4).out(ch_4, w_5)$$

where tr has been defined in Example 4. The attacker simply replays an old session. The resulting (uniquely defined) frames are:

- $\phi'_1 = \phi \cup \{w_4 \triangleright \mathsf{enc}(m_1, k), w_5 \triangleright \mathsf{enc}(m_1, k)\}$; and
- $\phi'_2 = \phi \cup \{w_4 \triangleright \mathsf{enc}(m_2, k'), w_5 \triangleright \mathsf{enc}(m_2, k'')\}$.

Then $(\mathsf{tr}', \phi'_1) \in \mathsf{trace}(P^1_{\mathsf{DS}})$ and $(\mathsf{tr}', \phi'_2) \in \mathsf{trace}(P^2_{\mathsf{DS}})$. However, we have that $\phi'_1 \not\sim \phi'_2$ since $w_4 = w_5$ in ϕ'_1 but not in ϕ'_2. Thus P^1_{DS} and P^2_{DS} are *not* in trace equivalence. To avoid this attack, the original protocol relies on timestamps.

3   Results

Our main goal is to show that we can safely consider a bounded number of agents. Our result relies in particular on the fact that constructor theories enjoy the property of being *b-blockable*, which is defined in Sect. 3.2. Our main reduction result is then stated in Sect. 3.3 with a sketch of proof provided in Sect. 3.4. We first start this section with a presentation of our model for an unbounded number of agents.

3.1   Modelling an Unbounded Number of Agents

In the previous section, for illustrative purposes, we considered a scenario that involved only 2 honest agents a and b. This is clearly not sufficient when performing a security analysis. To model an unbounded number of agents, we introduce some new function symbols $\Sigma_{\mathsf{ag}} = \{\mathsf{ag}, \mathsf{hon}, \mathsf{dis}\}$, each of arity 1. The term $\mathsf{ag}(a)$ with $a \in \mathcal{A}$ will represent the fact that a is an agent, $\mathsf{hon}(a)$ and $\mathsf{dis}(a)$ are intended to represent honest and compromised agents respectively. This distinction is used in protocol description to state the security property under study: typically, we wish to ensure security of data shared by *honest* agents. These symbols are private and not available to the attacker. We thus consider a term algebra as defined in Sect. 2. We simply assume in addition that $\Sigma_{\mathsf{ag}} \subseteq \Sigma_c \cap \Sigma_{\mathsf{priv}}$, and that our notion of messages contains at least $\{\mathsf{ag}(a), \mathsf{hon}(a), \mathsf{dis}(a) \mid a \in \mathcal{A}\}$.

Example 7. Going back to the Denning Sacco protocol presented in Example 3, we consider now a richer scenario.

$$P'_A = \mathsf{in}(c_1, \mathsf{ag}(z_A)).\mathsf{in}(c_1, \mathsf{ag}(z_B)).1 : P_A$$
$$P'_B = \mathsf{in}(c_2, \mathsf{ag}(z_A)).\mathsf{in}(c_2, \mathsf{ag}(z_B)).1 : P_B$$
$$P'_S = \mathsf{in}(c_3, \mathsf{ag}(z_A)).\mathsf{in}(c_3, \mathsf{ag}(z_B)).1 : P_S$$

where P_A, P_B, and P_S are as defined in Example 3 after replacement of the occurrences of a (resp. b) by z_A (resp. z_B). Then the process P'_{DS} models an unbounded number of agents executing an unbounded number of sessions:

$$P'_{\mathsf{DS}} = !\, \mathsf{new}\, c_1.\mathsf{out}(c_A, c_1).P'_A \mid !\, \mathsf{new}\, c_2.\mathsf{out}(c_B, c_2).P'_B \mid !\, \mathsf{new}\, c_3.\mathsf{out}(c_S, c_3).P'_S$$

It is then necessary to provide an unbounded number of honest and dishonest agent names. This is the purpose of the following frame.

Definition 5. *Given an integer n, the frame $\phi_{\mathsf{hd}}(n) = \phi_{\mathsf{a}}(n) \uplus \phi_{\mathsf{h}}(n) \uplus \phi_{\mathsf{d}}(n)$ is defined as follows:*

- $\phi_a(n) = \{w_1^h \triangleright a_1^h; \ \ldots; \ w_n^h \triangleright a_n^h; \ w_1^d \triangleright a_1^d; \ \ldots; \ w_n^d \triangleright a_n^d\};$
- $\phi_h(n) = \{w_1^{hag} \triangleright ag(a_1^h); \ w_1^{hon} \triangleright hon(a_1^h); \ \ldots; \ w_n^{hag} \triangleright ag(a_n^h); \ w_n^{hon} \triangleright hon(a_n^h)\};$
- $\phi_d(n) = \{w_1^{dag} \triangleright ag(a_1^d); \ w_1^{dis} \triangleright dis(a_1^d); \ \ldots; \ w_n^{dag} \triangleright ag(a_n^d); \ w_n^{dis} \triangleright dis(a_n^d)\};$

where a_i^h, and a_i^d $(1 \leq i \leq n)$ are pairwise different names in $\mathcal{A}$.

Of course, to model faithfully compromised agents, it is important to reveal their keys to the attacker. This can be modelled through an additional process K that should be part of the initial configuration.

Example 8. Going back to our running example, we may disclose keys through the following process.

$$K = ! \, new \, c'.out(c_K, c').in(c', dis(x)).out(c', shk_s(x)).$$

This process reveals all the keys shared between the server and a compromised agent. Strong secrecy of the exchanged key can be expressed by the following family of equivalences with $n \geq 0$:

$$(P'_{DS} \mid ! \, new \, c'_2.out(c'_B, c'_2).P'_1 \mid K; \ \phi_{hd}(n); \ 0)$$
$$\approx$$
$$(P'_{DS} \mid ! \, new \, c'_2.out(c'_B, c'_2).P'_2 \mid K; \ \phi_{hd}(n); \ 0)$$

where P'_1 and P'_2 are processes that are introduced to model our strong secrecy property as done in Example 6.

$P'_1 = in(c'_2, hon(z_A)).in(c'_2, hon(z_B)).$ $P'_2 = in(c'_2, hon(z_A)).in(c'_2, hon(z_B)).$
       $1: in(c'_2, enc(\langle y_{AB}, z_A \rangle, shk_s(z_B))).$ $1: in(c'_2, enc(\langle y_{AB}, z_A \rangle, shk_s(z_B))).$
       $2: out(c'_2, enc(m_1, y_{AB}))$ $2: new \, k'.out(c'_2, enc(m_2, k'))$

Our reduction result applies to a rather large class of processes. However, we have to ensure that their executions do not depend on specific agent names. Moreover, we consider processes with *simple* else branches: an else branche can only be the null process or the emission of an error message.

Definition 6. *A protocol P is a process such that $fv(P) = \emptyset$, and $fc(P) \cap Ch^{fresh} = \emptyset$. We also assume that P does not use names in $\mathcal{A}$. Moreover, the constants from Σ_{error} only occur in the* else *part of a* let *instruction in P.*

Example 9. Considering $\Sigma_{error} = \emptyset$, it is easy to see that the processes

$$P'_{DS} \mid ! \, new \, c'_2.out(c'_B, c'_2).P'_i \mid K$$

with $i \in \{1, 2\}$ are protocols. They only have trivial else branches.

3.2   Blocking Equational Theories

We aim at reducing the number of agents. To preserve equivalence, our reduction has to preserve equalities as well as disequalities. It also has to preserve the fact of being a message or not. We introduce the notion of b-*blockable* theories: a theory is b-blockable if it is always sufficient to leave b agents unchanged to preserve the fact of not being a message.

Definition 7. *A constructor theory $\mathcal{E}$ is b-blockable if for any term $t \in \mathcal{T}(\Sigma^+, \mathcal{N} \cup \mathcal{A}) \setminus \mathcal{M}_\Sigma$ in normal form, there exists a set of names $\mathsf{A} \subseteq \mathcal{A}$ of size at most b such that for any $\mathcal{A}$-renaming ρ with $(dom(\rho) \cup img(\rho)) \cap \mathsf{A} = \emptyset$, we have that $t\rho{\downarrow} \notin \mathcal{M}_\Sigma$.*

Example 10. Let $\mathsf{eq}_2 \in \Sigma_d$ be a symbol of arity 4, and $\mathsf{ok} \in \Sigma_c$ be a constant. Consider the two following rewriting rules:

$$\mathsf{eq}_2(x, x, y, z) \to \mathsf{ok} \ \text{ and } \ \mathsf{eq}_2(x, y, z, z) \to \mathsf{ok}$$

This theory can be used to model disjonction. Intuitively, $\mathsf{eq}_2(u_1, u_2, u_3, u_4)$ can be reduced to ok when either $u_1 = u_2$ or $u_3 = u_4$. Note that this theory is *not* 1-blockable. Indeed, the term $t = \mathsf{eq}_2(a, b, c, d)$ is a witness showing that keeping one agent name unchanged is not sufficient to prevent the application of a rewriting rule on $t\rho$ (for any renaming ρ that leaves this name unchanged). Actually, we will show that this theory is 2-blockable.

A constructor theory is actually always b-blockable for some b.

Proposition 1. *Any constructor theory $\mathcal{E}$ is b-blockable for some $b \in \mathbb{N}$.*

We note $b(\mathcal{E})$ the *blocking factor* of $\mathcal{E}$. This is the smallest b such that the theory $\mathcal{E}$ is b-blockable. Actually, not only all the theories are b-blockable for some b, but this bound is quite small for most of the theories that are used to model cryptographic primitives.

Example 11. The theory $\mathcal{E}_{\mathsf{std}}$ given in Example 2 is 1-blockable whereas the theory given in Example 10 is 2-blockable. These results are an easy consequence of Lemma 2 stated.

The blocking factor of a constructor theory is related to the size of critical tuples of the theory.

Definition 8. *A constructor theory $\mathcal{E}$ with a rewriting system $\mathcal{R}$ has a critical set of size k if there exist k distinct rules $\ell_1 \to r_1, \dots, \ell_k \to r_k$ in $\mathcal{R}$, and a substitution σ such that $\ell_1\sigma = \dots = \ell_k\sigma$.*

Lemma 2. *If a constructor theory $\mathcal{E}$ has no critical set of size $k+1$ with $k \geq 0$ then it is k-blockable.*

This lemma is a consequence of the proof of Proposition 1 (see [17]). From this lemma, we easily deduce that many theories used in practice to model security protocols are actually 1-blockable. This is the case of the theory $\mathcal{E}_{\mathsf{std}}$ and many variants of it. We may for instance add function symbols to model blind signatures, or zero-knowledge proofs.

3.3 Main Result

We are now able to state our main reduction result.

Theorem 1. *Let P, Q be two action-deterministic protocols built on a constructor theory $\mathcal{E}$. If $(P; \phi_{\mathsf{hd}}(n_0); 0) \approx (Q; \phi_{\mathsf{hd}}(n_0); 0)$ where $n_0 = 2b(\mathcal{E}) + 1$ and $b(\mathcal{E})$ is the blocking factor of $\mathcal{E}$, we have that*

$$(P; \phi_{\mathsf{hd}}(n); 0) \approx (Q; \phi_{\mathsf{hd}}(n); 0) \text{ for any } n \geq 0.$$

Moreover, when P and Q have only let construction with trivial else branches considering $n_0 = b(\mathcal{E}) + 1$ is sufficient.

This theorem shows that whenever two protocols are not in trace equivalence, then they are already not in trace equivalence for a relatively small number of agents that does not depend on the protocols (but only on the underlying theory).

Example 12. Continuing our running example, thanks to Theorem 1, we only have to consider 4 agents (2 honest agents and 2 dishonest ones) for the theory $\mathcal{E}_{\mathsf{std}}$ introduced in Example 2, that corresponds to the standard primitives. Therefore we only have to perform the security analysis considering $\phi_{\mathsf{a}}(2) \uplus \phi_{\mathsf{h}}(2) \uplus \phi_{\mathsf{d}}(2)$ as initial frame.

This reduction result bounds a priori the number of agents involved in an attack. However, due to our setting, the resulting configurations are not written in their usual form (*e.g.* compromised keys are emitted through process K instead of being included in the initial frame). We show that it is possible to retrieve the equivalences written in a more usual form, after some clean-up transformations and some instantiations. This step is formalised in Proposition 2. We first define the notion of key generator process. The purpose of such a process is to provide long-term keys of compromised agents to the attacker.

Definition 9. *A key generator is an action-deterministic process K with no phase instruction in it. Moreover, for any $n \in \mathbb{N}$, we assume that there exists $\phi_K(n)$ with no occurrence of symbols in Σ_{ag}, and such that:*

- *$\mathcal{C}_K^n = (K; \phi_{\mathsf{hd}}(n); 0) \xRightarrow{\mathsf{tr}} (K'; \phi_{\mathsf{hd}}(n) \uplus \phi_K(n); 0)$ for some tr and K';*
- *$img(\phi) \subseteq img(\phi_K(n))$ for any $(\mathcal{P}; \phi_{\mathsf{hd}}(n) \uplus \phi; 0)$ reachable from $\mathcal{C}_K^n$.*

Such a frame $\phi_K(n)$ is called a n-saturation of K, and its image, i.e. $img(\phi_K(n))$, is uniquely defined.

Intuitively, the attacker knowledge no longer grows once the frame $\phi_K(n)$ has been reached. Then two processes $P \mid K$ and $Q \mid K$ are in trace equivalence for some initial knowledge $\phi_{\mathsf{hd}}(n_0)$ if, and only if, P' and Q' are in trace equivalence with an initial knowledge enriched with $\phi_K(n_0)$ and P' and Q' are the instantiations of P and Q considering $2n_0$ agents (n_0 honest agents and n_0 dishonest ones).

Proposition 2. *Consider $2n$ processes of the form $(1 \leq i \leq n)$:*

$$P'_i = !\, \mathsf{new}\, c'_i.\mathsf{out}(c_i, c'_i).\mathsf{in}(c'_i, \mathsf{x}^1_i(z^1_i)).\ldots.\mathsf{in}(c'_i, \mathsf{x}^{k_i}_i(z^{k_i}_i)).1{:}\, P_i(z^1_i, \ldots, z^{k_i}_i)$$
$$Q'_i = !\, \mathsf{new}\, c'_i.\mathsf{out}(c_i, c'_i).\mathsf{in}(c'_i, \mathsf{x}^1_i(z^1_i)).\ldots.\mathsf{in}(c'_i, \mathsf{x}^{k_i}_i(z^{k_i}_i)).1{:}\, Q_i(z^1_i, \ldots, z^{k_i}_i)$$

where each P_i (resp. Q_i) is a basic process built on c'_i, and $\mathsf{x}^j_i \in \{\mathsf{ag}, \mathsf{hon}, \mathsf{dis}\}$ for any $1 \leq j \leq k_i$, and the c_i for $1 \leq i \leq n$ are pairwise distinct. Moreover, we assume that ag, hon and dis do not occur in P_i, Q_i $(1 \leq i \leq n)$. Let $n_0 \in \mathbb{N}$, and K be a key generator such that $fc(K) \cap \{c_1, \ldots, c_n\} = \emptyset$. We have that:

$$(K \uplus \{P'_i | 1 \leq i \leq n\}; \phi_{\mathsf{hd}}(n_0); 0) \approx (K \uplus \{Q'_i | 1 \leq i \leq n\}; \phi_{\mathsf{hd}}(n_0); 0)$$

$$if,\ and\ only\ if,$$

$$(\bigcup_{i=1}^{n} \mathcal{P}_i; \phi_{\mathsf{a}}(n_0) \uplus \phi_K(n_0); 0) \approx (\bigcup_{i=1}^{n} \mathcal{Q}_i; \phi_{\mathsf{a}}(n_0) \uplus \phi_K(n_0); 0)$$

where $\phi_K(n_0)$ is a n-saturation of K, and

$$\mathcal{P}_i = \{!\, \mathsf{new}\, c'_i.\mathsf{out}(c^i_{z^1_i, \ldots, z^{k_i}_i}, c'_i).1{:}\, P_i(z^1_i, \ldots, z^{k_i}_i) | \mathsf{x}^1_i(z^1_i), \ldots, \mathsf{x}^{k_i}_i(z^{k_i}_i) \in img(\phi_{\mathsf{hd}}(n_0))\};$$
$$\mathcal{Q}_i = \{!\, \mathsf{new}\, c'_i.\mathsf{out}(c^i_{z^1_i, \ldots, z^{k_i}_i}, c'_i).1{:}\, Q_i(z^1_i, \ldots, z^{k_i}_i) | \mathsf{x}^1_i(z^1_i), \ldots, \mathsf{x}^{k_i}_i(z^{k_i}_i) \in img(\phi_{\mathsf{hd}}(n_0))\}.$$

Example 13. Using more conventional notations for agent names and after applying Proposition 2, we deduce the following equivalence:

$$(\mathcal{P}_{\mathsf{DS}} \uplus \mathcal{P}'_1; \phi_0; 0) \approx (\mathcal{P}_{\mathsf{DS}} \uplus \mathcal{P}'_2; \phi_0; 0)$$

where

- $\phi_0 = \{\mathsf{w}_a \rhd a;\ \mathsf{w}_b \rhd b;\ \mathsf{w}_c \rhd c;\ \mathsf{w}_d \rhd d;\ \mathsf{w}_{kc} \rhd \mathsf{shk}_{\mathsf{s}}(c);\ \mathsf{w}_{kd} \rhd \mathsf{shk}_{\mathsf{s}}(d)\}$;
- $\mathcal{P}_{\mathsf{DS}} = \left\{ \begin{array}{l} !\, \mathsf{new}\, c_1.\mathsf{out}(c_{A,z_A,z_B}, c_1).P_A(z_A, z_B) \\ | \,!\, \mathsf{new}\, c_2.\mathsf{out}(c_{B,z_A,z_B}, c_2).P_B(z_A, z_B) \\ | \,!\, \mathsf{new}\, c_3.\mathsf{out}(c_{S,z_A,z_B}, c_3).P_S(z_A, z_B) \end{array} \middle| \; z_A, z_B \in \{a, b, c, d\} \right\}$
- $\mathcal{P}'_i = \{!\, \mathsf{new}\, c'_2.\mathsf{out}(c'_{B,z_A,z_B}, c'_2).P'_i(z_A, z_B) \mid z_A, z_B \in \{a, b\}\}$.

This corresponds to the standard scenario with 2 honest agents and 2 dishonest ones when assuming that agents may talk to themselves.

3.4   Sketch of proof of Theorem 1

First, thanks to the fact that we consider action-deterministic processes, we can restrict our attention to the study of the following notion of trace inclusion, and this is formally justified by the lemma stated below.

Definition 10. *Let $\mathcal{C}$ and $\mathcal{C}'$ be two configurations. We say that $\mathcal{C}$ is trace included in $\mathcal{C}'$, written $\mathcal{C} \sqsubseteq \mathcal{C}'$, if for every $(\mathsf{tr}, \phi) \in \mathsf{trace}(\mathcal{C})$, there exists $(\mathsf{tr}', \phi') \in \mathsf{trace}(\mathcal{C}')$ such that $\mathsf{tr} = \mathsf{tr}'$, and $\phi \sqsubseteq_s \phi'$.*

Lemma 3. *Let $\mathcal{C}$ and $\mathcal{C}'$ be two action-deterministic configurations. We have $\mathcal{C} \approx \mathcal{C}'$, if, and only if, $\mathcal{C} \sqsubseteq \mathcal{C}'$ and $\mathcal{C}' \sqsubseteq \mathcal{C}$.*

Given two action-deterministic configurations $\mathcal{C}$ and $\mathcal{C}'$ such that $\mathcal{C} \not\sqsubseteq \mathcal{C}'$, a *witness* of non-inclusion is a trace tr for which there exists ϕ such that $(\mathsf{tr}, \phi) \in$ trace($\mathcal{C}$) and:

- either there does not exist ϕ' such that $(\mathsf{tr}, \phi') \in$ trace($\mathcal{C}'$) (intuitively, the trace tr cannot be executed in $\mathcal{C}'$);
- or such a ϕ' exists and $\phi \not\sqsubseteq_s \phi'$ (intuitively, the attacker can observe that a test succeeds in ϕ and fails in ϕ').

Second, we show that we can restrict our attention to witnesses of non-inclusion that have a special shape: in case a constant from Σ_{error} is emitted, this happens only at the very last step. In other words, this means that we may assume that the rule LET-FAIL is applied at most once, at the end of the execution. More formally, a term t is Σ_{error}-*free* if t does not contain any occurrence of error for any error $\in \Sigma_{\text{error}}$. This notion is extended as expected to frames, and traces.

Lemma 4. *Let P and Q be two action-deterministic protocols, and ϕ_0 and ψ_0 be two frames that are Σ_{error}-free. If $(P; \phi_0; 0) \not\sqsubseteq (Q; \psi_0; 0)$ then there exists a witness tr of this non-inclusion such that:*

- *either tr is Σ_{error}-free;*
- *or tr is of the form tr'.out(c, error) with tr' Σ_{error}-free and error $\in \Sigma_{\text{error}}$.*

This lemma relies on the fact that else branches are simple: at best they yield the emission of a constant in Σ_{error} but they may not trigger any interesting process.

We can then prove our key result: it is possible to bound the number of agents needed for an attack. To formally state this proposition, we rely on the frame $\phi_{\mathsf{hd}(n)}$ as introduced in Definition 5. Theorem 1 then easily follows from Proposition 3.

Proposition 3. *Let $\mathcal{E}$ be a constructor theory, and P and Q be two action-deterministic protocols such that $(P; \phi_{\mathsf{hd}}(n); 0) \not\sqsubseteq (Q; \phi_{\mathsf{hd}}(n); 0)$ for some $n \in \mathbb{N}$. We have that*

$$(P; \phi_{\mathsf{hd}}(n)\rho; 0) \not\sqsubseteq (Q; \phi_{\mathsf{hd}}(n)\rho; 0)$$

for some $\mathcal{A}$-renaming ρ such that $\phi_{\mathsf{h}}(n)\rho$ (resp. $\phi_{\mathsf{d}}(n)\rho$) contains at most $2b(\mathcal{E})+1$ distinct agent names, and $\phi_{\mathsf{h}}(n)\rho$ and $\phi_{\mathsf{d}}(n)\rho$ do not share any name.

Proof. (sketch). Of course, when $n \leq 2b(\mathcal{E}) + 1$, the result is obvious. Otherwise, let tr be a witness of non-inclusion for $(P; \phi_{\mathsf{hd}}(n); 0) \not\sqsubseteq (Q; \phi_{\mathsf{hd}}(n); 0)$. Thanks to Lemma 4, we can assume that tr is either Σ_{error}-free or of the form tr'.out(c, error) for some error $\in \Sigma_{\text{error}}$. This means that the trace tr can be executed from $(P; \phi_{\mathsf{hd}}(n); 0)$ without using the rule LET-FAIL at least up to its last visible action.

Considering a renaming ρ_0 that maps any honest agent name h to h_0, and any dishonest agent name d to d_0, we still have that the trace $\mathsf{tr}\rho_0$ can be executed from $(P; \phi_{\mathsf{hd}}(n)\rho_0; 0)$ at least up to its last visible action. Indeed, this renaming preserves equality tests and the property of being a message. Now, to ensure that the trace can still not be executed in the Q side (or maintaining the fact that the test under consideration still fails), we may need to maintain some disequalities, and actually at most $b(\mathcal{E})$ agent names have to be kept unchanged for this (remember that our theory is $b(\mathcal{E})$-blockable). Moreover, in case P executes its else branch, we have also to maintain some disequalities from the P side, and again we need at most to preserve $b(\mathcal{E})$ agent names for that. We do not know whether those names for which we have to maintain distinctness correspond to honest or dishonest agents, but in any case considering $2b(\mathcal{E}) + 1$ of each sort is sufficient. □

The following example illustrates why we may need $2b(\mathcal{E}) + 1$ agents of a particular sort (honest or dishonest) to carry out the proof as explained above.

Example 14. We also consider two constants $\mathsf{error}_1, \mathsf{error}_2 \in \Sigma_{\mathsf{error}}$. In processes P and Q below, we omit the channel name for simplicity. We may assume that all input/outputs occur on a public channel c.

$$P = \mathsf{in}(\mathsf{hon}(x_1)).\mathsf{in}(\mathsf{hon}(x_2)).\mathsf{in}(\mathsf{hon}(x_3)).\mathsf{in}(\mathsf{hon}(x_4)).\mathsf{let}\ z_1 = \mathsf{eq}(x_1, x_2)\ \mathsf{in}$$
$$\mathsf{let}\ z_2 = \mathsf{eq}(x_3, x_4)\ \mathsf{in}\ 0\ \mathsf{else}\ \mathsf{out}(\mathsf{error}_1)$$
$$\mathsf{else}\ \mathsf{out}(\mathsf{error}_2)$$

The process Q is as P after having swapped the two tests, and the two constants error_1 and error_2.

$$Q = \mathsf{in}(\mathsf{hon}(x_1)).\mathsf{in}(\mathsf{hon}(x_2)).\mathsf{in}(\mathsf{hon}(x_3)).\mathsf{in}(\mathsf{hon}(x_4)).\mathsf{let}\ z_1 = \mathsf{eq}(x_3, x_4)\ \mathsf{in}$$
$$\mathsf{let}\ z_2 = \mathsf{eq}(x_1, x_2)\ \mathsf{in}\ 0\ \mathsf{else}\ \mathsf{out}(\mathsf{error}_2)$$
$$\mathsf{else}\ \mathsf{out}(\mathsf{error}_1)$$

We have that $P \not\approx Q$. To see this, we may consider a trace where $x_1, x_2, x_3,$ and x_4 are instantiated using distinct agent names. However, any trace where $x_1 = x_2$ or $x_3 = x_4$ (or both), does not allow one to distinguish these two processes. It is thus important to block at least one agent name among $x_1, x_2,$ and one among x_3, x_4. This will ensure that both P and Q trigger their first else branch. Then, the remaining agent names can be mapped to the same honest agent name. Thus, applying our proof technique we need $b + b + 1$ honest agent names (and here $b = 1$). Note however that a tighter bound may be found for this example since 2 distinct honest agent names are actually sufficient. Indeed, choosing $x_1 = x_3$ and $x_2 = x_4$ allows one to establish non-equivalence. But such a choice would not be found following our technique.

Actually, we can show that there is no attack that requires simultaneously $2b+1$ honest agents and $2b + 1$ dishonest agents. We could elaborate a tighter bound, at the cost of having to check more equivalences.

4   Tightness of Our Hypothesis

Our class of protocols is somewhat limited in the sense that we consider processes that are action-deterministic, with simple else branches, and constructor theories. The counter-examples developed in this section actually suggest that our hypotheses are tight. We provide impossibility results for protocols in case any of our hypotheses is removed, that is, we provide counter-examples for processes with complex else branches, or non constructor theories, or non action-deterministic protocols.

4.1 Complex Else Branches

A natural extension is to consider processes with more expressive else branches. However, as soon as messages emitted in else branches may rely (directly or indirectly) on some agent names, this may impose some disequalities between arbitrary many agent names. This negative result already holds for the standard secrecy property expressed as a reachability requirement.

Formally, we show that we can associate, to any instance of PCP (Post Correspondance Problem), a process P (that uses only standard primitives) such that P reveals a secret s for n agents if, and only if, the corresponding PCP instance has a solution of length smaller than n. Therefore computing a bound for the number of agents needed to mount an attack is as difficult as computing a bound (regarding the length of its smallest solution) for the PCP instance under study. Computing such a bound is undecidable since otherwise we would get a decision procedure for the PCP problem by simply enumerating all the possible solutions until reaching the bound.

Property 1. There is an execution $(P; \phi_{\mathsf{hd}}(n); 0) \xrightarrow{\mathsf{tr.out}(c,\mathsf{w})} (\mathcal{P}; \phi \uplus \{\mathsf{w} \triangleright \mathsf{s}\}; 0)$ if, and only if, the instance of PCP under study admits a solution of length at most n.

An instance of PCP over the alphabet A is given by two sets of tiles $U = \{u_i \mid 1 \le i \le n\}$ and $V = \{v_i \mid 1 \le i \le n\}$ where $u_i, v_i \in \mathsf{A}^*$. A solution of PCP is a non-empty sequence $i_1, \ldots, i_p$ over $\{1, \ldots, n\}$ such that $u_{i_1} \ldots u_{i_p} = v_{i_1} \ldots v_{i_p}$. Deciding whether an instance of PCP admits a solution is well-known to be undecidable, and thus there are instances for which a bound on the size of a solution is not computable. We describe here informally how to build our process P made of several parts. For the sake of clarity, we simply provide the informal rules of the protocol. It is then easy (but less readable) to write the corresponding process. First, following the construction proposed *e.g.* in [15], we write a process P_{PCP} that builds and outputs all the terms of the form:

$$\mathsf{enc}(\langle\langle u, v \rangle, \ell \rangle, k)$$

where $u = u_{i_1} \ldots u_{i_p}$, $v = v_{i_1} \ldots v_{i_p}$, and ℓ is a list of agent names of length p that can be encoded using pairs. The key k is supposed to be unknown from the attacker. This can be easily done by considering rules of the form (where concatenation can be encoded using nested pairs):

$$\mathsf{ag}(z), \mathsf{enc}(\langle\langle x, y \rangle, z_\ell \rangle, k) \to \mathsf{enc}(\langle\langle x.u_i, y.v_i \rangle, \langle z, z_\ell \rangle \rangle, k)$$

for any pair of tiles (u_i, v_i).

We then need to check whether a pair $\langle u, v \rangle$ embedded in the term $\mathsf{enc}(\langle \langle u, v \rangle, \ell \rangle, k)$ is a solution of PCP.

$$\mathsf{enc}(\langle \langle x, x \rangle, z \rangle, k), \ \mathsf{enc}(z, k_{\mathsf{diff}}) \ \rightarrow \ \mathsf{s}$$

Second, to build our counter-example, we write a process that relies on some else branches to ensure that a list ℓ is made of distinct elements. The idea is that $\mathsf{enc}(\ell, k_{\mathsf{diff}})$ is emitted if, and only if, elements in ℓ are distinct agent names.

$$\mathsf{ag}(x) \ \rightarrow \ \mathsf{enc}(\langle x, \bot \rangle, k_{\mathsf{diff}})$$
$$\mathsf{ag}(x), \ \mathsf{ag}(y), \ \mathsf{enc}(\langle x, z \rangle, k_{\mathsf{diff}}), \mathsf{enc}(\langle y, z \rangle, k_{\mathsf{diff}}) \ \xrightarrow{x \neq y} \ \mathsf{enc}(\langle x, \langle y, z \rangle \rangle, k_{\mathsf{diff}})$$

The first rule allows us to generate list of length 1 whereas the second rule gives us the possibility to build list of greater length, like $[a_1, a_2, \ldots, a_n]$ as soon as the sublists $[a_1, a_3, \ldots, a_n]$ and $[a_2, a_3, \ldots, a_n]$ have been checked, and a_1 and a_2 are distinct agent names. The rule $u \xrightarrow{t_1 \neq t_2} v$ is the informal description for the following process: on input u and if $t_1 \neq t_2$ then emit v. This can be encoded in our framework as explained in Sect. 2.3.

The formalisation of these rules yields a process P that satisfies Property 1, and it is not difficult to write a process P that satisfies in addition our action-determinism condition. This encoding can be adapted to show a similar result regarding trace equivalence. We may also note that this encoding works if we consider an execution model in which agents are not authorised to talk to themselves. In such a case, we even do not need to rely explicitly on else branches.

4.2   Pure Equational Theories

We now show that it is actually impossible to bound the number of agents for non constructor theories. This impossibility result already holds for the standard equational theory $\mathsf{E}_{\mathsf{enc}}$: $\mathsf{dec}(\mathsf{enc}(x, y), y) = x$.

To prove our result, given a list ℓ of pairs of agent names, we build two terms $t^P(\ell)$ and $t^Q(\ell)$ using the function symbols enc, dec, the public constant c_0, and some agent names $a_1, \ldots, a_n$ in $\mathcal{A}$. The terms $t^P(\ell)$ and $t^Q(\ell)$ are such that they are equal as soon as two agent names of a pair in ℓ are identical.

Property 2. The terms $t^P(\ell)$ and $t^Q(\ell)$ are equal modulo $\mathsf{E}_{\mathsf{enc}}$ if, and only if, there exists a pair (a, b) in ℓ such that $a = b$.

The terms $t^P(\ell)$ and $t^Q(\ell)$ are defined inductively as follows:

- $t^P(\ell) = \mathsf{dec}(\mathsf{enc}(c_0, a), b)$ and $t^Q(\ell) = \mathsf{dec}(\mathsf{enc}(c_0, b), a)$ when $\ell = [(a, b)]$;
- In case $\ell = (a, b) :: \ell'$ with ℓ' non-empty, we have that

$$t^X(\ell) = \mathsf{dec}(\mathsf{enc}(c_0, \mathsf{dec}(\mathsf{enc}(a, t_1), t_2)), \mathsf{dec}(\mathsf{enc}(b, t_1), t_2))$$

where m, t_1 and t_2 are such that $t^X(\ell') = \mathsf{dec}(\mathsf{enc}(c_0, t_1), t_2)$ and $X \in \{P, Q\}$.

For illustration purposes, the term $t^P(\ell_0)$ for $\ell_0 = [(a_2, a_3), (a_1, a_3), (a_1, a_2)]$ is depicted below. A subtree whose root is labelled with n having subtrees t_1 and t_2 as children represents the term $\mathsf{dec}(\mathsf{enc}(n, t_1), t_2)$. The term $t^Q(\ell_0)$ is the same as $t^P(\ell_0)$ after permutation of the labels on the leaves.

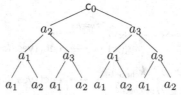

First, we may note that $t^P(\ell_0) = t^Q(\ell_0)$ when $a_1 = a_2$. Now, in case $a_1 = a_3$, we obtain $t^P(\ell_0) = t^Q(\ell_0) = \mathsf{dec}(\mathsf{enc}(c_0, a_2), a_3)$, and we have that $t^P(\ell_0) = t^Q(\ell_0) = c_0$ when $a_2 = a_3$. These are the only cases where $t^P(\ell_0)$ and $t^Q(\ell_0)$ are equal modulo $\mathsf{E_{enc}}$. More generally, we can show that $t^P(\ell)$ and $t^Q(\ell)$ enjoy Property 2.

Now we may rely on these terms to build two processes P_n and Q_n such that $(P_n; \phi_{\mathsf{hd}}(n_0); 0) \not\approx (Q_n; \phi_{\mathsf{hd}}(n_0); 0)$ if, and only if, $n_0 \geq n$. These processes are as follows:

$$P_n = \mathsf{in}(c, \mathsf{ag}(z_1)) \ldots \mathsf{in}(c, \mathsf{ag}(z_n)).\mathsf{out}(c, t^P(\ell))$$
$$Q_n = \mathsf{in}(c, \mathsf{ag}(z_1)) \ldots \mathsf{in}(c, \mathsf{ag}(z_n)).\mathsf{out}(c, t^Q(\ell))$$

where ℓ is a list of length $n(n - 1)/2$ which contains all the pairs of the form (z_i, z_j) with $i < j$.

Note that in case $n_0 < n$, in any execution, we are thus forced to use twice the same agent names, and thus the resulting instances of $t^P(\ell)$ and $t^Q(\ell)$ will be equal modulo $\mathsf{E_{enc}}$. In case we have sufficiently many distinct agent names, the resulting instances of $t^P(\ell)$ and $t^Q(\ell)$ will correspond to distinct public terms. Hence, in such a case trace equivalence does not hold.

Note that, for sake of simplicity, our encoding directly relies on the agent names, but a similar encoding can be done using for instance $\mathsf{shk_s}(a)$ instead of a so that agent names will not be used in key position.

4.3 Beyond Action-Deterministic Processes

Another natural extension is to get rid of the action-determinism condition, or at least to weaken it in order to consider processes that are determinate (as defined e.g. in [10]). This is actually not possible. The encoding is quite similar to the one presented in Sect. 4.1. Since we have no easy way to ensure that all the terms of the form $\mathsf{enc}(\ell, k_{\mathsf{diff}})$ will contain distinct elements, the encoding is more involved.

To prove our result, we show that given an instance of PCP, it is possible to build two processes P and Q (that use only standard primitives and no else branch) that are in equivalence for n agents if, and only if, the corresponding PCP instance has a solution of length at most n.

Property 3. $(P; \phi_{\mathsf{hd}}(n); 0) \not\approx (Q; \phi_{\mathsf{hd}}(n); 0)$ if, and only if, the instance of PCP under study admits a solution of length at most n.

Our process P is quite similar to the one described in Sect. 4.1. Note that the test $x \neq y$ has been removed, and a public constant yes has been added inside each encryption. The presence of such a constant is not mandatory when defining P but will become useful when defining Q.

$$\mathsf{enc}(\langle\langle\langle x, x\rangle, z\rangle, k), \ \mathsf{enc}(\langle\langle z_b, z\rangle, k_{\mathsf{check}}) \xrightarrow{z_b = \mathsf{yes}} \mathsf{ok} \tag{1}$$

$$\mathsf{ag}(x) \longrightarrow \mathsf{enc}(\langle \mathsf{yes}, \langle x, \perp\rangle\rangle, k_{\mathsf{check}}) \tag{2}$$

$$\mathsf{ag}(x), \ \mathsf{ag}(y), \ \mathsf{enc}(\langle z_b, \langle x, z\rangle\rangle, k_{\mathsf{check}}), \\ \mathsf{enc}(\langle z_b', \langle y, z\rangle\rangle, k_{\mathsf{check}}) \longrightarrow \mathsf{enc}(\langle \mathsf{yes}, \langle x, \langle y, z\rangle\rangle\rangle, k_{\mathsf{check}}) \tag{3}$$

Then, Q is quite similar except that we replace the test $z_b = \mathsf{yes}$ by $z_b = \mathsf{no}$ and we consider in addition three other versions of the last protocol rule (rule (3)) giving us a way to generate encryption containing the flag no. More precisely, we consider the following rule with φ equal to $x = y$ (rule 3a), $z_b = \mathsf{no}$ (rule 3b), and $z_b' = \mathsf{no}$ (rule 3c).

$$\mathsf{ag}(x), \ \mathsf{ag}(y), \ \mathsf{enc}(\langle z_b, \langle x, z\rangle\rangle, k_{\mathsf{check}}), \\ \mathsf{enc}(\langle z_b', \langle y, z\rangle\rangle, k_{\mathsf{check}}) \xrightarrow{\varphi} \mathsf{enc}(\langle \mathsf{no}, \langle x, \langle y, z\rangle\rangle\rangle, k_{\mathsf{check}})$$

Putting all these rules together and considering randomised encryption to avoid spurious equalities to happen, this yields two processes P and Q that actually satisfy Property 3.

Proof sketch. ($\Leftarrow$) if PCP has a solution of length at most n, it is possible to build the term $\mathsf{enc}(\langle\langle u, v\rangle, \ell\rangle, k)$ corresponding to this solution with $u = v$ and ℓ of length at most n. Moreover, we can assume that ℓ is made of distinct elements. Hence, the additional rules in Q will not be really useful to generate a certificate on the list ℓ with the flag set to no. Actually, only $\mathsf{enc}(\langle \mathsf{yes}, \ell\rangle, k_{\mathsf{check}})$ will be generated, and thus P will emit ok and Q will not be able to mimic this step.

($\Rightarrow$) Now, if PCP has no solution of length at most n, then either PCP has no solution at all, and in such a case, the part where P and Q differ is not reachable, and thus the processes are in trace equivalence. Now, assuming that PCP has a solution of length n' with $n' > n$, the only possibility to distinguish P from Q is to build the term $\mathsf{enc}(\langle \mathsf{yes}, \ell\rangle, k_{\mathsf{check}})$ with ℓ of length n'. This term will allow us to trigger the rule (1) in P but not in Q. The problem is that ℓ contains a duplicate entry, and due to this, at some point it would be possible to mimic what is done in P using rule (3) with the additional rule (3a), and to pursue the construction of this certificate relying on (3b) and (3c). This will allow Q to go through the rule (1) as P did.   □

5   Conclusion

We have shown that we can bound the number of agents for a large class of protocols: action-deterministic processes with simple else branches and constructor theories, which encompasses many primitives. The resulting bound is rather small in general. For example, 4 agents are sufficient for standard primitives and processes without else branches. Our assumptions are rather tight. Surprisingly, such a reduction result does not hold in case processes are not action-deterministic, or if they include more complex else branches, or else for more general equational theories. This draws a thin line between our result (where terms with destructors may not be sent) and a more general framework.

Our result applies for any equivalence between two processes. This allows us to cover various security properties such as strong secrecy or anonymity. However, assuming deterministic processes discards the encoding of some properties such as unlinkability. We devise in [17] an alternative encoding to check for unlinkability in our framework, considering only deterministic processes.

Our reduction result enlarges the scope of some existing decidability results. For example, [13] provides a decision procedure for an unbounded number of sessions, for processes that use at most one variable per rule. In case an arbitrary number of agents is considered, one or two variables are typically used simply to describe the agents. Bounding the number of agents is therefore needed to consider non trivial protocols.

The proof of our reduction result is inspired from [14], which shows how to bound the number of nonces. Taking advantage of the properties of agent names, we extend [14] to processes with simple else branches, action-determinism and general constructor theories. As future work, we plan to study how to generalize both results in a framework that would allow to bound several types of data.

References

1. Abadi, M., Fournet, C.: Mobile values, new names, and secure communication. In: Proceedings of the 28th Symposium on Principles of Programming Languages (POPL 2001). ACM Press (2001)
2. Arapinis, M., Chothia, T., Ritter, E., Ryan, M.: Analysing unlinkability and anonymity using the applied pi calculus. In: Proceedings of the 23rd Computer Security Foundations Symposium (CSF 2010), pp. 107–121. IEEE Computer Society Press (2010)
3. Armando, A., et al.: The AVISPA tool for the automated validation of internet security protocols and applications. In: Etessami, K., Rajamani, S.K. (eds.) CAV 2005. LNCS, vol. 3576, pp. 281–285. Springer, Heidelberg (2005)
4. Backes, M., Maffei, M., Unruh, D.: Zero-knowledge in the applied pi-calculus and automated verification of the direct anonymous attestation protocol. In: Proceedings of 29th IEEE Symposium on Security and Privacy, May 2008
5. Baelde, D., Delaune, S., Hirschi, L.: Partial order reduction for security protocols. In: Aceto, L., de Frutos-Escrig, D. (eds.) CONCUR 2015. Leibniz International Proceedings in Informatics, vol. 42, pp. 497–510. Leibniz-Zentrum für Informatik, Madrid (2015)
6. Blanchet, B.: Proverif 1.91. As downloaded on October 1st. See files in directory (2015). http://prosecco.gforge.inria.fr/personal/bblanche/examples/pitype/choice/

7. Blanchet, B.: An efficient cryptographic protocol verifier based on prolog rules. In: Proceedings of the 14th Computer Security Foundations Workshop (CSFW 2001). IEEE Computer Society Press, June 2001

8. Blanchet, B.: An automatic security protocol verifier based on resolution theorem proving (invited tutorial). In: Proceedings of the 20th International Conference on Automated Deduction (CADE-20), Tallinn, July 2005

9. Blanchet, B., Abadi, M., Fournet, C.: Automated verification of selected equivalences for security protocols. J. Logic Algebr. Program. **75**(1), 3–51 (2008)

10. Chadha, R., Ciobâcă, Ş., Kremer, S.: Automated verification of equivalence properties of cryptographic protocols. In: Seidl, H. (ed.) ESOP 2012. LNCS, vol. 7211, pp. 108–127. Springer, Heidelberg (2012)

11. Cheval, V., Cortier, V., Delaune, S.: Deciding equivalence-based properties using constraint solving. Theor. Comput. Sci. **492**, 1–39 (2013)

12. Chothia, T., Smirnov, V.: A traceability attack against e-passports. In: Proceedings of the 14th International Conference on Financial Cryptography and Data Security (FC) (2010)

13. Chrétien, R., Cortier, V., Delaune, S.: From security protocols to pushdown automata. In: Fomin, F.V., Freivalds, R., Kwiatkowska, M., Peleg, D. (eds.) ICALP 2013. LNCS, vol. 7966, pp. 137–149. Springer, Heidelberg (2013)

14. Chrétien, R., Cortier, V., Delaune, S.: Checking trace equivalence: how to get rid of nonces? In: Pernul, G., Ryan, P.Y.A., Weippl, E. (eds.) ESORICS 2015. LNCS, vol. 9327, pp. 230–251. Springer, Heidelberg (2015). doi:10.1007/978-3-319-24177-7_12

15. Comon-Lundh, H., Cortier, V.: Security properties: two agents are sufficient. Sci. Comput. Program. **50**(1–3), 51–71 (2004)

16. Comon-Lundh, H., Cortier, V.: Computational soundness of observational equivalence. In: Proceedings of the 15th ACM Conference on Computer and Communications Security (CCS 2008), pp. 109–118. ACM Press, Alexandria, October 2008

17. Cortier, V., Dallon, A., Delaune, S.: Bounding the number of agents, for equivalence too. Research report LSV-16-01, Laboratoire Spécification et Vérification, ENS Cachan, p. 37, January 2016

18. Cremers, C.J.F.: The scyther tool: verification, falsification, and analysis of security protocols. In: Gupta, A., Malik, S. (eds.) CAV 2008. LNCS, vol. 5123, pp. 414–418. Springer, Heidelberg (2008)

19. Delaune, S., Kremer, S., Ryan, M.D.: Verifying privacy-type properties of electronic voting protocols. J. Comput. Secur. **4**, 435–487 (2008)

20. Denning, D., Sacco, G.: Timestamps in key distributed protocols. Commun. ACM **24**(8), 533–535 (1981)

21. Schmidt, B., Meier, S., Cremers, C., Basin, D.: Automated analysis of Diffie-Hellman protocols and advanced security properties. In: Chong, S. (ed.) Proceedings of the 25th IEEE Computer Security Foundations Symposium, CSF 2012, IEEE, Cambridge, pp. 78–94, 25–27 June 2012

AIF-ω: Set-Based Protocol Abstraction with Countable Families

Sebastian Mödersheim[1] and Alessandro Bruni[2(✉)]

[1] DTU Compute, Lyngby, Denmark
[2] IT University of Copenhagen, Copenhagen, Denmark
brun@itu.dk

Abstract. Abstraction based approaches like ProVerif are very efficient in protocol verification, but have a limitation in dealing with stateful protocols. A number of extensions have been proposed to allow for a limited amount of state information while not destroying the advantages of the abstraction method. However, the extensions proposed so far can only deal with a *finite* amount of state information. This can in many cases make it impossible to formulate a verification problem for an unbounded number of agents (and one has to rather specify a fixed set of agents). Our work shows how to overcome this limitation by abstracting state into countable families of sets. We can then formalize a problem with unbounded agents, where each agent maintains its own set of keys. Still, our method does not loose the benefits of the abstraction approach, in particular, it translates a verification problem to a set of first-order Horn clauses that can then be efficiently verified with tools like ProVerif.

1 Introduction

A very successful idea in protocol verification, most prominently in the ProVerif tool, is an abstraction approach that over-approximates every possible protocol behavior by a set of first-order Horn clauses, rather than considering the set of reachable states [2,12]. The benefit is that one completely avoids the state-explosion problem (i.e., that the number of reachable state grows exponentially with the number of sessions) and allows one to even deal with an unbounded number of sessions. The fact that this approach "throws away" the state space does indeed not hurt the modeling and analysis for most protocols: typically, the amount of context needed to participate in a protocol is contained within a session, and all information that is shared across different sessions is immutable like agent names and long-term keys.

We run into limitations with this approach, however, when we consider protocols that use some kind of long-term information that can be changed across multiple sessions of the protocol. As an example, a web server maintains a database of ordered goods, or a key server stores valid and revoked keys. In the case of a key server, some actions can just be performed while the key is valid, but as soon as this key is revoked, the same actions are disabled. This behavior does not directly work with the Horn-clause approach, because they have

© Springer-Verlag Berlin Heidelberg 2016
F. Piessens and L. Viganò (Eds.): POST 2016, LNCS 9635, pp. 233–253, 2016.
DOI: 10.1007/978-3-662-49635-0_12

the monotonicity property of classic logics: what is true cannot become false by learning more information. This is at odds with any "non-monotonic" behavior, i.e., that something is no longer possible after a particular event has occurred.

Several works have proposed extensions of the abstraction approach by including a limited amount of state information, so as to allow the analysis of stateful protocols, without destroying the large benefits of the approach. The first was the AIF tool that allows one to declare a fixed number N of sets [10]. One can then specify a transition system with an unbounded number of constants. These constants can be added to, and removed from, each of the sets upon transitions, and transitions can be conditioned by set memberships. The main idea is here that one can abstract these constants by their set membership, i.e., partitioning the constants into 2^N equivalence classes for a system with N sets. The AIF tool generates a set of Horn clauses using this abstraction, and can use either ProVerif or the first-order theorem prover SPASS [13] to check whether a distinguished symbol *attack* can be derived from the Horn clauses. The soundness proof shows that if the specified transition system has an attack state then *attack* can be derived from the corresponding Horn clause model. There are two more approaches that similarly bring state information into ProVerif: StatVerif [1] and Set-π [4]. We discuss them in the related work.

While AIF is an infinite state approach, it has the limitation to a fixed number N of sets. For instance, when modeling a system where every user maintains its own set of keys, one needs to specify a fixed number of users, so as to arrive at a concrete number N of sets. The main contribution of AIF-ω is to overcome precisely this limitation and instead allow for specifying N *families* of sets, where each family can consist of a countably infinite number of sets. For instance, we may declare that *User* is an infinite set and define a family *ring*(*User*) of sets so that each user $a \in User$ has its own set of keys *ring*(*a*). To make this feasible with the abstraction approach, we however need to make one restriction: the sets of a family must be pairwise disjoint, i.e., $ring(a) \cap ring(b) = \emptyset$ for any two users a and b. In fact, we do allow for AIF-ω specifications that could potentially violate this property, but if the disjointness is violated, it counts as an attack.

The contributions of this work are the formal development and soundness proof of this countable-family abstraction. It is in fact a generalization of the AIF approach. Besides this generalization, AIF-ω has also a direct practical advantage in the verification tool: experiments show for instance that the verification for infinitely many agents in an example is more efficient than the finite enumeration of agents in AIF. In fact, the infinite agents specification has almost the same run time as the specification with a single agent for each role in AIF.

The rest of this paper is organized as follows. In Sect. 2 we formally define AIF-ω and introduce preliminaries along the way. In Sect. 3 we define the abstraction and translation to Horn clauses and prove the soundness in Sect. 4. We discuss how to encode the approach in SPASS and ProVerif as well as experimental results in Sect. 5. We discuss related work and conclude in Sect. 6.

2   Formal Definition of AIF-ω

We go right into the definition of the AIF-ω language, and introduce all preliminaries along the way. An AIF-ω specification consists of the following sections:
declaring user-defined types, declaring families of sets, declaring function and
fact symbols, and finally defining the transition rules. We explain these concepts
step-by-step and for concreteness illustrate it with the running example of a
keyserver adapted from our previous paper [10].

2.1   Types

An AIF-ω specification starts with a declaration of user-defined types. These
types can either be given by a complete enumeration (finite sets), or using the
operator "...." one can declare that the type contains a countable number of
elements. Finally, we can also build the types as the union of other types. For
the keyserver example, let us define the following types:

$$Honest = \{a, b, \ldots\} \quad Dishon = \{i, p, \ldots\} \qquad User \; = Honest \cup Dishon$$
$$Server \; = \{s, \ldots\} \qquad Agent \; = User \cup Server \quad Status = \{valid, revoked\}$$

This declares the type $Honest$ to be a countably infinite set that contains the
constants a and b. Similarly $Dishon$ and $Server$ are defined. It may be intuitively
clear that in this declaration, the sets $Honest$ and $Dishon$ should be disparate
types, but to make the "...." notation formally precise, we give each type T
an *extensional semantics* $[\![T]\!]$. To that end, for each "....", we introduce new
constants $t_1, t_2, \ldots$ so that for the running example we have for instance:

$$[\![Honest]\!] = \{a, b\} \cup \{honest_n \mid n \in \mathbb{N}\} \quad [\![Dishon]\!] = \{s, p\} \cup \{dishon_n \mid n \in \mathbb{N}\}$$

Comparing AIF-ω with the previous language AIF, the ability to define infinite types and families of sets over these types, are the essential new features.
Drastically speaking, "...." is thus what you could not do in AIF. The complexity
of this paper however suggests that it is not an entirely trivial generalization.

Besides the user-defined types, we also have two built-in types: $Value$ and
$Untyped$. The type $Value$ is the central type of the approach, because all sets
of the system can only contain elements of type value, and all freshly created
elements must be of type value. It is thus exactly those entities that we later
want to replace by abstract equivalence classes. Let thus $\mathfrak{A} = \{abs_n \mid n \in \mathbb{N}\}$ be
a countable set of constants (again disjoint from all others) and $[\![Value]\!] = \mathfrak{A}$.
Second, we have also the "type" $Untyped$. Below, we define the set of ground
terms $\mathcal{T}_\Sigma$ that includes all constants and composed terms that can be built using
function symbols. We want the type $Untyped$ to summarize arbitrary such terms,
and thus define $[\![Untyped]\!] = \mathcal{T}_\Sigma$.

2.2   Sets

The core concept of AIF-ω is using sets of values from $\mathfrak{A}$ to model simple "databases" that can be queried and modified by the participants of the protocols.

These sets can even be shared between participants, and the modeler has a great freedom on how to use them. For our running example we want to declare sets for the key ring of every user, and for every server a database that contains for all users the currently valid and revoked keys:

$$ring(\mathit{User}!) \quad db(\mathit{Server}!, \mathit{User}!, \mathit{Status}!)$$

This declares two *families* of sets, the first family consists of one set $ring(c)$ for every $c \in [\![\mathit{User}]\!]$ and the second family consists of one set $db(c_1, c_2, c_3)$ for every $c_1 \in [\![\mathit{Server}]\!]$, $c_2 \in [\![\mathit{User}]\!]$, and $c_3 \in [\![\mathit{Status}]\!]$.

The exclamation mark behind the types in the set declaration has a crucial meaning: with this the modeler defines a *uniqueness invariant* on the state space, namely that the sets of this family will be pairwise disjoint for that parameter. In the example, $ring(c_1) \cap ring(c_2) = \emptyset$ for any $c_1 \neq c_2$, and $db(c_1, c_2, c_3) \cap db(c_1', c_2', c_3') = \emptyset$ if $(c_1, c_2, c_3) \neq (c_1', c_2', c_3')$. This invariant is part of the definition of the transition system: it is an attack, if a state is reachable in which the invariant is violated.

An important requirement of AIF-ω is that *all family parameters of infinite type must have the uniqueness invariant*. Thus, it is not allowed to declare $ring(\mathit{Agent})$, because $[\![\mathit{Agent}]\!]$ is infinite. However, it *is* allowed to declare $db(\mathit{Server}!, \mathit{Agent}!, \mathit{Status})$ since $[\![\mathit{Status}]\!]$ is finite. This declaration with non-unique *Status* could be specified using two families $db_{valid}(\mathit{Server}!, \mathit{Agent}!)$ and $db_{revoked}(\mathit{Server}!, \mathit{Agent}!)$ instead. We thus regard non-unique arguments of a finite type as syntactic sugar that is compiled away in AIF-ω.

Since non-unique arguments are syntactic sugar, let us assume for the rest of the paper an AIF-ω specification (like in the running example) where all set parameters have the uniqueness invariant (i.e., the ! symbol). Let us denote the families of sets in general as $s_1, \ldots, s_N$ where N is the number of declared families, i.e., in the example, $N = 2$ with $s_1 = ring$ and $s_2 = db$. We thus have for every $1 \leq i \leq N$ the uniqueness invariant that $s_i(a_1, \ldots, a_n) \cap s_i(b_1, \ldots, b_n) = \emptyset$ whenever $(a_1, \ldots, a_n) \neq (b_1, \ldots, b_n)$.

2.3 Functions, Facts, and Terms

Finally the user can declare a set of functions and facts (predicates) with their arities. For the example let us have:

Functions: $inv/1$, $sign/2$, $pair/2$ Facts: $iknows/1$, $attack/0$

Intuitively, $inv(pk)$ represents the private key corresponding to public key pk, $sign(inv(pk), m)$ represents a digital signature on message m with private key $inv(pk)$, $pair$ is for building pairs of messages; $iknows(m)$ expresses that the intruder knows m, and $attack$ represents a flag we raise as soon as an attack has occurred (and we later ask whether $attack$ holds in any reachable state).

Definition 1. *Let Σ consist of all function symbols, the extension $[\![T]\!]$ of any user-defined type T, and the values $\mathfrak{A}$ (where all constants are considered as* *function symbols with arity 0). Let $\mathcal{V}$ be a set of variables disjoint from Σ. We define $T_{\Sigma}(V)$ to be the set of terms that can be built from Σ and $V \subseteq \mathcal{V}$, i.e., the least set that contains V and such that $f(t_1, \ldots, t_n) \in T_{\Sigma}(V)$ if $t_1, \ldots, t_n \in T_{\Sigma}(V)$ and $f/n \in \Sigma$. When $V = \emptyset$, we also just write T_{Σ}, and we call this the set of* ground terms*. A* fact *(over Σ and V) has the form $f(t_1, \ldots, t_n)$ where f/n is a fact symbol and $t_1, \ldots, t_n \in T_{\Sigma}(V)$.*

2.4 Transition Rules

The core of an AIF-ω specification is the definition of its transition rules that give rise to an infinite-state transition system, where each state is a set of facts and set conditions (as defined below). The initial state is simply the empty set of facts and set conditions. We proceed as follows: we first give the formal definition of syntax and semantics of rules. We then discuss the details at hand of the rules of the running example. Finally, we give a number of restrictions on rules that we need for the abstraction approach in the following section.

In the following we often speak of *the type* of a variable (and may write $X : T$); this is because variables occur only within rules (not within states) and are then always declared as part of the rule parameters.

Definition 2. *A* positive set condition *has the form $t \in s_i(A_1, \ldots, A_n)$ where t is either a constant of $\mathfrak{A}$ or a variable of type Value, the family s_i of sets has been declared as $s_i(T_1!, \ldots, T_n!)$, and each A_i is either an element of $[\![T_i]\!]$ or a variable of type T_i' with $[\![T_i']\!] \subseteq [\![T_i]\!]$. A positive set condition is called* ground *if it contains no variables. A* negative set condition *has the form $t \notin s_i(\_)$ where t and s_i are as before.*

A state *is a finite set of ground facts and ground positive set conditions. A* transition rule *r has the form*

$$r(X_1 : T_1, \ldots, X_n : T_n) = LF \cdot S_+ \cdot S_- =\![F]\!\Rightarrow RF \cdot RS$$

where

1. *$X_1, \ldots, X_n$ are variables and $T_1, \ldots, T_n$ are their types;*
   We often abbreviate $(X_1 : T_1, \ldots, X_n : T_n)$ by $\boldsymbol{X} : \boldsymbol{T}$;
2. *The X_i are exactly the variables that occur in the rule*
3. *LF and RF are sets of facts;*
4. *S_+ and RS are sets of positive set conditions;*
5. *S_- is a set of negative set conditions;*
6. *F is a set of variables that are of type Value and they do not occur in LF, S_+, or S_-.*
7. *For every untyped variable that occurs in RF, it also occurs in LF.*

Let $V_{\mathfrak{A}}$ denote the subset of the X_i that have type Value.

A rule r gives rise to a state-transition relation $\Rightarrow_r$ where $S \Rightarrow_r^{\sigma} S'$ holds for states S and S' and a substitution σ iff

- σ has domain $\{X_1, \ldots, X_n\}$ and $\sigma(X_i) \in [\![T_i]\!]$ for each $1 \leq i \leq n$;
- $(LF \cdot S_+)\sigma \subseteq S$,
- For every negative set condition $X \notin s_i(\_)$ of S_-, state S does not contain $\sigma(X) \in s_i(a_1, \ldots, a_m)$ for any $(a_1, \ldots, a_m)$.
- $S' = (S \setminus \sigma(S_+)) \cup \sigma(RF) \cup \sigma(RS)$,
- $\sigma(F)$ are fresh constants from $\mathfrak{A}$ (i.e. they do not occur in S or the AIF-ω specification).

A state S is called reachable using the set of transition rules R, iff $\emptyset \Rightarrow_R^* S$. Here $\Rightarrow_R$ is the union of $\Rightarrow_r$ for all $r \in R$ (ignoring substitution σ) and $\cdot^*$ is the reflexive transitive closure.   □

Intuitively, a rule r can be applied under *match* σ if the left-hand side facts $\sigma(LF)$ and positive set conditions $\sigma(S_+)$ are present in the current state, and none of the negative conditions $\sigma(S_-)$ holds. Upon transition we remove the matched set conditions $\sigma(S_+)$ and replace them with the right-hand side set conditions $\sigma(RS)$ and facts $\sigma(RF)$. The semantics ensures that all reachable states are ground, because σ must instantiate all variables with ground terms. The semantics defines facts to be *persistent*, i.e., when present in a state, then also in all successor states. Thus only set conditions can be "taken back".

To illustrate the AIF-ω rules more concretely, we now discuss the rules of the key server example. We first look at the three rules that describe the behavior of honest users and servers:

$keyReg(A: User, S: Server, PK: Value) =$
$\quad =\!\!|PK|\!\!\Rightarrow iknows(PK) \cdot PK \in ring(A) \cdot PK \in db(S, A, valid)$
$userUpdateKey(A: Honest, S: Server, PK: Value, NPK: Value) =$
$\quad PK \in ring(A) \cdot iknows(PK)$
$\quad =\!\!|NPK|\!\!\Rightarrow NPK \in ring(A) \cdot iknows(sign(inv(PK), pair(A, NPK)))$
$serverUpdateKey(A: User, S: Server, PK: Value, NPK: Value) =$
$\quad iknows(sign(inv(PK), pair(A, NPK))) \cdot PK \in db(S, A, valid) \cdot NPK \notin db(\_)$
$\quad \Rightarrow PK \in db(S, A, revoked) \cdot NPK \in db(S, A, valid) \cdot iknows(inv(PK))$

Intuitively, the *keyReg* rule describes an "out-of-band" key registration, e.g. a physical visit of a user A at an authority S. Here, the left-hand side of the rule is empty: the rule can be applied in any state. Upon the arrow, we have PK, meaning that in this transition we create a *fresh* value from $\mathfrak{A}$ that did not occur previously. Intuitively this is a new public key that the user A has created. We directly give the intruder this public key, as it is public. The two set conditions formalize that the key is added to the key ring of A and that the server S stores PK as a valid key for A in its database. Of course, the user A should also know the corresponding private key $inv(PK)$, but we do not explicitly express this (and rather later make a special rule for dishonest agents). Note that, having no prerequisites, this rule can be applied in any state, and thus every user can register an unbounded number of keys with every server.

The *userUpdateKey* rule now describes that an honest user (for the behavior of dishonest users, see below) can update any of its current keys PK (the requirement $iknows(PK)$ is explained below) by creating a new key NPK and sending an update message $sign(inv(PK), pair(A, NPK))$ to the server, signing the new key with the current key. As it is often done, this example does not explicitly model sending messages on an insecure channel and rather directly adds it to the intruder knowledge (see also the model of receiving a message in the next rule). Further, NPK is added to the key ring of A. Finally, observe that the set condition $PK \in ring(A)$ is not repeated on the right-hand side. This means that PK is actually removed from the key ring. Of course this is a simplistic example: in a real system, the update would include some kind of confirmation message from the server, and the user would not throw away the current key before receiving the confirmation.

The third rule $serverUpdateKey$ formalizes how a server processes such an update message: it will check that the signing key PK is currently registered as a valid key and that NPK is not yet registered, neither as valid nor as revoked. If so, it will register NPK as a valid key for A in its database. PK is now removed from the database of valid keys for A, because $PK \in db(S, A, valid)$ is not present on the right-hand side; PK is added to the revoked keys instead. Note that the check $NPK \notin db(\_)$ on the left-hand side actually models a server that checks that *no* server of *Server* has seen this key so far.[1] As a particular "chicane", we finally give the intruder the private key to every revoked key. This is modeling that we want the protocol to be secure (as we define shortly) even when the intruder can get hold of old private keys.

Remaining rules of the example model the behavior of dishonest agents and define what constitutes an attack:

$iknowsAgents(A: Agent) = \Rightarrow iknows(A)$
$sign(M1, M2: Untyped) = iknows(M1) \cdot iknows(M2) \Rightarrow iknows(sign(M1, M2))$
$open(M1, M2: Untyped) = iknows(sign(M1, M2)) \Rightarrow iknows(M2)$
$pair(M1, M2: Untyped) = iknows(M1) \cdot iknows(M2) \Rightarrow iknows(pair(M1, M2))$
$proj(M1, M2: Untyped) = iknows(pair(M1, M2)) \Rightarrow iknows(M1) \cdot iknows(M2)$
$dishonKey(A: Dishon, PK: Value) = iknows(PK) \cdot PK \in ring(A)$
    $\Rightarrow iknows(inv(PK)) \cdot PK \in ring(A)$
$attdef(A: Honest, S: Server) = iknows(inv(PK)) \cdot PK \in db(S, A, valid) \Rightarrow attack$

The first rules are basically a standard Dolev-Yao intruder for the operators we use (i.e., the intruder has access to all algorithms like encryption and signing, but cannot break cryptography and can thus apply the algorithms only to messages and keys he knows). The rule $dishonKey$ expresses that the intruder gets the private key to all public keys registered in the name of a dishonest agent. This reflects the common model that all dishonest agents work together. Finally the rule $attdef$ defines security indirectly by specifying what is an attack: when the intruder finds out a private key that some server S considers currently as a

---

[1] If one would rather like to model that servers cannot see which keys the other servers consider as valid or revoked, one runs indeed into the boundaries of AIF-ω here. This is because in this case one must accept that at least a dishonest agent can register the same key at two different servers, violating the uniqueness invariant. If one wants to model such systems, one must resort to finitely many servers.

valid key of an honest agent A. One may give more goals, especially directly talking about authentication—note that this secrecy goal implicitly refers to authentication, as the intruder would for instance have a successful attack if he manages to get a server S to accept as the public key of an honest agent any key to which the intruder knows the private key. For an in-depth discussion of formalizing authentication goals, see [4].

2.5 Restrictions and Syntactic Sugar

There are a few forms of rules that are problematic for the treatment in the abstraction approach later. Actually, problematic rules may also indicate that the modeler could have made a mistake (i.e. has something different in mind than what the rule formally means). Most of the problematic rules are either paradox (and thus useless) or can be compiled into non-problematic variants as syntactic sugar. We first define problematic, or inadmissible, rules, then discuss what is problematic about them and how they are handled. Afterwards, we assume to deal only with admissible rules.

Definition 3. *A rule* $r(\boldsymbol{X{:}Type}) = LF \cdot S_+ \cdot S_- =[F] \Rightarrow RF \cdot RS$ *is called* inadmissible, *if any of the following holds:*

1. *Either* $X \in s_i(\ldots)$ *occurs in* S_+ *or* $X \notin s_i(\_)$ *occurs in* S_-, *but* X *does not occur in* LF, *or*
2. $X \in s_i(A_1, \ldots, A_n)$ *occurs in* S_+ *and* $X \notin s_i(\_)$ *occurs in* S_-, *or*
3. *both* $X \in s_i(A_1, \ldots, A_n)$ *and* $X \in s_i(A'_1, \ldots, A'_n)$ *occur in* S_+ *for* $(A'_1, \ldots, A'_n) \neq (A_1, \ldots, A_n)$, *or*
4. *both* $X \in s_i(A_1, \ldots, A_n)$ *and* $X \in s_i(A'_1, \ldots, A'_n)$ *occur in* RS *for* $(A'_1, \ldots, A'_n) \neq (A_1, \ldots, A_n)$, *or*
5. $X \in S_i(A_1, \ldots, A_n)$ *occurs in* RS *and neither:*
   - $X \in F$, *nor*
   - $X \notin s_i(\_, \ldots, \_)$ *occurs in* S_-, *nor*
   - $X \in s_i(A'_1, \ldots, A'_n)$ *occurs in* S_+;

For the rest of this paper, we consider only admissible rules.

Also we define the distinguished semantics *as the following restriction of the* $\Rightarrow$ *relation:* $S \Rightarrow^\sigma_r S'$ *additionally requires that* $\sigma(X) \neq \sigma(Y)$ *for any distinct variables* $X, Y \in \mathcal{V}_{\mathfrak{A}}$.   □

Condition (1) is in fact completely fine in a specification and it only causes problems in the abstraction approach later (since set conditions are removed from the rules and put into the abstraction of the data). To "rule out" such an occurrence without bothering the modeler, the AIF-ω compiler simply introduces a new fact symbol $occurs/1$ and adds $occurs(X)$ on the left-hand and right-hand side of every rule for every $X \in \mathcal{V}_{\mathfrak{A}}$ of the rule. (In the running example, the rule $userUpdateKey$ has $iknows(PK)$ on the left-hand side, simply because without it, it would satisfy condition (1); since in this example the intruder knows all public keys, this is the easiest way to ensure admissibility without introducing *occurs.*)

Condition (2) means that the rule is simply never applicable. The compiler refuses it as this is a clear specification error.

An example for condition (3) is the rule: $r(\ldots) = X \in s_1(A) \cdot X \in s_1(B) \Rightarrow \ldots$ Recall that our uniqueness invariant forbids two distinct sets of the same family (like s_1 here) to have an element in common. So this rule cannot be applicable in any state that satisfies the invariant unless $\sigma(A) = \sigma(B)$. As this may be a specification error, the compiler also refuses this with the suggestion to unify A and B. Similarly, condition (4) forbids the same situation on the right-hand side, as for $\sigma(A) \neq \sigma(B)$ the invariant would be violated. Also in this case, the compiler refuses the rule with the suggestion to unify A and B.

An example of a rule that is inadmissible by condition (5) is the following:

$$r(X\colon \textit{Value}) = p(X) \implies X \in s_1(a)$$

The problem here is that we insert X into $s_1(a)$ without checking if possibly X is already member of another set of the s_1 family. Suppose for instance the state $S = \{p(c), c \in s_1(b)\}$ is reachable, then r is applicable and produces state $S = \{p(c), c \in s_1(a), c \in s_1(b)\}$ violating the invariant that the sets belonging to the same family are pairwise disjoint. However, note that r is only *potentially* problematic: it depends on whether we can reach a state in which both $p(c)$ and $c \in s_1(\ldots)$ holds for some constant $c \in \mathfrak{A}$, otherwise r is fine.

The AIF-ω compiler indeed allows for such inadmissible rules that potentially violate the invariant, but transforms them into the following two admissible rules:

$$r_1(X\colon \textit{Value}) = p(X) \cdot X \notin s_1(\_) \implies X \in s_1(a)$$
$$r_2(X\colon \textit{Value}, A\colon T) = p(X) \cdot X \in s_1(A) \implies \textit{attack}$$

where T is the appropriate type for the parameter of s_1. Thus, we have turned this into one rule for the "safe" case (r_1) where X is not previously in any set of s_1, and one for the "unsafe" case (r_2) where X is already in s_1 and applying the original rule r would lead to a violation of the invariant (unless $\sigma(A) = a$);[2] in this case we directly raise the attack flag. Note that neither r_1 nor r_2 still have the problem of condition (5). The compiler simply performs such case splits until no rule has the problem of condition (5) anymore. We thus allow the user to specify rules that would potentially violate the invariant, but make it part of the analysis that no reachable state actually violates it.

Finally, consider the restriction to a distinguished semantics of Definition 3. Here is an example why the standard semantics of Definition 2 can make things very tricky:

$$r(\ldots) = p(X, Y) \cdot X \in s_1(a) \cdot Y \in s_1(a) \to X \in s_1(a)$$

---

[2] In fact, we are here over-careful as the case $\sigma(A) = a$ in the second rule would still be fine; but a precise solution in general would require inequalities—which we leave for future work.

Suppose the state $S = \{p(c,c) \cdot c \in s_1(a)\}$ is reachable, then the rule clearly is applicable in S (with $\sigma(X) = \sigma(Y) = c$), but the rule tells us that Y should be removed from $s_1(a)$ while X stays in there. (Here, the semantics tells us that the positive $X \in s_1(a)$ "wins", and the successor state is also S.) However, it would be quite difficult to handle such cases in the abstraction and it would further complicate the already complex set of conditions of Definition 3.

Therefore we like to work in the following with the distinguished semantics of Definition 3, where the instantiation $\sigma(X) = \sigma(Y)$ in the above example is simply excluded. To make this possible without imposing the restriction on the modeler, the AIF-ω compiler applies the following transformation step. We check in every rule for every pair of variables $X, Y \in \mathcal{V}_{\mathfrak{A}}$ whether $\sigma(X) = \sigma(Y)$ is possible, i.e. neither X nor Y is in the fresh variables, and left-hand side memberships of X and Y do not contradict each other. (Observe that in none of the rules of the running example, such a unification of two $\mathcal{V}_{\mathfrak{A}}$ variables is possible.) If the rule does not prevent $X = Y$, the AIF-ω compiler generates a variant of the rule where Y is replaced by X. Thus, we do not loose the case $X = Y$ even when interpreting the rules in the distinguished semantics.

As a fruit of all this restriction we can prove that admissible rules cannot produce a reachable state that violates the invariant:

Lemma 1. *Considering only admissible rules in the distinguished semantics. Then there is no reachable state S and constant $c \in \mathfrak{A}$ such that S contains both $c \in s_i(a_1, \ldots, a_n)$ and $c \in s_i(a_1', \ldots, a_n')$ for any $(a_1, \ldots, a_n) \neq (a_1', \ldots, a_n')$.*

Proof. By induction over reachability. The property trivially holds for the initial state. Suppose S is a reachable state with the property, and $S \Rightarrow_r^\sigma S'$. Suppose S' contains both $c \in s_i(a_1, \ldots, a_n)$ and $c \in s_i(a_1', \ldots, a_n')$. Since S enjoys the property, at least one of the two set conditions has been introduced by the transition. Thus there is a value variable X in r and $\sigma(X) = c$, and $X \in s_i(A_1, \ldots, A_n)$ is in RS and either $\sigma(A_j) = a_j$ or $\sigma(A_j) = a_j'$, so without loss of generality, assume $\sigma(A_j) = a_j$. By excluding (4) of Definition 3, RS cannot contain another set condition $X \in s_i(A_1', \ldots, A_n')$ (such that $\sigma(A_j') = a_j'$), so $c \in s_i(a_1', \ldots, a_n')$ must have been present in S already. By excluding (5), we have however either of the following cases:

- $X \notin s_i(\_)$ is in S_-, but that clearly contradicts the fact that $\sigma(X) \in s_i(a_1', \ldots, a_n')$ is in S.
- $X \in s_i(B_1, \ldots, B_n)$ is in S_+, and by excluding (3) and (2) this is the only positive or negative condition for X on the s_i family. This means that only $\sigma(B_j) = a_j'$ is possible, so $c \in s_i(a_1', \ldots, a_n')$ actually gets removed from the state upon transition, and is no longer present in S'.
- $X \in F$, but that is also absurd since then $\sigma(X)$ cannot occur in S.

So in all cases, we get to a contradiction, so we cannot have c being a member of two sets of the s_i family.   □

3   Abstraction

We now define a translation from AIF-ω rules to Horn clauses augmented with a special kind of rules, called term implication. (We show in a second step how to encode these term implication rules into Horn clauses, to keep the approach easier to grasp and to work with.) The basic idea is that we abstract the constants of $\mathfrak{A}$ into equivalence classes that are easier to work with. In fact, in the classic AIF, we had finitely many equivalence classes, but in AIF-ω we have a countable number of equivalence classes, due to the countable families of sets.

The abstraction of a constant $c \in \mathfrak{A}$ for a state S shall be $(e_1, \ldots, e_N)$ where e_i represents the set membership for the family s_i: either $e_i = 0$ if c belongs to no member of s_i or $e_i = s_i(a_1, \ldots, a_n)$ if e_i belongs to set $s_i(a_1, \ldots, a_n)$ in S. For instance in a state with set conditions

$$\{c_1 \in db(a, s, revoked), c_2 \in db(b, s, valid), c_2 \in ring(b)\}$$

the abstraction of c_1 is $(0, db(a, s, revoked))$ and similarly the abstraction of c_2 is $(ring(b), db(b, s, valid))$. Thus, we do not distinguish concrete constants in the abstraction whenever they have the same set memberships.

The second main idea (as in other Horn-clause based approaches) is to formulate Horn clauses that entail all facts (under the abstraction) that hold in any reachable state. This is like merging all states together into a single big state.

3.1   Translation of the Rules

We first define how admissible AIF-ω rules are translated into Horn clauses and then show in the next section that this is a sound over-approximation (in the distinguished semantics).

Definition 4. *For the translation, we use the same symbols as declared by the user in AIF-ω plus the following:*

- *new untyped variables $E_{i,X}$ for $X \in \mathcal{V}_{\mathfrak{A}}$ and $1 \leq i \leq N$.*
- *a new function symbol val/N (where N is the number of families of sets)*
- *new fact symbols isT_i/1 for every user-defined type T_i,*
- *and finally the infix fact symbol $\twoheadrightarrow$ /2.*

For an admissible AIF-ω rule

$$r(X_1 : T_1, \ldots, X_m : T_m) = LF \cdot S_+ \cdot S_- =\!\![F]\!\!\Rightarrow RF \cdot RS$$

define its translation into a Horn clause $[\![r]\!]$ as follows.

$$L_i(X) = \begin{cases} s_i(A_1, \ldots, A_n) & \text{if } X \in s_i(A_1, \ldots, A_n) \text{ occurs in } S_+ \\ 0 & \text{if } X \notin s_i(\_) \text{ occurs in } S_- \\ E_{i,X} & \text{otherwise} \end{cases}$$

$$R_i(X) = \begin{cases} s_i(A_1, \ldots, A_n) & \text{if } X \in s_i(A_1, \ldots, A_n) \text{ occurs in } RS \\ E_{i,X} & \text{otherwise, if } L_i(X) = E_{i,X} \text{ and } t \notin F \\ 0 & \text{otherwise} \end{cases}$$

$$L(X) = (L_1(X), \ldots, L_N(X))$$
$$R(X) = (R_1(X), \ldots, R_N(X))$$
$$\lambda = [X \mapsto val(L(X)) \mid X \in \mathcal{V}_\mathfrak{A}]$$
$$\rho = [X \mapsto val(R(X)) \mid X \in \mathcal{V}_\mathfrak{A}]$$
$$C = \{\lambda(X) \twoheadrightarrow \rho(X) \mid X \in \mathcal{V}_\mathfrak{A} \setminus F, \text{ and } \lambda(X) \neq \rho(X)\}$$
$$Types = \{isT_i(X_i) \mid T_i \text{ is a user defined type}\}$$
$$[\![r]\!] = Types \cdot \lambda(LF) \to \rho(RF) \cdot C$$

where $\to$ is the "normal implication" in Horn clauses. We keep the set operator $\cdot$ from AIF-ω in our notation, denoting in Horn clauses simply conjunction. Finally, note that our Horn clauses have in general more than one fact as conclusion, but this is of course also just syntactic sugar.

We give the translation for the behavior of the honest agents in the running example (other rules are similar and shown in the appendix for completeness).

$[\![keyReg]\!] = isUser(A) \cdot isServer(S) \to iknows(val(ring(A), db(S, A, valid)))$
$[\![userUpdateKey]\!] = isHonest(A) \cdot isServer(S) \cdot iknows(val(ring(A), E_{db,PK}))$
$\quad \to iknows(sign(inv(val(0, E_{db,PK})), pair(A, val(ring(A), 0)))) \cdot$
$\quad (val(ring(A), E_{db,PK}) \twoheadrightarrow val(0, E_{db,PK}))$
$[\![serverUpdateKey]\!] = isUser(A) \cdot isServer(S) \cdot$
$\quad iknows(sign(inv(val(E_{ring,PK}, db(S, A, valid))), pair(A, val(E_{ring,NPK}, 0)))) $
$\quad \to iknows(inv(val(E_{ring,PK}, db(S, A, revoked)))) \cdot$
$\quad (val(E_{ring,PK}, db(S, A, valid)) \twoheadrightarrow val(E_{ring,PK}, db(S, A, revoked))) \cdot$
$\quad (val(E_{ring,NPK}, 0) \twoheadrightarrow val(E_{ring,NPK}, db(S, A, valid)))$

First note that all right-hand side variables of the Horn clauses also occur on the left-hand side; this is in fact the reason to introduce the typing facts like *isUser*. In fact, the variables of each Horn clause are implicitly universally quantified (e.g. in ProVerif) and we explicitly add these quantifiers when translating to SPASS. Thus, $[\![keyReg]\!]$ expresses that the intruder knows all those values (public keys) that are in the key ring of a user A and registered as valid for A at server S.

For the $[\![userUpdateKey]\!]$ rule, let us first look at the abstraction of the involved keys PK and NPK. We have $L(PK) = (ring(A), E_{db,PK})$ (we write the family name *db* rather than its index for readability) and $R(PK) = (0, E_{db,PK})$. This reflects that the rule operates on any key in the key ring of an honest agent A, where the variable $E_{db,PK}$ then is a placeholder for what status the key has in the database. The fact that in the original transition system, the key PK gets removed from the key ring when applying this rule, is reflected by the 0 component in the right-hand side abstraction: this is any key that is not in the key-ring but has the same status for *db* as on the left-hand side. Actually, in the key update message that the agent produces for the signing key $inv(PK)$ it holds that PK is no longer in the key ring. The Horn clause reflects that: for every value in the ring of an honest user, the intruder gets the key update message with the same key removed from the key ring (but with the same membership in db). Finally, the $\twoheadrightarrow$ fact here intuitively expresses that everything that is true about an abstract value $val(ring(A), E_{db,PK})$ is also true about $val(0, E_{db,PK})$. We formally define this special meaning of $\twoheadrightarrow$ below.

3.2 Fixedpoint Definition

We define the fixedpoint for the Horn clauses in a standard way, where we give a special meaning to the $s \twoheadrightarrow t$ facts: for every fact $C[s]$ that the fixedpoint contains, also $C[t]$ must be contained. We see later how to encode this (and the typing facts) for existing tools like ProVerif and SPASS.

Definition 5. *Let*

- *Types* $= \{isT_i(c) \mid c \in [\![T_i]\!]$ *for every user-defined type* $T_i\}$.
- *For a set of ground facts* Γ, *let* $Timplies(\Gamma) = \{C[t] \mid s \twoheadrightarrow t \in \Gamma \wedge C[s] \in \Gamma\}$ *where* $C[\cdot]$ *is a context, i.e. a "term with a hole", and* $C[t]$ *means filling the hole with term* t.
- *For any Horn clause* $r = A_1 \ldots A_n \rightarrow C_1 \ldots C_m$, *define* $Apply(r)(\Gamma) = \{\sigma(C_i) \mid \sigma(A_1) \in \Gamma, \ldots, \sigma(A_n) \in \Gamma, 1 \le i \le m\}$.

For a set of Horn clauses R, *we define the least fixed-point* $LFP(R)$ *as the least closed set* Γ *that contains Types and is closed under Timplies and Apply(r) for each* $r \in R$.

For our running example we can describe the "essential" fixedpoint as follows, for every $A \in [\![Honest]\!]$, $D \in [\![Dishon]\!]$ and $S \in [\![Server]\!]$:

$$val(ring(A), 0) \twoheadrightarrow val(ring(A), db(S, A, valid))$$
$$val(ring(A), 0) \twoheadrightarrow val(0, 0)$$
$$val(ring(A), db(S, A, valid)) \twoheadrightarrow val(0, db(S, A, valid))$$
$$val(0, 0) \twoheadrightarrow val(0, db(S, A, valid))$$
$$val(0, db(S, A, valid)) \twoheadrightarrow val(0, db(S, A, revoked))$$
$$val(ring(D), 0) \twoheadrightarrow val(ring(D), db(S, D, valid))$$
$$val(ring(D), db(S, D, valid)) \twoheadrightarrow val(ring(D), db(S, D, revoked))$$
$$iknows(val(ring(A), 0))$$
$$iknows(sign(inv(val(0, 0)), pair(A, val(ring(A), 0))))$$
$$iknows(inv(0, db(S, A, revoked)))$$
$$iknows(val(ring(D), 0)) iknows(inv(val(ring(D), 0)))$$

Here, we have omitted the type facts, "boring" intruder deductions, and consequences of $\twoheadrightarrow$ (i.e., when $C[s]$ and $s \twoheadrightarrow t$ omit $C[t]$). Note that the $\twoheadrightarrow$ facts reflect the "life cycle" of the keys.

4 Soundness

We now show that the fixedpoint of Definition 5 represents a sound over-approximation of the transition system defined by an AIF-ω specification: if an attack state is reachable in the transition system, then the fixedpoint will contain the fact *attack*. The inverse is in general not true, i.e., we may have *attack* in the fixedpoint while the transition system has no attack state. However, soundness thus gives us the guarantee that the system is correct, if the fixedpoint does not contain *attack*. To show soundness we take several steps:

- We first annotate in the transition system in every state all occurring constants $c \in \mathfrak{A}$ with the equivalence class that they shall be abstracted to.
- We then give a variant of the rules that correctly handles these labels.
- We can then eliminate all set conditions $s \in \ldots$ and $s \notin \ldots$ from the transition rules and states, since this information is also present in the labels.
- Finally, we show for any fact that occurs in a reachable state, the fixedpoint contains its abstraction (i.e., replacing any labeled concrete constant with just its label).

Note that the first three steps are isomorphic transformations of the state transition system, i.e., we maintain the same set of reachable states only in a different representation.

4.1 The Labeled Concrete Model

The basic idea of our abstraction is that every constant $c \in \mathfrak{A}$ shall be abstracted by what sets it belongs to, i.e., two constants that belong to exactly the same sets will be identified in the abstraction. The first step is that in every reachable state S, we shall label every occurring constant $c \in \mathfrak{A}$ with this equivalence class. Note that upon state transitions, the equivalence class of a constant can change, since its set memberships can.

Definition 6. *Given a state S and a constant $c \in \mathfrak{A}$ that occurs in S. Then the N-tuple $(e_1, \ldots, e_N)$ is called the* correct label *of c in S if for every $1 \le i \le N$ either*

- $e_i = 0$ *and $c \in s_i(a_1, \ldots, a_n)$ does not occur in S for any $a_1, \ldots, a_n$, or*
- $e_i = s_i(a_1, \ldots, a_n)$ *and $c \in s_i(a_1, \ldots, a_n)$ occurs in S and $c \in s_i(a'_1, \ldots, a'_n)$ does not occur in S for any $(a'_1, \ldots, a'_n) \ne (a_1, \ldots, a_n)$.*

We write $c@l$ for constant c annotated with label l.

Note that, at this point, the label is merely an annotation and it can be applied correctly to every constant $c \in \mathfrak{A}$ in every reachable state S, because by Lemma 1, c can never be in more than one set of the same family, i.e., $c \in s_i(a_1, \ldots, a_n)$ and $c \in s_i(a'_1, \ldots, a'_N)$ cannot occur in the same state S.

4.2   Labeled Transition Rules

While, in the previous definition, the labels are just an annotation that decorate each state, we now show that we can actually modify the transition rules so that they "generate" the labels on the right-hand side, and "pattern match" existing labels on the left-hand side.

Definition 7. *Given an AIF-ω rule r we define the corresponding labeled rule r' as the following modification of r:*

- *Every variable $X \in \mathcal{V}_{\mathfrak{A}}$ on the left-hand side is labeled with $L(X)$ and every variable $X \in \mathcal{V}_{\mathfrak{A}}$ on the right-hand side (including the fresh variables) is labeled with $R(X)$.*
- *All variables $E_{i,X}$ that occur in $L(X)$ and $R(X)$ are added to the rule parameters of r'.*
- *For each variable $X \in \mathcal{V}_{\mathfrak{A}}$ that occurs both on the left-hand side and the right-hand side and where $L(X) \neq R(X)$, we augment r' with the label modification $X@L(X) \mapsto X@R(X)$.*

The semantics of r' is defined as follows. First, the labeling symbol @ is not treated as a mere annotation anymore, but as a binary function symbol (so labels are treated as a regular part of terms, including variable matching on the left-hand side). To define the semantics of the label modifications, consider a rule

$$r' = r'_0 \cdot (X_1@l_1 \mapsto X_1@r_1) \cdot \ldots \cdot (X_n@l_n \mapsto X_n@r_n)$$

where r'_0 is the basis of r' that does not contain label modifications. We define $S \Rightarrow^{\sigma}_{r'} S'$ iff $S \Rightarrow^{\sigma}_{r'_0} S'_0$ and S' is obtained from S'_0 by replacing every occurrence of $\sigma(X_i@l_i)$ with $\sigma(X_i@r_i)$ for $i = 1, 2, \ldots, n$ (in this order).

Note that the order $i = 1, 2, \ldots, n$ does not matter: the distinguished semantics requires that all distinct variables $X, X' \in \mathcal{V}_{\mathfrak{A}}$ have $\sigma(X) \neq \sigma(X')$ and therefore the label replacements are on disjoint value-label pairs.

As an example, the second rule of our running example looks as follows in the labeled model:

$userUpdateKey'(A\colon Honest, S\colon Server, PK\colon Value, NPK\colon Value) =$
$\quad PK@(ring(A), E_{db,X}) \in ring(A) \cdot iknows(PK@(ring(A), E_{db,X}))$
$\quad =\!\![NPK@(ring(A), 0)] \Rightarrow NPK@(ring(A), 0) \in ring(A) \cdot$
$\quad iknows(sign(inv(PK@(0, E_{db,X})), pair(A, NPK@(ring(A), 0)))) \cdot$
$\quad (PK@(ring(A), E_{db,X}) \mapsto PK@(0, E_{db,X}));$

Lemma 2. *Given a set R of AIF-ω rules, and let R' be the corresponding labeled rules. Then R' induces the same state space as R except that all states are correctly labeled.*

Proof. This requires two induction proofs, one showing that every R-reachable state has its R'-reachable correspondent. The other direction, that every R'-reachable state has an R-reachable correspondent is similar and actually not necessary for the overall soundness, so we omit it here.

For the initial state $\emptyset$, the statement is immediate. Suppose now S_1 is an R-reachable state, S_1' is an R'-reachable state where S_1' is like S_1 but correctly labeled. Suppose further $S_1 \Rightarrow_r^\sigma S_2$ for some $r \in R$, some substitution σ, and some successor state S_2. We show that the corresponding rule $r' \in R'$ allows for a transition $S_1 \Rightarrow_{r'}^{\sigma'\tau} S_2'$ where S_2' is the correctly labeled version of S_2 and some substitutions σ' and τ.

The substitution σ' here is an adaption of σ, because untyped variables are substituted for terms that can contain constants from $\mathfrak{A}$ that are labeled in S_1' but unlabeled in S_1. In fact, this label may even change upon transition, in this case, σ' contains the label of S_1'. Thus, σ and σ' only differ on untyped variables.

The substitution τ is for all variables $E_{i,X}$ that occur in the label variables of r'. We show the statement for the following choice of τ: for each label variable $E_{i,X}$ that occurs in r' (where by construction $X \in \mathcal{V}_\mathfrak{A}$ is a variable that occurs in r' and $1 \leq i \leq N$), we set $\tau(E_{i,X}) = e_i(X)$ if $e(X) = (e_1(X), \ldots, e_N(X))$ is the correct label of $\sigma(X)$ in S_1. Note that τ is a grounding substitution and does not interfere with σ or σ'.

To prove that $S_1 \Rightarrow_{r'}^{\sigma'\tau} S_2'$, we first consider the matching of r on S_1 and r' on S_1'. We have to show that despite the additional labels, essentially the same match is still possible. Consider thus any variable $X \in \mathcal{V}_\mathfrak{A}$ that occurs on the left-hand side of r and thus $X@L(X)$ occurs correspondingly on the left-hand side of r'. We have to show that the correct label for $\sigma(X)$ in S_1 is indeed $\sigma(\tau(L(X)))$. For $1 \leq i \leq N$, we distinguish three cases:

- $L_i(X) = s_i(A_1, \ldots, A_n)$, then S_+ of r contains the positive set condition $X \in s_i(A_1, \ldots, A_n)$ and thus $\sigma(X \in s_i(A_1, \ldots, A_n))$ occurs in S_1. Thus $\sigma(\tau(L_i(X))) = \sigma(s_i(A_1, \ldots, A_n))$ is the i-th part of the correct label of $\sigma(X)$.
- $L_i(X) = 0$, then S_- of r contains the negative set condition $X \notin s_i(\_)$ and thus $\sigma(X) \in s_i(a_1, \ldots, a_n)$ does not occur in S_1 for any a_i. Thus $\sigma(\tau(L_i(X))) = 0$ is the i-th part of the correct label of $\sigma(X)$.
- $L_i(X) = E_{i,X}$. In this case the rule neither requires nor forbids X to be member of some set of family s_i. Since $\tau(E_{i,X}) = e_i(X)$ where $e_i(X)$ is i-th component of the correct label for $\sigma(X)$, we have that $\sigma(\tau(L_i(X))) = e_i(X)$ is the i-th component of the correct label for $\sigma(X)$.

Thus in all cases, $\sigma(\tau(L(X))$ is the correct label for $\sigma(X)$ in S_1. Since S_1' is correctly labeled, all occurrences of $\sigma(X)$ in S_1' are labeled $\sigma(\tau(L(X)))$, and thus the rule r' is applicable to S_1' under $\sigma'\tau$ (where σ' adapts to labels in the substitution of untyped variables). It remains to show that under this match we obtain the desired successor state S_2'.

To that end, we first show that for any variable $X \in \mathfrak{A}$ that occurs in the right-hand side of r, $\sigma(\tau(R(X))$ is the correct label for $\sigma(X)$ in S_2. For $1 \leq i \leq N$, we distinguish three cases:

- $R_i(X) = s_1(A_1, \ldots, A_n)$. Then $X \in s_i(A_1, \ldots, A_n)$ occurs in RS of r and thus $\sigma(X \in s_i(A_1, \ldots, A_n))$ is in S_2. Thus $\sigma(\tau(R_i(X))) = \sigma(s_i(A_1, \ldots, A_n))$ is the i-th component of the correct label for $\sigma(X)$ in S_2.

- $R_i(X) = 0$. Then either $X \in s_i(\ldots)$ occurs in S_+ or $X \in s_i(\_)$ occurs in S_-, or X is a fresh variable, and but $X \in s_i(\ldots)$ does not occur in RS, so $\sigma(X \in s_i(a_1, \ldots, a_n))$ is not contained in S_2 for any a_j, and therefore $\sigma(\tau(R_i(X))) = 0$ is the i-th component of the correct label for $\sigma(X)$ in S_2.
- $R_i(X) = E_{i,X}$. Then the set membership of X with respect to family s_i does not change on the transition, and $\sigma(\tau(R_i(X))) = e_i(X)$ is the correct label for $\sigma(X)$ also in S_2.

Thus in all cases, $\sigma(\tau(R(X)))$ is the correct label for $\sigma(X)$ in S_2. Finally, the label replacements of r' ensure that for all $c@l$ that occur in S_1' and where the label of c has changed upon transition to S_2' to label l' will be updated. Thus S_2' is the correctly labeled version of S_2. $\square$

4.3   Labeled Concrete Model Without Set Conditions

Since every label correctly represents the set memberships of the involved constants, we can just do without set membership facts, i.e., remove from the labeled rules the S_+, S_- and RS part. We obtain states that do not contain any $s \in s_i(\cdot)$ conditions anymore, but only handle this information in the labels of the constants. It is immediate from Lemma 2 that this changes the model only in terms of representation:

Lemma 3. *The labeled model without set conditions has the same reachable states as the labeled model, except that states have no more explicit set conditions.*

4.4   Reachable Abstract Facts

All the previous steps were only changing the representation of the model, but besides that the models are all equivalent. Now we finally come to the actual abstraction step that transforms the model into an abstract over-approximation.

We define a representation function η that maps terms and facts of the concrete model to ones of the abstract model:

Definition 8.

$$\eta(t@(e_1, \ldots, e_N)) = val(e_1, \ldots, e_N) \; for \; t \in \mathfrak{A} \cup \mathcal{V}_{\mathfrak{A}}$$
$$\eta(f(t_1, \ldots, t_n)) = f(\eta(t_1), \ldots, \eta(t_n))$$
$$for \; any \; function \; or \; fact \; symbol \; f \; of \; arity \; n$$

We show that the abstract rules allow for the derivation of the abstract representation of every reachable fact f of the concrete model:

Lemma 4. *For an AIF-ω rule set R, let R' be the corresponding rule set in the labeled model without, f be a fact in a reachable state of R' (i.e. $\emptyset \to_{R'}^* S$ and $f \in S$ for some S). Let $[\![R]\!]$ be the translation into Horn clauses of the rules R according to Definition 4, and $\Gamma = LFP([\![R]\!])$. Then $\eta(f) \in \Gamma$.*

This lemma is simply adapting the corresponding result for AIF [10], which we omit due to the lack of space. From Lemmas 2, 3 and 4 immediately follows that the over-approximation is sound:

Theorem 1. *Given an AIF-ω specification with rules R. If an attack state is reachable with R, then attack ∈ LFP([[R]]).*

5   Encoding in SPASS and ProVerif

We now want to use SPASS and ProVerif for checking the property *attack* ∈ *LFP*([[R]]). Three aspects in our definition of *LFP* need special considerations.

First, SPASS is a theorem prover for standard first-order logic FOL (and the Horn clause resolution in ProVerif is very similar, but more geared towards protocol verification). The problem here is that the Horn clauses [[R]] always have the trivial model where the interpretation of all facts is set simply to true, and in this model, *attack* holds. We are interested in the "least" model and terms to be interpreted in the Herbrand universe, i.e., the free term algebra $\mathcal{T}_\Sigma$. The common "Herbrand trick" is to try to prove the FOL formula [[R]] $\Longrightarrow$ *attack*, i.e., that in *every* model of the Horn clauses, *attack* is true. If that is valid, then also in the least Herbrand model, *attack* is true. Vice-versa, if the formula is not valid, then there are some models in which *attack* does not hold, and then also in the least Herbrand model. This trick is also part of the setup of ProVerif.

The second difficulty is the encoding of the user-defined types. For instance, the declaration $A = \{\ldots\}$ leads to the extension $[\![A]\!] = \{a_n \mid n \in \mathbb{N}\}$ for some new constant symbols a_n, and then by definition, *LFP*([[R]]) contains the infinite set $\{isA(a_n) \mid n \in \mathbb{N}\}$. We could encode this by Horn clauses

$$isA(mkA(0)) \quad \wedge \quad \forall X.isA(mkA(X)) \rightarrow isA(mkA(s(X)))$$

for new function symbols *mkA* and *s*. Note that this encoding only makes sense in the least Herbrand model (standard FOL allows to interpret *s* as the identity). However, it easily leads to non-termination in tools. A version that works however, is simply saying $\forall X.isA(mkA(X))$. Interpreting this in the least Herbrand model, *X* can be instantiated with any term from $\mathcal{T}_\Sigma$ (which is countable).

The third and final difficulty are the ↠ facts that have a special meaning in *LFP*([[R]]): whenever both $C[s]$ and $s ↠ t$ in *LFP*([[R]]) then also $C[t]$ (for any context $C[\cdot]$). We can encode this into Horn clauses because we can soundly limit the set of contexts $C[\cdot]$ that need to be considered: it is sufficient to consider right-hand side facts of rules in *R* in which a variable $X \in \mathcal{V}_\mathfrak{A}$ occurs (note that a fact may have more than one such occurrence). Define thus the finite set $Con = \{C[\cdot] \mid C[X] \text{ is a RHS fact in } R, X \in \mathcal{V}_\mathfrak{A}\}$. We generate the additional Horn clauses: $\{\forall X, Y.C[X] \wedge (X ↠ Y) \rightarrow C[Y] \mid C[\cdot] \in Con\}$.

Lemma 5. *The encoding of ↠ into Horn clauses is correct.*

Proof. Suppose $C[s]$ and $s ↠ t$ are in the fixedpoint. Then $C[s]$ is the consequence of some Horn clause $A \rightarrow B$, i.e., $C[s] = \sigma(B)$ such that $\sigma(A)$ is part of the fixedpoint. We distinguish two cases. First $B = C'[X]$ for some $X \in \mathcal{V}_\mathfrak{A}$, some context $C'[\cdot]$ and $\sigma(C'[\cdot]) = C[\cdot]$, i.e., $s = \sigma(X)$ is directly the instance of a $\mathcal{V}_\mathfrak{A}$ variable, and thus our Horn clause encoding covers $C[\cdot]$. Second, the only other possibility for $\sigma(B) = C[s]$ is that B contains an untyped variable that matches s or a super-term of it in $C[s]$. By the rule shape, this untyped variable is also part of the assumptions A. Since $\sigma(A)$ is already in the fixedpoint, we can by an inductive argument conclude that for every $C_0[s]$ of $\sigma(A)$ also $C_0[t]$ is in the fixedpoint. In both cases, we conclude that $C[t]$ is derivable.   □

5.1   Experimental Results

Table 1 compares the run times of our key-server example for AIF and AIF-ω, taken on a 2.66 GHz Core 2 Duo, 8 GB of RAM. In AIF we have to specify a fixed number of honest and dishonest users and servers, while in AIF-ω we can have an unbounded set for each of them (denoted ω in the Figure). Observe that in AIF the run times "explode" when increasing the number of agents. It is clear why this happens when looking at an example: when we specify the sets $ring(User)$ in AIF, $User$ needs to be a finite set (the honest and dishonest users) and this gets first translated into n different sets when we specify n users. Since these sets are by construction all disjoint, we can specify in AIF-ω instead $ring(User!)$ turning the n sets of the AIF abstraction into a single family of sets in the AIF-ω abstraction—and then allowing even for a countably infinite set $User$. Observe that the run times for AIF-ω for infinitely many agents are indeed very close to the ones of AIF with one agent. Thus, even when dealing with finitely many agents, AIF-ω allows for a substantial improvement of performance whenever we can exploit the uniqueness, i.e., can specify $set(Type!)$ instead of $set(Type)$.

Table 1. AIF vs. AIF-ω on the key-server example.

	Number of Agents			Backend	
	Honest	Dishon	Server	ProVerif	SPASS
AIF	1	1	1	0.025 s	0.891 s
	2	1	1	0.135 s	324.696 s
	2	2	1	0.418 s	Timeout
	3	3	1	2.057 s	Timeout
AIF-ω	ω	ω	ω	0.034 s	0.941 s

The key server is in fact our simplest example, a kind of "NSPK" of stateful protocols. We updated our suite of case studies for AIF to benefit in the same way from the AIF-ω extension [3]. These include the ASW protocol (one of the original motivations for developing AIF and also for extending it to AIF-ω), an in-depth analysis of the Secure Vehicle Communication protocols SEVECOM [11], and a model of and analysis of PKCS#11 tokens [9] that replicates the attacks reported in [6] and verifies the proposed fixes.

6   Conclusions

In this paper we introduced the language AIF-ω and showed how it can be used to model cryptographic systems with unbounded numbers of agents and databases pertaining to these agents. AIF-ω extends our previous language AIF by introducing types with countably infinite constants and allowing families of sets to range over such types. The only requirement to this extension is that the sets of all infinite families are kept pairwise disjoint.

We defined the semantics of this extension and proposed an analysis technique that translates AIF-ω models into Horn clauses, which are then solved by standard off-the-shelf resolution-based theorem provers. We proved that our analysis is sound w.r.t. the transition system defined by the semantics: if an attack is reachable, then it is also derivable in the Horn clause model.

Finally, the experimental results show that the clauses produced by AIF-ω, for the protocol with unbounded agents, can be solved in running times similar to their AIF counterparts for just one agent of each type, both in ProVerif and SPASS. In contrast, adding agents to the bounded AIF model produces an exponential increase in running times.

To our knowledge, this is the first work that proposes a fully automated technique for analyzing stateful cryptographic protocols with unbounded agents. This work is a direct extension of our previous work on AIF [10], which allows to model infinite transition systems with bounded agents. Its relation with AIF-ω has been extensively described throughout this paper. Another work that uses the set-abstraction is our work on Set-π [4], which extends the Applied π-calculus by similarly introducing a notion of a fixed number of sets. Set-π presents a modeling interface that is more familiar to the user, and the process-calculus specification exposes a great deal of details (e.g. locking, replications) that are abstracted away by the AIF rules. This reduces the gap to the system implementation, but as a modeling language Set-π has essentially the same expressive power of AIF. We believe that a similar extension can be devised for our process algebraic interface, possibly using AIF-ω as an intermediate representation.

Another related work is StatVerif [1], which extends the Applied π-calculus with global cells that can be accessed and modified by the processes. As the number of cells is finite and fixed for a model, the amount of state that one can finitely represent is limited. However, the particular encoding of StatVerif is more precise in capturing state transitions synchronized over multiple cells. We claim that the two approaches are orthogonal, and we have not succeeded so far in combining the advantages of both with an encoding into Horn clauses.

The Tamarin prover [8] and its process calculus interface SAPIC [7] use multiset rewriting rules to describe cryptographic protocols, and a semi-automated search procedure to find a solution for the models. This formalism is very expressive and allows to prove security properties in stateful protocols with unbounded agents, but expressiveness comes at the price of usability, as the search procedure needs to be guided by introducing lemmas in the models.

Finally, we believe that bounded-agents results like [5] can be also derived for AIF-ω, since the resolution will never run into distinguishing single agents.

The experimental results, however, suggest that for our verification it is more efficient to avoid the enumeration of concrete agents where possible.

The authors would like to thank Luca Viganò for the helpful comments.

References

1. Arapinis, M., Phillips, J., Ritter, E., Ryan, M.D.: Statverif: verification of stateful processes. J. Comput. Secur. **22**(5), 743–821 (2014)
2. Blanchet, B.: An efficient cryptographic protocol verifier based on prolog rules. In: Computer Security Foundations Workshop (2001)
3. Bruni, A., Modersheim, S.: The AIF-ω Compiler and Examples. http://www. compute.dtu.dk/~samo/aifom.html
4. Bruni, A., Mödersheim, S., Nielson, F., Nielson, H.R.: Set-pi: set membership p-calculus. In: IEEE 28th Computer Security Foundations Symposium, CSF 2015 (2015)
5. Comon-Lundh, H., Cortier, V.: Security properties: two agents are sufficient. Sci. Comput. Program. **50**(1–3), 51–71 (2004)
6. Fröschle, S., Steel, G.: Analysing PKCS#11 key management apis with unbounded fresh data. In: Degano, P., Viganò, L. (eds.) ARSPA-WITS 2009. LNCS, vol. 5511, pp. 92–106. Springer, Heidelberg (2009)
7. Kremer, S., Künnemann, R.: Automated analysis of security protocols with global state. In: Security and Privacy (2014)
8. Meier, S., Schmidt, B., Cremers, C., Basin, D.: The TAMARIN prover for the symbolic analysis of security protocols. In: Sharygina, N., Veith, H. (eds.) CAV 2013. LNCS, vol. 8044, pp. 696–701. Springer, Heidelberg (2013)
9. Ye, M.: Design and analysis of PKCS#11 key management with AIF. Master's thesis, DTU Compute (2014). www2.compute.dtu.dk/~samo
10. Mödersheim, S.: Abstraction by set-membership: verifying security protocols and web services with databases. In: Computer and Communications Security (2010)
11. Mödersheim, S., Modesti, P.: Verifying sevecom using set-based abstraction. In: Proceedings of the 7th International Wireless Communications and Mobile Computing Conference, IWCMC 2011, Istanbul, Turkey, 4–8 July 2011 (2011)
12. Weidenbach, C.: Towards an automatic analysis of security protocols in first-order logic. In: Ganzinger, H. (ed.) CADE 1999. LNCS (LNAI), vol. 1632, pp. 314–328. Springer, Heidelberg (1999)
13. Weidenbach, C., Dimova, D., Fietzke, A., Kumar, R., Suda, M., Wischnewski, P.: SPASS version 3.5. In: Schmidt, R.A. (ed.) CADE-22. LNCS, vol. 5663, pp. 140–145. Springer, Heidelberg (2009)

Computational Soundness Results for Stateful Applied π Calculus

Jianxiong Shao, Yu Qin$^{(\boxtimes)}$, and Dengguo Feng

Trusted Computing and Information Assurance Laboratory,
Institute of Software, Chinese Academy of Sciences, Beijing, China
{shaojianxiong,qin_yu,feng}@tca.iscas.ac.cn

Abstract. In recent years, many researches have been done to establish symbolic models of stateful protocols. Two works among them, the SAPIC tool and StatVerif tool, provide a high-level specification language and an automated analysis. Their language, the stateful applied π calculus, is extended from the applied π calculus by defining explicit state constructs. Symbolic abstractions of cryptography used in it make the analysis amenable to automation. However, this might overlook the attacks based on the algebraic properties of the cryptographic algorithms. In our paper, we establish the computational soundness results for stateful applied π calculus used in SAPIC tool and StatVerif tool.

In our approach, we build our results on the CoSP framework. For SAPIC, we embed the non-monotonic protocol states into the CoSP protocols, and prove that the resulting CoSP protocols are efficient. Through the embedding, we provide the computational soundness result for SAPIC (by Theorem 1). For StatVerif, we encode the StatVerif process into a subset of SAPIC process, and obtain the computational soundness result for StatVerif (by Theorem 2). Our encoding shows the differences between the semantics of the two languages. Our work inherits the modularity of CoSP, which allows for easily extending the proofs to specific cryptographic primitives. Thus we establish a computationally sound automated verification result for the input languages of SAPIC and StatVerif that use public-key encryption and signatures (by Theorem 3).

Keywords: Computational soundness · Applied π calculus · Stateful protocols

1 Introduction

Manual proofs of security protocols that rely on cryptographic functions are complex and known to be error-prone. The complexity that arises from their distributed nature motivates the researches on automation of proofs. In recent

Y. Qin—The research presented in this paper is supported by the National Basic Research Program of China (No. 2013CB338003) and National Natural Science Foundation of China (No. 91118006, No. 61202414).

F. Piessens and L. Viganò (Eds.): POST 2016, LNCS 9635, pp. 254–275, 2016.
DOI: 10.1007/978-3-662-49635-0_13

years, many efficient verification tools [1–3] have been developed to prove logical properties of protocol behaviors. To eliminate the inherent complexity of the cryptographic operations in formal analysis, these verification tools abstract the cryptographic functions as idealized symbolic terms that obey simple cancelation rules, i.e., the so-called Dolev-Yao models [4,5]. Unfortunately, these idealizations also abstract away from the algebraic properties a cryptographic algorithm may exhibit. Therefore a symbolic formal analysis may omit attacks based on these properties. In other words, symbolic security does not immediately imply computational security. In order to remove this limitation, the concept of Computational Soundness (CS) is introduced in [6]. From the start, a large number of CS results over the past decade were made to show that many of the Dolev-Yao models are sound with respect to actual cryptographic realizations and security definitions (see, e.g., [7–15]).

More recently, formal analysis methods have been applied to stateful protocols, i.e., protocols which require *non-monotonic global state* that can affect and be changed by protocol runs. Stateful protocols can be used to model hardware devices that have some internal memory and security APIs, such as the RSA PKCS#11, IBM's CCA, or the trusted platform module. There are many formal methods that have been used to establish symbolic model of stateful protocols [16–22]. Two works among them, the SAPIC tool [20] and StatVerif tool [21], can provide an automated analysis of stateful protocols. Their language, the stateful applied π calculus, is extended from the applied π calculus [23] by defining constructs for explicitly manipulating global state. One advantage of the stateful applied π calculus is that it provides a high-level specification language to model stateful protocols. Its syntax and semantics inherited from the applied π calculus can arguably ease protocol modeling. Another advantage is that the formal verification can be performed automatically by these tools.

However, no CS works have been done for the stateful applied π calculus. Although there are many for the original applied π calculus, e.g., see [11,15,24]. Our purpose is to establish the CS results for the input languages of the two verification tools SAPIC and StatVerif. With our results, we can transform their symbolically automated verification results of stateful protocols (with some restrictions) to the computationally sound one with respect to actual cryptographic realizations and security definitions. We want to establish the CS results directly for the input languages of SAPIC and StatVerif. To achieve this, we choose to embed them into the CoSP work [11], a general framework for conceptually modular CS proofs. Since the stateful applied π calculus used in SAPIC and StatVerif are slightly different, in the following we call the former SAPIC calculus and the latter StatVerif calculus.

Our Work. We present two CS results respectively for the stateful applied π calculus used in SAPIC tool and StatVerif tool. In our approach, we first provide the method to embed SAPIC calculus into the CoSP framework. Note that the CoSP framework does not provide explicit state manipulation. We need to embed the complex state constructs of stateful applied π calculus into the CoSP protocols and make sure that the resulting CoSP protocol is efficient. By the embedding, we prove that the CS result of applied π calculus implies that of SAPIC calculus (by Theorem 1). For StatVerif, we provide an encoding of StatVerif processes into a subset of SAPIC processes and build the CS result of StatVerif calculus (by Theorem 2). Our encoding shows the differences between the semantics of these two languages. Finally, we establish a computationally sound automated verification result for the input languages of SAPIC and StatVerif that use public-key encryption and signatures (by Theorem 3).

For SAPIC, we use the calculus proposed by [20] as the SAPIC calculus. It extends the applied π calculus with two kinds of state: the functional state and the multiset state. We set two restrictions respectively for the pattern matching in the input constructs and for the multiset state constructs. They are necessary for the computational execution model. We embed the SAPIC calculus into the CoSP framework. The two kinds of state are encoded into the CoSP protocol state (as part of the CoSP node identifiers). We have met two challenges in the embedding. First is for the functional state. If we encode them directly as π-terms, the resulting CoSP protocol is not efficient. Thus we transform them into the CoSP terms which are treated as black boxes by CoSP protocols. The second problem is for the encoding of multiset state. By our restriction of multiset state constructs, we can transform the arguments of facts into CoSP terms and limit the growth of the size of multiset state. We also provide an efficient CoSP subprotocol to implement the pattern matching in the multiset state constructs. At last, we prove that our embedding is an efficient and safe approximation of the SAPIC calculus, and build the CS result of SAPIC calculus upon that of applied π calculus (by Theorem 1).

For StatVerif, we use the calculus proposed by [21] as the StatVerif calculus. It has minor differences to SAPIC calculus. We first provide an encoding of the StatVerif processes into a subset of SAPIC processes. Then we prove that by using SAPIC trace properties our encoding is able to capture secrecy of stateful protocols. With the CS result of SAPIC, we can directly obtain the CS result of StatVerif calculus (by Theorem 2). Our encoding shows the differences between the semantics of state constructs in these two calculi.

Note that our contribution is a soundness result for the execution models that can manipulate state, rather than a soundness result for any new cryptographic primitives. The advantage of our CS result is its extensibility, since we build it on the CoSP framework and involve no new cryptographic arguments. It is easy to extend our proofs to additional cryptographic abstractions phrased in CoSP framework. Any computationally sound implementations for applied π calculus that have been proved in CoSP framework can be applied to our work. To explain its extendibility, we establish a computationally sound automated verification result for the input languages of SAPIC and StatVerif that use public-key encryption and signatures (by Theorem 3). We have verified the classic left-or-right protocol presented in [21] by using these tools in a computationally sound way to show the usefulness of our result.

The paper is organized as follows. In Sect. 2 we give a brief introduction to the CoSP framework and the embedding of applied π calculus. In Sects. 3 and 4 we respectively show the CS results of stateful applied π calculus in SAPIC and StatVerif work. Section 5 contains a case study of the CS result of public-key encryption and signatures. We conclude in Sect. 6.

2   Preliminaries

2.1   CoSP Framework

Our CS results are formulated within CoSP [11], a framework for conceptually modular CS proofs. It decouples the treatment of cryptographic primitives from the treatment of calculi. The results in [15,24] have shown that CoSP framework is capable of handling CS with respect to trace properties and uniformity for ProVerif. Several calculi such as the applied π calculus and RCF can be embedded into CoSP [11,25] and combined with CS results for cryptographic primitives. In this subsection, we will give a brief introduction to the CoSP framework.

CoSP provides a general symbolic model for abstracting cryptographic primitives. It contains some central concepts such as constructors, destructors, and deduction relations.

Definition 1 (Symbolic Model). A symbolic model $\mathbf{M} = (\mathbf{C}, \mathbf{N}, \mathbf{T}, \mathbf{D}, \vdash)$ consists of a set of constructors $\mathbf{C}$, a set of nonces $\mathbf{N}$, a message type $\mathbf{T}$ over $\mathbf{C}$ and $\mathbf{N}$ with $\mathbf{N} \subseteq \mathbf{T}$, a set of destructors $\mathbf{D}$ over $\mathbf{T}$, and a deduction relation $\vdash$ over $\mathbf{T}$. A constructor $C/n \in \mathbf{C}$ is a symbol with (possible zero) arity. A nonce $N \in \mathbf{N}$ is a symbol with zero arity. A message type $\mathbf{T}$ is a set of terms over constructors and nonces. A destructor $D/n \in \mathbf{D}$ of arity n over a message type $\mathbf{T}$ is a partial map $\mathbf{T}^n \to \mathbf{T}$. If D is undefined on a list of message $\underline{t} = (t_1, \cdots, t_n)$, then $D(\underline{t}) = \bot$.

To unify notation of constructor or destructor $F/n \in \mathbf{C} \cup \mathbf{D}$ and nonce $F \in \mathbf{N}$, we define the partial function $eval_F : \mathbf{T}^n \to \mathbf{T}$, where $n = 0$ for the nonce, as follows: If F is a constructor, $eval_F(\underline{t}) := F(\underline{t})$ if $F(\underline{t}) \in \mathbf{T}$ and $eval_F(\underline{t}) := \bot$ otherwise. If F is a nonce, $eval_F() := F$. If F is a destructor, $eval_F(\underline{t}) := F(\underline{t})$ if $F(\underline{t}) \neq \bot$ and $eval_F(\underline{t}) := \bot$ otherwise.

A *computational implementation* A of a symbolic model $\mathbf{M}$ is a family of algorithms that provide computational interpretations to constructors, destructors, and specify the distribution of nonces.

A *CoSP protocol* Π is a tree with labelled nodes and edges. Each node has a unique identifier. It distinguishes 4 types of nodes. *Computation nodes* describe constructor applications, destructor applications, and creations of nonce. *Output* and *input nodes* describe communications with the adversary. *Control nodes* allow the adversary to choose the control flow of the protocol. The computation nodes and input nodes can be referred to by later computation nodes or output nodes. The messages computed or received at these earlier nodes are then taken as arguments by the later constructor/destructor applications or sent to the adversary. A CoSP protocol is *efficient* if it satisfies two conditions: for any node, the length of the identifier is bounded by a polynomial in the length of the path (including the total length of the edge-labels) from the root to it; there is a deterministic polynomial-time algorithm that, given the labels of all nodes and edges on the path to a node, computes the node's identifier.

Given an efficient CoSP protocol Π, both its *symbolic* and *computational executions* are defined as a valid path through the protocol tree. In the symbolic execution, the computation nodes operate on terms, and the input (resp. output) nodes receive (resp. send) terms to the symbolic adversary. The successors of control nodes are chosen by the adversary. In the computational execution, the computation nodes operate on bitstrings by using a computational implementation A, and the input (resp. output) nodes receive (resp. send) bitstrings to the polynomial-time adversary. The successors of control nodes are also chosen by the adversary. The symbolic (resp. computational) *node trace* is a list of node identifiers if there is a symbolic (resp. computational) execution path with these node identifiers.

Definition 2 (Trace Property). A trace property $\wp$ is an efficiently decidable and prefix-closed set of (finite) lists of node identifiers. Let $\mathbf{M} = (\mathbf{C}, \mathbf{N}, \mathbf{T}, \mathbf{D}, \vdash)$ be a symbolic model and Π be an efficient CoSP protocol. Then Π symbolically satisfies a trace property $\wp$ in $\mathbf{M}$ *iff* every symbolic node trace of Π is contained in $\wp$. Let A be a computational implementation of $\mathbf{M}$. Then (Π, A) computationally satisfies a trace property $\wp$ in $\mathbf{M}$ *iff* for all probabilistic polynomial-time interactive machines $\mathcal{A}$, the computational node trace is in $\wp$ with overwhelming probability.

Definition 3 (Computational Soundness). A computational implementation A of a symbolic model $\mathbf{M} = (\mathbf{C}, \mathbf{N}, \mathbf{T}, \mathbf{D}, \vdash)$ is computationally sound for a class P of CoSP protocols *iff* for every trace property $\wp$ and for every efficient CoSP protocol $\Pi \in P$, we have that (Π, A) computationally satisfies $\wp$ whenever Π symbolically satisfies $\wp$.

2.2 Embedding Applied π Calculus into CoSP Framework

Stateful applied π calculus is a variant of applied π calculus. We need to review the original applied π calculus first. We provide its syntax in Table 1. It corresponds to the one considered in [11].

In the following, we call the terms in process calculus the π-terms and terms in CoSP the CoSP-terms, in order to avoid ambiguities. It is similar for the other homonyms such as π-constructors. We will use $fn(P)$ (resp. $fv(P)$) for free names (resp. free variables) in process P, i.e., the names (resp. variables) that are not protected by a name restriction (resp. a let or an input). The notations can also be applied to terms in process. We call a process closed or a term ground if it has no free variables.

The calculus is parameterized over a set of π-constructors $\mathbf{C}_\pi$, a set of π-destructors $\mathbf{D}_\pi$, and an equational theory E over ground π-terms. It requires that the equational theory is compatible with the π-constructors and π-destructors

Table 1. Syntax of applied π calculus

$\langle M, N \rangle ::=$	terms	$\langle P, Q \rangle ::=$	processes
$a, b, m, n, \dots$	names	0	nil
$x, y, z, \dots$	variables	$P \vert Q$	parallel
$f(M_1, \dots, M_n)$	constructor applications	$!P$	replication
		$\nu n; P$	restriction
$D ::=$	destructor terms	$\mathrm{out}(M, N); P$	output
$M, N, \dots$	terms	$\mathrm{in}(M, x); P$	input
$d(D_1, \dots, D_n)$	destructor applications	$\mathrm{let}\ x = D\ \mathrm{in}\ P\ \mathrm{else}\ Q$	let
$f(D_1, \dots, D_n)$	constructor applications	$\mathrm{event}\ e; P$	event

as defined in [11]. The symbolic model of applied π-calculus can be embedded into the CoSP framework.

Definition 4 (Symbolic Model of the Applied π Calculus). For a π-destructor $d \in \mathbf{D}_\pi$, the CoSP-destructor d' is defined by $d'(\underline{t}) := d(\underline{t}\rho)\rho^{-1}$ where ρ is any injective map from the nonces occurring in the CoSP-terms $\underline{t}$ to names. Let $\mathbf{N}_E$ for adversary nonces and $\mathbf{N}_P$ for protocol nonces be two countably infinite sets. The symbolic model of the applied π calculus is given by $\mathbf{M} = (\mathbf{C}, \mathbf{N}, \mathbf{T}, \mathbf{D}, \vdash)$, where $\mathbf{N} := \mathbf{N}_E \cup \mathbf{N}_P$, $\mathbf{C} := \mathbf{C}_\pi$, $\mathbf{D} := \{d' \vert d \in \mathbf{D}_\pi\}$, and where $\mathbf{T}$ consists of all terms over $\mathbf{C}$ and $\mathbf{N}$, and where $\vdash$ is the smallest relation such that $m \in S \Rightarrow S \vdash m$, $N \in \mathbf{N}_E \Rightarrow S \vdash N$, and such that for any $F \in \mathbf{C} \cup \mathbf{D}$ and any $\underline{t} = (t_1, \dots, t_n) \in \mathbf{T}^n$ with $S \vdash \underline{t}$ and $eval_F(\underline{t}) \neq \bot$, we have $S \vdash eval_F(\underline{t})$.

The if-statement can be expressed using an additional destructor $equal$, where $equal(M, N) = M$ if $M =_E N$ and $equal(M, N) = \bot$ otherwise. We always assume $equal \in \mathbf{D}_\pi$. The destructor $equal'$ induces an equivalence relation $\cong$ on the set of CoSP-terms with $x \cong y$ iff $equal'(x, y) \neq \bot$.

For the symbolic model, we can specify its computational implementation A. It assigns the deterministic polynomial-time algorithms A_f and A_d to each π-constructors and π-destructors, and chooses the nonces uniformly at random.

We introduce some notations for the definitions of computational and symbolic π-executions. Given a ground destructor CoSP-term D', we can evaluate it to a ground CoSP-term $eval^{CoSP}(D')$ by evaluating all CoSP-destructors in the arguments of D'. We set $eval^{CoSP}(D') := \bot$ iff any one of the CoSP-destructors returns $\bot$. Given a destructor π-term D, an assignment μ from π-names to bitstrings, and an assignment η from variables to bitstrings with $fn(D) \subseteq dom(\mu)$ and $fv(D) \subseteq dom(\eta)$, we can computationally evaluate D to a bitstring $ceval_{\eta, \mu} D$. We set $ceval_{\eta, \mu} D := \bot$ if the application of one of the algorithms A_f^π or A_d^π fails. For a partial function g, we define the function $f := g \cup \{a := b\}$ with $dom(f) = dom(g) \cup \{a\}$ as $f(a) := b$ and $f(x) := g(x)$ for $x \neq a$.

The computational and symbolic execution models of a π-process are defined in [11] by using evaluation contexts where the holes only occur below parallel compositions. The adversary is allowed to determine which process in parallel should be proceeded by setting the evaluation context for each step of proceeding. The execution models of π calculus are defined as follows. We take the writing way in [11] and mark the symbolic execution model by $[\![\ldots]\!]$.

Definition 5 [6] (Computational $[\![$Symbolic$]\!]$ Execution of π Calculus).
Let P_0 be a closed process (where all bound variables and names are renamed such that they are pairwise distinct and distinct from all unbound ones). Let $\mathcal{A}$ be an interactive machine called the adversary. $[\![$For the symbolic model, $\mathcal{A}$ only sends message m if $K \vdash m$ where K are the messages sent to $\mathcal{A}$ so far.$]\!]$ We define the computational $[\![$symbolic$]\!]$ execution of π calculus as an interactive machine $Exec_{P_0}(1^k)$ that takes a security parameter k as argument $[\![$interactive machine $SExec_{P_0}$ that takes no argument$]\!]$ and interacts with $\mathcal{A}$:

Start: Let $\mathcal{P} := \{P_0\}$. Let η be a totally undefined partial function mapping π-variables to bitstrings $[\![$CoSP-terms$]\!]$. Let μ be a totally undefined partial function mapping π-names to bitstrings $[\![$CoSP-terms$]\!]$. Let $a_1, ..., a_n$ denote the free names in P_0. Pick $\{r_i\}_{i=1}^n \in \text{Nonces}_k$ at random $[\![$Choose a different $r_i \in \mathbf{N}_P]\!]$. Set $\mu := \mu \cup \{a_i := r_i\}_{i=1}^n$. Send $(r_1, ..., r_n)$ to $\mathcal{A}$.
Main loop: Send $\mathcal{P}$ to $\mathcal{A}$ and expect an evaluation context E from the adversary. Distinguish the following cases:

- $\mathcal{P} = E[\text{in}(M, x); P_1]$: Request two bitstrings $[\![$CoSP-terms$]\!]$ c, m from the adversary. If $c = \text{ceval}_{\eta,\mu}(M)$ $[\![c \cong \text{eval}^{CoSP}(M\eta\mu)]\!]$, set $\eta := \eta \cup \{x := m\}$ and $\mathcal{P} := E[P_1]$.
- $\mathcal{P} = E[\nu a; P_1]$: Pick $r \in \text{Nonces}_k$ at random $[\![$ Choose $r \in \mathbf{N}_P \backslash \text{range } \mu]\!]$, set $\mu := \mu \cup \{a := r\}$ and $\mathcal{P} := E[P_1]$.
- $\mathcal{P} = E[\text{out}(M_1, N); P_1][\text{in}(M_2, x); P_2]$: If $\text{ceval}_{\eta,\mu}(M_1) = \text{ceval}_{\eta,\mu}(M_2)$ $[\![\text{eval}^{CoSP}(M_1\eta\mu) \cong \text{eval}^{CoSP}(M_2\eta\mu)]\!]$, set $\eta := \eta \cup \{x := \text{ceval}_{\eta,\mu}(N)\}$ $[\![\eta := \eta \cup \{x := \text{eval}^{CoSP}(N\eta\mu)\}]\!]$ and $\mathcal{P} := E[P_1][P_2]$.
- $\mathcal{P} = E[\text{let } x = D \text{ in } P_1 \text{ else } P_2]$: If $m := \text{ceval}_{\eta,\mu}(D) \neq \bot$ $[\![m := \text{eval}^{CoSP}(D\eta\mu)$
$\neq \bot]\!]$, set $\mu := \mu \cup \{x := m\}$ and $\mathcal{P} := E[P_1]$. Otherwise set $\mathcal{P} := E[P_2]$
- $\mathcal{P} = E[\text{event } e; P_1]$: Let $\mathcal{P} := E[P_1]$ and raise the event e.
- $\mathcal{P} = E[!P_1]$: Rename all bound variables of P_1 such that they are pairwise distinct and distinct from all variables and names in $\mathcal{P}$ and in domains of η, μ, yielding a process $\tilde{P}_1$. Set $\mathcal{P} := E[\tilde{P}_1|!P_1]$.
- $\mathcal{P} = E[\text{out}(M, N); P_1]$: Request a bitstring $[\![$CoSP-term$]\!]$ c from the adversary. If $c = \text{ceval}_{\eta,\mu}(M)$ $[\![c \cong \text{eval}^{CoSP}(M\eta\mu)]\!]$, set $\mathcal{P} := E[P_1]$ and send $\text{ceval}_{\eta,\mu}(N)$ $[\![\text{eval}^{CoSP}(N\eta\mu)]\!]$ to the adversary.
- In all other cases, do nothing.

We say that a closed process computationally satisfies a π-trace property $\wp$ if the list of events raised by its computational execution is in $\wp$ with overwhelming probability. Then the theorem in [11] states that for any given computationally sound implementation of the applied π-calculus (embedded in the CoSP model), the symbolic verification of a closed process P_0 satisfying a π-trace property $\wp$ implies P_0 computationally satisfies $\wp$.

3   Computational Soundness Results for SAPIC

3.1   SAPIC

The SAPIC tool was proposed in [20]. It translates SAPIC process to multiset rewrite rules, which can be analyzed by the tamarin-prover [18]. Its language extends the applied π calculus with two kinds of explicit state constructs. The first kind is functional. It provides the operation for defining, deleting, retrieving, locking and unlocking the memory states. The second construct allows to manipulate the global state in the form of a multiset of ground facts. This state manipulation is similar to the "low-level" language of the tamarin-prover and offers a more flexible way to model stateful protocols. Moreover, the security property of SAPIC process is expressed by trace formulas. It is expressive enough to formalize complex properties such as injective correspondence.

Table 2. State constructs of SAPIC calculus

$\langle P, Q \rangle ::=$	processes
...	standard processes
insert $M, N; P$	insert
delete $M; P$	delete
lookup M as x in P else Q	retrieve
lock $M; P$	lock
unlock $M; P$	unlock
$[L] - [e] \rightarrow [R]; P \quad (L, R \in \mathcal{F}^*)$	multiset state construct

Syntax. We list the two kinds of state constructs in Table 2. Tables 1 and 2 together compose the full syntax of SAPIC language. Let Σ_{fact} be a signature that is partitioned into *linear* and *persistent* fact symbols. We can define the set of facts as

$$\mathcal{F} := \{F(M_1, ..., M_n) | F \in \Sigma_{fact} \text{ of arity } n\},$$

Given a finite sequence or set of facts $L \in \mathcal{F}^*$, $lfacts(L)$ denotes the multiset of all linear facts in L and $pfacts(L)$ denotes the set of all persistent facts in L. $\mathcal{G}$ denotes the set of ground facts, i.e., the set of facts that do not contain variables. Given a set L, we denote by $L^\#$ the set of finite multisets of elements from L. We use the superscript $\#$ to annotate usual multiset operation, e.g. $L_1 \cup^\# L_2$ denotes the multiset union of multisets L_1, L_2.

Note that we do our first restriction in the input construct. In [20], the original SAPIC language allows the input of a term in the input construct in$(M, N); P$. We use the standard construct in$(M, x); P$ instead in Table 1. We will explain it later in Sect. 3.2.

Operational Semantics. A semantic configuration for SAPIC calculus is a tuple $(\tilde{n}, \mathcal{S}, \mathcal{S}^{MS}, \mathcal{P}, \mathcal{K}, \mathcal{L})$. $\tilde{n}$ is a set of names which have been restricted by the protocol. $\mathcal{S}$ is a partial function associating the values to the memory state cells. $\mathcal{S}^{MS} \subseteq \mathcal{G}^{\#}$ is a multiset of ground facts. $\mathcal{P} = \{P_1, ..., P_k\}$ is a finite multiset of ground processes representing the processes to be executed in parallel. $\mathcal{K}$ is the set of ground terms modeling the messages output to the environment (adversary). $\mathcal{L}$ is the set of currently acquired locks. The semantics of the SAPIC is defined by a reduction relation $\rightarrow$ on semantic configurations. We just list the semantics of state constructs in Fig. 1. By $\mathcal{S}(M)$ we denote $\mathcal{S}(N)$ if $\exists N \in dom(\mathcal{S}), N =_E M$. By $\mathcal{L}\backslash_E\{M\}$ we denote $\mathcal{L}\backslash\{N\}$ if $\exists N \in \mathcal{L}, M =_E N$. The rest are in [20].

$$\left(\tilde{n}, \mathcal{S}, \mathcal{S}^{MS}, \mathcal{P} \cup^{\#} \{\text{insert } M, N; P\}, \mathcal{K}, \mathcal{L}\right) \rightarrow \left(\tilde{n}, \mathcal{S} \cup \{M := N\}, \mathcal{S}^{MS}, \mathcal{P} \cup^{\#} \{P\}, \mathcal{K}, \mathcal{L}\right)$$

$$\left(\tilde{n}, \mathcal{S}, \mathcal{S}^{MS}, \mathcal{P} \cup^{\#} \{\text{delete } M; P\}, \mathcal{K}, \mathcal{L}\right) \rightarrow \left(\tilde{n}, \mathcal{S} \cup \{M := \bot\}, \mathcal{S}^{MS}, \mathcal{P} \cup^{\#} \{P\}, \mathcal{K}, \mathcal{L}\right)$$

$$\left(\tilde{n}, \mathcal{S}, \mathcal{S}^{MS}, \mathcal{P} \cup^{\#} \{\text{lookup } M \text{ as } x \text{ in } P \text{ else } Q\}, \mathcal{K}, \mathcal{L}\right) \rightarrow \left(\tilde{n}, \mathcal{S}, \mathcal{S}^{MS}, \mathcal{P} \cup^{\#} \{P\{V/x\}\}, \mathcal{K}, \mathcal{L}\right) \text{ if } \mathcal{S}(M) =_E V$$

$$\left(\tilde{n}, \mathcal{S}, \mathcal{S}^{MS}, \mathcal{P} \cup^{\#} \{\text{lookup } M \text{ as } x \text{ in } P \text{ else } Q\}, \mathcal{K}, \mathcal{L}\right) \rightarrow \left(\tilde{n}, \mathcal{S}, \mathcal{S}^{MS}, \mathcal{P} \cup^{\#} \{Q\}\}, \mathcal{K}, \mathcal{L}\right) \text{ if } \mathcal{S}(M) = \bot$$

$$\left(\tilde{n}, \mathcal{S}, \mathcal{S}^{MS}, \mathcal{P} \cup^{\#} \{\text{lock } M; P\}, \mathcal{K}, \mathcal{L}\right) \rightarrow \left(\tilde{n}, \mathcal{S}, \mathcal{S}^{MS}, \mathcal{P} \cup^{\#} \{P\}, \mathcal{K}, \mathcal{L} \cup \{M\}\right) \text{ if } M \notin_E \mathcal{L}$$

$$\left(\tilde{n}, \mathcal{S}, \mathcal{S}^{MS}, \mathcal{P} \cup^{\#} \{\text{unlock } M; P\}, \mathcal{K}, \mathcal{L}\right) \rightarrow \left(\tilde{n}, \mathcal{S}, \mathcal{S}^{MS}, \mathcal{P} \cup^{\#} \{P\}, \mathcal{K}, \mathcal{L}\backslash_E\{M\}\right) \text{ if } M \in_E \mathcal{L}$$

$$\left(\tilde{n}, \mathcal{S}, \mathcal{S}^{MS}, \mathcal{P} \cup^{\#} \{[L] - [e] \rightarrow [R]; P\}, \mathcal{K}, \mathcal{L}\right) \xrightarrow{e} \left(\tilde{n}, \mathcal{S}, \mathcal{S}^{MS}\backslash lfacts(L') \cup^{\#} R', \mathcal{P} \cup^{\#} \{P\tau\}, \mathcal{K}, \mathcal{L}\right)$$

if $\exists \tau, L', R'$. τ grounding for L, R such that $L' =_E L\tau, R' =_E R\tau$, and $lfacts(L') \subseteq^{\#} \mathcal{S}^{MS}, pfacts(L') \subset \mathcal{S}^{MS}$

Fig. 1. The semantics of SAPIC

Security Property. With the operational semantics, we can give out the definition of SAPIC trace property. The set of traces of a closed SAPIC process P, written $traces(P)$, defines all its possible executions. In SAPIC, security properties are described in a two-sorted first-order logic, defined as the trace formula. Given a closed SAPIC process P, a trace formula ϕ is said to be *valid* for P, written $traces(P) \vDash^{\forall} \phi$, if all the traces of P satisfies ϕ. ϕ is said to be *satisfiable* for P, written $traces(P) \vDash^{\exists} \phi$, if there exists a trace of P satisfies ϕ. Note that $traces(P) \vDash^{\exists} \phi$ *iff* $traces(P) \nvDash^{\forall} \neg\phi$. It means the verification of satisfiability can be transformed to the falsification of validity. Thus in the following, we only consider the validity of trace formula. We can transform its definition to trace property in the sense of Definition 2 by requiring that $\wp := \{tr|tr \vDash \phi\}$. Then we get the following definition of SAPIC trace property.

Definition 7 (SAPIC Trace Property). Given a closed SAPIC process P, we define the set of traces of P as

$$traces(P) = \{[e_1, ..., e_m] \mid (\emptyset, \emptyset, \emptyset, \{P\}, fn(P), \emptyset) \to^* \xrightarrow{e_1} (\tilde{n}_1, \mathcal{S}_1, \mathcal{S}_1^{MS}, \mathcal{P}_1, \mathcal{K}_1, \mathcal{L}_1)$$
$$\to^* \xrightarrow{e_2} \cdots \to^* \xrightarrow{e_m} (\tilde{n}_m, \mathcal{S}_m, \mathcal{S}_m^{MS}, \mathcal{P}_m, \mathcal{K}_m, \mathcal{L}_m)\}$$

A SAPIC trace property $\wp$ is an efficiently decidable and prefix-closed set of strings. A process P symbolically satisfies the SAPIC trace property $\wp$ if we have $traces(P) \subseteq \wp$.

3.2   CS Results of the Calculus

SAPIC language only has semantics in the symbolic model. We need to introduce the computational execution model of SAPIC process. It is not a trivial extension of the computational execution model of the applied π calculus in Definition 5. We first restrict the pattern matching in the original SAPIC input construct because for some cases, it cannot be performed by any sound computational model. Then we set up the computational execution model for the two kinds of global states in SAPIC. Note that the CoSP framework does not immediately support nodes for the operation of functional states and multiset states. We will encode them into the CoSP protocol node identifiers and mechanize the two kinds of state constructs by using CoSP protocol tree.

First, we need to explain the restriction of the input construct. Note that we use the standard syntax of applied π calculus as part of the syntax of SAPIC language in Table 2. In [20], the original SAPIC process allows the input of a term in the input construct $in(M, N); P$ where it receives a ground term N' on the channel M, does a pattern matching to find a substitution τ such that $N' =_E N\tau$, and then proceeds by $P\tau$. However, we find that it is impossible to embed it into the CoSP framework. As in Definition 5, the computational execution of the calculus receives the bitstring m from the adversary. Then the interactive machine $Exec_{P_0}(1^k)$ should extract from m the sub-bitstrings corresponding to the subterms in the range of τ. This is impossible for some cases. One example is the input process $P := in(c, h(x))$ where the adversary may generate a name t, compute and output the term $h(t)$ on the channel c. It has no computational execution model since the protocol does not know how to bind the variable x ($h(\cdot)$ is not invertible). Thus in the following, we do our *first restriction* that the SAPIC input construct should be in the form $in(M, x)$.

Then we show how to embed the two kinds of states into the CoSP framework and mechanize the state constructs. Our computational execution model maintains a standard protocol state that consists of the current process $\mathcal{P}$, an environment η, and an interpretation μ as in Definition 5. Moreover, we extend the protocol state with a set S including all the pairs (M, N) of the functional state cells M and their associated values N, a set Λ of all the currently locked state cells, and a multiset S^{MS} of the current ground facts. We denote by

$dom(S) := \{m|(m,n) \in S\}$ the set of state cells in S (S can be seen as a partial function and $dom(S)$ is its domain). In each step of the execution, the adversary receives the process $\mathcal{P}$ and sends back an evaluation context E where $\mathcal{P} = E[\mathcal{P}_1]$ to schedule the proceeding to $\mathcal{P}_1$. In addition to the standard cases operated in Definition 5, we need to mechanize the functional and multiset state constructs according to the protocol states S, Λ, and S^{MS}. We implement the procedures as CoSP sub-protocols. Note that our encoding should keep the efficiency of the resulting CoSP protocol and cannot introduce an unacceptable time cost for computational execution. In the following, we respectively explain how to embed the two kinds of state constructs.

Embedding the Functional State. For the functional state constructs in SAPIC, the state cells and their associated values are π-terms. If we encode them directly as π-terms in the set S, its size would grow exponentially, and the resulting CoSP protocol is not efficient. To solve this problem, we store the state cell M and its value N as CoSP-terms in the sets S and Λ. The CoSP-terms can be encoded by the indexes of the nodes in which they were created (or received). In this setting, the CoSP-terms are treated as black boxes by the CoSP protocol with a linear size.

However, we have to pay extra cost for this setting. For a finite set of CoSP terms, such as $dom(S)$ or Λ, we need to formalize the decision of set-membership. It can be done with the help of *parameterized CoSP protocols*, which act as sub-protocols with formal parameters of CoSP nodes and can be plugged into another CoSP protocol tree. Its definition is introduced in [24]. We denote by f_{mem} the decision of set-membership relation: if $\exists r_i \in \Lambda, r_i \cong r$, where r is a CoSP-term, $\Lambda = \{r_1, ..., r_n\}$ is a set of CoSP-terms. It can be accomplished by a sequence of n CoSP computation nodes for the destructor $equal'$ as in Fig. 2. The success-edge of $f_{\mathrm{mem}}(\Lambda; r)$ corresponds to each **yes**-edge. The failure-edge corresponds to the **no**-edge of the last computation node. With this sub-protocol, we can embed the functional state constructs in the execution model of SAPIC. The computation steps of the embedding would not grow exponentially. Decision of set-membership costs no more than the size of the set, which is bounded by the reduction steps t. Thus there exists a polynomial p, such that the computation steps of embedding is bounded by $p(t)$.

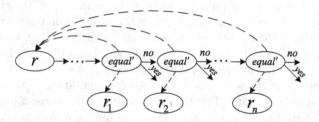

Fig. 2. Sub-protocol f_{mem} for decision of set-membership

Embedding the Multiset State. For the multiset state, we keep a multiset S^{MS} of the current ground facts. In the execution model, we need to encode the multiset state construct $[L] - [e] \rightarrow [R]; P$ by using CoSP sub-protocol f_{match}. As in Fig. 1, the SAPIC process tries to match each fact in the sequence L to the ground facts in S^{MS} and, if successful, adds the corresponding instance of facts R to S^{MS}. We denote by $fv(L)$ the set of variables in L that are not under the scope of a previous binder. The variables $x \in fv(L)$ should be bound by the pattern matching. For the reason of efficiency, we store the arguments of ground facts in S^{MS} as CoSP-terms rather than π-terms[1], as we have done in the case of functional state. S^{MS} can only be altered using the multiset state construct $[L] - [e] \rightarrow [R]; P$. Given a closed SAPIC process, the maximum length of R (counted by the number of fact symbols in R) is a constant value. In each execution step, the multiset state construct can proceed at most once. Thus the size of S^{MS} is bounded by a polynomial in the number of execution steps (taken CoSP-terms as blackboxes).

When designing the sub-protocol f_{match} for the multiset state construct, we should solve the pattern matching problem, which is similar to the previous one in the input construct. To solve this problem, we need to do our *second restriction*. In the multiset state construct $[L] - [e] \rightarrow [R]; P$, we require that: (i) it is well-formed (Definition 12 in [20]); (ii) $\forall F(M_1, ..., M_n) \in L$, either $M_i \in fv(L)$ or $fv(M_i) = \emptyset$ for all $1 \le i \le n$. It means that the free variables of L can only occur as the arguments of the facts in L. By (i), the well-formed requirement, we have $fv(R) \subseteq fv(L)$. Thus all the facts added into the current multiset state S^{MS} are ground. By (ii), we can match each variable in $fv(L)$ to the corresponding arguments of the ground facts in S^{MS} and find the substitution τ for $fv(L)$ in the execution. Note that our second restriction is necessary for the CS results. Otherwise, if we allow the free variables in $fv(L)$ occur as the subterms of the arguments of facts, it might lead to a mismatch case as we have described in the input construct.

The second restriction does not make the multiset state construct useless. All the examples in [20] using this construct meet our requirements. Moreover, this style of state manipulation is the underlying specification language of the tamarin tool [18]. Even considering our restriction, the tamarin tool is still useful to model security protocols. The example is the NAXOS protocol for the eCK model formalized in [18].

In the following, we will give out the sub-protocol f_{match} of the pattern matching. Since f_{match} is plugged in the execution model of SAPIC, it assumes an initial protocol state which includes an environment η, an interpretation μ, and a multiset S^{MS} of the current ground facts. For each multiset state construct $[L] - [e] \rightarrow [R]$, f_{match} tries to find a substitution τ' from $fv(L)$ to CoSP-terms, such that $lfacts(L)\eta'\mu \subseteq^{\#} S^{MS}$ and $pfacts(L)\eta'\mu \subset S^{MS}$, where $\eta' = \eta \cup \tau'$. For simplicity, we denote by $f/(n,k)$ a π-fact such that $f/(n,k) = F(M_1, ..., M_k) \in \mathcal{F}$ and $\{M_i\}_{i=1}^k$ are π-terms including n variables. A π-fact $f/(0,k)$ is ground.

---

[1] Otherwise, the length of π-terms may grow exponentially by the iterated binding of variables. One example is the construct $!([Iter(x)] - [] \rightarrow [Iter(fun(x,x))])$.

Definition 8 (Sub-protocol of Pattern Matching). Let η be a partial function mapping variables to CoSP-terms, let μ be a partial function mapping π-names to CoSP-terms, let S^{MS} be a multiset of facts whose arguments are CoSP-terms. Let $[L] - [e] \to [R]; P$ be a multiset state construct with our restriction. We define the sub-protocol f_{match} which contains two stages respectively for the pattern matching of linear and persistent facts in L:

Start. For stage 1, let τ' be a totally undefined partial function mapping variables to CoSP-terms. Set $S_{rest} := S^{MS}$. Let $L_{rest} := lfacts(L)$ and $L_{linear} := \emptyset$ be two multisets of π-facts.

Loop. Choose a π-fact $l/(n,k) \in^{\#} L_{rest}$, match it to all the fact $f \in^{\#} S_{rest}$ with the same fact symbol by performing the following steps (i)–(iii). If any check in step (ii) is failed, choose the next $f \in^{\#} S_{rest}$ to match. If there is no matching with $l/(n,k)$ for any facts in S_{rest}, stop and go to the failure-edge.

(i) For n variables x_i in $l/(n,k)$, pick up $x_i \notin dom(\eta) \cup dom(\tau')$ (i.e., the free variables in l), set $\tau'' := \tau' \cup \{x_i \mapsto s_i | 1 \le i \le n, x_i \notin dom(\eta) \cup dom(\tau')\}$ by mapping x_i to the CoSP-term s_i with the same position in f. This can be done since we require free variables should be the arguments of facts.

(ii) For k arguments of $l/(n,k) = F(M_1, ..., M_k)$, use the CoSP computation node to check whether $t_j \cong eval^{CoSP}(M_j \eta' \mu)$ for $j = 1, ..., k$, where t_j is the argument of f with the same position, $\eta' = \eta \cup \tau''$. This can be done since $dom(\eta) \cap dom(\tau'') = \emptyset$.

(iii) If all the checks in step (ii) pass, we set $L_{rest} := L_{rest} \backslash^{\#} \{l/(n,k)\}$, $S_{rest} := S_{rest} \backslash^{\#} \{f\}$, $L_{linear} := L_{linear} \cup^{\#} \{l/(n,k)\}$, and $\tau' = \tau''$. Loop while $L_{rest} \ne \emptyset$.

Stage 2 is similar. We perform the above algorithm of stage 1 without $^{\#}$. In the Start, let τ' be the one we have achieved in stage 1, set $L_{rest} := pfacts(L)$, $S_{rest} := S^{MS}$, and do not change S_{rest} in step (iii) of the Loop. If both the two stages are successful, f_{match} goes to the success-edge.

All the steps in f_{match} can be performed by CoSP nodes. By the conditions in step (ii), if successful, f_{match} will find τ' and $\eta' = \eta \cup \tau'$ such that $lfacts(L)\eta'\mu \subseteq^{\#} S^{MS}$ and $pfacts(L)\eta'\mu \subset S^{MS}$. Thus we encode the pattern matching of multiset state construct into the CoSP sub-protocol f_{match}.

Then we need to explain that the embedding way does not cost unacceptably high. The time complexity of the above sub-protocol (measured by the CoSP nodes) is approximately the size of S^{MS} times the size of L. Given a closed SAPIC process, the maximum size of L is a constant number and the size of S^{MS} is polynomial in the execution steps t. Thus there exists a polynomial p, such that the computation steps of encoding is bounded by $p(t)$.

Now we could give out the definition of computational execution model of SAPIC in Definition 9. It is an interactive machine $Exec^{S}_{P_0}(1^k)$ that executes the SAPIC process and communicates with a probabilistic polynomial-time adversary. The model maintains a protocol state as 6-tuple $(\mathcal{P}, \eta, \mu, S, \Lambda, S^{MS})$. The definition of the evaluation context is similar to that of the applied π calculus. We write $E[P] = \mathcal{P} \cup \{P\}$.

In order to relate the symbolic and the computational semantics of a SAPIC process, we also define an additional symbolic execution for closed SAPIC processes as a technical tool as in [11]. It is a direct analogue of the computational execution model and denoted by $SExec_{P_0}^S$. The difference between $Exec_{P_0}^S(1^k)$ and $SExec_{P_0}^S$ is that the latter one operates on CoSP-terms rather than bitstrings: It computes CoSP-terms $M\eta\mu$ and $eval^{CoSP}D\eta\mu$ instead of bitstrings $ceval_{\eta,\mu}(M)$ and $ceval_{\eta,\mu}(D)$, it compares the CoSP-terms using CoSP-destructor $\cong$ instead of checking for equality of bitstrings, and it chooses a fresh nonce $r \in N_P$ instead of choosing a random bitstring r as value for a new protocol name.

Due to the limited space, we merge the Definition 10 of the symbolic execution of SAPIC into the Definition 9 of the computational one. It is marked by [...]. In the main loop, we only present the cases of SAPIC state constructs. For the standard cases, the execution model performs in the same way as the applied π calculus model does.

Definition 9 [10] (Computational [Symbolic] Execution of SAPIC).
Let P_0 be a closed SAPIC process (where all bound variables and names are renamed such that they are pairwise distinct and distinct from all unbound ones). Let $\mathcal{A}$ be an interactive machine called the adversary. We define the computational [symbolic] execution of SAPIC calculus as an interactive machine $Exec_{P_0}^S(1^k)$ that takes a security parameter k as argument [interactive machine $SExec_{P_0}^S$ that takes no argument] and interacts with $\mathcal{A}$:
Start: Let $\mathcal{P} := \{P_0\}$. Let η be a totally undefined partial function mapping π-variables to bitstrings [CoSP-terms], let μ be a totally undefined partial function mapping π-names to bitstrings [CoSP-terms], let S be an initially empty set of pairs of bitstrings [CoSP-terms]. Let S^{MS} be an initially empty multiset of facts whose arguments are bitstrings [CoSP-terms]. Let Λ be an initially empty set of bitstrings [CoSP-terms]. Let $a_1, ..., a_n$ denote the free names in P_0. Pick $\{r_i\}_{i=1}^n \in Nonces_k$ at random [Choose a different $r_i \in N_P$]. Set $\mu := \mu \cup \{a_i := r_i\}_{i=1}^n$. Send $(r_1, ..., r_n)$ to $\mathcal{A}$.

Main loop: Send $\mathcal{P}$ to $\mathcal{A}$ and expect an evaluation context E from the adversary. Distinguish the following cases:

- For the standard cases, the execution model performs the same way as in Definition 5 [6].
- $\mathcal{P} = E[\text{insert } M, N; P_1]$: Set $m := ceval_{\eta,\mu}(M), n := ceval_{\eta,\mu}(N)$ [$m := eval^{CoSP}(M\eta\mu), n := eval^{CoSP}(N\eta\mu)$]. Plug in f_{mem} to decide if $\exists(r',r) \in S, r' = m$ [$r' \cong m$]. For the success-edge, set $\mathcal{P} := E[P_1]$ and $S := S\backslash\{(r',r)\} \cup \{(m,n)\}$. For the failure-edge, set $\mathcal{P} := E[P_1]$ and $S := S \cup \{(m,n)\}$.
- $\mathcal{P} = E[\text{delete } M; P_1]$: Set $m := ceval_{\eta,\mu}(M)$ [$m := eval^{CoSP}(M\eta\mu)$]. Plug in f_{mem} to decide if $\exists(r',r) \in S, r' = m$ [$r' \cong m$]. For the success-edge, set $\mathcal{P} := E[P_1]$ and $S := S\backslash\{(r',r)\}$. For the failure-edge, set $\mathcal{P} := E[P_1]$.
- $\mathcal{P} = E[\text{lookup } M \text{ as } x \text{ in } P_1 \text{ else } P_2]$: Set $m := ceval_{\eta,\mu}(M)$ [$m := eval^{CoSP}(M\eta\mu)$]. Plug in f_{mem} to decide if $\exists(r,r) \in S, r' = m$ [$r' \cong m$]. For the

success-edge, set $\mathcal{P} := E[P_1]$ and $\eta := \eta \cup \{x := r\}$. For the failure-edge, set
$\mathcal{P} := E[P_2]$.

- $\mathcal{P} = E[\text{lock } M; P_1]$: Set $m := \text{ceval}_{\eta,\mu}(M)$ $[\![m := \text{eval}^{CoSP}(M\eta\mu)]\!]$. Plug in
  f_{mem} to decide if $\exists r' \in \Lambda, r' = m$ $[\![r' \cong m]\!]$. For the success-edge, do nothing.
  For the failure-edge, set $\mathcal{P} := E[P_1]$ and $\Lambda := \Lambda \cup \{m\}$.

- $\mathcal{P} = E[\text{unlock } M; P_1]$: Set $m := \text{ceval}_{\eta,\mu}(M)$ $[\![m := \text{eval}^{CoSP}(M\eta\mu)]\!]$. Plug
  in f_{mem} to decide if $\exists r' \in \Lambda, r' = m$ $[\![r' \cong m]\!]$. For the success-edge, set
  $\mathcal{P} := E[P_1]$ and $\Lambda := \Lambda \backslash \{r'\}$. For the failure-edge, do nothing.

- $\mathcal{P} = E[[L] - [e] \rightarrow [R]; P_1]$: Plug in f_{match} to find a substitution τ' from
  $fv(L)$ to bitstrings $[\![\text{CoSP-terms}]\!]$, such that $lfacts(L)\eta'\mu \subseteq^{\#} S^{MS}$ and
  $pfacts(L)\eta'\mu \subset S^{MS}$, where $\eta' = \eta \cup \tau'$. For the success-edge, set $\mathcal{P} := E[P_1]$,
  $S^{MS} := S^{MS}\backslash^{\#} lfacts(L)\eta'\mu \cup R\eta'\mu$, $\eta := \eta'$, and raise the event e. For the
  failure-edge, do nothing.

- In all other cases, do nothing.

For a given polynomial-time interactive machine $\mathcal{A}$, a closed SAPIC process
P_0, and a polynomial p, let $Events^S_{\mathcal{A},P_0,p}(k)$ be the distribution for the list of
events raised within the first $p(k)$ computational steps (jointly counted for $\mathcal{A}(1^k)$
and $Exec^S_{P_0}(1^k)$). Then the computational fulfillment of SAPIC trace properties
can be defined as follows.

Definition 11 (Computational SAPIC Trace Properties). Let P_0 be a
closed process, and p a polynomial. We say that P_0 computationally satisfies a
SAPIC trace property $\wp$ if for all polynomial-time interactive machines $\mathcal{A}$ and
all polynomials p, we have that $\Pr[Events^S_{\mathcal{A},P_0,p}(k) \in \wp]$ is overwhelming in k.

Then we should explain that $SExec^S_{P_0}$ can be realized by a CoSP protocol
tree. The state of the machine $SExec^S_{P_0}$ includes a tuple $(\mathcal{P}, \mu, \eta, S, S^{MS}, \Lambda)$. It
is used as a node identifier. CoSP-terms should be encoded by the indexes in
the path from the root to the node in which they were created (or received).
The process $\mathcal{P}$, the fact symbols in S^{MS}, and the π-names in $dom(\mu)$ will be
encoded as bitstrings. We plug two sub-protocols, f_{mem} and f_{match}, into the
CoSP protocol respectively for the decision of set-membership in the functional
state constructs, and for the pattern matching in the multiset state constructs.
We have explained that these two sub-protocols do not introduce an unacceptable cost. The operation of raising event e can be realized using a control node
with one successor that sends $(event, e)$ to the adversary. Given a sequence of
nodes $\underline{\nu}$, we denote by $events(\underline{\nu})$ the events $\underline{e}$ raised by the event nodes in $\underline{\nu}$. We
call this resulting CoSP protocol $\Pi^S_{P_0}$.

Definition 12. $SExec^S_{P_0}$ satisfies a SAPIC trace property $\wp$ if in a finite interaction with any Dolev-Yao adversary, the sequence of events raised by $SExec^S_{P_0}$
is contained in $\wp$.

Theorem 1 states the CS result of SAPIC. We present its proof in the full
version of this paper [26].

Theorem 1 (CS in SAPIC). Assume that the computational implementation of the applied π calculus is a computationally sound implementation (in the sense of Definition 3) of the symbolic model of applied π calculus (Definition 4) for a class **P** of protocols. If a closed SAPIC process P_0 symbolically satisfies a SAPIC trace property $\wp$ (Definition 7), and $\Pi_{P_0}^S \in \mathbf{P}$, then P_0 computationally satisfies $\wp$ (Definition 11).

4   Computational Soundness Result for StatVerif

StatVerif was proposed in [21]. Its process language is an extension of the ProVerif process calculus with only functional state constructs. StatVerif is limited to the verification of secrecy property.

In this section, we first encode the StatVerif processes into a subset of SAPIC processes. Then we prove that our encoding is able to capture secrecy of stateful protocols by using SAPIC trace properties. Finally with the CS result of SAPIC, we can directly obtain the CS result for StatVerif calculus. Note that our encoding way shows the differences between the semantics of state constructs in these two calculi.

Table 3. State constructs of StatVerif calculus

$\langle P, Q \rangle ::=$	processes
...	standard processes
$[s \mapsto M]$	initialize
$s := M; P$	assign
read s as $x; P$	read
lock; P	lock state
unlock; P	unlock state

Syntax. We first review the StatVerif calculus proposed in [21]. We list the explicit functional state constructs in Table 3. Tables 1 and 3 together compose the full syntax of StatVerif calculus. Note that the state constructs are subject to the following two additional restrictions:

- $[s \mapsto M]$ may occur only once for a given cell name s, and may occur only within the scope of name restriction, a parallel and a replication.
- For every lock; P, the part P of the process must not include parallel or replication unless it is after an unlock construct.

Operational Semantics. A semantic configuration for StatVerif is a tuple $(\tilde{n}, \mathcal{S}, \mathcal{P}, \mathcal{K})$. $\tilde{n}$ is a finite set of names. $\mathcal{S} = \{s_i := M_i\}$ is a partial function mapping cell names s_i to their associated values M_i. $\mathcal{P} = \{(P_1, \beta_1), ..., (P_k, \beta_k)\}$ is a finite multiset of pairs where P_i is a process and $\beta_i \in \{0, 1\}$ is a boolean indicating whether P_i has locked the state. For any $1 \leq i \leq k$, we have at most one $\beta_i = 1$. $\mathcal{K}$ is a set of ground terms modeling the messages output to the environment (adversary). The semantics of StatVerif calculus is defined by transition rules on semantic configurations. We do a little change to the original semantics by adding two labelled transitions for the input and output of adversary. With these rules, we can define secrecy property without explicitly considering the adversary processes. We list these two rules and the semantics of state constructs in Fig. 3. The rest are in [21].

$(\tilde{n}, S, \mathcal{P} \cup \{([s \mapsto M], 0)\}, \mathcal{K}) \rightarrow (\tilde{n}, S \cup \{s := M\}, \mathcal{P}, \mathcal{K})$ if $s \in \tilde{n}$ and $s \notin dom(S)$

$(\tilde{n}, S, \mathcal{P} \cup \{(s := N; P, \beta)\}, \mathcal{K}) \rightarrow (\tilde{n}, S \cup \{s := N\}, \mathcal{P} \cup \{(P, \beta)\}, \mathcal{K})$ if $s \in dom(S)$ and $\forall (Q, \beta') \in \mathcal{P}, \beta' = 0$

$(\tilde{n}, S, \mathcal{P} \cup \{(\text{read } s \text{ as } x; P, \beta)\}, \mathcal{K}) \rightarrow (\tilde{n}, S, \mathcal{P} \cup \{(P\{S(s)/x\}, \beta)\}, \mathcal{K})$ if $s \in dom(S)$ and $\forall (Q, \beta') \in \mathcal{P}, \beta' = 0$

$(\tilde{n}, S, \mathcal{P} \cup \{(\text{lock}; P, 0)\}, \mathcal{K}) \rightarrow (\tilde{n}, S, \mathcal{P} \cup \{(P, 1)\}, \mathcal{K})$ if $\forall (Q, \beta') \in \mathcal{P}, \beta' = 0$

$(\tilde{n}, S, \mathcal{P} \cup \{(\text{unlock}; P, 1)\}, \mathcal{K}) \rightarrow (\tilde{n}, S, \mathcal{P} \cup \{(P, 0)\}, \mathcal{K})$

$(\tilde{n}, S, \mathcal{P} \cup \{(\text{out}(M, N); P, \beta)\}, \mathcal{K}) \xrightarrow{K(N)} (\tilde{n}, S, \mathcal{P} \cup \{(P, \beta)\}, \mathcal{K} \cup \{N\})$ if $\nu\tilde{n}.\mathcal{K} \vdash M$

$(\tilde{n}, S, \mathcal{P} \cup \{(\text{in}(M, x); P, \beta)\}, \mathcal{K}) \xrightarrow{K(M, N)} (\tilde{n}, S, \mathcal{P} \cup \{(P\{N/x\}, \beta)\}, \mathcal{K})$ if $\nu\tilde{n}.\mathcal{K} \vdash M$ and $\nu\tilde{n}.\mathcal{K} \vdash N$

Fig. 3. The semantics of Statverif

Security Property. StatVerif is limited to the verification of secrecy property. The secrecy property of StatVerif is defined as follows.

Definition 13 (StatVerif Secrecy Property). Let P be a closed StatVerif process, M a message. P preserves the secrecy of M if there exists no trace of the form:

$$(\emptyset, \emptyset, \{(P, 0)\}, fn(P)) \xrightarrow{\alpha}{}^{*} (\tilde{n}, S, \mathcal{P}, \mathcal{K}) \text{ where } \nu\tilde{n}.\mathcal{K} \vdash M$$

In the following, we encode the StatVerif processes into a subset of SAPIC processes and obtain the CS result directly from that of SAPIC, which has been proved in Sect. 3.2. With this encoding, we can easily embed the StatVerif calculus into the CoSP framework. Thus we do not need to build another computational execution model for StatVerif like what we have done for SAPIC.

There are many differences between the semantics of these two calculi. The lock construct is the place in which they differ the most. For a StatVerif process $P := \text{lock}; P_1$, it will lock the state and all the processes in parallel cannot access the current state cells until an unlock in P_1 is achieved. For a SAPIC process $P := \text{lock } M; P_1$, it will only store the π-term M in a set Λ and make sure it cannot be locked again in another concurrent process $Q := \text{lock } M'; Q_1$ where $M' =_E M$ until an unlock construct is achieved. Moreover, the state cells in StatVerif calculus should be initialized before they can be accessed. It is not required in SAPIC. Thus we should do more for a SAPIC process to simulate the state construct in a StatVerif process.

We first define the encoding $\lfloor P \rfloor_b$ for StatVerif process P with the boolean b indicating whether P has locked the state. Note that we only need to encode the

$\lfloor 0 \rfloor_0 = 0$ $\quad \lfloor P|Q \rfloor_0 = \lfloor P \rfloor_0 \| \lfloor Q \rfloor_0$ $\quad \lfloor \nu n; P \rfloor_b = \nu n; \lfloor P \rfloor_b$ $\quad \lfloor !P \rfloor_0 = \, !\lfloor P \rfloor_0$
$\lfloor \text{in}\,(M,x)\,; P \rfloor_b = \text{in}\,(M,x)\,; \lfloor P \rfloor_b$ $\quad \lfloor \text{out}\,(M,N)\,; P \rfloor_b = \text{out}\,(M,N)\,; \lfloor P \rfloor_b$
$\lfloor \text{let}\ x = D\ \text{in}\ P\ \text{else}\ Q \rfloor_b = \text{let}\ x = D\ \text{in}\ \lfloor P \rfloor_b\ \text{else}\ \lfloor Q \rfloor_b$ $\quad \lfloor \text{event}\ e; P \rfloor_b = \text{event}\ e; \lfloor P \rfloor_b$
$\lfloor [s \mapsto M] \rfloor_0 = \text{insert}\ s, M$
$\lfloor \text{lock}; P \rfloor_0 = \text{lock}\ l; \lfloor P \rfloor_1$ $\quad \lfloor \text{unlock}; P \rfloor_1 = \text{unlock}\ l; \lfloor P \rfloor_0$

$$\lfloor s := M; P \rfloor_b = \begin{cases} \text{lock}\ l; \text{lookup}\ s\ \text{as}\ x_s\ \text{in insert}\ s, M; \text{unlock}\ l; \lfloor P \rfloor_0 & \text{for}\ b = 0 \\ \text{lookup}\ s\ \text{as}\ x_s\ \text{in insert}\ s, M; \lfloor P \rfloor_1 & \text{for}\ b = 1 \\ & \text{where}\ x_s\ \text{is a fresh variable} \end{cases}$$

$$\lfloor \text{read}\ s\ \text{as}\ x; P \rfloor_b = \begin{cases} \text{lock}\ l; \text{lookup}\ s\ \text{as}\ x\ \text{in unlock}\ l; \lfloor P \rfloor_0 & \text{for}\ b = 0 \\ \text{lookup}\ s\ \text{as}\ x\ \text{in}\ \lfloor P \rfloor_1 & \text{for}\ b = 1 \end{cases}$$

Fig. 4. Encoding Statverif process

StatVerif state constructs by using SAPIC functional state constructs. We leave the standard constructs unchanged. For the sake of completeness, we list them all in Fig. 4. The state cell initialization $[s \mapsto M]$ is represented by the construct insert s, M. To encode the lock operation, we set a free fresh cell name l. The lock is represented by lock l and turning the boolean b from 0 to 1. The unlock construct is done in the opposite direction. To write a new value into an unlocked state cell ($s := M$ for $b = 0$), we need to perform 4 steps. We first lock l before the operation. It is to ensure the state is not locked in concurrent processes. We then read the original value in s to ensure s has been initialized. We complete the writing operation by the construct insert s, M and finally unlock l. When the state has been locked ($s := M$ for $b = 1$), we omit the constructs lock l and unlock l because it has been locked before and the boolean b could be turned from 1 to 0 only by an unlock construct. The reading operation is similar where we bind the value to x instead of a fresh variable x_s.

Let $O = (\tilde{n}, \mathcal{S}, \mathcal{P}, \mathcal{K})$ be a StatVerif semantic configuration where $\mathcal{P} = \{(P_i, \beta_i)\}_{i=1}^{k}$ and $\beta_i \in \{0, 1\}$ indicating whether P_i has locked the state. We define the encoding $\lfloor O \rfloor$ as SAPIC semantic configuration.

$$\lfloor O \rfloor = \begin{cases} (\tilde{n}, \mathcal{S}, \emptyset, \{\lfloor P_i \rfloor_{\beta_i}\}_{i=1}^{k}, \mathcal{K}, \{l\}) & \text{if}\ \exists (P_i, \beta_i) \in \mathcal{P}, \beta_i = 1, \\ (\tilde{n}, \mathcal{S}, \emptyset, \{\lfloor P_i \rfloor_{\beta_i}\}_{i=1}^{k}, \mathcal{K}, \emptyset) & \text{if}\ \forall (P_i, \beta_i) \in \mathcal{P}, \beta_i = 0. \end{cases}$$

Lemma 1 states that our encoding is able to capture secrecy of StatVerif process. Then by Theorem 2 we obtain the CS result of StatVerif through our encoding. We present the proofs in the full version of this paper [26].

Lemma 1. Let P_0 be a closed StatVerif process. Let M be a message. Set $P' := \text{in}(attch, x); \text{let}\ y = equal(x, M)$ in event $NotSecret$, where x, y are two fresh variables that are not used in P_0, $attch \in \mathbf{N}_E$ is a free channel name which is known by the adversary. We set $\wp := \{e | NotSecret\ \text{is not in}\ e\}$. $Q_0 := \lfloor P'|P_0 \rfloor_0$ is a closed SAPIC process and $\wp$ is a SAPIC trace property. Then we have that P_0 symbolically preserves the secrecy of M (in the sense of Definition 13) *iff* Q_0 symbolically satisfies $\wp$ (in the sense of Definition 7).

Theorem 2 (CS in StatVerif). Assume that the computational implementation of the applied π calculus is a computationally sound implementation (Definition 3) of the symbolic model of the applied π calculus (Definition 4) for a class **P** of protocols. For a closed StatVerif process P_0, we denote by Q_0 and $\wp$ the same meanings in Lemma 1. Thus if the StatVerif process P_0 symbolically preserves the secrecy of a message M (Definition 13) and $\Pi^S_{Q_0} \in \mathbf{P}$, then Q_0 computationally satisfies $\wp$.

5   Case Study: CS Results of Public-Key Encryption and Signatures

In Sects. 3 and 4, we have embedded the stateful applied π calculus used in SAPIC and StatVerif into the CoSP framework. CoSP allows for casting CS proofs in a conceptually modular and generic way: proving x cryptographic primitives sound for y calculi only requires $x + y$ proofs (instead of $x \cdot y$ proofs without this framework). In particular with our results, all CS proofs that have been conducted in CoSP are valid for the stateful applied π calculus, and hence accessible to SAPIC and StatVerif.

We exemplify our CS results for stateful applied π calculus by providing the symbolic model that is accessible to the two verification tools, SAPIC and StatVerif. We use the CS proofs in [15] with a few changes fitting for the verification mechanism in these tools. The symbolic model allows for expressing public-key encryption and signatures.

Let $\mathbf{C} := \{enc/3, ek/1, dk/1, sig/3, vk/1, sk/1, pair/2, string_0/1, string_1/1, empty/0, garbageSig/2, garbage/1, garbageEnc/2\}$ be the set of constructors. We require that $\mathbf{N} = \mathbf{N_E} \uplus \mathbf{N_P}$ for countable infinite sets $\mathbf{N_P}$ of protocol nonces and $\mathbf{N_E}$ of attacker nonces. Message type $\mathbf{T}$ is the set of all terms T matching the following grammar, where the nonterminal N stands for nonces.

$$T ::= enc(ek(N), T, N) | ek(N) | dk(N) | sig(sk(N), T, N) | vk(N) | sk(N) |$$
$$\qquad pair(T, T) | S | N | garbage(N) | garbageEnc(T, N) | garbageSig(T, N)$$
$$S ::= empty | string_0(S) | string_1(S)$$

Let $\mathbf{D} := \{dec/2, isenc/1, isek/1, isdk/1, ekof/1, ekofdk/1, verify/2, issig/1, isvk/1, issk/1, vkof/2, vkofsk/1, fst/1, snd/1, unstring_0/1, equal/2\}$ be the set of destructors. The full description of all destructor rules is given in [15]. Let $\vdash$ be defined as in Definition 4. Let $\mathbf{M} = (\mathbf{C}, \mathbf{N}, \mathbf{T}, \mathbf{D}, \vdash)$ be the symbolic model.

In StatVerif, the symbolic model $\mathbf{M}$ can be directly achieved since the term algebra is inherited from ProVerif, whose CS property has been proved in [15]. In SAPIC, we formalize the symbolic model by a signature $\Sigma :=$ $\mathbf{C} \cup \mathbf{D}$ with the equational theories expressing the destructor rules. Note that 3 destructor rules are filtered out including: (i) $ekofdk(dk(t)) = ek(t)$; (ii) $vkof(sig(sk(t_1), t_2, t_3)) = vk(t_1)$; (iii) $vkofsk(sk(t)) = vk(t)$, since they are not subterm-convergent, which is required by SAPIC (by verification mechanism of tamarin-prover). Note that these rules are all used to derive the public key. We require that for all the signatures and private keys in communication, they should be accompanied by their public keys. In this way, both the adversary and the protocol will not use these rules. To show the usefulness of our symbolic model in this section, we have verified the left-or-right protocol presented in [21] by using SAPIC and StatVerif. In the full version of this paper [26], we provide the scripts for the protocol.

To establish CS results, we require the protocols to fulfill several natural conditions with respect to their use of randomness. Protocols that satisfy these protocol conditions are called *randomness-safe*. Additionally, the cryptographic implementations needs to fulfill certain conditions, e.g., that the encryption scheme is PROG-KDM secure, and the signature scheme is SUF-CMA. Both the protocol conditions and the implementation conditions could be found in [15]. Then we conclude CS for protocols in the stateful applied π calculus that use public-key encryption and signatures.

Theorem 3 (CS for Enc. and Signatures in SAPIC and StatVerif). Let **M** be as defined in this section and A of **M** be an implementation that satisfies the conditions from above. If a randomness-safe closed SAPIC or StatVerif process P_0 symbolically satisfies a trace property $\wp$, then P_0 computationally satisfies[2] $\wp$.

6 Conclusion

In this paper, we present two CS results respectively for the stateful applied π calculus used in SAPIC tool and StatVerif tool. We show that the CS results of applied π calculus implies the CS results of SAPIC calculus and of StatVerif calculus. Thus for any computationally sound implementation of applied π calculus, if the security property of a closed stateful process is verified by SAPIC tool or StatVerif tool, it is also computationally satisfied. The work is conducted within the CoSP framework. We give the embedding from the SAPIC calculus to CoSP protocols. Furthermore, we provide an encoding of the StatVerif processes into a subset of SAPIC processes, which shows the differences between the semantics of these two calculi. As a case study, we provide the CS result for the input languages of StatVerif and SAPIC with public-key encryption and signatures.

References

1. Blanchet, B.: An efficient cryptographic protocol verifier based on Prolog rules. In: 2001 Proceedings of the 14th IEEE Computer Security Foundations Workshopp, pp. 82–96 (2001)

---

[2] For a closed StatVerif process P_0, we denote by Q_0 and $\wp$ the same meanings in Lemma 1. We say P_0 computationally satisfies $\wp$ iff Q_0 computationally satisfies $\wp$.

2. Armando, A., et al.: The AVISPA tool for the automated validation of internet security protocols and applications. In: Etessami, K., Rajamani, S.K. (eds.) CAV 2005. LNCS, vol. 3576, pp. 281–285. Springer, Heidelberg (2005)
3. Escobar, S., Meadows, C., Meseguer, J.: Maude-NPA: cryptographic protocol analysis modulo equational properties. In: Aldini, A., Barthe, G., Gorrieri, R. (eds.) FOSAD 2007/2008/2009. LNCS, vol. 5705, pp. 1–50. Springer, Heidelberg (2009)
4. Dolev, D., Yao, A.C.: On the security of public key protocols. In: Proceedings of the 22nd Annual Symposium on Foundations of Computer Science, SFCS 1981, pp. 350–357. IEEE Computer Society, Washington, DC (1981)
5. Even, S., Goldreich, O.: On the security of multi-party ping-pong protocols. In: 24th Annual Symposium on Foundations of Computer Science, pp. 34–39, November 1983
6. Abadi, M., Rogaway, P.: Reconciling two views of cryptography. In: Watanabe, O., Hagiya, M., Ito, T., van Leeuwen, J., Mosses, P.D. (eds.) TCS 2000. LNCS, vol. 1872, pp. 3–22. Springer, Heidelberg (2000)
7. Janvier, R., Lakhnech, Y., Mazaré, L.: Completing the picture: soundness of formal encryption in the presence of active adversaries. In: Sagiv, M. (ed.) ESOP 2005. LNCS, vol. 3444, pp. 172–185. Springer, Heidelberg (2005)
8. Micciancio, D., Warinschi, B.: Soundness of formal encryption in the presence of active adversaries. In: Naor, M. (ed.) TCC 2004. LNCS, vol. 2951, pp. 133–151. Springer, Heidelberg (2004)
9. Cortier, V., Warinschi, B.: Computationally sound, automated proofs for security protocols. In: Sagiv, M. (ed.) ESOP 2005. LNCS, vol. 3444, pp. 157–171. Springer, Heidelberg (2005)
10. Cortier, V., Kremer, S., Küsters, R., Warinschi, B.: Computationally sound symbolic secrecy in the presence of hash functions. In: Arun-Kumar, S., Garg, N. (eds.) FSTTCS 2006. LNCS, vol. 4337, pp. 176–187. Springer, Heidelberg (2006)
11. Backes, M., Hofheinz, D., Unruh, D.: CoSP: a general framework for computational soundness proofs. In: Proceedings of the 16th ACM Conference on Computer and Communications Security, CCS 2009, pp. 66–78. ACM, New York (2009)
12. Backes, M., Bendun, F., Unruh, D.: Computational soundness of symbolic zero-knowledge proofs: weaker assumptions and mechanized verification. In: Basin, D., Mitchell, J.C. (eds.) POST 2013 (ETAPS 2013). LNCS, vol. 7796, pp. 206–225. Springer, Heidelberg (2013)
13. Cortier, V., Warinschi, B.: A composable computational soundness notion. In: Proceedings of the 18th ACM Conference on Computer and Communications Security, CCS 2011, pp. 63–74. ACM, New York (2011)
14. Böhl, F., Cortier, V., Warinschi, B.: Deduction soundness: prove one, get five for free. In: Proceedings of the 2013 ACM SIGSAC Conference on Computer & Communications Security, CCS 2013, pp. 1261–1272. ACM, New York (2013)
15. Backes, M., Malik, A., Unruh, D.: Computational soundness without protocol restrictions. In: Proceedings of the 2012 ACM Conference on Computer and Communications Security, CCS 2012, pp. 699–711. ACM, New York (2012)
16. Arapinis, M., Liu, J., Ritter, E., Ryan, M.: Stateful applied Pi Calculus. In: Abadi, M., Kremer, S. (eds.) POST 2014 (ETAPS 2014). LNCS, vol. 8414, pp. 22–41. Springer, Heidelberg (2014)
17. Guttman, J.D.: State and progress in strand spaces: proving fair exchange. J. Autom. Reason. **48**, 159–195 (2012)
18. Schmidt, B., Meier, S., Cremers, C., Basin, D.: Automated analysis of Diffie-Hellman protocols and advanced security properties. In: 2012 IEEE 25th Computer Security Foundations Symposium (CSF), pp. 78–94, June 2012

19. Delaune, S., Kremer, S., Ryan, M.D., Steel, G.: Formal analysis of protocols based on TPM state registers. In: Proceedings of the 2011 IEEE 24th Computer Security Foundations Symposium, CSF 2011, pp. 66–80. IEEE Computer Society, Washington, DC (2011)
20. Kremer, S., Künnemann, R.: Automated analysis of security protocols with global state. In: Proceedings of the 35th IEEE Symposium on Security and Privacy, SP 2014. IEEE Computer Society, Washington (2014)
21. Arapinis, M., Ritter, E., Ryan, M.D.: StatVerif: verification of stateful processes. In: 2011 IEEE 24th Computer Security Foundations Symposium (CSF), pp. 33–47, June 2011
22. Mödersheim, S.A.: Abstraction by set-membership: verifying security protocols and web services with databases. In: Proceedings of the 17th ACM Conference on Computer and Communications Security, CCS 2010, pp. 351–360. ACM, New York (2010)
23. Abadi, M., Fournet, C.: Mobile values, new names, and secure communication. In: Proceedings of the 28th ACM SIGPLAN-SIGACT Symposium on Principles of Programming Languages, vol. 36, pp. 104–115, January 2001
24. Backes, M., Mohammadi, E., Ruffing, T.: Computational soundness results for ProVerif: bridging the gap from trace properties to uniformity. In: Abadi, M., Kremer, S. (eds.) POST 2014 (ETAPS 2014). LNCS, vol. 8414, pp. 42–62. Springer, Heidelberg (2014)
25. Backes, M., Maffei, M., Unruh, D.: Computationally sound verification of source code. In: Proceedings of the 17th ACM Conference on Computer and Communications Security, CCS 2010, pp. 387–398. ACM, New York (2010)
26. Shao, J., Qin, Y., Feng, D.: Computational Soundness Results for Stateful Applied π Calculus. http://arxiv.org/abs/1601.00363

Author Index

Printed in the United States
By Bookmasters